THE CLASSICS
OF WESTERN
SPIRITUALITY

PHILO of ALEXANDRIA
THE CONTEMPLATIVE LIFE, THE GIANTS, AND SELECTIONS

TRANSLATION AND INTRODUCTION
BY
DAVID WINSTON

PREFACE
BY
JOHN DILLON

PAULIST PRESS

Cover Art
The Artist LIAM ROBERTS was born in Ireland and now lives in New York City.
After attending the National College of Art in Dublin, he studied at the Academy of
Fine Arts in Florence, at the Royal Academy of San Fernando in Madrid, and at the
Academy of Fine Art in Rome. In this cover Mr. Roberts has produced an up-dated
version of the ancient image of Philo.

Design: Barbini, Pesce & Noble, Inc.

Library of Congress
Catalog Card Number: 80-84499

ISBN 0-8091-2333-9

Published by Paulist Press
545 Island Road, Ramsey, N.J. 07446

Printed and bound in the
United States of America

CONTENTS

Author of the Preface

John Dillon is Regius Professor of Greek Trinity College, Dublin. After earning his B.A. and M.A. at Oriel College, Oxford, he continued his studies at the University of California, Berkeley, where he received his Ph.D. He taught at Berkeley from 1969 to 1980, and was Chairman of its Classics Department from 1978 to 1980. He has published innumerable articles and reviews. His books include *The Fragments of Iamblichus: Text, Translation, and Commentary* (1973), and *The Middle Platonists* (1977). Born in Madison, Wisconsin, he lives with his wife Jean at Drumnigh House, Dublin, Ireland.

PREFACE

Philo of Alexandria seems destined to remain a battleground of scholars for some time to come. This remarkable figure, poised as he is between the Greek and Jewish thought-worlds, attracts interest from a variety of sources, each of which is inclined to claim him for itself. Is he an essentially Jewish thinker, clothing his doctrines in Greek terminology? Or is he, on the contrary, essentially Hellenic in his cast of mind, Jewish only by ancestral loyalty, making of Moses the archetypal Greek philosopher? Has he a coherent philosophy, derived from whatever sources, or is he essentially a commentator on the Pentateuch, making use of philosophical doctrines and terminology piecemeal, to suit his exegetical purposes?

It is hardly suitable for me, I think, to impose my views on these vexed questions here. I have made them clear, for what they are worth, elsewhere (cf. *The Middle Platonists*, pp. 139–183). The fact that they are still live issues after generations of modern scholarship is an indication of the complexity of the character who is the subject of the present study. While H. A. Wolfson may have been excessive in seeing Philo as the founder of a new mode in European philosophy, Religious Philosophy, he is certainly drawing attention to a truth. Philo is a man between two worlds, the Jewish and the Greek, and in the process of his attempt to reconcile the Greek philosophical *paideia* on which, in his thoroughly Hellenized family, he had been brought up, with the faith inherited from his ancestors, he did, without perhaps intending to, produce a new synthesis. This had no discernible effect on either the Greek or the Jewish traditions, but was picked up ea-

xi

gerly by the Alexandrian Christian theologians, Clement and Origen, and through them passed on to later times, both to Medieval European and to Arab and Medieval Jewish thinkers. In this sense, Wolfson's great vision of Philo as the founder of a tradition of which Spinoza is the dismantler has considerable justification.

Philo is, for this reason, a key figure in the development of Western Spirituality, even though he is only drawing existing threads together. The contrast between soul and body, spirit and matter, dominates his work. As a commentator, for a start, he explains his allegorical method as a laying bare of the *soul* of the Pentateuch, by contrast with its body, the actual words of the text, and the overtly historical incidents they describe. This is the activity for which he praises the Therapeutae (*Vit. Cont.* 78) and it is what he saw himself as doing. In moral philosophy, he consistently advocates the separation of the soul from earthly concerns. A good passage occurs in the present selection, at *Gig.* 12–15, where we are presented with a picture of the soul plunged into the realm of matter as into a raging torrent (a thoroughly Platonic image), and the soul of the philosopher coming to the surface as soon as possible, and then soaring back to the heavens from which it came. Again, the message he derives from an allegorizing of Leviticus 18:6, at *Gig.* 32ff., is that of spurning contact with the flesh and this world.

For Philo, the human intellect, the *nous,* is an entity from a higher world, not bound by the laws of this one. "It is the mind alone," he says at *Deus* 47, "which the Father who begat it deemed worthy of freedom, and, loosening the bonds of necessity, allowed it to range free, and of that power of volition which constitutes his most intimate and fitting possession presented it with such a portion as it was capable of receiving." The *nous* is actually a part of God, or, more properly, of his *logos,* and is thus able to rise above the realm of cosmic necessity. Those who are "men of God" (*Gig.* 61), that is, who have made God-inspired intellect their dominant element, "have entirely transcended the sensible sphere, and have migrated to the intelligible world, and dwell there enrolled as citizens of the commonwealth of Ideas, which are imperishable and incorporeal."

On one controversial subject, however, I will take a stand, and that is the question of Philo's relation to Greek philosophy. Philo has been seen as an "eclectic," choosing a concept here and a formulation there from the Presocratics, Plato, Aristotle, the Stoics, and even from Epicureans and Skeptics. He has been presented, also, as essentially unconcerned with matters philosophical, using philosophical language simply in the service of exegesis. Both these views I find quite implausible.

To address the second first, Philo's whole position is based on the premise that Greek philosophy is a development from the God-given teaching of Moses, and thus that it is quite proper for him to claim it back, as it were, accepting it as the best mode of expressing to a "modern" audience (one influenced by Greek modes of thought) the substance of Moses' message.

As to the first view (that, notably, of H. A. Wolfson), to view Philo as an eclectic because of the apparent amalgam of Platonist, Aristotelian and Stoic doctrines observable in his works is to ignore the developments which had taken place within Platonism itself by Philo's time. Two generations before (c. 90 B.C.E.), Antiochus of Ascalon had propounded, in Athens, a revived dogmatic Platonism, incorporating a good deal of Stoic doctrine and terminology, on the argument that Zeno and his successors were in fact the truest successors of the Old Academy, rather than the Skeptic Arcesilaus and his followers, Antiochus' own immediate predecessors. Peripatetic elements, especially in logic and ethics, had already penetrated the Academy in the first generations after Plato's death, and Antiochus does not reject these.

His rather materialistic version of Platonism (he does not seem to have differed from the Stoics on this question) was modified in the next generation, in the direction of transcendentalism and the immaterial nature of the divine, by Eudorus of Alexandria, who was probably a pupil of a pupil of Antiochus. Eudorus was influenced by the revival of interest in Pythagoreanism which took place in the first century B.C.E. This combination of Stoicizing Platonism with a Pythagorean-influenced view of the transcendence of God, and of the significance of Number, together with a more austere ethics than that of Antiochus (who was inclined to peripatetic broad-mindedness about bodily and worldly goods) is the Platonism which Philo inherited. It is unclear through what medium he inherited this form of Platonism but it may have been from attending the lectures of contemporary Platonists. Though Philo is certainly less than consistent in his terminology, it is not necessary, in my view, to go outside of the spectrum of contemporary Platonism to explain his position, and I am glad to say that David Winston is in agreement with me on this.

PREFACE

Philo did contribute enormously, through the Christian thinkers of the Alexandrian School, to the tradition of spirituality both in Western Europe and in the Eastern Orthodox world, and the magnificent intellectual tour-de-force constituted by his Platonizing allegory of the Pentateuch deserves due recognition and honor. This excellent selection of his works will give the reader a vivid picture of the essential Philo in all his aspects.

John Dillon
University of California
Berkeley

FOREWORD

It is somewhat surprising that in the face of a corpus of writings as large as that of Philo, marked by a verbose and often repetitious style, only one meager anthology (*Philo: Selections,* edited by Hans Lewy, in *Three Jewish Philosophers* [Cleveland, New York, Philadelphia, 1961]) has thus far been produced for the benefit of the modern reader. Although all florilegia are inevitably compromises, if the present work, which purports to cover most of the important themes of Philo's thought and includes two of the shorter treatises in their entirety, should goad the reader to turn to the main body of his writings, it shall have served its purpose.

In preparing my own translation, I have consulted with great profit the German and French translations of Philo's works (see bibliography), and am especially indebted to the splendid English version of Colson and Whitaker. I have sought to make my own version conform as closely as possible to the original Greek without violating the spirit of English style or idiom. Others will have to judge to what extent I have succeeded in this endeavor. In appending notes to the passages selected, I gratefully acknowledge my debt to the annotations accompanying the earlier translations, although I have added much new material. I trust that the reader who seeks to understand the Greek and Jewish sources that lie behind Philo's multidomed construction will find them useful. I am also indebted to Professors John Dillon and Valentin Nikiprowetzky with whom I have been collaborating in the production of a commentary on the pair of Philonic treatises *De Gigantibus—Quod Deus.* I have incorporated in a considerably abbreviated form some of the material that will appear in that forth-coming work.

I owe a very special debt of gratitude to my colleague and friend Professor Abraham Terian of Andrews University, who graciously undertook to translate directly from the Armenian those passages I had selected from the *De Providentia,* and to revise (on the basis of the Armenian) Ralph Marcus's translation of the passages I had selected from the *Quaestiones in Genesim et Exodum.* Terian also kindly consent-ed to allow the inclusion of three passages from his English transla-tion of the *De Animalibus,* which, together with an introduction and notes, will soon be published by the Philo Institute and Scholars Press.

I have sought in my selections from Philo to include those pas-sages that are the most significant and representative of his religious philosophy, although my choices necessarily reflect my own reading of his thought. Moreover, it often happened that the same passage could readily have been included under more than one rubric, and the heading chosen in such cases was determined by considerations of mere convenience. Though generally avoiding the inclusion of par-allel passages unless they added something particularly significant, I have been especially careful to list copious references to them in the notes.

Given the complexity of Philo's thought and the sharply diver-gent expositions of its fundamental nature, it seemed to me best to avoid providing yet another broad summary of its basic principles, which would skirt the chief areas of controversy. I have chosen in-stead to utilize the brief space of the introduction for a closer look at some of the central issues that inevitably determine the entire sweep of Philo's world view, and have thus concentrated my analysis on those elements of his thought that ultimately ground and define the character of what I consider to be a rational, mystical monism in the service of Mosaic Scripture. The bibliographical note at the end of the book will guide the curious reader to a selection of works that will allow him to consider alternative interpretations.

I wish to thank Claude Welch, president and dean of the Grad-uate Theological Union, for providing funds for the typing of my manuscript. I should also like to express my appreciation to my wife Irene for successfully deciphering my handwriting and doing a large part of the typing.

PRINCIPAL ABBREVIATIONS

AAJR	American Academy of Jewish Research
ANRW	*Aufstieg und Niedergang der römischen Welt,* Philosophie und Wissenschaften, ed. W. Haase. Berlin, 198?
AP	*Anthologia Palatina,* eds. H. Stadmüller and F. Bucherer, 1906
A.Z.	*Aboda Zara*
BR	*Bereshith Rabbah,* ed. J. Theodor, with additional corrections by C. Albeck, 3 vols. Jerusalem, 1965
BT	*Babylonian Talmud*
CD	*Codex Damascus* or *Damascus Document* (older designation: CDC *Cairo Damascus Covenant*)
CH	*Corpus Hermeticum*
DK	H. Diels and W. Kranz, *Die Fragmente der Vorsokratiker,* 8th ed., 3 vols., Berlin, 1956. (Pagination remains the same in later editions.)
Dox. Graec.	*Doxographi Graeci,* ed. H. Diels. Berlin, 1958
FGH	*Die Fragmente der griechischen Historiker,* ed. F. Jacoby. Berlin and Leiden, 1923ff.
Gr. Fr.	Greek Fragment
HR	*History of Religions*
HTR	*Harvard Theological Review*

ABBREVIATIONS

HUCA	*Hebrew Union College Annual*
JBL	*Journal of Biblical Literature*
JHS	*Journal of Hellenic Studies*
JQR	*Jewish Quarterly Review*
JSJ	*Journal for the Study of Judaism in the Persian, Hellenistic, and Roman Period*
JTS	*Journal of Theological Studies*
LCL	Loeb Classical Library
LSJ	H. G. Liddell and R. Scott, *A Greek-English Lexicon* (1843), 9th ed., rev. by H. S. Jones. Oxford, 1948
Lyon	*Les Oeuvres de Philon d'Alexandrie publiées sous le patronage de l'Université de Lyon,* par R. Arnaldez, J. Pouilloux, C. Mondésert. Paris 1961ff., vols. 1–34ᴬ, and 35
M.	*Mishnah*
Mek.	*Mekilta De-Rabbi Ishmael,* ed. H. S. Horovitz and I. A. Rabin. Jerusalem, 1960. English trans. by J. Lauterbach. 3 vols. Philadelphia, 1933
MGWJ	*Monatsschrift für Geschichte und Wissenschaft des Judentums*
Mid. Teh.	*Midrash Tehillim,* ed. S. Buber. Reprint, New York, 1947
PAL	*Philon d'Alexandrie,* Lyon 1966: Colloque. Centre national de la recherche scientifique. Paris, 1967
PRK	*Pesikta de Rav Kahana,* ed. B. Mandelbaum. 2 vols. New York, 1962. English trans. by W. G. Braude and I. J. Kapstein. Philadelphia, 1975
PT	*Palestinian Talmud*
PW	A. Pauly and G. Wissowa, *Real-Enzyklopädie der classischen Altertumswissenschaften.* 1892ff.
REJ	*Revue des Études Juives*
RHR	*Revue de l'histoire des religions*
R.	*Rabbah*

ABBREVIATIONS

RR	*Review of Religion*
SBL	Society of Biblical Literature
ShR	*Shemoth Rabbah*
Sib Or	*Sibylline Oracles*
Sir	The Wisdom of Ben Sira
SP	*Studia Philonica*
SVF	*Stoicorum Veterum Fragmenta*, ed. H. von Arnim. 4 vols. Reprint, Stuttgart, 1964
Tanḥ.	*Midrash Tanḥuma*. Wilna 1885. Reprint, Jerusalem, 1965. ed. S. Buber. 2 vols. Reprint, New York, 1946
Tosef.	*Tosefta*, ed. M. S. Zuckermandel. Reprint, Jerusalem, 1963
TrGF	*Tragicorum Graecorum Fragmenta*, ed. B. Snell. Göttingen, 1971
Wisd.	The Wisdom of Solomon
ZAW	*Zeitschrift für die alttestamentliche Wissenschaft*
ZKG	*Zeitschrift für Kirchengeschichte*

ABBREVIATIONS OF PHILO'S TREATISES

Abr.	*De Abrahamo*
Aet.	*De Aeternitate Mundi*
Agr.	*De Agricultura*
Anim.	*De Animalibus*
Cher.	*De Cherubim*
Conf.	*De Confusione Linguarum*
Congr.	*De Congressu Eruditionis Gratia*
Cont.	*De Vita Contemplativa*
Decal.	*De Decalogo*
Det.	*Quod Deterius Potiori Insidiari Soleat*
Deus	*Quod Deus Sit Immutabilis*

ABBREVIATIONS

Ebr.	*De Ebrietate*
Flac.	*In Flaccum*
Fug.	*De Fuga et Inventione*
Gig.	*De Gigantibus*
Her.	*Quis Rerum Divinarum Heres Sit*
Hypoth.	*Hypothetica*
Jos.	*De Josepho*
LA	*Legum Allegoriarum*
Legat.	*Legatio ad Gaium*
Mig.	*De Migratione Abrahami*
Mos.	*De Vita Mosis*
Mut.	*De Mutatione Nominum*
Op.	*De Opificio Mundi*
Plant.	*De Plantatione*
Post.	*De Posteritate Caini*
Praem.	*De Praemiis et Poenis*
Prob.	*Quod Omnis Probus Liber Sit*
Prov.	*De Providentia*
QE	*Quaestiones et Solutiones in Exodum*
QG	*Quaestiones et Solutiones in Genesim*
Sacr.	*De Sacrificiis Abelis et Caini*
Sobr.	*De Sobrietate*
Somn.	*De Somniis*
Spec.	*De Specialibus Legibus*
Virt.	*De Virtutibus*

REFERENCE WORKS

The following books are cited by the author's name alone:

Baer, R. C. *Philo's Use of the Categories Male and Female*. Leiden, 1970.
Billings, T. H. *The Platonism of Philo Judaeus*. Chicago, 1919.
Bréhier, E. *Les idées philosophiques et religieuses de Philon d'Alexandrie*, 3rd. ed. Paris, 1950.

ABBREVIATIONS

Dillon, J. *The Middle Platonists.* London, 1977.

Dodds, E. R. *Pagan and Christian in an Age of Anxiety.* Cambridge, 1965.

Festugière, A. J. *La Révélation d'Hermès Trismégiste,* 4 vols., 3rd. ed. Paris, 1950.

Hahm, H. E. *The Origins of Stoic Cosmology.* Columbus, Ohio, 1977.

Heinemann, I. *Philons griechische und jüdische Bildung.* Breslau, 1932.

Lilla, S. R. C. *Clement of Alexandria.* Oxford, 1971.

Nikiprowetzky, V. *Le commentaire de l'écriture chez Philon d'Alexandrie.* Leiden, 1977.

Thesleff, H. *The Pythagorean Texts of the Hellenistic Period.* Åbo, 1965.

Urbach, E. *Hazal. Pirke Emunot We-Deot.* Jerusalem (Hebrew), 1969.

Winston, D. *The Wisdom of Solomon.* New York, 1979.

Wolfson, H. A. *Philo,* 2 vols. Cambridge, Mass., 1947.

INTRODUCTION

Philo of Alexandria (c. 20 B.C.E.–50 C.E.) stands at the apex of the
cultural activity of the Jewish-Alexandrian community, his literary
work climaxing a long chain of Jewish-Hellenistic writings whose
aim was to establish the validity and integrity of Jewish religious
thought in the face of the counterclaims of the intellectually powerful
Greek tradition.[1] Philo's Atticizing Greek is unexceptionable, and his
vast knowledge of classical Greek literature is dazzling.[2] Employing
a copious vocabulary, and a wide variety of Greek rhetorical techniques of composition, he tends to amplify and elaborate his themes
in a manner that strikes the modern reader as overly wrought and laborious, although his more successful passages are quite impressive.
Standing on the shoulders of a complex Jewish exegetical tradition,
he succeeded in forging a strikingly new synthesis of Jewish and Hellenic thought patterns, which undoubtedly exercised great attraction
for his fellow Jewish intellectuals. He was a convinced and ardent
Platonist, passionately goaded by the charms of philosophy to attempt to lead others into her delightful embrace (*Cher.* 73–80; *Prov.*
2.115; *Spec.* 3.1–6). At the same time, he cherished a deep and devoted
loyalty to his ancestral tradition, and believed he could bridge the
chasm that seemed to sunder the Greek and Jewish realms from one
another. Dillon (p. 141) has detected in his writing the zeal of a convert, and has suggested that he may have had an exclusively Hellenic
education in his youth, and that only in his maturer years did he conceive a new interest in his native tradition. However that may be he
certainly belonged to a wealthy, aristocratic Jewish family that was

1

readily attracted by the glitter of the Hellenistic world. The wealth
of his brother Alexander (mistakenly surnamed Lysimachus) brought
the latter into contact with prominent personalities in both the Roman and Jewish worlds. A letter of credit for the large sum of 200,000
drachmae (about $54,000) granted to Agrippa, grandson of Herod the
Great, and the provision of silver and gold plates for nine gates of the
Temple, attest to his great wealth (Josephus *Ant.* 18.159–60; *JW* 5.205).
He acted as customs agent (if we may equate alabarch and arabarch)
for the collection of dues on all goods imported into Egypt from the
East, and it is probable that he was given the Roman citizenship by
the Emperor whose *praenomen* and *nomen* were borne by his sons
Marcus and Tiberius Julius Alexander. The latter was described by
Josephus (*Ant.* 20.101) as "not remaining true to his ancestral prac-
tices," and served as procurator of the province of Judaea, Prefect of
Egypt under Nero, and perhaps Prefect of the Praetorian Guard in
Rome.[3]

I. PHILOSOPHICAL EXEGETE OF ALEXANDRIAN JEWRY

Philo remains for us a highly enigmatic figure. Aside from his
heading the Jewish delegation to Gaius (apparently together with his
brother Alexander and his nephew Tiberius Julius Alexander) in 39–
40 C.E., and a visit to the Jerusalem Temple, we know exceedingly little about the man or the chronology of his voluminous writings and
their respective audiences. The enigma is compounded by the fact
that he chose to cast the greater part of his treatises in the form of
a detailed philosophical exegesis of the Pentateuch. He certainly
could have fashioned his synthesis of Judaism and Hellenism in the
form of philosophical essays dealing with the major themes of biblical
thought, thus providing his readers with a precise and systematic exposition of his views. That he preferred the role of philosophical exegete of Hebrew Scripture is therefore of capital importance.[4] It may
be helpful in this regard to recall the mode of exposition adopted by
Philo's philosophical master, "the most holy Plato" (*Prob.* 13). Choosing the dramatic form of the philosophical dialogue, Plato's teasing
dialectic frequently leaves the reader utterly baffled and desperately

uncertain of his real views. Yet Plato clearly felt that the dialectical form was essential to the philosophical enterprise as he had conceived it, and that however great the degree of obscurity that resulted therefrom, it was a price well worth paying. In the case of Philo, we might similarly conclude that he too had apparently felt that the exegetical mode was so essential to his grand design that it more than counterbalanced the considerable obscurity it inevitably occasioned. Perhaps he felt that the success of his enterprise was largely dependent on his ability to convince his readers through a detailed scriptural commentary that the mystical Platonism he championed was not a farfetched philosophical construct attached to the Bible by threads of gossamer, but could readily be deduced from virtually every one of its verses. In any case, once having adopted this mode of writing, he could no more avoid the resulting ambiguities and inconsistencies than could Plato in the wake of his choice of the dramatic dialogue. But just as it is possible to extract from their dialogical context the fundamental presuppositions of Plato's thought and the main thrust of his philosophical construction, it is not very difficult to do the same for Philo. Willy Theiler and, more recently, John Dillon[5] have clearly demonstrated that Philo's philosophical views are Middle Platonist, that is, a highly Stoicized form of Platonism, streaked with Neopythagorean concerns. Many apparent inconsistencies thus turn out to be variations allowed in the Middle Platonic tradition, although there is no need to deny that some are undoubtedly generated by the exigencies of his exegetical requirements.

It is now abundantly clear that the extreme positions of both Wolfson and Völker with regard to Philo are almost certainly wrong. The former forces his thought into an artificially rigid Jewish "orthodoxy" that bears no semblance to the true character of his work, while the latter converts him into a simple-minded Jewish exegete unduly enamored of the tinsel of Greek philosophical terminology and motifs. Unlike Plato, however, Philo is not to be seen as an original philosopher intent on leaving his mark on philosophy. He must be regarded instead as a highly competent student of the entire range of the Greek philosophical tradition available to his generation, fully acquainted with the texts at firsthand and in no way restricted to handbooks and secondary digests. If there are serious gaps in his scholarship, they inhere rather in the Judaic side of his training, where he is almost totally reliant on Greek translations of the Bible, unable apparently to consult the Hebrew original.[6] He conceived, very likely late in his career[7] (although this remains uncertain), an all-consuming desire to put his hand to the great task of reconciling Judaism and Hellenism. Although passionately devoted to a mystical form of Platonism, he was convinced that it was possible to assimilate this way of thinking to his Jewish heritage. (We shall see in the course of the Introduction that his resolution of the major tensions inherent in this enterprise involved him in a series of subtle maneuvers that successfully camouflaged his preference for the philosophical through a deliberate ambiguity in his mode of presentation.) He was fully aware of the earlier, and probably less ambitious, attempts made by Alexandrian Jews who preceded him (such as Ps-Aristeas and Aristobulus),[8] and was also fully alert to the techniques employed by many of the Middle Platonists in their attempt to foist the Pythagorean doctrines of later men, including even their own, on Pythagoras himself. This tendency began in Platonism with Speusippus, if not with Plato himself, but is observable especially beginning with Eudorus and most later Platonists to a greater or lesser degree. As Dillon points out, "there was a good deal of simple 'one-upmanship' involved in the Neopythagorean movement (Plato can now be viewed as a mere pupil of Pythagoras), and it is a game in which Philo joined with a will, putting forward Moses as the greatest authority of all, as being the teacher of Pythagoras, and indeed of all Greek philosophers and lawgivers, Hesiod, Heraclitus and Lycurgus, for example" (pp. 38, 120). Philo was indeed no innovator in this matter even within the Alexandrian Jewish tradition. Artapanus (second century B.C.E.) had already identified Moses with Musaeus, with Orpheus becoming his disciple, and according to Aristobulus of Paneas (first half of second century B.C.E.), Homer and Hesiod drew from the books of Moses, which had already been translated into Greek long before the Septuagint version (Eusebius *PE* 9.27, 13.11).[9]

The crucial exegetical technique for Philo's vast enterprise, however, was provided by the Greek allegorical tradition. Initiated by Theagenes of Rhegium (second half of sixth century B.C.E.) in order to justify Homer against the detractors of his theology, it involved both physical and psychological interpretation. The myths concerning the gods' struggles with one another were said to refer to the fundamental opposition between the elements, and the names of the gods were also made to refer to various dispositions of the soul, Athena, for example, being reflection, Aphrodite desire, and Hermes elocution (DK A. 1–2). Anaxagoras (c. 500–420) could thus explain the Homeric poems as discussions of virtue and justice. The Sophist Prodicus of Ceos (contemporary of Socrates) inaugurated the theme later found among the Stoics that the gods of Homeric mythology personified those natural substances that are useful to human life, bread becoming Demeter, wine Dionysus, water Poseidon, and fire Hephaestus (DK B.5). Prodicus also employed ethical allegory. His treatise *The Seasons* contained the celebrated "Parable of Heracles," a paraphrase of which is found in Xenophon's *Memorabilia* (2.1.21–34), which tells the story of Heracles at the crossroads, attracted by Virtue and Vice in the form of two women of great stature (cf. Philo *Sacr.* 20–44). More significant is the use made of Homeric allegory by the Cynic Antisthenes (contemporary of Plato) to support his Cynic philosophy. Of special interest is the distinction according to which the poet sometimes spoke according to δόξα, opinion, sometimes according to ἀλήθεια, truth, which, according to Dio Chrysostom, goes back to Antisthenes, although he did not make as full a use of it as did Zeno. We are also told that Diogenes the Cynic explained Medea's use of sorcery in restoring old men to youth as the work of gymnastics (Stobaeus 3.29.92). The Cynics, then, were not content merely to defend Homer's piety, but annexed him into their own philosophy, converting Heracles and Odysseus, Medea and Circe, into Cynic heroes (Dio Chrysostom *Orat.* 8, 20–21).

It was the Stoics, to whom we have already alluded above, who considerably expanded the Cynics' employment of Homeric allegory in the interests of a philosophical system. Zeno, who composed five books of *Homeric Problems*, blamed nothing in Homer and said that the poet wrote some things in accordance with truth, others in accordance with opinion (*SVF* 1.274). Cicero describes the Stoic method of explaining the gods as personified natural forces as follows:

> This subject was handled by Zeno and was later explained
> more fully by Cleanthes and Chrysippus. For example, an
> ancient belief prevailed throughout Greece that Caelus (i.e.,
> Uranus) was mutilated by his son Saturn, and Saturn him-
> self thrown into bondage by his son Jove: now these immor-
> al fables enshrined a decidedly clever scientific theory. Their
> meaning was that the highest element of celestial aether or

fire, which by itself generates all things, is devoid of that bodily part which requires union with another for the work of procreation. [*ND* 2.63–64]

The Stoics also made extensive use of etymologizing in their allegorical interpretations, a procedure that had a great impact on Philo.

For Zeno, the Titans always represent the elements of the cosmos. In the name Koeos (Κοῖον) he sees in effect "quality" (ποιότης) in accordance with the Aeolic replacement of "π" by "κ"; Kreios is the regent and dominant element [probably through the resemblance of κρεῖος with κρείων, sovereign]; Hyperion indicates ascendant movement, in virtue of the expression "to go up higher" (ὑπεράνω ἰέναι). [*SVF* 1.100][10]

Armed with Greek allegorical exegesis, which seeks out the hidden meanings that lie beneath the surface of any particular text, and given the Middle Platonist and Neopythagorean penchant to read back new doctrines into the works of a venerable figure of the past, Philo was fully prepared to do battle for his ancestral tradition.[11] A novice in the use of Hebrew texts, he relied on the LXX, which he happily considered inspired. The enormous variety, the great subtlety, and the sheer quantity of his exegesis, in addition to his own many attestations to his predecessors, make it virtually certain that much of his commentary derived from a rich body of scholastic tradition.[12] None of this, however, can detract from his own genius, which selected, modified, refined, amplified, and synthesized this great mass of material and placed it in the service of an elaborate religious-philosophical world view. Human talents are considerably diverse, and the fact that Philo was neither a Plato, nor even a Xenocrates, in no way diminishes the magnitude of his own peculiar achievement.

It is customary to divide Philo's exegetical works into three categories. The first comprises the *Questions and Answers to Genesis and Exodus* (aside from Greek fragments—preserved only in Armenian), which invariably begin with a brief literal answer to a scriptural problem, followed by a lengthy allegorical explanation. These treatises are generally less sophisticated than Philo's other exegetical works and give the appearance of being rough compilations of raw material (neither Genesis nor Exodus is completely covered) to be utilized in future writings. The second great series of exegetical works is known as the *Allegory of the Law*,[13] and comprises those treatises that begin with a series of biblical verses by which they are closely shaped, generally proceeding verse by verse, but constantly incorporating related texts that are in turn investigated in great detail. The third series is constituted of those treatises whose structure is shaped by a broad theme indicated in the title and is known as the *Exposition of the Law*.[14]

II. PHILO'S THEORY OF CREATION[15]

1. Creation *ex nihilo* or from Primordial Matter?

A philosopher's theory of creation invariably reveals the fundamental presuppositions of his thought and is inextricably intertwined with his doctrine of God. Our exposition of Philo's theory of cosmogony will therefore be of pivotal importance for the correct interpretation of his entire metaphysical construction. Unfortunately there is little agreement on the twin key points in his theory, namely, whether it asserts a doctrine of creation *ex nihilo* or creation out of primordial matter, and whether creation constitutes a temporal act or an eternal process.

It is indeed explicitly stated by Philo that God created the world out of a preexistent matter, but it is exceedingly unclear whether that matter was itself, in Philo's view, a product of God's creative act. Thus Philo insists that Moses had anticipated Plato by teaching in Genesis that there was water, darkness, and chaos before the world came into existence (*Prov.* 1.22; cf. Justin *Apol.* 1.59). Having attained philosophy's summit, Moses recognized that there are two fundamental principles of being, the one active, the other passive, the former an absolutely pure universal mind, the latter something lifeless and motionless (*Op.* 7–9).[16] The nature of this preexistent matter is further described as "having of itself nothing lovely," and "being without order, quality, homogeneity, and full of discord and disharmony" (*Op.* 22).[17] It is often designated as either ὕλη or ο ὐσία, and possibly as μὴ ὄν, nonbeing.[18] The latter depends on how we interpret a number of passages containing this expression. We read, for example, in *Mos.* 2.267: "For as God brought into the light of being his most perfect

7

work, the world, out of nonbeing, so did he produce abundance in the desert, altering the elements to meet the urgent need, so that instead of the earth the air bore food, nourishment without labor or pain for those who had no means of retreat for the leisurely readying of their provisions" (*Mos.* 2.267). This description of the mannah produced miraculously from the air implies that the μὴ ὄν of the analogy from creation refers to a preexistent matter.

A similar implication may be drawn from the analogy used in the following passage:

> For parents are midway between divine and human nature, sharing in both; the human, as is evident, because they have been born and will perish, the divine because they have brought others to birth and have brought forth the nonexistent (τὰ μὴ ὄντα) into being. For what God is to the universe, I believe parents are to their children, since just as he has achieved existence for the nonexistent (τῷ μὴ ὑπάρχον τι), so they, in imitation of his power, as far as they are capable, immortalize the race. (*Spec.* 2.225; cf. *Deus* 119; *Virt.* 130)

On the other hand, the sun analogy in *Somn.* 1.76 has been taken by some to refer to a creation *ex nihilo:* "And above all, just as the rising sun exhibits bodies that were hidden, so God when he generated all things, not only made them visible, but also brought into being that which did not exist before (ἃ πρότερον οὐκ ἦν), acting not only the artificer (δημιουργός) but also the creator (κτίστης)." This passage, however, may simply mean that God not only made things visible, but, acting the creator rather than a mere artificer (who fashions things out of formed elements), established the very structure of matter, thereby bringing into being forms that did not exist before.[19]

Furthermore, it is Philo's view that, in shaping the primordial matter, God conferred benefits only "according to the capacities of the recipients. For creation is unable in its nature to receive the good in the same way that it is the nature of God to confer it, since his powers exceed all bounds, whereas creation, being too feeble to take in their magnitude, would have given out, had not God weighed and appropriately measured out that which falls to the share of each" (*Op.* 23; cf. *Test. Napht.* 2:2). Moreover, God created all things from the preelemental matter "without laying hold of it himself, since it was not lawful for the happy and blessed One to touch limitless chaotic matter. Instead he employed his incorporeal powers, truly designated Forms, so that each genus assume its fitting shape" (*Spec.* 1.328).

Philo brings scriptural support (Gen. 1:27) to indicate that the sensible world was created by God after the pattern of an intelligible world, which served as its model (*Op.* 19, 25). God created on the first day Ideas or Forms of heaven, earth, air (= darkness), void (= abyss), water, pneuma (= mind), and, "topping them all in the seventh place," light, the intelligent pattern of the sun and stars (*Op.* 29).[20] Days two through six witness the creation of the sensible world, though Philo insists that the number six is not to be taken literally, and that creation was in reality an instantaneous event that did not take place in time, "for time there was not before there was a world" (*Op.* 26, 67; *LA* 1.2; *Sacr.* 65).

The creation of the four elements is described by Philo as taking place by means of God's all-incising Logos, which divided the formless primordial matter into heavy and light, or dense and rare. The rare was further divided into air and fire, and the dense into water and earth (*Her.* 134–40). This process of division was carried out with superhuman and meticulous accuracy, so that the halves are always equal to the last atom (*Her.* 143; cf. *BR* 10.10, Th-Alb, p. 85). As in Plato, the elements are described as possessing certain geometrical figures, the fire being assigned the pyramid, while air is an octahedron, water an icosahedron, and the earth a cube (*QG* 3.49). Finally, we are told that the resulting four elements are proportionately equal, and that God's creative act is "insusceptible of any heightening or lowering of intensity but, remaining always in its supreme perfection, it fashioned every being perfectly, every number and every form that tends to perfection being used to the full by the Creator" (*Her.* 152, 156).[21]

In his valiant attempt to fill in the gaps and remove the ambiguities in Philo's creation account, H. Wolfson has provided a detailed interpretation that may serve as a convenient springboard for my own analysis. Despite the prodigal employment of long chains of adjectives and expressions, Philo's descriptions of preexistent matter appear to be almost deliberately vague. On the reasonable assumption that Philo was following closely in the footsteps of Plato's *Timaeus*, Wolfson explains the nature of his primordial matter as consisting of copies (μιμήματα) or traces ἴχνη) of the ideal four elements, and of the empty space (χώρα) that contained them as a sort of receptacle

9

(ὑποδοχή). Although there is no explicit mention of this in Philo, it seems to me that his descriptive adjectives must imply such a concept. How else explain that the primordial matter is disordered, confused, contentious, and full of dissimilars and inequality? These words imply differentiation and would jibe well with a receptacle in which the copies of the four elements are flashing in and out in haphazard disarray. Such a matter is qualityless and formless in the sense of not yet possessing any determinate character; motionless, as not yet possessing rational motion;[22] and dissoluble or perishable in itself, as lacking any stable character.

Wolfson notes further that, in describing the intelligible world, Philo has made some important modifications in Plato's theory. Whereas Plato had no special form for soul or mind, Philo does introduce such a form (i.e., *pneuma*). Although Wolfson makes no mention of them, there are two further modifications that ought to be pointed out. For Plato, the Form is contrasted with Space in that the Form "never receives anything else into itself from elsewhere." There is no archetype of Space that exists in its own right, and is apprehended not by sense but by a sort of bastard reasoning. "It is not, like the Form, an object of genuine rational understanding, because it has no status in the world of Forms."[23] Philo, on the other hand, has an ideal Form of Space. Moreover, Plato never designated the ὑποδοχή or ἐκμαγεῖον as a κενόν, whereas Philo does use the latter designation.[24] A modification of more crucial importance, however, as Wolfson has correctly indicated, is Philo's ascribing of the creation of the Forms to God, whereas for Plato they were ungenerated. But if the Forms are created by God, argues Wolfson, then the copies of those Forms must also be created, and so it becomes "unmistakably clear" that preexistent matter was, in Philo's opinion, created by God (1.308). Finding Plato either vague or inconsistent on the question of the creation of the Forms and the copies of the Forms, Philo clarified these matters for himself through his own interpretation. This is the crux of Wolfson's argument for ascribing to Philo a double creation theory, and I shall now proceed to show why I find it unconvincing.[25]

Wolfson admits at the very outset that "no light can be thrown on Philo's position (on whether preexistent matter was itself created) through the help of Scripture or postscriptural Jewish tradition. . . . If, therefore, an answer is to be found, it will have to be found in some passage in which he defines and unmistakably states that the preexistent matter out of which the world was created was itself created by God" (1.302–303). With this I heartily agree. Since no explicit theory of creation *ex nihilo* had ever been formulated either in Jewish or Greek tradition before Philo,[26] we should expect an emphatic and unambiguous statement from Philo on this matter, if that were indeed his position. I shall now attempt to demonstrate that Wolfson's inference from Philo's modifications of Plato's theory that Philo must have thought that the copies of the four elements were created, is, first of all, unwarranted, and second, would involve Philo's theory in a series of inner contradictions.

Plato was certainly vague on the manner in which the copies of the eternal Forms came into being, and his promise to "follow the matter up on another occasion" (*Tim.* 50C) was apparently never fulfilled. As a matter of fact, no philosophy that declares the intelligible alone to be real and all else relatively unreal (cf. Philo *Det.* 160) has ever successfully bridged the gap between these two realms. On the other hand, Plato admits that the "impressions are taken from the Forms (μιμήματα τυπωθέντα ἀπ' αὐτῶν) in a strange manner that is hard to express" (*Tim.* 50C), and makes no attempt to attribute their creation to the Demiurge. To have done so would have been contrary to his conception of the latter as "good" and "desiring that all things should come as near as possible to being like himself" (29E). Why should the Demiurge create semblances (φαντάσματα) that barely "cling to existence on pain of being nothing at all?" Most scholars have therefore understood the emergence of the Platonic εἴδωλα as some sort of automatic reflection of the Forms in the Receptacle. The whole point of the Platonic construction is that our sensible world is only a shadow-image of the truly existent, whose very shadowy existence is a constant embarrassment that needs to be glossed over as inconspicuously as possible.[27] Wolfson's inference, then, that according to Philo God must have created the copies is by no means a necessary one. We might just as well conclude that for Philo, as for Plato, the copies are mere shadow-reflexes of the Forms, and that the precise explanation for their production was as nonchalantly brushed aside by Philo as it was by Plato.

Furthermore, to attribute to Philo the view that God created preexistent matter would be incongruous with his whole language of creation. First, if God created the copies of the four elements according to the pattern of the divine Forms, why should they be disordered? Second, how could God who, according to Philo, is never the source of evil, and is always introducing harmony and order, be the source of a preexistent matter that is "contentious," "disordered," "dead," "chaotic," and "out of tune"?[28] Moreover, the argument that God created the cosmos because he did not begrudge a share in his own excellence to an existence that in itself had nothing fair or lovely would completely miss its mark if this "unlovely existence" was itself created by God. Philo's assertion that God did not confer benefits on preexistent matter in proportion to his own bounties, but rather in proportion to the capacities of the recipients (*Op.* 23), implies an inherent limitation in the nature of this matter. Why, then, should God have created copies of the Forms in the first place? If, as we have just seen, the copies are inherently disordered and disharmonious and can be rendered ordered and harmonious only up to a point, what reason could there be for the all-beneficent Deity to initiate the production of such limited phantoms, a "faulted reality" from a faultless one? Indeed, Philo virtually says as much when he poignantly states that "it was not the matter subjected to his creative activity, material inanimate, discordant and dissoluble, and what is more in itself perishable, irregular and unequal, that God praised, but the works of his own art accomplished by a power unique, equal, and uniform, and through knowledge ever one and the same" (*Her.* 160). Logically, of course, God is, for Philo, indirectly the source of preexistent matter, but Philo would have recoiled from ascribing it to the *creative* activity of God, just as he recoiled from ascribing even the *shaping* of matter directly to God.[29]

Wolfson further asserts that God's creation of preexistent matter must have been *ex nihilo*.[30] This, however, would appear to contradict Philo's explicit statement in *Aet.* 5 that "nothing comes into being from the nonexistent and nothing is destroyed into the nonexistent."[31] Nor is it possible to assume that this represented only an early view of Philo's, since it is repeated in *Spec.* 1.266: "For nothing is made as to disappear into nonexistence; whence it came in the beginning, thither will it return in the end."[32]

Summing up, Wolfson asserts that Philo indirectly alludes to God's creation of preexistent matter in his statement that God "created space (χώρα) and place (τόπος) simultaneously with bodies (σώματα)." By the term "bodies," Wolfson thinks Philo means both extended bodies, that is, the elements, and the copies of the four ideal elements, for the term body has also the meaning of matter in the sense of not being an idea. "It is because of the double meaning of the term 'bodies' used by him here that he uses the two terms 'space' and 'place,' meaning thereby that 'space' was created simultaneously with the 'matter from which,' whereas 'place' by its Aristotelian definition implies the existence of extended bodies" (*Phys.* 4.4.212a, 5–6). Grant, de Vogel, and Arnaldez have accepted Wolfson's interpretation, and Grant thinks that the Philonic statement quoted above contains a clear allusion to God's creation of the receptacle or space, which was a component of the Platonic preexistent matter.[33] But the use of σώματα to refer to primordial matter is highly unlikely, and Philo's statement is clearly susceptible of an alternative interpretation. The term χώρα had been used by Chrysippus as essentially synonymous with τόπος except that the former referred to the τόπος of a large body (*SVF* 2.503, 505). Philo may therefore simply be saying that with the creation of determinate matter (σώματα), God thereby also created both χώρα and τόπος.[34]

2. Creation Temporal or Eternal?

In his discussion of the origin and duration of the world, Aristotle asserts that all his predecessors held it to have had a beginning (γενόμενον), but some (like Plato) had maintained that having begun it was everlasting, others (such as the Atomists) that it was perishable, and others again (such as Empedocles and Heraclitus) that it was subject to an eternal sequence of cyclic genesis and destruction (*De Cael.* 1.10). The Platonic view Aristotle held to be impossible. He was aware, however, that some Platonists interpreted Plato's cosmology differently, though he considered their interpretation to be untrue.

> They claim that what they say about the generation of the world is analogous to the diagrams drawn by mathematicians: their exposition does not mean that the world ever was generated (οὐχ ὡς γενομένου ποτέ), but is used for instructional purposes (διδασκαλίας χάριν), since it makes things easier to understand just as the diagram does for those who see it in process of construction. (*De Cael.* 279b30)

With the exception of Plutarch and Atticus, this interpretation of Plato's *Timaeus* was steadily maintained by virtually all Platonists down to the time of Plotinus. Moreover, according to Atticus, the motivation for this exegesis was the inability of its authors to resist the Aris-

INTRODUCTION

totelian argument for the eternity of the universe, while yet shrinking in their pious devotion to the Master from ascribing to him a doctrine considered false by Aristotle (Euseb. *PE*. 15.6.6).[35]

It should be noted, however, that there was some disagreement among the Platonists as to the precise formulaton of the Platonic theory of cosmogony. Some were willing to assert that according to Plato the world was in reality ἀγένητος, uncreated, but could, for pedagogical reasons, be characterized as γενητός, created, insofar as it is ultimately derived from higher principles (e.g., the One and the Indefinite Dyad, and secondarily, the Ideas and Mathematicals). Others however (such as Crantor and his followers) insisted that according to Plato the world was γενητός, though this was not to be understood in a temporal sense. Proclus, for example, attacks Platonists like Xenocrates and Speusippus for asserting that according to Plato the world was γενητός only κατ᾽ ἐπίνοιαν, conceptually, or was feigned to be so σαφηνείας ἕνεκα διδασκαλικῆς, for clarity of instruction, for Timaeus, he insists, infers the existence of the Maker from the premise that the world is γενητός, and if the premise is merely conceptual, the Demiurge must be so too. It would appear that Proclus's objection rests on semantic considerations. In his view, the formulations of Xenocrates and Speusippus and their like are misleading and may result in the branding of their ultimate principles (the One and the Indefinite Dyad)[36] as empty abstractions. Proclus, therefore, prefers to say that the world is γενητός, though in the sense that it is ἀεὶ γιγνόμενον καὶ γεγενημένον, ever being produced and in a state of having been produced (*In Plat. Tim.* 290.3–25). This semantic distinction is of some importance for our understanding of Philo's position in this matter, for if our thesis that he taught a doctrine of eternal creation is correct, it would strike one as not a little perverse that he should accept Aristotle's literalist interpretation of Plato's creation doctrine in the *Timaeus* in preference to that of Xenocrates and Speusippus (*Aet.* 14–16). He apparently did so, however, in order to substantiate the view that Plato did think that the world was γενητός in the sense that it was the product of a real Demiurgic creativity (cf. *Op.* 171), yet at the same time rejecting Aristotle's temporal understanding of it.[37]

In the light of this debate over the meaning of the *Timaeus* doctrine of creation, we may now examine Philo's discussion of the eternity of the world in *Prov.* 1.6–9.[38] After noting that superficial observation often results in the belief that the world has existed from

14

eternity independent of any creative act (the Aristotelian view), he immediately proceeds to attack the "sophistic" view[39] "elaborated with drawn-out quibbles," that God did not begin to create the world at a certain moment, but was "eternally applying himself to its creation." The intent of this formulation, says Philo, was to avoid imputing to God a most unbecoming inactivity, which would otherwise have characterized his precreative state.[40] But in this case, the absurdity of this hypothesis becomes immediately evident; for those who have espoused it in order to remove a minimal accusation against the deity have actually attached to him a maximal one. Their conception of God's creative act consists, in the last analysis, of the bestowal of order and form on a primordial matter that lacked all previous determination. Is this not equivalent, argues Philo, to making matter into a principle of creation alongside of God? While solicitously clearing God of the accusation of temporary inactivity they have thus nonchalantly overlooked the more genuine threat to his sovereign creative power.

Philo now states his own position:

> God is continuously ordering matter by his thought. His thinking was not anterior to his creating and there never was a time when he did not create, the ideas themselves having been with him from the beginning. For God's will is not posterior to him, but is always with him, for natural motions never give out. Thus ever thinking he creates, and furnishes to sensible things the principle of their existence, so that both should exist together: the ever-creating Divine Mind and the sense-perceptible things to which beginning of being is given. (1.7)[41]

At first sight this passage seems baffling. Having concluded his denunciation of those who teach a doctrine of eternal creation on the grounds of their converting the Creator into the mere orderer of a primordial principle, Philo now seems to espouse just such a doctrine in turn. God, in Philo's view, is eternally creating inasmuch as he is ever thinking, and his creativity is constituted by nothing more than the meticulously accurate division of a formless matter through his all-incising Logos (cf. *Her.* 134, 140). The solution, however, is not far to seek, if we focus our attention on some important modifications Philo has introduced into his own theory of eternal creation. In the mystical monotheism of Philo nothing really exists or acts except God;[42] all else is but a shadow reality ultimately deriving from the truly Existent. Unlike Plato, who was a pluralist, Philo was thus unwilling to allow even for a self-existing void, and therefore made its pattern an eternal idea within the Divine Mind.[43] In Plato's conception of matter, the self-existing Receptacle is its most stable and permanent constituent: "It must be called always the same, for it never departs at all from its own character" (*Tim.* 50BC).[44] For Philo, however, not only are the phantasmagoric copies of the ideal four elements indirectly derived from God[45] (whether they are similarly derived for any of the Middle Platonists preceding Philo would depend on whether or not they had anticipated him in making the eternal Forms ideas in the mind of God),[46] but even the virtually nonexistent void is but a shadow reflection of an idea in God. Hence what in Philo's view was the crucial defect in the Platonists' doctrine of eternal creation (i.e., the elevation of matter into an autonomous albeit passive principle) has carefully been eliminated from his own version of that theory.[47]

Continuing his argument with the Platonists, Philo now confronts them with what he considers to be an inner contradiction in their doctrine. If, says Philo, one refuses to acknowledge the simultaneity of God's thinking and creating, how can one explain the fact that matter that existed from all time was never found in a disordered state? What Philo seems to be arguing is that if one considers matter as an autonomous primordial element, rather than an indirect product of God's thinking, how could it be maintained that it never was in a disordered state? Only if God's thinking is eternally bringing matter into being and simultaneously ordering it can one avoid a primordially formless state of matter. But, continues Philo, if there was a time when matter was disordered, then the origin of the world began when order was imposed on it, and the Platonists can no longer speak of eternal creation.

Philo's theory of eternal creation can now be stated succinctly. Insofar as God is always thinking the intelligible Forms, he is eternally creating the Intelligible World or Logos, and thereby also indirectly causing its shadow reflection, the sensible world, which he is constantly making to conform as closely as possible to its intelligible counterpart.[48] Corroboration for this interpretation may be found in an oft-repeated principle of Philo's theology that God is unchangeable, so that a temporal creation involving as it does a change in God's nature would thus stand in open contradiction to a fundamental assumption of Philo's thought. Nor is it possible to say as Saint Thomas later would that God willed freely from eternity that the world should come into existence in time (or have *esse post non-esse: Contr. Gent.* 2.31–7; *S.T.* 1.46.1; *De Potent.* 3.7), for Philo has already stated (*Prov.* 1.7) that God's thinking is simultaneous with his acting or creating (cf. *Sacr.* 65; *Mos.* 1.283). In the light of all this we should have to conclude that the many passages in which Philo speaks of creation in temporal terms are not to be taken literally, but only as accommodations to the biblical idiom.[49]

A strangely dissonant note, however, is struck in *Decal.* 58, where it is explicitly stated that "there was a time when the world was not" ($\mathring{\eta}\nu$ $\pi o\tau\epsilon$ $\chi\rho\acute{o}\nu o\varsigma$, $\acute{o}\tau\epsilon$ $o\mathring{v}\kappa$ $\mathring{\eta}\nu$). It may be that in a polemical context in which the target is a form of idolatry (worship of the Universe itself: cf. Wisd. 13:1–9) dangerously attractive even for a Jew if he belonged to the enlightened Hellenized class,[50] Philo did not hesitate to use locutions that explicitly negated his precise technical position. Moreover, it is not entirely out of keeping with Philo's usual style of exposition to use the phrase $\mathring{\eta}\nu$ $\pi o\tau\epsilon$ $\chi\rho\acute{o}\nu o\varsigma$ in a context such as this. For analytical purposes, Philo speaks, for example, of the mind's condition as it would have been, had it no connection with the sense perceptions transmitted to it by bodily sense organs. Allegorizing the biblical text concerning the creation of Eve, he naturally describes this state of the mind in temporal terms:

> For there was a time ($\mathring{\eta}\nu$ $\gamma\acute{a}\rho$ $\pi o\tau\epsilon$ $\chi\rho\acute{o}\nu o\varsigma$) when Mind neither had sense perception, nor held converse with it. . . . It was but half the perfect soul, lacking the power whereby it is the nature of bodies to be perceived, a mere unhappy section bereft of its mate without the support of the sense perceiving organs. . . . God, then, wishing to provide the Mind with perception of material as well as immaterial things, thought to complete the soul by weaving into the part first made the other section, which he called by the general name of "woman" and the proper name of "Eve," thus symbolizing sense. (*Cher.* 58–60; cf. *LA* 2.73)

We may conclude, then, that it is unnecessary to take the passage in *Decal.* 58 *au pied de la lettre*.[51]

We must now test our interpretation of Philo's creation doctrine by an examination of his theory of miracles to see whether the latter is consistent with the former. One of Philo's favored phrases is πάντα θεῷ δυνατά, a doctrine he never fails to intone as emphatically as he can whenever the opportunity presents itself. According to Philo, God created the heaven only after he had created the earth, so that

> none would suppose that the regular movements of the heavenly bodies are the causes of all things. For he has no need of his heavenly offspring on which he bestowed powers but not independence: for like a charioteer grasping the reins or a pilot the tiller, he guides all things in what direction he pleases as law and right demand, standing in need of no one besides: for all things are possible to God. (*Op.* 46; cf. *QG* 4.51)

This passage makes it clear that the formula "all things are possible to God" does not include what is not κατὰ νόμον καὶ δίκην, so that God evidently cannot act arbitrarily, that is, in a way that might be contrary to his own nature. Nor would it be correct to interpret Philo's position (as Wolfson does)[52] in the light of Saint Thomas's view, which would allow God to act outside the order of nature:

> If we consider the order of things according as it depends on any secondary causes, God can do something outside such order (e.g., produce the effects of secondary causes without them). For he is not subject to the order of secondary causes, but, on the contrary, this order is subject to him, as proceeding from him, not by a natural necessity, but by the choice of his own will; for he could have created another order of things.

Moreover,

> God fixed a certain order in things in such a way that at the same time he reserved to himself whatever he intended to do otherwise than by a particular cause. So when he acts outside this order, he does not change. (*S.T.* 1.105.6)

18

Philo, however, gives every indication of explaining God's miraculous acts within the framework of the existing natural order by simply expanding its parameters. Since our knowledge of the physical world is extremely limited, as Philo often emphasizes with a gusto that leads him on occasion to reproduce the Skeptical tropes (τρόποι or "modes") designed to bring about suspense of judgment (ἐποχή),[53] we easily mistake the biblically recorded miracles for events in contravention of the laws of nature. This is clearly indicated by Philo when he writes of the Israelites' incredulity concerning the ability of God to rescue them from a seemingly endless sequence of crises:

> For after experiencing strange events outside the customary without number, they should have ceased to be guided by anything that is specious and plausible (ὤφειλον ὑπὸ μηδενὸς ἔτι τῶν εὐλόγων καὶ πιθανῶν ἄγεσθαι) but should have put their trust in him [i.e., Moses] of whose unfailing truthfulness they had received the clearest proofs. (Mos. 1.196)

The speciousness of our perceptions, which leads to a narrow-minded view of what is physically possible, is expressed again in the following passage:

> To think that after witnessing wonders so many and so great, impossibilities no doubt as judged by what to outward appearance is credible and reasonable (πρὸς μὲν τὰς πιθανὰς καὶ εὐλόγους φαντασίας ἀδύνατα πραχθῆναι) but easily accomplished by the dispensations of God's providence, they not only doubted, but in their incapacity for learning actually disbelieved (Mos. 2.261).[54]

Although Philo does not explicitly invoke the physical principles involved in the Stoic theory of *pneuma* in order to explain God's ability to transform the elements at will, he very likely has this doctrine in the back of his mind.[55] Nevertheless, one cannot avoid the feeling that in expanding the natural order to encompass the biblical miracles, Philo has strained it to the breaking point, and has compromised the credibility of his philosophical position. He had, however, before him a striking example of this kind of intellectual legerdemain in the attempt of the Stoics to incorporate divination into their philosophical system. Cicero offers a sharp critique of the Stoic effort to explain the miracles associated with divination:

> Between that divine system of nature whose great and glorious laws pervade all space and regulate all motion what possible connection can there be with—I shall not say the gall of a chicken, whose entrails, some men assert, give very clear indications of the future, but—the liver, heart, and lungs of a sacrificial ox? (*Divinat.* 2.29)

He especially pokes fun at their explanation of how the sacrificer, in his search for favorable signs, is able to choose the proper victim by means of the divine power that pervades the entire universe:

> But even more absurd is that other pronouncement of theirs which you adopted: "At the moment of sacrifice a change in the entrails takes place; something is added or something is taken away; for all things are obedient to the Divine Will." Upon my word, no old woman is credulous enough now to believe such stuff. Do you believe that the same bullock, if chosen by one man, will have a liver without a head, and if chosen by another will have a liver with a head? ... Upon my word, you Stoics surrender the very city of philosophy while defending its outworks! For, by your insistence on the truth of soothsaying, you utterly overthrow physiology. There is a head to the liver and a heart in the entrails, presto! they will vanish the very second you have sprinkled them with meal and wine! Aye, some God will snatch them away! Some invisible power will destroy them or eat them up! Then the creation and destruction of all things are not due to nature, and there are some things which spring from nothing or suddenly become nothing. Was any such statement ever made by any natural philosopher? (*Divinat.* 2.35–37)

In the light of this Stoic caper,[56] it is no longer surprising that Philo felt free to exhibit the biblical miracles as emphatically as he did, although he occasionally tried to inject a possible explanation for them that coincided with the normal course of nature (the plague of

20

darkness, says Philo, may have been a total eclipse of the sun: *Mos.*
1.123),[57] and attempted to fit the ten plagues into a neat cosmological
pattern. Moreover, just as the Stoics believed that the miracles of divination were included among the causes foreordained by Destiny, so
Philo must have considered the biblical miracles as part of the complex patterns of an unchanging and eternal Logos, in which past,
present, and future are one.[58] If, nevertheless, Philo's exegetical devices are as unconvincing in this matter as those of the Stoics, we
should hasten to point out that his procedure seems to have been to
speak to his different audiences on various levels of comprehension,
a technique he projected into the biblical narrative itself.[59] In addressing a general audience, for example, he usually sacrifices philosophical rigor to the larger religious need of preserving the integrity
of the biblical tradition in the face of the Greek philosophical chal-
lenge without appearing to compromise any essentials on either side.
It is the nature of such a pedagogical approach that it renders well-
nigh impossible any effort to determine with precision which of the
two traditions ultimately has the upper hand when irreconcilable differences between them can no longer be adequately suppressed. In
the last analysis, it is the subtle inner flow of Philo's general thought
that must guide our interpretation of any particular issue that is obscured by the almost deliberate ambiguity projected by so much of his
writing.

III. PHILO'S MYSTICISM[60]

Although it is notoriously difficult to define mysticism, most students of the subject agree that it involves a timeless apprehension of
the transcendent through a unifying vision that gives bliss or serenity
and normally accrues on a course of self-mastery and contemplation.[61] This minimal description may serve as an adequate criterion
for our analysis of Philo's mystical passages, if in addition to the distinction between complete or undifferentiated identity with the transcendent as opposed to mere union with it, we further distinguish
between a union with the ultimate itself and one that is limited to
only an aspect of it, for we shall soon see that man's highest union
with God, according to Philo, is limited to the Deity's manifestation
as Logos, and is thus in a sense similar to the later mystical notion

of the contact or conjunction *(ittiṣāl)* of man's "acquired" intellect with the transcendent "active" intellect associated with philosophers such as Ibn Bājjah (d. 1138) and Ibn Rushd (1126–1198), and derived from Aristotle's famous commentator Alexander of Aphrodisias (fl. early third century C.E.).[62] This is obviously quite different from the Plotinian absorption into the Ineffable One, which is beyond Intellect, and is described in terms of a "touching" (ἀφή, ἐπαφή, θίξις) or "blending" (συακρῖναι) or the converging centers of circles.[63] Since Philo's barring of the way to God's essence is rooted in his concept of the utter divine transcendence, we shall begin our discussion with an analysis of that concept and its sources.

1. Divine Transcendence

It has already been noted that the notion of the absolute transcendence of the supreme First Principle may go back to Speusippus, the successor of Plato as head of the Old Academy, according to whom the primary principle of all things is not identical with any of them, but is prior to them and their attendant qualities (fr. 34, Lang). It would appear that this principle was already operative to some extent in early Greek philosophy. Simplicius, for example, explains Anaximander's choice of the ἄπειρον as the ἀρχή in the following manner: "It is clear that, having observed the change of the four elements into one another, he did not think fit to make any one of these the material substratum (ὑποκείμενον), but something else beside these" (DK A.9).[64] A similar doctrine to that of Speusippus was propounded by some of the Neopythagoreans, as well as by the Middle Platonist Eudorus of Alexandria (fl. 25 B.C.E.), with their postulation of a supranoetic First Principle above a pair of opposites: the Monad, representing Form, and the Dyad, representing Matter (Simplic. *In Phy.* 181, 10ff., Diels).[65] In the light of this evidence it should be apparent that Philo's prophetic inheritance, which emphasized the incomparability and unnameability of God, had converged in this instance with his philosophical inheritance to lead him to an emphatic doctrine of divine transcendence. It should be equally clear, however, that (pace Wolfson) it was his philosophic commitment that was the decisive element in his sharp distinction between God's existence and his essence, and his insistence on man's total inability to cognize the latter, for the use of such categories of thought was completely alien to both biblical and rabbinic tradition. Many scholars, however, have found Philo's utterances on this subject contradictory, and we must therefore examine his doctrine of transcendence in further detail.

Philo explicitly states on numerous occasions that God is absolutely ἄποιος, qualityless (*LA* 3.36, 1.36, 51; 3.206; *Deus* 55–56; *Cher.* 67), and Drummond and Wolfson have shown that not only does this mean that God is without accidental quality, but that it may be taken to imply also indirectly that in God there is no distinction of genus and species, that is, he is τὸ γενικώτατον, the most generic (*Gig.* 52), and since he belongs to no class, we do not know what he is.[66] Moreover, all the predicates that are predicated of God are strictly speaking "properties" (ἰδιότητες), that is, they are derivative of his essence, but unlike definitions, do not indicate the essence itself, and unlike qualities are not shared by him with others. Furthermore, since the essence of God is one and single, whatever belongs to it as a property must be one and single, and Philo therefore reduces all the divine properties to one single property, that of acting (*Cher.* 77).[67] In Philo's hierarchical construction of reality the essence of God, though utterly concealed in its primary being, is nevertheless made manifest on two secondary levels: the intelligible universe of Logos, which is God's image (*Somn.* 1.239; *Conf.* 147–48), and the sensible universe, which in turn is an image of that Logos (*Op.* 25). Thus, though the essence of God as it is in itself remains forever undisclosed, its effects, images, or shadows (or, to use the Plotinian term, traces: 6.7.17) may be perceived. Philo further attempts to delineate the dynamics of the Logos's activity by defining and describing its two constitutive polar principles: Goodness or the Creative Power (ποιητικὴ δύναμις), and Sovereignty (ἐξουσία) or the Regent Power (βασιλικὴ δύναμις) (*Cher.* 27–28; *Sacr.* 59; *Her.* 166; *Abr.* 124–25; *QE* 2.68; *Fug.* 95). It is not difficult to recognize in these two powers the ἄπειρον and πέρας or the Unlimited and Limit of Plato's *Philebus* (23C–31A),[68] which reappear in Plotinus's two moments in the emergence of *Nous*, where we find undefined or unlimited Intelligible Matter proceeding from the One and then turning back to its source for definition (2.4.5; 5.4.2; 6.7.17. cf. Proclus, *Elements*, props. 89–92, 159). Now, the various positive properties attributed to God by Philo may all be subsumed under either of these two polar forces, and are therefore all expressions of the one Logos, which constitutes the manifestation of God as thinking-acting (*Prov.* 1.7; *Sacr.* 65; *Mos.* 1.283). However, since God's essence as it is in itself is beyond any possibility of human experience or cognition, including the experience of mystic vision, the only attributes that may be applied to God in his supreme state of concealment are those of the *via negativa* (e.g. ἀγένητος, ἀδέκαστος, ἀκατάληπτος, ἀκατονόμαστος, ἀόρατος, ἀπερίγραφος, ἄρρητος, ἀσύγκριτος), or of the *via eminentiae*.[69]

Although at the summit the powers of the Logos may be grasped as constituting an indivisible unity, at lower levels there are those who cognize the Logos exclusively as the Creative Power, and those beneath them who cognize it as the Regent Power (*Fug.* 94ff.; *Abr.* 124–25). Lower still are those who, sunk in the mire of sensible being, are unable to perceive the intelligible realities with any degree of continuity (*Gig.* 20). At each successively lower level of divine knowledge the image of God's essence is increasingly dimmed or veiled.

2. Rational Mysticism: Faith, Reason, and Intuition

If we are to determine the function of mystic vision in the philosophy of Philo, we must first clarify his views concerning the relationship between faith, reason, and intuition. Wolfson has claimed that Philo sought to diminish Philosophy's stature by reducing it to the status of a bondwoman in contrast to the Torah, which is seen as the mistress, and has argued that when Philo represents philosophy as the bondwoman of wisdom, he thereby indicates that she is the bondwoman of the Torah:

> Philo compares the relation of philosophy, in the sense of Greek philosophy, to "wisdom" in the sense of the revealed Law, to the relation of the "encyclical studies" to philosophy, for he says, "just as the encyclical culture is the bondwoman of philosophy, so also is philosophy the bondwoman of wisdom" (*Congr.* 79). . . . This subservience of philosophy to wisdom or the Law is explained by him in a passage in which he says that "philosophy teaches the control of the belly and the control of the parts below the belly," but while all these qualities are desirable in themselves, still they "will assume a grander and loftier aspect if practised for the honor and service of God"; for the service and worship of God, as we have seen constitutes wisdom, and wisdom is the revealed Law embodied in Scripture. When, therefore, Philo speaks of philosophy as being the bondwoman or handmaid

of wisdom, he means thereby that it is the bondwoman or
handmaid of Scripture. [*Philo* 1.149–50]

The fact is, however, that a distinction between philosophy and wisdom was quite common among many Stoic thinkers according to Seneca's testimony (*Ep.* 89.4–9), and this distinction probably goes back
to the Middle Stoa.[70] It is therefore quite evident that when Philo,
following in the footsteps of the Stoa, defines philosophy as "devotion
to wisdom" (ἐπιτήδευσις σοφίας) and wisdom as the "knowledge of
things divine and human and their causes" (*Congr.* 79),[71] and then
concludes that just as the ἐγκύκλια are subservient to philosophy, so
philosophy is subservient to wisdom, that by wisdom he means philosophy consummated, which in turn is identical in his scheme of
things with the Torah, whose laws are in agreement with the eternal
principles of nature.[72] Far from subordinating philosophy to Scripture, Philo is rather identifying the Mosaic Law with the summit of
philosophical achievement. Thus, for example, Philo can equate Moses "who had attained philosophy's summit" with Moses "who had
been divinely instructed in the greater and most essential part of nature's lore" (*Op.* 8).[73]

Wolfson continues his argument by insisting that "the subordination of philosophy to Scripture means to Philo the subordination
of reason to faith." This is clearly expressed by him in his comment
on the verses "Abraham believed God and it was counted to him for
justice," and "not so my servant Moses; he is faithful in all my
house." Commenting on these verses, he says that "it is best to have
faith in the immediate knowledge given by God through revelation
rather than in the result of our reason" (Wolfson 1.151–52). The Philonic passage under discussion (*LA* 3.228–29), however, is not contrasting reason and faith, but faulty reason with firm, secure
knowledge. Philo employs four emphatic adjectives to draw his sharp
distinction between "trust in God" on the one hand, and the use of
obscure (ἀσαφέσι), empty (κενοῖς), plausible (πιθανοῖς) arguments,
or unreliable conjectures (ἀβεβαίοις εἰκασίαις), on the other. Abraham's faith in God is paradigmatic for Philo of the "unswerving and
firm assumption" that is attained when the mind has a vision of the
First Cause, the truly Existent.[74] The exuberant variety of physical
speculations is frequently the butt of Philo's biting critique,[75] when
he wishes to contrast the utter uncertainty of man's knowledge of reality with the infinite splendor of the divine wisdom, which alone is

perfect and self-secure. It is not the denigration of philosophic reason and the attempt to escape into the bosom of divine revelation that motivates Philo's skeptical flights (*Cher.* 65, 113; *Her.* 246; *Somn.* 1.21; *Ebr.* 166–205; *Jos.* 125–43; *Mig.* 134–38) but rather his unshakable conviction that our knowledge of the modal or finite aspect of reality belongs to the contingent and unabiding, whereas our unmediated intuition of infinite divinity, limited though it be by the inherent finitude of the human mind, is vastly more effective than discursive reason in affording us a glimpse of the eternally and truly real (*Praem.* 28–30). It is only as a consequence of such an intuitive vision that one begins to read Scripture correctly and in accord with its deeper meaning. Wolfson's attempt, therefore, to foist on Philo "the ancillary conception of philosophy which prevailed for many centuries in European philosophy" is essentially misguided.[76]

We must now determine the exact nature of this unmediated intuitive vision in whose praise Philo's efforts are so unflagging. In Philo's philosophy, the Logos is the Divine Mind, the Idea of Ideas, the first-begotten Son of the Uncreated Father, eldest and chief of the angels, the man or shadow of God, or even the second God, the pattern of all creation and archetype of human reason.[77] The Logos is God immanent, holding together and administering the entire chain of creation (*Mos.* 2.134; *Her.* 188), and man's mind is but a tiny fragment of this all-pervading Logos:

> For how was it likely that the human mind being so tiny, hemmed in by such puny masses as brain or heart, should be able to contain such an immense magnitude of sky and universe, had it not been an inseparable portion of that divine and blessed soul? For nothing is severed or detached from the divine, but only extended. When the mind, therefore, which has received its share in the perfection of the whole, conceives of the universe, it stretches out as widely as the bounds of tne whole, for its force is susceptible of attraction. (*Det.* 90; cf. *Gig.* 27; *LA* 1.37; Ps-Plato *Axioch.* 370B)

To the mind as yet uninitiated into the highest mysteries and still unable to apprehend the Existent alone by itself, but only through its actions, God appears as a triad constituted by himself and his two potencies, the Creative and the Regent. To the purified mind, on the other hand, God appears as One (*Abr.* 119–23). Philo thus dis-

26

tinguishes between the mind that apprehends God through his creation, and the mind that elevates itself beyond the physical universe and perceives the Uncreated One through a clear vision. Following in the footsteps of Plato, Aristotle, and the Stoa,[78] he vividly expounds the teleological proof for God's existence[79] (LA 3.97–103; see p. 124 below). At Praem. 40, he speaks of those who have apprehended God through his works as advancing from down to up (κάτωθεν ἄνω) by a sort of heavenly ladder[80] and conjecturing (στοχασάμενοι) his existence through plausible inference (εἰκότι λογισμ ῷ). But the genuine worshipers and true friends of God, he continues, are those who apprehend him through himself without the cooperation of reasoned inference, as light is seen by light. This formula is precisely that of Plotinus, when he speaks of "seeing the Supreme by the Supreme and not by the light of any other principle, for that which illumines the Soul is that which it is to see, just as it is by the sun's own light that we see the sun" (5.3.17; cf. idem 5.5.10; Apoc. Abr. chap. 7: "Yet may God reveal himself to us through himself." Both Philo and Plotinus are undoubtedly dependent for this sun image on Plato Rep. 507Cff. Cf. Mut. 4–6.) (See pp. 127–29 below.)

It is therefore quite clear that according to Philo, there is in addition to inferential reason, which provides an indirect mode for the apprehension of God, a direct approach requiring no mediation whatsoever. Wolfson believed that Philo is here referring to a direct divine revelation that bypasses the powers of human reason and is utterly dependent on God's grace, whose illumination flashes into the human psyche from without (cf. Bréhier, p. 134). Such an interpretation is, in my opinion, very unlikely. Philo does indeed speak elsewhere of prophetic revelation mediated through either ecstatic possession or the divine voice, a theory couched by him in the standard language of Greek theories of divination, but there is no mention of ecstasy or the eviction of the mind at the arrival of the Divine Spirit (Her. 265), or any form of prophecy at all, in the passages dealing with the direct vision of God.[81] Instead, Philo speaks of a "purified mind" capable of seeing God through Himself (cf. Deus 2). Moreover, as I have attempted to demonstrate above, Philo understands God's creative act as constituting an eternal process. God's revelation must therefore be seen as continuous, and as encompassing the ideas taking shape within the human mind, which as we have seen is nothing but an inseparable portion of the Divine Mind (cf. Op. 146; Mut. 223; Spec. 4.123).

Having thus eliminated a revelation that bypasses human reason,

27

we have yet to specify the precise nature of Philo's theory concerning the direct approach to God. The latter can be elucidated, however, by the examination of a well-known tradition in the history of philosophy that distinguishes between the cosmological and the ontological proofs for the existence of God. Whereas the former is based on inferential or deductive reasoning, the latter constitutes an analytical truth and its function is to clarify those propositions that are implied by our definitions. It would appear then that, according to Philo, the concept of God's existence is contained within certain definitions of human reason and needs but an inner illumination to reveal it. It is this inner intuitive illumination, constituting a rational process of an analytical type, that is to be identified with the divine revelation taking shape in the human mind and enabling it to have a direct vision of God. In Philo's figurative language, this experience is expressed as follows: "He in his love for mankind, when the soul came into his presence, did not turn away his face, but came forward to meet him and revealed his nature, so far as the beholder's power of sight allowed" (*Abr.* 79–80). Elsewhere he puts it that "the invisible Deity stamped on the invisible soul the impression of itself, to the end that not even the terrestrial region should be without a share in an image of God. . . . Having been struck in accord with the Pattern, it entertained ideas not now mortal but immortal" (*Det.* 86ff.; *LA* 38).

Although Philo does not specify the definitions that in his view contained the concept of God's existence, we may surmise that he is undoubtedly thinking of the various definitions of the *archē* out of which all things arise. Diogenes of Apollonia, for example, explained why the various elements of the cosmos could not be really different from one another in their own nature, so that they must all be modifications of one *archē*. "This is obvious," he writes, "for if the things now existing in this cosmos—earth, water, air, fire and all the other things which manifestly exist in this cosmos—if one of these was different from another, different, that is, in its own proper nature, and not the same thing changed and altered in many ways, they could in no way mix with one another, nor affect one another for good or ill" (*DK.* B.2; cf. *QE* 2.88). One can easily transpose this into Spinozistic terms: The various elements cannot be *archai* or substances, for substances having different attributes have nothing in common with one another (*Eth.* 1.2), whereas the elements interchange and therefore must have something in common. They therefore constitute but one substance modified in different ways. The immediate origin, however, of Philo's second way of knowing God, is undoubtedly to be found in Plato's well-known remarks at the end of *Rep.* 6 to the effect that dialectical reasoning (νόησις) can arrive at the intuition of a First Principle by "treating its assumptions not as absolute beginnings but literally as hypotheses, underpinnings, footings, and springboards so to speak, to enable it to rise to that which requires no assumption and is the starting point of all, and after attaining to that again taking hold of the first dependencies from it, so to proceed downward to the conclusion, making no use whatever of any object of sense but only of pure ideas moving on through ideas to ideas and ending with ideas" (511BC; cf. 532AB: "When anyone by dialectics attempts through discourse of reason and apart from all perceptions of sense to find his way to the very essence of each thing and does not desist till he apprehends by thought itself the nature of the good in itself, he arrives at the limit of the intelligible"). The exact nature of this upward-downward dialectical path has been much debated, but the most likely interpretation is that it involves a sudden intuition of the First Principle (cf. *Symp.* 210E; *Ep.* 7.341CD) at the end of a series of analyses of various hypotheses, which then permits a downward series of deductions from that Principle.[82] It may be recalled that Spinoza's third kind of knowledge, *scientia intuitiva*, by means of which man knows God, is similarly independent of sense perception and deductive reasoning.

Finally, according to the testimony of Cicero (*ND* 2.12), the Stoics taught that God's existence is imprinted in man. Among the many proofs they adduced there are some that appear to have constituted analytical truths. One series of arguments, for example, revolves around the central notion of the world's perfection, which necessarily includes the highest form of reason. "There is nothing else beside the world that has nothing wanting, but is fully equipped and complete and perfect in all its details and parts" (ibid. 2.37). Since "it embraces all things and since nothing exists that is not within it, it is entirely perfect; how then can it fail to possess that which is best?" (2.38). (Cf. Sextus *Math.* 9.88-91, where a similar argument is ascribed to Cleanthes, and Aristotle *De Philosophia*, fr. 16 Ross.)[82a] Although the Stoic arguments cited by Cicero are not quite identical with the ontological argument as classically formulated by thinkers such as Saint Anselm, Descartes, and Spinoza, we do have at one point a locution that appears to be an incipient form of Saint Anselm's famous "*aliquid quo nihil maius cogitari potest*" (*Proslogion*, chaps. 2 and 3). The Stoics point out that not only does nothing exist that is superior to the world, but nothing superior can even be conceived *(ne cogitari quidem quicquam melius potest)* (2.18). The ontological proof is essentially constituted by the argument that man possesses the notion of that "than which nothing greater can be conceived," or that which necessarily exists, or that "whose essence involves existence," or a being who exists through his own power, or a being of the highest power or perfection. The Stoic arguments referred to above all endeavor to demonstrate that universal nature is an absolutely perfect being and therefore perfectly intelligent or divine. The human mind thus possesses the notion of a being of the highest power or perfection, and may thus be said to have the existence of God engraved within.

It is now clear that the direct vision of God is attributed by Philo to the workings of intuitive reason, and in no way serves as a bypass of man's rational faculties. Following Plato's lead *(Phaedr.* 249 CD), however, Philo repeatedly asserts that this unmediated vision may at times culminate in an experience of mystical union accompanied by a Bacchic frenzy, an ecstatic condition that shakes the soul to its very foundations. As with most mystics, however, he is convinced that this longed-for experience can come only after long and arduous preparations. We must therefore now turn our attention to a description of the psychic state that in Philo's view is a prerequisite for the mystic experience and the ascetic path leading to it.

3. *Apatheia/Eupatheia*

Imitating God, who is completely *apathēs*,[83] the wise man must achieve a state of *apatheia*, that is, he must convert all his *pathē*, diseased or irrational emotions, into *eupatheiai*, rational emotions.[84] Thus, for example, the wise man would never experience the morbid emotion of fear, but only the completely rational feeling of caution or wariness, which requires no further moderation or modification. Grief, on the other hand, he would not be subject to in any form, experiencing at most a mental sting or minor soul contractions, which are morally neutral and betray not the slightest trace of irrationality. In his state of *apatheia/eupatheia* the *sophos*, symbolized for Philo by Isaac, acts out of a fixity of disposition, no longer having to struggle to make rational decisions.[85]

In Philo's view, the body is by no means to be neglected, nor is its well-being deliberately to be compromised in any way. Those who needlessly fast or refuse the bath and oil, or are careless about their clothing and lodging, thinking that they are thereby practicing self-control, are to be pitied for their error. They are similar to those counterfeits who never cease making sacrificial and costly votive offerings in their mistaken belief that piety consists in ritual rather than holiness, and thus attempt to flatter One who cannot be flattered and who abhors all counterfeit approaches (*Det.* 19–21). Moreover, it is false strategy to oppose irrational desires by taking off in the opposite direction and practicing austerities, "for in this way you will rouse your adversary's spirit and stimulate a more dangerous foe to the contest against you" (*Fug.* 25). Better to indulge in the various pursuits for external goods, but to do so with skillful moderation and self-control. "Begin, then," advises Philo, "by getting some exercise and practice in the business of life both private and public; and when by means of the sister virtues, household-management and statesmanship, you have become masters in each domain, enter now, as more than qualified to do so, on your migration to a different and more excellent way of life" (*Fug.* 36–38). As a matter of fact, even the wise man will indulge in heavy drinking, though in the more moderate manner of the ancients rather than in the style of the moderns who drink "till body and soul are unstrung." For "the countenance of wisdom is not scowling and severe, contracted by deep thought and depression of spirit, but on the contrary cheerful and tranquil, full of joy and gladness" (*Plant.* 167–68).[86]

If the body is thus not to be neglected in any way, neither is it to be allowed to become the central focus of human concern or to usurp the higher dignity reserved for the rational element. Pleasure plays an important role in the life of ensouled creatures, but it must be accepted for what it really is and not elevated into a self-validating principle motivating human behavior. Following the teaching of Aristotle and the Stoics, Philo insists that joy, as well as pleasure, has no intrinsic importance, but is purely adventitious, a supervening aftermath or by-product of virtue (*Det.* 124; *LA* 3.80).[87] Moreover, although *hēdonē* in the sense of agreeable physical feelings is permitted even to the wise man, this is not the case when it denotes that type of mental pleasure which is accounted a *pathos* by the Stoics, and is the result of a faulty judgment:[88]

> But the serpent, pleasure, is of itself evil and is therefore not found at all in a good man, the bad man enjoying it all to

31

himself. Most appropriately, then, does God impose the curse, without allowing her a defense, since she contains no seed of virtue, but always and everywhere is found culpable and abominable. (*LA* 3.68)[89]

The body is for Philo, at best, a necessary evil (*LA* 3.72–73), for it is a corpse, a shell-like growth, "the dwelling place of endless calamities" (*Conf.* 177), wicked by nature and a plotter against the soul (*LA* 3.69). It is the source both of *agnoia*, lack of knowledge, and *amathia*, fundamental ignorance (cf. Plato *Rep.* 585B; *Tim.* 86B; *Soph.* 228ff.).

> For souls unfleshed and disembodied pass their days in the theater of the universe and enjoy unhindered sights and sounds divine, possessed by an insatiate love for them. But those who bear the load of the flesh are unable, thus weighed down and oppressed, to gaze upward at the revolving heavens, but with necks wrenched downward are forcibly rooted to the ground like four-footed beasts. (*Gig.* 31)

Philo quotes with approval Heraclitus's saying "we live their death, and are dead to their life" (*LA* 1.108). The soul that loves God will therefore disrobe itself of the body and its senses (*Ebr.* 69–70), and, devoting itself to genuine philosophy, will "from first to last study to die to the life in the body" (*Gig.* 14).[90]

In sum, like any good Platonist, Philo would much prefer to dispense with material reality and the human body that constitutes an inseparable part of it. As a philosophical realist, however, he must accept it and, on occasion, justify its existence within the divine scheme of things. He consequently never loses track of the body's legitimate needs and functions, though he is keenly aware of its capacity to entrap and entice the higher self. He believes that most men must wean themselves away from the physical aspect of things only very gradually and with the expenditure of much effort and toil, though he is aware of the psychological contamination that may result from too extended an exposure to bodily concerns. He is convinced, however, that some, though not many, may ultimately succeed in focusing their minds much of the time on the eternal realities, while yet going through the motions of somatic activity, which will have finally faded away into insignificance.

INTRODUCTION

4. The Mystical Experience

We are now prepared to evaluate the mystical passages in Philo. Like most mystics, he is convinced that man's goal and ultimate bliss lie in the knowledge or vision of God (*Decal.* 81; *Det.* 86; *Abr.* 58; *Praem.* 14; *QE* 2.51). Indeed, the mere quest is sufficient of itself to give a foretaste of gladness (*Post.* 20; *QG* 4.4; see pp. 164–65 below). The soul has a natural longing and love for God and is drawn to him by a surpassing beauty (*Somn.* 2.232; see p. 165–67 below). The first step leading to God is man's recognition of his own nothingness, which induces him to depart from himself (*Somn.* 1.60; *Her.* 69; see pp. 168–69 below). Having gone out of himself, the devotee is now asked to attach himself completely to God (*Plant.* 64; see p. 169 below). This attachment to God involves the realization that it is God alone who acts, and as long as the mind "supposes itself to be the author of anything it is far away from making room for God" (*LA* 1.82). In the fragment from the lost fourth book of his *Legum Allegoria*, Philo writes:

> "But when [Moses] affirms the first and better principle, namely, that God acts not as man, he ascribes the powers and causes of all things to God, leaving no work for a created being but showing it to be inactive and passive." Those uninitiated, however, "in the great mysteries about the sovereignty and authority of the Uncreated and the exceeding nothingness of the created," do not as yet recognize this truth. [Harris, *Fragments*, p. 8; cf. *Cher.* 77, 128]

Moreover, in abandoning body and sense perception, the mind is now absorbed in a form of intellectual prayer that is wordless and unencumbered by petition (*Fug.* 92; see pp. 170–71 below.[91] In *Her.* 71 Philo writes:

> Great indeed was [speech's] audacity, that it should attempt the impossible task to use shadows to point me to substances, words to point me to facts. And, amid all its blunders, it chattered and gushed about, unable to present with clear expression those distinctions in things which baffled its vague and general vocabulary.

The mystic vision of God is a timeless experience that carries the soul to the uttermost bounds of the universe and enables it to gaze on the Divine Logos (*Conf.* 95; *Ebr.* 152; see pp. 171–72 below). Still, the notion of actual union with God appears in only one passage: "He bids them 'cleave to Him' (Deut. 30:20), bringing out by the use of this word how constant and continuous and unbroken is the concord and union (ἑνώσεως) that comes through making God our own" (*Post.* 12; cf. *QG* 4.188: The wise man tries to unite the created with the uncreated). In the exceptional case of Moses, however, Philo's language occasionally oversteps its usual restraints and not only describes him as having been resolved into the nature of unity (*QE* 2.29), but also as having been "divinized" by ascending to God (ibid. 2.40; cf. however, *Det.* 161).[92]

The mystic state is further described by Philo as producing tranquility and stability (*Gig.* 49; *Deus* 12; *LA* 1.16; *Abr.* 58; *Post.* 27–28; cf. *Rep.* 532E2–3; *Somn.* 2.227–28, 236ff.), and it is sometimes indicated that it supervenes suddenly (*Sacr.* 78; *Somn.* 1.71; *Mig.* 35; cf. Plato, *Symp.* 210E; *Ep.* 7.341CD). It is also frequently described as a condition of sober intoxication,[93] which is invariably depicted in a highly spirited and enthusiastic manner. (The best known passage is at *Op.* 70; see p. 173 below).[94] Finally, like most mystics, Philo is keenly aware of the inability of man to maintain a steady vision of the divine and he speaks of the consequent ebb and flow that characterize that type of experience:

> But when the inspiration is stayed, and the strong yearning abates, it hastens back from the divine and becomes a man and meets the human interests that lay waiting in the vestibule ready to seize upon it, should it but show its face for a moment from within. [*Somn.* 2.233; cf. ibid. 1.115–15, 150; *QG* 4.29.]

Philo occasionally exhibits a tendency to compare the mystic experience to that of prophetic ecstasy (*Her.* 69–70; see p. 169 below), and in an autobiographical vein, describing his own personal experiences, he speaks of an inner voice within his soul that is God-possessed and divines where it does not know (*Cher.* 27). At *Mig.* 34–35, he describes such an experience more spaciously (see p. 76 below). It is significant that Philo has in this passage assimilated the mind's sudden attainment of clear insight to instances of divine possession and corybantic frenzy, thus providing a further indication that the latter terminol-

34

ogy was freely applied by him to all extraordinary experiences of intuitive clarity.[95]

It has been pointed out that one possible motive behind Philo's lyrical descriptions of the mystic condition of the soul is his desire to vindicate prophetic inspiration and thereby authenticate Scripture as inspired writing. Some interpreters of Philo have consequently played down the mystical passages and have regarded them not as a reflection of true mystical experience but rather as a combination of poetic flourishes and clever apologetic. An analogy to this would be the well-known use of "mystery" terminology by many Greek philosophers in order to indicate the more esoteric levels of their teachings.[96] Our detailed examination of Philo's mystical passages, however, has clearly revealed that they contain most of the characteristic earmarks of mystical experience. These may now be briefly summarized as follows: Knowledge of God is man's supreme bliss (with the corollary that separation from God is the greatest of evils); the soul's intense yearning for the divine; recognition of man's nothingness and the need to go out of oneself; attachment to God; the realization that it is God alone who acts; a preference for contemplative prayer; a timeless union with the All; the serenity that results from the mystic experience; the suddenness with which the vision appears; the notion of sober intoxication; the ecstatic condition of the soul in the mystic state; and finally the ebb and flow of mystical experience. If this evidence is added to the autobiographical remarks quoted above, it becomes abundantly clear that Philo was at least a "mystical theorist" (if not a "practicing mystic")[97] in the very core of his being and that his philosophical writings cannot be adequately understood if this signal fact is in any way obscured.

IV. PHILO'S SIGNIFICANCE

The preservation of the very extensive Philonic corpus by the Church is due to the notion of the fourth-century church historian Eusebius that the monastic group described in Philo's *The Contemplative Life* was Christian (*HE* 2.17.1).[98] Eusebius mentions a tradition to the effect that Philo met Peter on a journey to Rome during the reign of Claudius, and he regards him as teaching the doctrine of the trinity. Jerome even includes Philo in the list of Church Fathers (*Virt. Il-lust.* 11).[99] Had it been left to Jewish tradition, Philo's work would undoubtedly have perished. The Jewish Middle Ages had access at best only to a partial translation of Philo's works in either Arabic or Syriac,[100] and it was not until the sixteenth century that Philo was rediscovered by Azariah dei Rossi.[101] Philo thus had virtually no direct influence on the Jewish philosophical tradition. Yet Philo was the only Jewish philosopher who possessed an unmediated knowledge of the original Greek texts, both literary and philosophical, and had elaborated a philosophy of Judaism that radically transformed its inner structure.

If my reading of Philo is correct, his world view is in many respects astonishingly similar to that of Spinoza,[102] despite the Platonic chasm that divides them. Like Spinoza, Philo teaches a doctrine of eternal creation[103] and places at the forefront of his proofs for God's existence a version of what appears to be the ontological argument. The human mind is for him a fragment of the Divine Mind (in Spinoza's terminology, a finite mode of the absolutely infinite intellect), and its highest knowledge is its direct knowledge of God (in Spinoza, *scientia intuitiva: Eth.* 5.25, 27). God's nature is absolutely unchangeable (Spinoza would say that "things could have been produced by God in no other manner and in no other order than that in which they have been produced" [*Eth.* 1.33]), and the human will is ultimately determined by the Divine (*Eth.* 1.27, 29). The authentic law is rooted in Nature or God *(Deus sive Natura)*, and man's highest goal is to attach himself completely to God, his mind absorbed in intellectual prayer (Spinoza's *amor dei intellectualis: Eth.* 5.33–42). The path leading to this goal entails the conversion of man's irrational emotions into rational ones (Spinoza's active and passive emotions: *Eth.* 3), until he rises to a state of union with the Divine Logos, seized by a sober intoxication. Here Philo's path converges completely with that of the God-intoxicated Spinoza. Still, while Spinoza's thought in the *Theological Political Tractate* is garbed in the rhetoric of confrontation and his precisely formulated propositions in the *Ethics* are calculated to effect a clean break with traditional theism, Philo's philosophy is couched in the conciliatory idiom of Platonic mysticism and is further deliberately disguised to camouflage its more radical dimensions. Had Philo's writings been accessible to the Jewish philosophical tradition, they would undoubtedly have left an indelible mark on it, and his profound insights would have imprinted themselves deeply within the Jewish psyche. But the Palestinian Jewry contemporary with Philo was not much interested in philosophy, particularly when written in Greek,[104] and the Alexandrian Jewish community was virtually annihilated after the revolt of Egyptian Jewry against Trajan (115–117 C.E.). Philo's great contribution to Judaism was thus relegated by the fortunes of history to the limbo of philosophy's untimely abortions whose impact is primarily channeled through the subterranean underworld of intellectual history, whereas his significance for Christian spirituality proved to be of primary importance.

THE
CONTEMPLATIVE
LIFE

INTRODUCTORY NOTE TO
THE CONTEMPLATIVE LIFE

In this treatise Philo presents an encomiastic account of an ascetic community devoted to the contemplative life, with which he had personal acquaintance. Having placed the Therapeutae ("healers" or "worshipers"), the name by which this sect was known, not far from Alexandria, where he himself lived, it is clear that he could not have invented them. Utopias are usually located at remote distances, safe from any effort at verification. As for the relationship of the Therapeutae to the Essenes, the consensus is that, although originating from the same root, they nevertheless represent separate developments. Vermes, however, believes that there is a close bond between them, and he interprets the opening sentence of the treatise as implying that the Therapeutae were contemplative Essenes.

The Therapeutae are not extreme ascetics (although considerably more ascetic than the Essenes), and do not practice mortifications. They do not live in the true desert, and seek only the philosophical tranquillity that will lead them to a mystic vision of the one God. Philo sharply contrasts their sober banquets with their pagan counterparts, and his account ends with a vivid and highly enthusiastic depiction of their festive symposia and night vigils, with their edifying disquisitions on questions of Holy Writ, culminating with choral hymns in a wide variety of modes, and the gradual blending of their male and female choirs into one, while rising to a crescendo of exquisite intoxication.

THE CONTEMPLATIVE LIFE
OR SUPPLIANTS[1]

Mode of Exposition

I. After discussing the Essenes[2] who zealously cultivated the ac- 1
tive life, and excelled in all or, to put it more acceptably, in most of its spheres, I shall now proceed at once, following the sequence demanded by the treatment of this subject, to say what is fitting con-

cerning those who have espoused the life of contemplation. I will add nothing of my own for the sake of embellishment, as is customarily done by all poets and historians through a dearth of noble life-styles in the subjects they treat, but shall absolutely hold to the truth itself, in the face of which I well know even the most eloquent orator would abandon the effort. We must nevertheless struggle through and bring the contest to its close, for the grandeur of these men's virtue ought not mute the tongue of those who hold that nothing excellent should be passed over in silence.

Explanation of the Name Therapeutae

2   The vocation of these philosophers is disclosed at once by their name, for they are called, according to the true meaning or etymology of the words, Therapeutae and Therapeutrides [literally, "healers," male and female], either insofar as they profess an art of healing[3] better than that practiced in the cities—for the latter cures only the body, while theirs treats also souls mastered by grievous and virtually incurable diseases, inflicted by pleasures and lusts, mental pains and fears, by acts of greed, folly, and injustice, and the endless multitude of the other mental disturbances and vices—or else they are so called because they have been taught by nature and the holy laws to worship the Existent who is better than the Good, purer than the One, and more primal then the Monad.

Incomparable Superiority of the Therapeutae

3   Who among those who profess piety may properly be compared with these? Can we compare those who revere the elements, earth, water, air, fire? To these elements different names have been assigned by different people, some, for example, calling fire Hephaestus, presumably because of its kindling ($\dot{\epsilon}\xi\dot{\alpha}\pi\tau\omega$), the air Hera because it is elevated ($\alpha\dot{\iota}\rho\omega$) and rises to a height; water Poseidon perhaps because it is potable ($\pi o\tau\acute{o}\varsigma$),[4] and earth Demeter, inasmuch as it appears to

4   be the mother of all plants and animals. These names, however, are the inventions of Sophists, whereas the elements are lifeless matter[5] incapable of self-movement and laid down by the Artificer as a substrate for every sort of form and quality.

5   What of those who worship the finished products of creation, sun, moon, or the other stars wandering or fixed, or the entire heaven

and universe? But these too did not come to be of themselves, but through a craftsman most perfect in his knowledge.

What of those who worship the demigods? Surely this is even a 6 matter for ridicule. How could the same being be both immortal and mortal, not to mention that the very source of their generation is open to reproach, infected as it is with youthful debauchery that they impiously dare to attribute to the blessed and divine powers, supposing that the thrice blessed beings who have no share in any passion were mad after mortal women and mated with them?

What of the worshipers of carved images and statues? Their sub- 7 stance is stone and wood, till a short while ago utterly shapeless. Quarrymen and woodcutters cut them out of their congenital structure while their kindred and cognate parts have become urns and footbasins and some other vessels of a yet ignobler sort, which serve for use in darkness rather than in the light.

As for the gods of the Egyptians, even to mention them is inde- 8 cent. The Egyptians have advanced to divine honors brute animals, not only of the tame sort but also beasts of the utmost savagery, from every sublunar species; from land creatures the lion, from those of the water the native crocodile, from those that roam the air the kite and the Egyptian ibis. And although they see these animals begotten, in 9 need of nourishment, insatiate in their eating, crammed with ordure, venom-spraying and man-devouring, the prey of all sorts of diseases, and perishing not only by a natural but often by a violent death, they make obeisance to them, they the civilized to the untamed and wild, the rational to the irrational, they who are akin to the Deity to those not even on a par with [the ape-like] Thersites,[6] the lords and masters of creation to the naturally subservient and slavish.

II. Since these men infect with their folly not only their fellow- 10 countrymen but also the neighboring peoples, let them remain incurable, bereft of vision, the most necessary of all the senses. And I do not mean the vision of the body, but that of the soul, through which alone the true and false are recognized. But let the sect of the Ther- 11 apeutae, taught in advance to exercise their sight, aim at the vision of the Existent, and soar above the sense-perceptible sun and never abandon this post which leads to perfect happiness. And those who 12 come to this service neither through force of habit nor on the advice or exhortation of others but because they have been ravished by a heavenly passion are possessed like Bacchants and Corybants until they behold the object of their longing.

Renunciation of Property

13   Then, through their yearning for the deathless and blessed life, believing that their mortal existence is already over, they leave their property to their sons or daughters or even to other kinsfolk, freely making them their heirs in advance, while those who have no kinsfolk bestow them on comrades and friends. For it was right that those who have received in ready form the wealth that has sight[7] should
14 surrender the blind wealth to those still mentally blind. The Greeks celebrate Anaxagoras and Democritus[8] because, smitten with the desire for philosophy, they allowed their property to be laid waste by sheep. I too myself admire these men who showed themselves superior to wealth, but how much better are those who did not allow their lands to become feeding grounds for cattle but supplied the needs of men, whether kinsfolk or friends, and so converted their indigence into affluence. For the former was a thoughtless act, not to say "mad," speaking of men whom Greece admired, but the latter was a
15 sober act, precisely arranged, and with exceeding good sense. What more does an enemy force do than to ravage their opponents' land and cut down its trees, in order to force their surrender through a shortage of necessaries? This is what Democritus did to those of his own blood, preparing for them artificial want and poverty, not perhaps maliciously but through not taking thought and careful consid-
16 eration for the interest of others. How much better and more admirable are they who, influenced by no lesser impulse toward philosophy, preferred magnanimity to negligence and cheerfully gave away their property instead of destroying it, in this way benefiting both others and themselves, others by furnishing them with plentiful resources, themselves by their devotion to philosophy. For the management of wealth and possessions is time-consuming, and it is well to husband one's time since according to the physician Hippocrates,
17 "life is short but art is long."[9] Homer, too, it seems to me, hints at this in the Iliad at the beginning of the thirteenth book in the following verses:

> And the Mysians who fight at close quarters, and the illustrious Hippomolgoi, drinkers of mare's milk, having no fixed subsistence, most righteous of men.[10]

The idea conveyed is that the effort to gain a livelihood and make money breeds injustice through the inequality entailed, while the opposite principle of action begets justice through equality, in accordance with which nature's wealth is delimited and thus surpasses the wealth derived through empty imaginings.[11]

Rejection of Family and City Life

So when they have given up possession of their property, with 18
nothing further to entice them, they flee without turning to look back, abandoning brothers, children, wives, parents, numerous kin, dear companions, the fatherlands in which they were born and reared, since the familiar has a great power of attraction and is the 19
most powerful of baits.[12] They do not emigrate to another city like unfortunate or worthless slaves who demand to be sold by their owners, thus obtaining for themselves a change of masters but not freedom.[13] For every city, even the best governed, teems with tumult and indescribable disturbances that no one could abide after having been once guided by wisdom. Instead they spend their time outside the 20
walls pursuing solitude in gardens or solitary places, not from having cultivated a cruel hatred of men, but because they know that intercourse with persons of dissimilar character is unprofitable and injurious.

THE THERAPEUTAE OF THE MAREOTIC LAKE

Description of Site

III. Now this kind exists in many parts of the inhabited world, 21
for both Greece and the non-Greek world must share in the perfect good, but it abounds in Egypt in each of the so-called nomes and particularly around Alexandria. But those who excel in every way settle 22
in a certain favorable spot as in their fatherland. This place is situated above the Mareotic Lake on a rather low-lying hillock, very well located both because of its security and its mild-tempered air. The safe- 23
ty is afforded by the homesteads and villages round about, and the mild-tempered air by the breezes continuously sent up both from the lake that opens into the sea and from the open sea hard by. For the sea breezes are light; those of the lake dense, and the blending of the two produces a most healthful condition of climate.[14]

The houses of those thus banded together are quite simple, af- 24 fording protection against the two things requiring it most, the blazing heat of the sun and the frostiness of the air. They are neither contiguous as in towns, since close proximity is troublesome and displeasing to those assiduously striving for solitude, nor yet far apart, because of the fellowship to which they cleave, and in order to render each other aid in the event of a piratical attack.

Spiritual Activities: Prayer and Study

25   In each house there is a sacred chamber, which is called a sanctuary or closet,[15] in which in isolation they are initiated into the mysteries of the holy life. They take nothing into it, neither drink, nor food, nor anything else necessary for bodily needs, but laws and oracles delivered through the prophets, and psalms and the other books through which knowledge and piety are increased and perfected.
26   They always remember God and never forget him, so that even in their dreams[16] no images are formed other than the loveliness of divine excellences and powers. Thus many of them, dreaming in their sleep,
27   divulge the glorious teachings of their holy philosophy. Twice daily they pray, at dawn and at eventide; at sunrise they pray for a joyful day, joyful in the true sense, that their minds may be filled with celestial light. At sunset, they pray that the soul may be fully relieved from the disturbance of the senses and the objects of sense, and that retired to its own consistory and council chamber it may search out
28   the truth. The entire interval between early morning and evening is devoted to spiritual exercise. They read the Holy Scriptures and apply themselves to their ancestral philosophy by means of allegory, since they believe that the words of the literal text are symbols of a hidden nature, revealed through its underlying meanings.
29   They have also writings of men of old, who were the founders of their sect and had left behind many memorials of the type of treatment employed in allegory, and taking these as a sort of archetype they imitate the method of this principle of interpretation. And so they not only apply themselves to contemplation, but also compose chants and hymns to God in all kinds of meters and melodies, which they perforce indite in rather solemn rhythms.

Sabbath Meetings

30   For six days they each live apart in seclusion in the aforementioned closets and pursue philosophy, without stepping beyond the

outer door or even seeing it from afar. But on the seventh day they get together as for a general assembly and seat themselves in order according to their age with the proper dignity, keeping their hands inside their robes,[17] the right hand between the breast and the chin and the left drawn in along the flank. Then the eldest who is also best 31 versed in their doctrines comes forward, and composed both in expression and in voice, holds forth with reasoned argument and wisdom. He makes no display of clever rhetoric like the orators or sophists of today, but after close examination he carefully expounds the precise meaning of his thoughts, which does not settle on the edge of the audience's ears, but passes through the hearing into the soul, and there remains securely ensconced. All the others listen quietly, showing their approval by their looks or nods.

This common sanctuary in which they meet every seventh day 32 is a double enclosure, one part set off for the men, the other for the women. For women too customarily form part of the audience, possessed by the same fervor and sense of purpose. The partition be- 33 tween the two chambers is built up to three or four cubits above the floor in the form of a breastwork, while the space above up to the roof is left open. This serves two purposes: that the modesty proper to women's nature be maintained and that the women seated within earshot with nothing to obstruct the voice of the speaker may obtain easy apprehension.[18]

Moderation and Self-Control

IV. They lay down self-control as a sort of foundation of the soul 34 and on this build the other virtues. None of them would take food or drink before sunset, since it is their view that the pursuit of philosophy is worthy of the light, but the needs of the body of darkness, wherefore they assign the day to the one and a brief portion of the night to the other.[19] Some, in whom there is a more deep-seated longing for knowledge, remember to take food even after only every third day. Others so revel and delight in being banqueted by wisdom, 35 which richly and lavishly supplies her teachings, that they hold out double that time and scarcely after every sixth day partake of necessary sustenance. They have become accustomed as, it is said, the grasshoppers have,[20] to feed on air, since their singing, I suppose, makes their lack of food easy. But the seventh day, since they consider 36 it all holy and a high festival, they have deemed worthy of singular

47

honor, and on it, after attention to the soul, they also anoint the body,[21] releasing it, just as they naturally do their cattle, of its con-
37 tinuous toils. Still they eat nothing sumptuous, only simple bread with salt as a condiment further seasoned by the more fastidious with hyssop,[22] and their drink is spring water. For the mistresses nature has set over mortal kind, hunger and thirst, these they appease, though adding nothing by way of fawning except what is useful and without which life is impossible. They therefore eat to keep from hunger and drink to keep from thirst, but satiety they shun as a treacherous enemy of both soul and body.[23]

38 As for the two forms of shelter, clothing and housing, we have already indicated that their dwelling is unadorned and improvised, constructed for utility alone. Their clothing likewise is of the simplest kind, with a view to protection from frost and heat, a thick cloak of shaggy hide[24] in winter, and in summer a single-sleeved tunic or
39 a fine linen shirt. For they practice a thorough lack of affectation, knowing that affectation is the source of falsehood, the absence of it that of truth, and that both bear the signification of a fountainhead since from falsehood flow the manifold forms of evil, and from truth the abundance of goods both human and divine.

Pagan Banquets

40 V. I wish also to speak of their common gatherings and their cheerful modes of entertainment at banquets, after contrasting them with those of other people. For some people, when they have filled themselves with strong drink, act as if they had drunk not wine but some arousing and maddening magical potion, and anything more grievous yet that can be imagined to distract the mind. They bellow and rave like wild dogs, attack and bite each other and chew off noses, ears, fingers, and some other parts of the body,[25] so that they demonstrate the truth of the story of the Cyclops and the comrades of Odysseus, by eating "gobbets of men's flesh,"[26] as the poet says, and
41 with greater savagery than the Cyclops. For he avenged himself on those whom he suspected as enemies, they on their intimates and friends and sometimes even on their kin while partaking of their salt and board, and as they pour the libation of peace they commit deeds of war,[27] like the acts of men in gymnastic contest, counterfeiting the genuine coinage of training, no wrestlers but wretches,[28] for that is
42 the name we must give them. For what the athletes do in the arena

48

while sober in the daytime with all Greece as spectators, for the sake of victory and crowns, and with applied skill, the counterfeiting revelers do at their banquets by night in darkness, drunken and besotted, unintelligently, and with malicious art, in order to dishonor, insult, and sorely outrage their victims. And if no one intervenes as an umpire[29] and parts them, they carry on their knock-down grappling with increased license, thirsty alike for the kill or for being killed. For they suffer no less than what they deal out to others though they have no awareness of it, these madmen who dare to drink wine, as the comic poet says, not only for the injury of their neighbors but to their own as well. Consequently, those who but shortly before came to the banquet in good bodily form and in friendship leave soon after as foes, with bodies mutilated; some in need of advocates and judges, others of apothecaries and doctors and the help they bring. Others, who appear to belong to the more moderate type of boon companion, on whom draughts of strong wine have the effect of mandragora, are in a state of effervescence. They thrust their left elbow forward, turn their neck at an angle, belch into the cups, and are oppressed by a deep sleep, seeing and hearing nothing, as if possessing only one sense, and the most slavish one at that, taste. I know of some who when mellow with wine,[30] before having completely gone under, arrange in advance the next day's carousal through voluntary contributions and subscriptions, in the belief that a part of their present cheer consists in the hope of future intoxication. In this way they spend their whole lives ever homeless and hearthless, enemies of their parents, their wives, and their children, enemies too of their native land, and hostile to their own selves. For a voluptuous and spendthrift life is a menace to all.

Banquets Italian Style

VI. Some may perhaps approve the style of banqueting now fashionable everywhere, out of love for Italian sumptuousness and luxury, which both Greeks and barbarians have affected, making their arrangements for ostentation rather than for good cheer. Dining rooms with three and more couches made of tortoise shell or ivory or even more costly material, most of them inlaid with precious stones; coverlets wrought in genuine purple dye with gold interwoven, others in bright and varied colors to attract the eye; a multitude of drinking cups arranged according to each kind, pointed drinking horns,

phials, wine cups, and other Theriklean goblets of various kinds fashioned most artistically and elaborately chased by scientific crafts-
50   men. In attendance are slaves of the utmost shapeliness and comeliness, giving the impression of having come not so much for service as to please through their appearance the eye of the beholders. Those of them who are still boys pour the wine, while the water is carried by the big lads well scrubbed and smoothly shaved, their faces rubbed with cosmetics and penciled under the eyelids, and the hair
51   of the head neatly pleated and tightly bound. For they have thick long hair, either not cut at all, or with their forelocks trimmed only at the ends to make them equal and to take on exactly the form of a circular line. They wear fine-spun tunics of dazzling white girt high up; the front falls below the genitals,[31] the back a little below the hips and they draw both parts together along the line of join of the tunics with twisted bows of ribbon[32] and then let the folds hang down obliquely,
52   broadening out the hollows along the sides. Others wait in the background, striplings in the bloom of youth, with the down just showing on their cheeks, recently become the playthings of pederasts, very elaborately tricked out for the heavier services, a proof of their hosts' wealth, as those who use them know, but in reality of their vulgarity.
53   Besides all this there are the varieties of sweet meat, dainties, and seasonings, slaved over by bakers and confectioners who are solicitous to please not only the sense of taste, which was a matter of necessity, but sight too through their elegant preparation. [The assembled guests] crane their necks this way and that, greedily eyeing the fullness and abundance of the meat and nosing the steamy savor given forth from it. When they have become surfeited with both sight and smell, they urge [one another] to eat, with considerable praise for
54   the preparation and the lavish expenditure of the host. Seven tables at least and more are brought in filled with everything that land, sea, rivers, and air produce, land animals, fish and birds, all choice and in prime condition, each table differing in mode of preparation and seasoning. In order that no natural species be unrepresented, the last tables brought in are loaded with fruits, in addition to those reserved
55   for the revels and the so-called after-dinners or desserts. Then while some tables are removed empty through the insatiate appetite of those present, who gorge themselves like cormorants[33] and eat so voraciously that they even consume the bones, other courses are mutilated and torn to pieces, and left half eaten. And when they finally give up, having crammed their bellies up to the gullet, but still unsatisfied in

their lust, weary of eating, [they turn to the drink].[34] But why enlarge 56
on these doings now condemned by many of the more moderate sort
as unleashing the lusts whose reduction would be to our advantage?
For one may well pray for what are most to be deprecated, hunger
and thirst, than for the lavish abundance of food and drink found in
festivities of this kind.

The Two Banquets at Which Socrates Was Present

VII. Of the banquets held in Greece, the most celebrated and re- 57
markable examples are the two in which Socrates too was present, the
one held at the house of Callias and hosted by him in honor of the
victory in which Autolycus won the crown, the other at the house of
Agathon. These were banquets that men, both of whose character
and words showed them to be philosophers, Xenophon and Plato,
thought worthy of commemoration, for they described them as worthy to be recorded, surmising that future generations would use them
as models of the proper amusements at banquets. Yet even these if 58
compared with those of our people who cleave to the contemplative
life will prove to be an occasion for laughter. Both have their delights,
but Xenophon's banquet is closer to common humanity. There are
flute girls, dancers, jugglers, fun-makers, proud of their ability for
jesting and being witty, and other features inducing yet greater cheer
and relaxation.

Plato's banquet is almost entirely concerned with love, not mere- 59
ly with men madly in love with women, or women with men, lusts
subject to the laws of nature, but of men for males differing from
them only in age.[35] For even if it appears that there is some contrived
subtlety concerning Eros and Heavenly Aphrodite, it is brought in
by way of jest. The greater part is taken up with common and vulgar 60
love, which not only robs men of courage, the virtue most useful for
life in peace as well as war, but produces in their souls the disease of
effeminacy and renders androgynous those who should have been
trained in all the pursuits making for valor. And having ruined their 61
years of boyhood, and degraded them to the class and condition of sex
objects, it injures the lovers, too, in the most essential respects, body,
mind, and property. For the mind of the boy-lover is necessarily
aimed at his darling, and is keen-sighted for him only, blind to all other interests, private and public; his body wastes away through lust,
especially if he fail in his suit, while his property is diminished from

62 either end by his neglecting it and expending it on his beloved. As a side-effect there is another still greater evil touching everyone; for they artificially contrive the desolation of cities, the scarcity of the best sort of men, and barrenness and sterility, by imitating those ignorant of the science of husbandry, sowing not in the deep soil of the plain but in briny fields and stony-hard places, which are not only of such a nature as to allow nothing to grow, but even destroy the seed deposited in them.[36]

63 I say nothing of the mythical fabrications, the two-bodied creatures[37] who originally clung fast to one another through unitive forces and later were sundered like a mere assemblage of parts, when the bonding that held them was dissolved. All these are seductive enough, capable by the novelty of their conception of enticing the ears, but the disciples of Moses, in their vast superiority, trained as they are from earliest youth to love the truth, hold them in contempt and continue undeceived.

The Banquets of the Therapeutae

64 VIII. But since these widely known banquets are filled with such nonsense and stand self-convicted, given one's willingness to disregard conventional opinions and the widely circulated report that considers them great successes, I shall set in contrast with them the festal gatherings of those who have dedicated their own lives and themselves to knowledge and contemplation of the realities of nature, in accordance with the most sacred instructions of the prophet Moses.

65 In the first place these people gather together every seven weeks,[38] for not only do they stand in amazement before the simple seven but its square too, since they know it to be pure and perpetually virgin. This is however a prelude to the greatest festival, to which the number fifty has been allotted, the most sacred of numbers and most in conformity with nature, being formed from the square of the right-angled triangle, which is the source of the generation of the All.[39]

66 When once assembled, garbed in white and radiant, but with the greatest solemnity, before reclining, at a signal from one of the Ephemereutae (for this is the name commonly given to those in charge of these services), they take their places in rows in orderly fashion, with eyes and hands raised up toward heaven, eyes because they were trained to gaze on things worthy of contemplation, hands because

they are pure of unjust gains and undefiled by any motive of the prof-it-making kind. Thus standing they pray to God that their feasting turn out to be well-pleasing and in accord with his wish.

After the prayers the elders recline in accordance with the order 67 of their admission; for they regard as elders not those who are rich in years and of silvery brow [but consider them as mere children][40] if they have only in later years come to conceive a passion for this way of life, but those who from their earliest years have spent the prime of their youth and the flower of their maturity in the contem-plative branch of philosophy, which is indeed the most beautiful and most godlike part.

The women, too, take part in the feast; most of them are aged vir- 68 gins who have maintained their purity not under constraint, like some of the priestesses among the Greeks, but voluntarily through their zealous desire for wisdom. Eager to enjoy intimacy with her,[41] they have been unconcerned with the pleasures of the body, desiring a progeny not mortal but immortal, which only the soul that loves God is capable of engendering unaided, since the Father has sown in her intelligible rays whereby she can behold the teachings of wisdom.

Service at the Tables

IX. The seating arrangement is so apportioned that the men sit 69 apart on the right, and the women apart on the left. Perhaps it might be supposed that couches, even if not expensive ones, yet at least of a softer kind, would have been provided for people of noble birth and refinement and well practiced in philosophy. The fact is that they are plain beds of the most ordinary wood, covered with very cheap mats of native papyrus, raised slightly at the elbows that they may lean on them. For they somewhat relax the rigorous Spartan training, but al-ways and everywhere they practice an easygoing contentedness befit-ting free men, and resist with might and main the love charms of pleasure. They use no slaves to minister to their needs, since they 70 consider the possession of servants to be entirely contrary to nature. For nature has created all men free, but the acts of injustice and greed of some who have energetically pursued inequality, the beginning of mischief, harnassed the power over the weaker and fastened it on the stronger. In this holy banquet there is as I have said no slave, but free 71 men do the serving, performing their menial chores not under com-pulsion or awaiting orders but freely anticipating the demands with

53

72   eagerness and zeal. Nor is it any and every free man who is appointed to these services, but young members of the society selected with all care and according to merit, in the manner necessary for men of good character and nobility, who are pressing on to reach the summit of virtue. These give their services gladly and eagerly as true sons do to their fathers and mothers, regarding them as their common parents, as more their own than those who are so by blood, since to the right-minded there is no closer tie than nobility of character.[42] Ungirt and with loose-flowing tunics they enter to do their serving, so that no trace of servile mien be introduced.

Nature of Drink and Food

73   In this banquet—I know that some will be amused at this, though only those whose actions are a matter for tears and lamentations[43]—wine is not brought in during those days, but only water of the most translucent clarity, cold for the majority, but warm for those of the elders who live delicately. The table too is kept clear of animal flesh, but on it are loaves of bread for nourishment, with salt as a seasoning, to which hyssop is sometimes added as a relish to satisfy the fastid-
74   ious. For as right reason instructs the priest to sacrifice while sober, so it enjoins them to spend their lives in the same state. For wine is the drug of folly, and sumptuous cuisine arouses that most insatiable of animals, desire.[44]

The Discourse

75   X. Such are the preliminaries. But when the banqueters have taken their places according to the arrangement that I have set forth and the attendants have taken their stand in good order ready for service, their president, after all are hushed in deep silence—here one might ask when is there not silence, but at this point there is silence even more than before, so that no one dares to utter a sound or breathe more forcefully than usual—in this silence, I say, he makes inquiry into some problem arising in the Holy Scriptures, or solves one propounded by someone else.[45] In so doing he is unconcerned with making a display, since he is not reaching out for a reputation for clever oratory, but only longs to gain a more precise vision of certain matters, and having gained it not to begrudge it to those who,
76   if not as quick-sighted as he, have at least a similar desire to learn. He

employs a leisurely mode of instruction, lingering and drawing things out through constant recapitulation, thus imprinting the thoughts in the souls of his hearers. For in the course of an exposition of one who discourses fluently without pausing for breath, the mind of the audience is unable to keep pace, lags behind, and fails to grasp what is said. His audience listens with ears pricked up and eyes fixed   77
on him always in one and the same posture, signifying understanding and comprehension by nods and glances, praise of the speaker by a cheerful mien and a slow turning about of their faces, perplexity by a gentler movement of the head and by the raising of the fingertip of the right hand. The youths standing by attend no less than those who have reclined.

Allegory

The interpretations of the Holy Scripture are made in accor-   78
dance with the deeper meanings conveyed in allegory. For the whole of the Law seems to these people to resemble a living being[46] with the literal commandments for its body, and for its soul the invisible meaning stored away in its words.[47] It is in the latter that the rational soul begins especially to contemplate the things akin to itself and, beholding the extraordinary beauties of the concepts through the polished glass of the words, unfolds and reveals the symbols, and brings forth the thoughts bared into the light for those who are able by a slight jog to their memory to view the invisible through the visible.

When it seems, then, that the president has spoken sufficiently   79
and that, in regard to the respective goals of speaker and audience, both the discourse and the response to it were right on target, there are rounds of applause from all, as if rejoicing together in what was yet to follow.

Then the president rises and sings a hymn composed in honor   80
of the Deity, either a new one of his own composition, or an old one by poets of an earlier age. For they have bequeathed many meters and melodies, iambic verse, hymns suited for processions, libations, and the altar, odes sung by the chorus when either stationary or dancing, well arranged metrically for its various evolutions. After him the others too sing in their places and in proper order while all the rest listen in deep silence, except when they need to chant the choral refrains, for then they all sing out, men and women alike.

When each has finished his hymn, the young men bring in the   81 table mentioned a little above on which is the supremely hallowed food, leavened bread seasoned with salt mixed with hyssop, out of reverence for the holy table set up in the sacred vestibule.[48] For on the latter lie loaves and salt without condiments, the bread unleav-

82 ened and the salt unmixed.[49] For it was fitting that the simplest and purest food be assigned to the highest class, that of the priests, as a reward for their ministry, and that the others, while aspiring to similar things, should desist from identical ones, so that their superiors may retain their privilege.

83   After the meal they hold the sacred vigil, which is celebrated in the following manner. They all rise up in a body and at the center of the refectory they first form two choirs, one of men, the other of women, the leader and precentor chosen for each being the most highly esteemed among them and the most musical. They then sing

84 hymns to God composed in many meters and melodies,[50] now chanting together, now moving hands and feet in concordant harmony, and full of inspiration they sometimes chant processional odes, and sometimes the lyrics of a chorus in standing position as well as executing the strophe and antistrophe of the choral dance.

85   Then when each choir has completed for itself its own part in the feasting, having drunk as in Bacchic revelries of the strong wine of God's love, they mix, and the two choirs become one, a copy of the choir organized at the Red Sea on the occasion of the wonders there

86 wrought. For at the divine command, the sea became a cause of salvation to the one side and of utter destruction to the other. For as the sea was rent asunder, drawn downward by the violent recoil of its waves, and on either side, facing each other, the waters virtually walled up in solid form, the intervening space thus opened up broadened into a highway fully dry, through which the people marched to the opposite mainland, safely escorted to higher ground. But when the waters came rushing in with the returning tide, and from either side poured over the dried sea floor, the pursuing enemy were over-

87 whelmed and perished. After witnessing and experiencing this act, which went beyond word, thought, and hope, men and women alike were filled with divine ecstasy, formed a single choir, sang hymns of thanksgiving to God their Savior, the men led by the prophet Moses and the women by the prophetess Miriam.

88   Modeled above all on this, the choir of the Therapeutae, both male and female, singing in harmony, the soprano of the women blending with the bass of the men, produces true musical concord.

Exceedingly beautiful are the thoughts, exceedingly beautiful are the words, and august the choristers, and the end goal of thought, words, and choristers alike is piety. Thus they continue till dawn intoxicated 89 with this exquisite intoxication and then, not with heavy head or drowsy eyes, but more alert than when they came to the banquet, they stand with their faces and whole body turned to the east, and when they behold the rising sun,[51] with hands stretched heavenward they pray for a joyous day, truth, and acuity of thought. And after the prayers they retire each to his own sanctuary once more to ply the trade and cultivate the field of their wonted philosophy.

Conclusion

So much then for the Therapeutae who have embraced the con- 90 templation of nature and its constituent parts, and have lived in the soul alone, citizens of Heaven and the universe, truly commended to the Father and Creator of all by virtue, which has secured for them God's friendship[52] in addition to the most fitting prize of nobility, which excels all good fortune and attains to the very summit of joy.

THE GIANTS

INTRODUCTORY NOTE TO THE GIANTS

The Giants contains a beautiful evocation of the spiritual dimensions of being. The nature of souls, angels, and daemons is explored, and the literal notion of evil angels is allegorized to indicate souls that have sunk into corporeality in contrast with those that have scorned embodiment. Flesh and spirit are sharply opposed, and the expansive nature of the divine spirit is shown to involve no diminution whatever in its own essence. The treatise concludes with a fine distinction between three classes of souls: the earth-born (the "giants" of Gen. 6:4, who pursue fleshly pleasure), the heaven-born (artists and lovers of learning), and the God-born (priests and prophets who have migrated to the Intelligible World to become citizens of the Commonwealth of Ideas).

THE GIANTS[1]

Correlation of Just and Unjust

I. "And it came to pass when men began to become numerous on earth and daughters were born to them" (Gen. 6:1). It is, I think, worth raising the difficulty, why after the birth of Noah and his sons, our race grows populous.[2] Yet perhaps it is not difficult to expound the reason. For it is always the case that when the rarity appears, its opposite is found in abundance.[3] The natural ability of the individual thus shows up the lack of ability in the multitude, and things artful, scientific, good, and beautiful, though few, unveil from their state of concealment the prodigiously vast throng of things inartistic, unscientific, unjust, and generally worthless. Note that in the universe, too, the sun, though a single entity, irradiates and scatters the deep and manifold darkness poured over sea and land. It is reasonable, therefore, that the birth of just Noah and his sons sets forth the multitude of the unjust; for it is in the nature of opposites to be best recognized through their contraries.[4] No unjust man, in any case, begets male offspring in his soul; instead, those whose thoughts are by nature unmanly, emasculate, and effeminate engender females. They plant no tree of virtue, whose fruit must be trueborn and excellent,

5   only trees of vice and passions, whose shoots are feminine. It is on this account that these men are said to have begotten daughters, but none of them a son. For since just Noah, who pursues the perfect, the right, truly masculine reason, begets males, the injustice of the crowd appears evidently to generate the female.[5] For it is impossible that from opposites there should arise things similar, rather than those that are opposite in turn.[6]

Angels, Souls, and Daemons

6   II. "And when the angels of God saw the daughters of men that they were beautiful, they took to themselves wives from among all those whom they chose" (Gen. 6:2). Those whom the philosophers

7   designate "daemons," Moses is accustomed to call angels.[7] These are souls that fly in the air.[8] And let no one assume that what is said here is a myth. For the universe must be animated through and through and each of its primary and elementary parts encompasses the life forms that are akin and suited to it.[9] The earth contains the land creatures, and the sea and the rivers those that are aquatic, fire the fire-engendered,[10] said to be located especially in Macedonia, and heaven

8   the stars. For the latter are souls, divine and pure throughout,[11] for which reason they move in a circle, the trajectory most akin to mind. The air, too, must therefore be filled with living things, though they

9   are invisible to us, since even the air itself is not visible to sense. We ought not conclude, however, inasmuch as our vision is incapable of forming images of souls, that there are consequently no souls in the air, but they must be apprehended by the mind, that like may be dis-

10   cerned in conformity with its similars. Moreover, do not all land and water creatures live by air and breath? And is it not true that when the air is polluted pestilential conditions usually arise,[12] suggesting that it is the principle of animation for all and each? Furthermore, when it is propitious and harmless, which is especially the case when the north wind blows, do not these same creatures, inhaling as they do a pure atmosphere, advance to a life of greater and more vigorous

11   permanence? Is it then likely that the element through which the others, denizens of land and water, possess the breath of life should be desolate and have no share in animate existence? On the contrary, even if all the other elements were unproductive of animal life, air alone ought to have given birth to it, since it had received the seeds of vitality from the Creator through his exceptional grace.

III. Now some of the souls have descended into bodies, but oth- 12
ers have never deigned to associate with any of the parts of earth.
Since the latter are consecrated and devoted to the service of the Father, they customarily serve their Creator as ministers and helpers in
his care for mortal man. The former, however, descending into the 13
body as though into a stream,[13] have sometimes been caught up in the
violent rush of its raging waters and swallowed up; at other times,
able to withstand the rapids, they have initially emerged at the surface and then soared back up to the place whence they had set out.
These, then, are the souls of the genuine philosophers, who from first 14
to last practice dying to the life in the body in order to obtain the portion of incorporeal and immortal life in the presence of the Uncreated
and Immortal. But the souls that have been plunged into the surf be- 15
low are the souls of the others who have had no regard for wisdom.
They have surrendered themselves to unstable and chance concerns,
none of which relate to our noblest part, the soul or mind, but all are
related to that corpse[14] which was our birth-fellow, the body, or to
objects even more lifeless than it—glory, wealth, offices, and honors,
and whatever else is molded or painted through the deceit of false
opinion by those who have never had a vision of the truly beautiful.

IV. If, then, you have in mind that souls, daemons, and angels 16
are but variant names for one and the same underlying object, you will
put away that most oppressive burden, superstition.For as the multitude speak of good and bad daemons and similarly of good and bad
souls, so you too will not err with regard to angels if you take some
as worthy of that designation, inasmuch as they serve as ambassadors
of men to God and of God to men,[15] and are rendered sacred and inviolate by reason of that glorious and blameless ministry, but others
in contrary fashion as unholy and unworthy of that name.

As testimony for my argument I have the following words of the 17
Psalmist in one of his psalms: "He despatched against them the wrath
of his anger, anger and wrath and affliction, a mission by evil angels"
(Ps. 77:49; [Ps. 78:49 in A.V.]). These are the evil ones who, taking on
the name of angels, know not the daughters of right reason, the sciences and virtues, but seek out the mortal descendants of mortal men,
the pleasures that bring with themselves not the genuine beauty discerned by the mind alone but a spurious shapeliness, through which
sense is deceived.[16] They do not all take all the daughters, but out of 18
countless many they have chosen for themselves some choose these,
some those. Some take the pleasures deriving from sight, others those

arising from hearing, others again those of the palate and the belly, others still those of sex, while many, stretching their inward desires to the limit, lay hold of pleasures ranging the outer bounds. For the choices of diversified pleasures must likewise be diversified, since their affinities are diverse.

Fleshly Concerns Drive the Divine Spirit Away

19   V. In such beings as these it is impossible that the spirit of God should remained fixed and dwell forever, as the Lawgiver himself makes clear. For he says: "The Lord God said, My spirit shall not
20 abide forever among men, because they are flesh" (Gen. 6:3). It sometimes tarries, but does not abide forever among us, the mass of men. Who indeed is so deprived of reason or soul that he has never, either willingly or unwillingly, had a conception of the best?[17] Even over the moral lepers there often hovers an unexpected vision of the excellent, but to grasp it and preserve it for themselves they have not the
21 capacity. Straightway it is gone and removes elsewhere, having turned away from visiting migrants who had gone astray from law and justice, to whom it could never have come save to convict those
22 who choose the base instead of the noble. The "pneuma of God" means according to one sense the air that flows up from the earth,[18] the third element that rides on the water, for which reason he says in the creation account, "the spirit of God was borne above the water" (Gen. 1:2), for the air, which is light, rises and is borne upward, using the water as its base. In another sense it is the pure[19] knowl-
23 edge that every wise man duly shares. The prophet shows this in regard to the craftsman and artificer of the sacred works when he says: "God summoned Bezalel and filled him with divine spirit, with wisdom, understanding, and knowledge to devise in every work" (Exod. 31:2f.). In these words we have an indication of the definition of the spirit of God.
24   VI. Such too is the spirit of Moses, which visits the seventy elders that they may surpass others and be made better. They would not have truly been even elders if they had no share in that spirit of perfect wisdom. For it is written, "I will take of the spirit that is on
25 thee and lay it upon the seventy elders" (Num. 11:17). But think not that this taking away comes about through severance or disjoining, but rather what happens when fire is taken from fire, for though it should kindle a thousand torches, it remains the same and is in no

way diminished.[20] Such too is the nature of knowledge. Although it makes all its disciples and devotees into men of skill, it is undiminished in any of its parts, and often even improves just as they say springs do when we draw water from them. For, as the story goes, they then become sweeter. Thus continuous intercourse with others 26 entails practice and training and makes for the sum of perfection. If, then, it were Moses' own spirit or that of some other engendered being that was to be distributed to so large a mass of disciples, it would be shredded into so many pieces and lessened. But, in fact, the spirit 27 that is on him is the wise, the divine, the indivisible, the unseverable, the excellent, filling all things entirely, the spirit that while conferring benefit remains unharmed, that though it be shared with or be added to others remains undiminished in understanding and knowledge and wisdom.

VII. The divine spirit may therefore tarry awhile in the soul, as 28 we have said, though it cannot abide there. And why wonder at this? For there is nothing else of which we enjoy firm and secure possession, since human affairs sway up and down, tilt the scale on either side, and suffer vicissitudes from hour to hour. But the chief cause of 29 ignorance is the flesh and our affinity for it. Moses himself affirms this when he says "because they are flesh" the divine spirit cannot abide. Marriage, indeed, and the rearing of children, the provision of necessities, the ill repute that comes in the wake of poverty, business both private and public, and a host of other things wilt the flower of wisdom before it blooms.[21] Nothing, however, so thwarts its growth 30 as our fleshly nature. For this is the primary and main underlying foundation of ignorance and the diseased condition of an unknowing mind, on which each of the aforementioned qualities is constructed. For souls unfleshed and disembodied pass their days in the theater of 31 the universe and enjoy unhindered sights and sounds divine, possessed by an insatiate love for them. But those who bear the load of the flesh are unable, thus weighed down and oppressed,[22] to gaze upward at the revolving heavens, but with necks wrenched downward are forcibly rooted to the ground like four-footed beasts.[23]

VIII. It is for the same reason that the legislator, having deter- 32 mined to abolish all lawless and illicit intercourse and union, says by way of preface thus, "a man, a man shall not go near to any that is akin to his flesh to uncover their shame. I am the Lord" (Lev. 18:6). How could one better urge the spurning of the flesh and what is akin to flesh than in this manner? And indeed he does not only deter, but 33 positively asserts that he who is truly a man[24] will not voluntarily come nigh to the pleasures that are friends and kin of the body, but

34 will always practice estrangement from them. The fact that he says not once but twice, "a man, a man,"[25] is a sign that it is not the man constituted of body and soul that is meant, but the man who exercises virtue. For he indeed is the true man, and it was with him in view that one of the ancients[26] lit a candle at midday and told those who inquired that he was seeking a man. Now, the precept not to go near to anything akin to the flesh has a cogent reason.[27] For some things we must admit, as, for example, the actual necessaries[28] whose use will enable us to live sound and healthy. But we must scornfully dismiss the superfluities by which are kindled the lusts that with a single

35 flare consume every good thing. Let not our appetites, then, be inflamed for anything that is dear to the flesh. For the wild pleasures[29] often fawn on us like dogs, then wheel around and inflict fatal bites.[30] Therefore let us embrace that spirit of frugal contentment[31] which is the friend of virtue rather than the things that are akin to the body, and thus let us destroy the endlessly vast host of her implacable foes. But if some opportune occasion compel us to receive more than a moderate sufficiency, let us not approach it on our own. For he says, "He shall not of himself go near to uncover shame."

36 IX. The significance of these words it is worthwhile to unfold. Frequently, men who were never money-makers have acquired an enormous profusion of wealth, while others who have not sought glory have been held worthy of receiving civic eulogies and honors. Others, again, who had no expectation of even slight bodily strength have

37 found themselves endowed with the greatest vigor. Let all these learn not to "go near" with deliberate intent to any of the things mentioned, that is, not to admire them or approve them unduly, judging that each of them—money, glory, and bodily strength—is not only not a good, but a very great evil. For to the money-lovers the approach to money is natural, to the glory-lovers glory, to lovers of athletics and gymnastics bodily strength. They have abandoned the

38 better to the worse, the soul to the soulless. Those who are in their right minds bring the splendid and highly prized gifts of fortune in subjection to the mind as to a captain. If they come their way they accept them with a view to improving their lives, but if they remain far off, they do not approach them, judging that even without them

39 they would be capable of living a happy life.[32] He who pursues them and wishes to track them down gives philosophy a bad name and

therefore is said to "uncover shame." For manifestly clear is the disgrace of those who claim to be wise, yet haggle over the sale of their wisdom, as they say they do who hawk their wares in the market,[33] sometimes through a low margin of profit, sometimes through a pleasingly seductive speech, sometimes through an insecure and ungrounded hope, sometimes again through promises differing in no way from dreams.

X. The words that follow, "I am the Lord," are most instructively and beautifully put. Contrast, good friend, he says, the fleshly good with that of the soul and that of the All. Now the former is irrational pleasure, the latter the mind of the universe, even God. The comparison of these two incomparables is, indeed, a serious match,[34] [so that one could be deceived] through their tight resemblance, if one were also to insist that the animate are in reality identical with the inanimate, reasoning beings with unreasoning ones, ordered with disordered, odd with even, light with darkness, day with night, and all opposites with their contraries. And yet, even if these opposites, because they have been the subject of genesis, possess a certain fellowship and kinship, still God has no likeness even to what is noblest of things born, since the latter has come into being and will suffer change in the future, but God is uncreated and ever active. 40 41 42

It is well not to abandon one's post[35] in the divine order in which all those so arrayed must be distinguished for bravery, and desert to cowardly and effeminate pleasure, who harms her friends and helps her enemies. Her nature is indeed exceedingly strange. On those whom she wishes to confer a share of her own proper goods, she inflicts immediate damage, whereas those whom she wishes to deprive she profits most. She harms when she bestows, she benefits when she takes away. Therefore, my soul, if any of the love charms of pleasure beckon you, turn aside, shift your view, and fix your gaze continuously on the genuine beauty of virtue, till yearning sinks in deeply and like a magnet draws you on and brings you near and attaches you to the object you desire. 43 44

XI. The words "I am the Lord" must be understood not only in the same sense as "I am the perfect, the imperishable, the truly good," which whoso embraces will turn away from the imperfect, the perishable, and what is attached to the flesh. They mean also "I am the ruler and king and master."[36] Neither for subjects in the presence of their rulers nor for slaves in the presence of their masters is it safe to do wrong. For when the ministers of punishment are near, those 45 46

47 who lack the natural faculty of self-reproof exercise self-control through fear. For God, whose fullness is everywhere, is near; therefore, since he watches over us and is close by,[37] let us refrain from wrongdoing, preferably out of reverence, but if not out of caution for the invincible power of his sovereignty, fearful and inexorable in its vengeance, when he is minded to use his power of chastisement.[38] Thus may the divine spirit of wisdom[39] not lightly migrate and be gone, but abide with us for a long period of time, since he did so with

48 Moses the wise. For whether standing or seated, he maintained a most peaceful stance, possessing a nature that did not undergo change or vicissitude. For it is said, "Moses and the ark were not moved" (Num. 14:44), either because the sage is inseparable from virtue,[40] or because virtue is not subject to movement nor the good man to change, but both are grounded in the firmness[41] of right reason. Again, it is said elsewhere, "Stand thou here with me" (Deut. 5:31).

49 Here we have an oracle delivered to the prophet; stability[42] and steadfast serenity is that which is found by the side of God who stands immutable. For all that is set beside a sound standard must be made

50 straight. This is why, it seems to me, excessive vanity called Jethro, astounded at the unwavering, exceedingly even-keeled, unvarying, and constant course of life of the sage,[43] protests and makes inquiry

51 in the following manner: "Why do you sit alone?" (Exod. 18:14). For one who observes man's continual war-in-peace joined not only among nations, countries, and cities, but also in the household, and still more in each individual man—the indescribably severe storm within the soul fanned by the violent force of life's events—can rightly wonder that another should find fair weather in the storm, or calm

52 amid the surf of a seething sea. Note that not even the high priest reason,[44] though capable of continuous devotion to the sacred doctrines, has obtained license to visit them at every season, but scarcely once a year (Lev. 16:2, 34). For that which comes through reason in the form of utterance[45] is uncertain, since it is dual, but the contemplation of the Existent without speech within the soul alone is firmly secured, because it arises in accordance with the Indivisible Monad.

53 XII. Thus we find that among the multitude—they, that is, that have set before them multiple life goals—the divine spirit does not abide, even though it dwell there for a short space of time. One sort of men only does it come to, those who, having doffed all that belongs to created being and the innermost veil and cloak of mere opinion,

54 with mind disengaged and naked[46] will come to God. So too Moses

pitched his own tent outside the encampment (Exod. 33:7) and the entire host of bodily things, that is, he rendered his judgment immovable, and then he begins to worship God, and, entering into the dark cloud,[47] the invisible region, abides there while being initiated into the most holy mysteries. He becomes, however, not only an initiate, but also hierophant and instructor of divine rites, which he will impart to those pure of ear.

He, then, has ever the divine spirit at his side, leading him in every right way, but from the others, as I have said, it swiftly disengages itself, from those whose span of life he has also brought to completion by the number of a hundred and twenty years, for he says, "Their days shall be a hundred and twenty years" (Gen. 6:3). But Moses too migrates from his mortal life when he has reached that same number of years (Deut. 34:7). How then is it likely that the guilty enjoy a life span equal that of the wise man and prophets? For the moment it will suffice to say the following: that things designated by the same name are not in every way similar, but often completely different in kind, and that the bad may have numbers and times matched with the good since they are brought forth as twins, but powers that are detached and widely separated from each other. The precise interpretation of these one hundred twenty years, however, we will defer until our inquiry concerning the prophet's life as a whole, when we have become fit to be initiated into its mystery.[48] As for now, let us speak of the words that follow next. 55 56 57

The Giants Symbolize the Men of Earth
(Who Are Contrasted with the Men of Heaven
and the Men of God)

XIII. "Now the giants were on the earth in those days" (Gen. 6:4). Some may think that the Lawgiver is alluding to what was fabled of the giants by the poets, although he is actually greatly at variance with mythmaking, and deems it right to follow in the tracks of truth itself. And therefore, he has expelled from his own commonwealth painting and sculpture,[49] for all their repute and finished artistry, because they falsify the nature of truth and contrive deceits and artifices through the eyes for souls easily led astray. In no way, then, is he introducing a myth about giants, but wishes to set this in your mind, that some men are earth-born, some heaven-born, and some God-born.[50] The earth-born are those who chase after the pleasures of the 58 59 60 body, who are preoccupied with their enjoyment and indulgence and provide the things that contribute to each. The heaven-born are those who are artists, men of skill, and lovers of learning. For the heavenly element in us, the mind (indeed every heavenly being also constitutes a mind) pursues the school studies and the other arts one and all, whetting and sharpening itself,[51] exercising and training in the realm

61 of the intelligible. But the men of God are priests and prophets, who have not deigned to obtain rights in the universal commonwealth and become world citizens but have entirely transcended[52] the sensible sphere and have migrated to the intelligible world and dwell there enrolled as citizens of the Commonwealth of Ideas, which are imperishable and incorporeal.

62   XIV. Thus Abraham,[53] while he sojourned in the land of the Chaldeans and their notions before his name was changed from Abram, was a "man of heaven." He inquired into the nature of the lofty and ethereal region, and investigated the events occurring there, and their causes and the like, for which reason he received a name suitable to the studies he pursued. For "Abram" interpreted means the "lofty father," the name of the father-mind that surveys on every side all that is lofty and celestial, for it is the father of our compound

63 being, which reaches out to the ether and even further. But when he is made more excellent and is on the verge of being called by a new name, he becomes a man of God in accordance with the oracle proclaimed to him, "I am your God: be well pleasing before me and be

64 blameless" (Gen. 17:1). Now if the God of the universe, the only God, is also, through a singular grace, his God in a special way, he must himself necessarily be a man of God. For he is called Abraham, which interpreted signifies "the elect father of sound,"[54] that is, "the good man's reasoning"; for it is elect and purified and father of the voice through which we produce concordant sound. Such a reasoning is attached to the one and only God, it becomes God's companion and makes straight the path of its whole life, using the true "King's way,"[55] the way of the sole king, all-powerful, deflecting and deviating neither to the right nor to the left.

65   XV. The sons of the earth, on the other hand, have derailed the mind from the tracks of reason and have converted it into the lifeless and inert nature of the flesh—for "the two became one flesh," as the lawgiver says (Gen. 2:24). They have adulterated the best coinage[56] and have abandoned the superior home position and deserted to one

66 that is inferior and of a contrary sort, Nimrod leading the way. For

the lawgiver says that "he began to be a giant on the earth" (Gen. 10:8), and Nimrod means "desertion."[57] For that exceedingly wretched soul was not content with a neutral stand, but going over to the enemy he took up arms against his friends and withstood them in open war. And therefore to Nimrod Moses ascribes Babylon as the beginning of his kingdom, for Babylon means "change," a thing akin to desertion both in name and fact. For the preface to every act of desertion involves transformation and change. It would therefore follow that according to Moses, holiest of men, even as the wicked man is a fugitive without home, city, or fixed abode, so too is he a deserter, while the good man is a firm ally. Enough has been said for the present about the giants. Let us turn to the words that follow in the text. They are as follows:

[Here the text breaks off and Philo's exegesis of Genesis 6:4 continues in the next treatise, *That God Is Immutable*. The two treatises apparently originally constituted one work which was called by Eusebius *On the Giants or That God Is Immutable*.]

SELECTIONS FROM PHILO'S OTHER WORKS

I. AUTOBIOGRAPHICAL

Paradise Lost

There was a time when I devoted myself to philosophy and the contemplation of the universe and its contents, when I enjoyed the beauty, extreme loveliness, and true felicity of its [all-encompassing] Mind, when I consorted constantly with divine principles and doctrines, wherein I rejoiced with a joy that knew no surfeit or satiety. I entertained no mean or lowly thought nor did I go crawling[1] after fame, riches, or bodily delights, but seemed always to be borne upward into the heights to the accompaniment of some soul-possessing inspiration and to revolve with the sun and moon,[2] and the whole heaven and universe. It was then, ah then, that I crouched down from above the ethereal heights, and straining the mind's eye, as if from some heavenly lookout,[3] beheld the innumerable spectacles of all things that are on earth and accounted myself happy in that I had escaped by main force the grievous calamities of mortal life. But here there lay in wait for me the worst of evils, envy, hater of the good, which suddenly assailed me and ceased not to drag me violently downward till it had hurled me into the vast sea of civil cares,[4] in which I am tossed about, unable even to rise to the surface. Yet in spite of my groans I endure, thanks to my longing for culture, rooted in my soul from my earliest youth, which ever has pity and compassion for me, rouses me, and raises me up. It is on its account that I sometimes raise my head and with the soul's eyes—dimly indeed, for the mist of strange affairs has obscured their acuity of vision[5]—I yet look around at the things about me as best I can, in my yearning to draw in a breath of life pure and unmixed with evil. And if unexpectedly I obtain a brief spell of fair weather and a calm from civil tumult, with wings I float on the waves and virtually traverse the air,[6] wafted by the breezes of knowledge that often persuade me to come and spend my days with her, and slip away as it were from harsh masters, not only men but also affairs, which pour in on me like a torrent from various sides. Yet it is fitting to render thanks to God even for this,[7] that though overwhelmed by the surf I am not swallowed up in the deep, but can also open the soul's eyes, which in my despair of every good hope I thought had become incapacitated, and am illuminated by the light of wisdom, and am not for the whole of my life delivered into darkness. Here I am, then, daring not only to read the sacred interpretations of Moses, but also in my fondness for knowledge to peer into each of them and unfold and bring to light what is unknown to the multitude.[8] (*Spec.* 3.1–6)

Literary Inspiration

I feel no shame in describing my own experience, a thing I know from its having occurred numberless times. On occasion, after deciding to follow the standard procedure of writing on philosophical doctrines and knowing precisely the elements of my composition, I have found my understanding sterile and barren and have abandoned my project without result, while reproaching my thought for its self-conceit, and struck with amazement at the might of Him that Is, on whom depend the opening and closing of the soul-wombs.[9] At other times, I have come empty and have suddenly[10] become full, the ideas descending like snow and invisibly sown, so that under the impact of divine possession I had been filled with corybantic frenzy and become ignorant of everything, place, people present, myself, what was said and what was written. For I acquired expression, ideas, an enjoyment of light, sharp-sighted vision, exceedingly distinct clarity of objects, such as might occur through the eyes as the result of the clearest display. (*Mig.* 34–35)[11]

Philo's Education

When first I was aroused by the goads of philosophy to desire her, I consorted while yet quite young with one of her handmaids,[12] Grammar, and all that I engendered by her, writing, reading, and inquiry into the writings of the poets, I dedicated to her mistress. And again I kept company with another, namely Geometry, and though I admired her beauty, for she exhibited symmetry and proportion in every part, still I appropriated none of her offspring but brought them as a gift to the true-born wife. I was also eager to keep company with a third; she had rhythm, harmony, and melody, and her name was Music, and from her I begat diatonics, chromatics and enharmonics, conjunct and disjunct melodies,[13] in accordance with the concord of the fourth, fifth, and octave intervals. And again none of these did I hide from sight, so that the lawful wife became a lady of wealth, ministered to by a host of servants. (*Congr.* 74–76)

SELECTIONS

The Virtuous Man Compared with a Good Pancratiast

I have already once observed in a contest of pancratiasts[14] how one of the combatants inflicted blows with hands and feet, all well aimed, and omitted nothing that could lead to his victory, but then exhausted and weakened ultimately quit the arena without the crown, whereas the one receiving the blows, a firm mass of compact flesh, dour, solid, full of the elasticity[15] of the true athlete, all muscle, hard as rock or iron, gave no ground in the face of the blows, but by his patient and steadfast endurance reduced the strength of his adversary until he had attained complete victory. Much the same, it seems to me, is the situation of the virtuous man; his soul well fortified through firm reasoning, he compels the one who acts with violence to sink in exhaustion, sooner than himself submit to do anything contrary to his judgment.[16] (*Prob.* 26–27)

Enthusiastic Applause for the Name of Freedom

Recently, when some players were putting on a tragedy and reciting those lines of Euripides,[17]

The name of freedom is worth all the world;
If one has little, let him think it much,

I saw the entire audience rise in a burst of enthusiasm on tiptoe, and outshouting the actors with continuous exclamations, combine the praise of the maxim with the praise of the poet, who glorified for its actions not only freedom but even its name. (*Prob.* 141)

Philo at the Chariot Races

Thus, for example,[18] I have already seen in chariot races people giving way to thoughtlessness who instead of remaining seated in their places as they ought, observing in orderly fashion, stood in the middle of the course and, pushed over by the rush of the chariots, were crushed under the feet and wheels and thus received the wages of their folly. (*Prov.* 2.103 [58])

PHILO OF ALEXANDRIA

Philo's Visit to the Jerusalem Temple

There is a Syrian city by the sea called Ascalon. While I was there, at a time that I was journeying to our ancestral temple to offer prayer and sacrifice, I observed an enormous multitude of pigeons at the crossroads and in each house. When I inquired into the cause of this, they informed me that it was unlawful to catch them, because their use had been of old forbidden to the inhabitants.[19] The animal has become so tame through its security that it not only lives under their roof but regularly eats at their table and revels in its state of truce. (*Prov.* 2.107 [64])

Philo's Behavior at Banquets

I know this from frequent personal experience. For when I attended an unrestrained gathering or sumptuous banquet, and did not arrive there accompanied by reason, I became the slave of what had been provided, the sport of wild masters, sights and sounds and all that produces pleasure through smell and taste. But whenever I arrive with persuasive reason, I become master instead of slave, and with main force win the noble victory of endurance and self-control, by resisting and striving against all that excites uncontrollable desires. (*LA* 3.156)

Soul Dispositions Determined
Not by Physical Environment But by God

For I have myself often left kinsmen, friends, and country to come into the wilderness to reflect on something worthy of contemplation and gained nothing from it, but my mind scattered or bitten by passion withdrew to matters of a contrary sort. There are times, however, when I am unmoved amidst a huge crowd. God has routed the mob thronging my soul and has taught me that it is not differences of place that effect good and bad dispositions, but God who moves and leads the vehicle of the soul whichever way he pleases. (*LA* 2.85)[20]

SELECTIONS

II. SCRIPTURAL EXEGESIS

A. ALLEGORY AND MYTH

The Contents of the Torah Are Symbolic

This is the reason that is generally and widely stated, but I have heard another from inspired men who take most of the contents of the Law to be visible symbols of things invisible, expressing the inexpressible. (*Spec.* 3.178)[21]

The Cosmopolitan and Open-Eyed Mind Pursues the Allegorical Interpretation of Scripture

It may be that some micropolites ("small townsmen") will suppose that the Legislator gives this lengthy discourse regarding the digging of wells, but those on the roll of a greater country, this universe, men endowed with more perfect thought, will clearly know that the investigation of the four things proposed to open-eyed lovers of contemplation concerns not four wells but the four parts of the universe, earth, water, air, and heavens. (*Somn.* 1.39)[22]

The Literalists Are Not Censured But Urged On to Higher Things

This is our explanation, but those who follow only the manifest and ordinary think that we have here a sketch of the origin of the Greek and barbarian languages. I would not censure such persons, for perhaps they too speak the truth, but would encourage them not to come to a halt at that point, but to go forward in quest of the allegorical interpretation,[23] in the conviction that the words of the oracles are as it were shadows cast by bodies,[24] whereas the significations therein revealed are the things that have true existence. Indeed the legislator himself gives openings for this genre of interpretation to those unblind in spirit, as he undoubtedly does in the matter now under discussion, by his designation of what had taken place as a "confusion." (*Conf.* 190)[25]

Scoffing Literalists

Some of the contentious type of people who wish always to attach blame to what is blameless, not so much in things material as in matters spiritual,[26] and wage war to the end against what is holy, vilify and slander all [the scriptural passages] that do not appear to preserve what is seemly in expression, though in reality they constitute symbols of the nature that loves concealment,[27] a nature into which these critics make no precise inquiry.[28] This vilification they pursue especially with the changes of names.

Recently I heard the scoffing and violent railing of a godless and impious fellow who dared to speak as follows: "Great indeed and extraordinary are the gifts that Moses says are held out by the Ruler of all." Through the addition of a letter, a single alpha,[29] and again by the addition of a rho, what an extraordinarily great kindness does he seem to have provided; for he [turned Abram ('Aβράμ) into Abraham ('Aβραάμ) through an additional alpha, and] Abraham's wife Sarai (Σάρα) into Sarah (Σάρρα) by doubling the rho.[30] And stringing similar cases together he went through them sneeringly without pausing for breath. It was not long before he paid the penalty appropriate to his folly. For a slight and trifling cause he rushed forth to hang himself, so that the filthy blackguard should not even die a clean death. (*Mut.* 60–61)[31]

The Literal Interpretation of Scriptural Myth Rejected

Narrated in this fashion, these things are like prodigies and wonders, one serpent projecting a human voice, playing the sophist with an utterly guileless character, and deceiving a woman with seductive persuasions; and another becoming the instrument of perfect salvation for those who beheld it. But by deploying explanations derived from the deeper sense, the mythical vanishes from sight, and the truth becomes manifest. (*Agr.* 96–97)[32]

The Literal Sense Is Impossible

"So Cain went forth from the face of God, and dwelt in the land of Naid, over against Eden" (Gen. 4:16). Let us here raise the problem whether we ought to understand the content of the books in which

SELECTIONS

Moses acts as God's interpreter figuratively, since the immediate impression made by his words is far from being in accord with the truth. For if the Existent has a face, and he who wishes to forsake it may remove elsewhere most easily, why do we deprecate the impious views of the Epicureans[33] or the atheism of the Egyptians,[34] or the mythical tales of which life is full? (*Post.* 1.1)[35]

The Historical Samuel Is of Little Interest

Now Samuel was probably an actual man; but he has been taken by us not as a vital complex of body and soul, but as a mind that rejoices solely in the service and worship of God. For his name signifies "appointed to God," because he believes that all actions that have their origin in empty imaginings constitute a grievous disorder. (*Ebr.* 144)

Philo Faults the Extreme Allegorists

There are some who, taking the laws in their literal sense as symbols of intelligible realities, are overprecise in their investigation of the symbol, while frivolously neglecting the letter. Such people I, for my part, should blame for their cool indifference, for they ought to have cultivated both a more precise investigation of things invisible and an unexceptionable stewardship of things visible. As it is, as if living alone by themselves in a wilderness, or as if they had become discarnate souls, knowing neither city nor village nor household nor any company of humans at all, transcending what is approved by the crowd, they track the absolute truth in its naked self. These men are taught by Sacred Scripture to be concerned with public opinion, and to abolish no part of the customs ordained by inspired men, greater than those of our own day.

For all that the Seventh Day teaches us the power of the unoriginate and the nonaction of created beings, let us by no means annul the laws laid down for its observance, kindling fire, tilling the earth, carrying burdens, instituting charges, sitting in judgment, demanding the return of deposits, recovering loans, or doing all else that is permitted in nonfestal seasons. And though it is true that the Feast is a symbol of spiritual joy and of thankfulness to God, let us not bid adieu to the annual seasonal gatherings. And though it is true that circumcision indicates the excision of pleasure and all passions and the removal of the godless conceit under which the mind supposed itself capable of engendering through its own powers, let us not abrogate the law laid down for circumcising. For we shall be neglecting the Temple service and a thousand other things if we are to pay sole regard to that which is revealed by the inner meaning. We ought rather look on the outward observances as resembling the body, and their inner meaning as resembling the soul. Just as we then provide for the body, inasmuch as it is the abode of the soul, so we must attend to the letter of the laws. If we keep these, we shall obtain an understanding of those things of which these are the symbols, and in addition we shall escape the censure and accusations of the multitude. (*Mig.* 89–93)

Scripture Contains No Myth

In God's work you will find no mythical fiction but the uncompromised rules of truth all well engraved. Nor will you find metrical speech, rhythms, and melodies beguiling the ear with their music, but nature's own consummate works, possessing their own proper harmony. And even as the mind that lends its ear to the poems of God is glad, so the speech that is in harmony with the conceptions of the understanding, and in some measure attendant to them, must necessarily rejoice. (*Det.* 125)[36]

B. MYSTERIES

The Divine Mysteries Must Be Kept from the Superstitious

But that I may speak of the conception and birth-throes of the virtues, let the superstitious stop up their ears or depart. For we teach mysteries divine to the initiates worthy of the holiest mysteries, they who practice the true and veritably unadorned piety without affectation. But we do not reveal the mysteries to those who, held fast by the incurable evil of vanity, measure what is pure and holy by no other standard than the "birdlime" of verbiage and pretentious claptrap of ceremonial. (*Cher.* 42)[37]

SELECTIONS

The Pagan Mysteries Denounced

Furthermore, he wipes out from sacred legislation[38] the lore of initiatory rites and mysteries and all such claptrap and buffoonery. He does not deem it fitting that people bred in such a commonwealth as ours celebrate secret rites and, clinging to mystical fictions, make light of the truth and pursue what has been assigned to darkness and night, disregarding what is worthy of the light of day. Let none, therefore, of Moses' disciples and followers perform or undergo initiatory rites; for both the teaching and the learning of such rites is no petty act of impiety. For why, O initiates, if these things are good and profitable, do you shut yourselves up in deep darkness and render services to three or four individuals alone, when you can render it to all by presenting these advantages in the public market, and thus enable all confidently to share a better and happier life? For envy does not dwell with virtue.[39] Let those who work harm feel shame and seek out holes and earth's crannies and thick darkness and there be concealed, and cloak their lawlessness from the sight of all. But let those whose actions are of benefit to all enjoy freedom of speech and walk in daylight through the central market square to converse with massed throngs, to illuminate their own life with pure sunlight, and through the most sovereign senses serve those assembled by enabling them to behold the most pleasing and most astonishing spectacles, and to hear and feast on pleasant discourse, which is wont to cheer the minds of those not wholly uncultured. Note that nature, too, does not conceal any of her storied and admirable works, but displays the stars and the whole heaven to delight us by the sight and to stir our longing for philosophy; so too the seas and fountains and rivers and the air made mild by tempering winds and breezes[40] with a view to producing the annual seasons, and the innumerable species of plants and animals and again of fruit, for the use and pleasure of man. Ought we not then follow her designs and display all that is necessary and useful for the benefit of those who are worthy of them? As a matter of fact, it often happens that no decent men are initiated into the mysteries, while thieves and pirates and companies of abominable and licentious women, when they provide money to whose who conduct the initiating rites, are accepted. Let all such be banished beyond the bounds of the state or constitution in which morality and truth are honored for their own sakes. So much for this subject. (*Spec.* 1.319–324)

83

C. PRECISION AND UNITY OF SCRIPTURE

There Is No Tautology in Scripture

It is worth raising the question why now Moses again calls Sarah the wife of Abraham, when he has already often before so designated her; for Moses did not practice the worst form of verbosity, namely, tautology. (*Congr.* 73)

There Is Nothing Superfluous in Scripture

Clearly aware that he never inserts a superfluous word,[41] in view of his powerful impulse to state the facts, I began to raise the issue with myself why he said that the intentional killer is not only to be put to death, but "by death to be put to death." (*Fug.* 54)[42]

The Most Far-Fetched Inquiry into Scripture
Defended as "Seasoning" to Holy Writ

Next, we might reasonably further raise the question why Moses spoke of the river of Egypt alone as having "lips," but not of the Euphrates and other holy rivers. . . . Yet some perhaps may say mockingly that we ought not introduce such matters into our researches, since they smack of hair-splitting rather than anything profitable. I take it, however, that such matters are like condiments added as seasoning to Holy Writ for the edification of its readers, and that the inquirers should not be charged with sophistical ingenuity, but on the contrary of laziness if they did not make inquiry. (*Somn.* 2. 300–301)

The Organic Unity of Scripture

The divine legislation is then in a manner a unified creature, which one must examine carefully through and through with wide-open eyes and carefully observe the design of the whole with utter precision and clarity, neither destroying its harmony nor breaking its unity. For deprived of what they have in common, things appear of diverse form and kind. (*QG* 3.3, Gr. fr., Harris, p. 29, LCL Supp. II, p. 207)

SELECTIONS

D. ARITHMOLOGY

The Marvelous Properties of the Number Seven

When the whole world had been completed in accordance with the nature of six, a perfect number, the Father exalted the following Seventh Day, praising it and calling it holy; for it is the festival, not of a single city or country, but of the universe, for it alone strictly deserves to be called a general holiday and the birthday of the world. I doubt whether anyone could adequately celebrate the nature of the number seven[43] since it is beyond all words. Indeed, the fact that it is more marvelous than all that is said of it is no reason for maintaining silence, but we must venture to disclose at least all that is accessible to our understandings, even if it be impossible to indicate all or even the most important points. (*Op.* 89–90)

Seven Neither Engenders Nor Is Engendered

Such is the holiness inherent by nature in the number seven that it has a singular value in relation to all the numbers within the decade: for some of these engender without being engendered, some are engendered but do not engender, some do both, both engender and are engendered: Seven alone is seen in none of these divisions.[44] This assertion must be confirmed through demonstration. The one engenders all the successive numbers, but is engendered by none whatever; eight is engendered by twice four, but engenders no number within the decade; four again holds the place of both, both of parents and of offspring, for it engenders eight when doubled, and is engendered by twice two. Seven alone, as I have said, is of such nature as neither to engender nor be engendered. It is on this account that other philosophers compare this number to the motherless and virgin Nike,[45] who is said to have appeared out of the head of Zeus, while the Pythagoreans compare it to the leader of all things: for that which neither engenders nor is engendered remains unmoved; for generation is encompassed by movement, since both that which engenders and that which is engendered are not without movement, the one that it may engender, the other that it may be engendered. The sole thing that neither moves nor is moved is the senior Ruler and Commander, of whom it may properly be said that seven is his image. Philolaos tes-

85

tifies to what I say in these words: "There exists, he says, a Commander and Ruler of all things, God, ever One, abiding, unmoved, himself like unto himself, different from all others." (*Op.* 99–100)

The Number Ten in Scripture

The matter of the decade has been carefully investigated by the musicians, but Moses, the holiest of men, has celebrated it at great length, referring to it things of outstanding excellence, beginnings, first fruits, the continued gifts of the priests, the observance of the Passover, the atonement, the release and the return to the ancient allotments in every period of fifty years, the furnishing of the permanent tabernacle, and many others it would take too long to mention. The principal ones, however, must not be passed over.

He introduces Noah, for example, the first man pronounced just in Holy Scripture, as tenth in line from the man molded from the earth; not that he wishes to set before us a specific number of years, but to clearly show that just as ten is the perfect term of the numbers derived from the monad, so justice in the soul is perfect and truly the term of our life's actions. (*Congr.* 89–90)[46]

E. ETYMOLOGIZING

Jerusalem Signifies "Vision of Peace"

The city of God is called by the Hebrews Jerusalem and its name when translated is "vision of peace." Therefore do not seek the city of the Existent in earthly latitudes for it is not constructed of wood or stone, but in a soul without war, whose sight is keen, which has set before it as its goal the contemplative and peaceful life. (*Somn.* 2.250)

Meaning of Ahiman, Sheshai, and Talmai

Ahiman means "my brother"; Sheshai "outside me";[47] Talmai "someone hanging": body-loving souls necessarily look to the body as a brother, and bestow preeminent honor on external goods; and all souls so disposed hang upon lifeless things and are, like those impaled, fixed to perishable materials until they die. (*Post.* 61)

SELECTIONS

III. THE DIVINE MIND:
THE MANY-NAMED LOGOS

A. IDEAS

The Eternity of the Ideas

When a musician or a scholar has died, the music or scholarship within him perishes together with him; but their Forms remain and in a way their life is of equal duration with the world, and in accordance with these both present and future generations in perpetual succession will become musicians or scholars. Similarly, if the practical sense or balanced self-control or bravery or justice or in a word the wisdom within an individual be destroyed, nonetheless there stand inscribed in the immortal nature of the universe undying wisdom and virtue entire and indestructible, and in accordance with these some men are wise today and will be so in the future. Such must be the case, unless we say that the death of an individual man has entailed the destruction of mankind. What "mankind" is, whether a genus or a Form, or a conception[48] or whatever name it must be called, they will know who investigate the precise use of terms. A single seal has often stamped its mark on innumerable substances, and at times all the impressions have faded together with the very substances on which they were made, while the seal has suffered no harm in its own nature, but remains in place. Must we then not believe that the virtues will forever maintain their nature inviolate and incorruptible, even if all the distinctive marks they have stamped on souls that have approached them should become effaced by reason of a corrupt way of life or some other cause? (*Det.* 75–77)[49]

Moses Seeks a Vision of God's Glory,
That Is, the Divine Forms Shaping All Things

When Moses heard this, he addressed to God a second entreaty and said, "I have been persuaded by your instructions that I could not have the power to receive a clear form of your appearance, but I beseech you that I may at least see the glory that surrounds you,[50] and by your glory I understand the powers that keep guard about you, whose apprehension has hitherto eluded me though it produces in me a great yearning to have knowledge of them." To this God says in response, "The powers that you seek are invisible and intelligible, belonging to me who am [equally] invisible and intelligible, and by intelligible I speak not of those effectively apprehended by mind but mean that if these powers could be apprehended, it would not be by sense but by mind at its purest. But though inapprehensible in their essence they show a sort of impress and copy of their activity: like your seals, which when wax or similar material is brought into contact with them stamp on them innumerable impressions without suffering loss in any part, but remaining as they were. Such you must assume my powers to be, procuring qualities for things qualityless and shapes for things shapeless, and neither altering nor lessening anything of their eternal nature. Some among you, without missing the mark, call them Forms,[51] since they provide everything that exists with form, ordering the disordered, bounding, limiting, and shaping the unbounded, the unlimited, and the shapeless, and generally transforming the worse into something better. Do not, then, entertain the hope ever to be able to apprehend me or any of my powers in our essence. But of what is attainable, as I have said, I readily and willingly grant you a share, which means that I invite you to contemplate the universe and its contents, a vision apprehended not by the eyes of the body but by the unsleeping eyes of the mind. Only let there be a continuous and constant longing for wisdom, which fills its devotees and disciples with glorious doctrines of exceeding loveliness." When Moses heard this, he did not cease from his desire, but kept kindling his yearning for the invisible. (*Spec.* 1.45–50)

A Critique of Those Who Deny the Theory of Forms

Some assert that the incorporeal Forms are a vacuous term[52] devoid of true reality, and thus they annul the indispensable essence of existent things, namely the archetypal model of all the qualities of being, in accordance with which everything was endowed with form and measure. These the holy tablets of the Law speak of as "crushed,"[53] for just as anything crushed has lost its quality and form and is properly speaking nothing more than shapeless matter, so the doctrine that annuls the Forms confuses everything and reduces it to that state of being anterior to the existence of elements, a state shapeless and qualityless. What could be more preposterous than this? For from the pre-elemental matter God created all things, without laying

88

hold of it himself, since it was not lawful for the happy and blessed One to touch limitless chaotic matter. Instead he employed his incorporeal powers, truly designated Forms, so that each genus assume its fitting shape. The other doctrine, however, introduces great disorder and confusion; for by annulling the agencies that produce the qualities, it annuls the qualities along with them. (*Spec.* 1.327–329)

B. POWERS

The Cherubim and Flaming Sword Symbolize God's Two Powers Goodness and Sovereignty, United by His Logos

But I also once heard a more excellent explanation from a voice within my soul, which frequently is inspired and divines concerning that of which it has no knowledge. This thought, if I can, I will disclose from memory. The voice told me that with the one God who truly Is are two all-high and primary powers, Goodness and Sovereignty. Through his Goodness he engendered all that is, through his Sovereignty he rules what he has engendered, but a third uniting both is intermediating Logos, for it is through Logos that God is both ruler and good. Of these two powers, Sovereignty and Goodness, the cherubim are symbols, but of Logos, the flaming sword is the symbol. For exceedingly swift and of glowing heat is Logos,[54] and especially so the Logos of the primal Cause, for this it was that preceded and outstripped all things, conceived before them all, and before all manifest. (*Cher.* 27–28)[55]

The Beneficent and Regent Powers Are Called God and Lord Respectively

The primary powers of the Existent, namely the Bounteous, through which he framed the world, and which is named God, and the Punitive, by which he rules and commands what is created, and which is called Lord, are, Moses tells us, separated by God himself standing above in the midst of them. "I will speak to you," it says, "above the mercy-seat in the midst of the two Cherubim" (Exod. 25:21), in order to show that the senior powers of the Existent, the Munificent and the Punitive, are equal, having him to divide them. (*Her.* 166)[56]

PHILO OF ALEXANDRIA

The Creative Power Passes through Every Part of the Universe

God is everywhere because he has stretched out his powers through earth and water, air and heaven, and left no part of the universe void of his presence,[57] and joining all with all has bound them fast with invisible bonds, that they should never be loosed. . . . [58] That aspect of him which transcends his powers cannot be conceived of at all in terms of place,[59] but only as pure being, but that power of his by which he made and ordered all things, called God in accordance with the etymology of that name, enfolds the whole and passes through the parts of the universe. (*Conf.* 136–137)[60]

God and His Two Ministering Powers Are in Reality One

What is the meaning of "He saw, and behold, three men were standing over him"? (Gen. 18:2)

What is most in accord with reality to those who are able to see does (Scripture) present, (namely) that it is reasonable for one to be three and for three to be one, for they were one by a higher principle. But when counted with the chief powers, the creative and kingly, he makes the appearance of three to the human mind. For this cannot be so keen of sight that it can see him who is above the powers that belong to him, (namely) God, distinct from everything else. For so soon as one sets eyes on God, there also appear, together with his being, the ministering powers, so that in place of one he makes the appearance of a triad. (*QG* 4.2)

Two Powers Enter Every Soul at Birth

(Exod. 12:23c) (Why) does (Scripture) say that He will not let "the destroyer enter your houses to strike"?

. . . As for the deeper meaning this must be said. Into every soul at its very birth there enter two powers, the salutary and the destructive. If the salutary one is victorious and prevails, the opposite one is too weak to see. And if the latter prevails, no profit at all or little is obtained from the salutary one. Through these powers the world, too, was created. People call them by other names: the salutary (power) they call powerful and beneficent, and the opposite one (they call) unbounded and destructive. Thus, the sun and moon and the appropriate positions of the other stars and their ordered functions and the whole heaven together came into being and exist through the two (powers). And they are created in accordance with the better part of these, namely when the salutary and beneficent (power) brings to an end the unbounded and destructive nature. Wherefore also to those who have attained such a state and a nature similar to this is immortality given. But the nation is a mixture of both (these powers), from which the heavens and the entire world as a whole received this mixture. Now, sometimes the evil becomes greater in this mixture, and hence (all creatures) live in torment, harm, ignominy, contention, battle, and bodily illness together with all the other things in human life, as in the whole world, so in man. And this mixture is in both the wicked man and the wise man but not in the same way. For the souls of foolish men have the unbounded and destructive rather than the powerful and salutary (power), and it is full of misery when it dwells with earthly creatures. But the prudent and noble (soul) rather receives the powerful and salutary (power) and, on the contrary, possesses in itself good fortune and happiness, being carried around with the heaven because of kinship with it. Most excellently, therefore, does (Scripture) say that He will not let "the destroyer enter your houses to strike," and this is what (actually) happens, for the force that is the cause of destruction strives, as it were, to enter the soul, but is prevented by the divine beneficences from striking (it), for these are salutary. But those from whom the favors and gifts of God are separated and cut off suffer the experience of desertion and widowhood. . . . [61] (*QE* 1.23)

The Creative Power Is Logically Prior to the Regent Power

The Creative is conceptually older than the Regent Power. For all the powers surrounding God are of equal age, but the Creative is in a way prior in thought to the Regent Power, since one is king not of the nonexistent but of what has already come into being.[62] (*QE* 2.62, Gr. fr., Harris, pp. 63–64, LCL Supp. II, pp. 253–254)

The Respective Functions of the Creative and Regent Powers

(Exod. 25:17c–18 [Hebrew, 18c–19]) Why did he fit the Cherubim to either side of the mercy-seat?

[This indicates that] the bounds of the whole heaven and the world are fortified by the two highest guards, both that through which God created all things, and that through which he is ruler over what has come into being. For each was destined to take care of the world as its most fitting and cognate possession, the Creative Power being concerned that the things that came into being through it should not be dissolved, and the Regent Power that nothing either exceed or be robbed of its due, all being arbitrated by the laws of equality, through which things continue everlasting. For excess and inequality are the incentives for war, the destroyers of existing things. But good order and equality are the seeds of peace, and the causes of preservation and perpetual survival. (*QE* 2.64)[63]

C. LOGOS/SOPHIA

Heavenly Wisdom Is Many-named

"And God planted a pleasure ground eastward in Eden, and placed there the man whom he had fashioned" (Gen. 2:8). Through the employment of many terms Moses has disclosed that the lofty and heavenly wisdom is many-named;[64] for he calls it "beginning"[65] and "image" and "vision of God"; and now by the planting of the pleasure ground he presents earthly wisdom as the copy of this as of an archetype. Let not so great impiety take possession of man's reason that it assume that God tills the ground and plants pleasure grounds, for we should immediately be at a loss to discover his motivation. Certainly not to provide himself with pleasant relaxation and pleasures. Let not such mythic inventions ever enter our mind. . . . God accordingly sows and plants terrestrial virtue for the race of mortals as a copy and representation of the heavenly. (*LA* 1.43, 45–46)[66]

The Flinty Rock, Symbol of God's Wisdom

But the soul falls in with a scorpion, which is "scattering," in the wilderness, and the thirst for the passions takes told of it, until God send forth the stream from his flinty wisdom and irrigate the changed soul with unchanging health. For the flinty rock is the wisdom of God, which he hewed out as the highest and most primary of his powers, from which he irrigates god-loving souls. And after they have been watered, they are filled also with the manna, the most generic of things, for the manna is called "something," the genus of all things. But the supremely generic is God, and next is the Logos of God; the other things subsist in word only, though in their effects they are at times equivalent to the nonsubsistent. (*LA* 2.86)[67]

The Tabernacle Is a Representation of Wisdom

When God willed to send down the image of divine excellence from heaven to earth in pity for our race so that it not fail to receive a better portion, he symbolically constructs the holy tabernacle and its contents as a representation and copy of wisdom. For the oracle tells us that the tabernacle "was set up in the midst of our uncleanness" (Lev. 16:16) in order that we have wherewith we may be clean after washing off and purging away all that sullies our life, wretched and laden with ignominy as it is. (*Her.* 112–113)[68]

The Divine Logos, Though Indivisible Itself, Divides Others

For the Divine Logos is a lover of the alone and the solitary, never mixing with the crowd of things created and destined to perish, but accustomed to roaming the heights and taking thought to attend on One alone. The two natures, then, that of the reasoning power within us and that of the Divine Logos above us, though indivisible, divide countless others. The Divine Logos separated and apportioned all that is in nature, and our mind, whatever things material or immaterial[69] it mentally ascertains, it divides infinitely into an infinite number of parts and never ceases dividing. This is the result of their likeness to the Father and Creator of all. For the Deity, though without mixture or blending and absolutely without parts, has become to the whole world the cause of mixture, blending, division, and multiplicity of parts. It naturally follows that these entities too that resemble God, the mind within us and the one above us, though without parts and indivisible, will be capable stoutly to divide and distinguish everything that is. (*Her.* 234–236)[70]

The Logos, Bond of the Universe, Mediates between Opposites

The Logos, extending himself from the center to its furthest bounds and from its extremities to the center again, runs nature's unvanquished course joining and binding fast all its parts. For the Father who begat him constituted him an unbreakable bond of the universe. It is therefore reasonable that all the earth will not be dissolved by all the water contained within its bosom-like hollows; nor fire be quenched by air; nor, on the other hand, air be rekindled by fire. The Divine Logos marshals himself between, like a vowel amid consonants, that the universe may produce a harmony like that of literary art,[71] for he mediates and moderates the threatenings[72] of the opponents through conciliatory persuasion.[73] (*Plant.* 9–10)[74]

The Mediatory Role of the Logos, Which Is Neither Uncreated as God, Nor Created as Man

To his chief messenger and most venerable Logos, the Father who engendered the universe has granted the singular gift, to stand between and separate the creature from the Creator. This same Logos is both suppliant of ever anxiety-ridden mortality before the immortal and ambassador of the ruler to the subject. He glories in this gift and proudly describes it in these words, "And I stood between the Lord and you" (Deut. 5:5), neither unbegotten as God, nor begotten as you, but midway between the two extremes, serving as a pledge for both; to the Creator as assurance that the creature should never completely shake off the reins and rebel, choosing disorder rather than order; to the creature warranting his hopefulness that the gracious God will never disregard his own work. For I am an ambassador of peace to creation from the God who has determined to put down wars, who is ever the guardian of peace. (*Her.* 205)[75]

Wisdom, the Daughter of God, Is in Reality Masculine

For you will find the house of wisdom a calm and serene haven that will readily welcome you as you enter; and it is wisdom's name that is celebrated in the oracles by "Bethuel" (Gen. 28:2), which translated means "Daughter of God"; indeed, a true-born and ever-virgin daughter, who has obtained a nature intact and undefiled, both because of her own propriety and the dignity of him that begot her.

He called Bethuel Rebecca's father (Gen. 28:2). But how can Wisdom, the daughter of God, be rightly said to be a father? Is it because, though Wisdom's name is feminine, her nature is masculine? Indeed all the virtues have women's designations, but powers and activities of truly perfect men. For that which comes after God, even if it were the most venerable of all other things, holds second place, and was called feminine in contrast to the Creator of the universe, who is masculine, and in accordance with its resemblance to everything else. For the feminine always falls short and is inferior to the masculine, which has priority.

Let us then pay no attention to the discrepancy in the terms, and say that the daughter of God, Wisdom, is both masculine and the father,[76] inseminating and engendering in souls a desire to learn discipline, knowledge, practical insight, noble and laudable actions. (*Fug.* 50–52)[77]

Wisdom Flows in a Perpetual Stream from the Divine Logos

When the Israelites sought what it is that nourished the soul (for as Moses says, "they knew not what it was") (Exod. 16:15), they learned and discovered that it was the word of God, the Divine Logos, from which all forms of instruction and wisdom flow in perpetual stream. This is the heavenly nourishment, and it is revealed in the sacred records on the part of[78] the First Cause when he says, "Lo, it is I that am raining upon you bread out of the heaven" (Exod. 16:4); for in truth God distills from on high the ethereal wisdom on minds well endowed and fond of contemplation. (*Fug.* 137–138)[79]

The Logos, Cupbearer of God, Pours Himself into Happy Souls

And into the happy soul, which holds out the truly holy chalice, its own reason, who is it that pours the sacred measures of true gladness but the Logos, the Cupbearer of God and Toastmaster of the feast, who differs not from the draught he pours, but is himself the undiluted drink, the gaiety, the seasoning, the effusion, the cheer, and, to make poetic expression our own, the ambrosian drug of joy and gladness? (*Somn.* 2.249)[80]

IV. COSMOGONY

A. CREATION FROM PRIMORDIAL MATTER

The Active and Passive Causes

Some people, admiring the world rather than its Creator, proclaimed it uncreated and eternal, while impiously feigning a vast inaction in God,[81] whereas we ought on the contrary to be astounded at his powers as Creator and Father, and not overglorify the world. But Moses, who had both attained philosophy's summit and had been taught through oracles the greater and most essential truths of nature, recognized that at the very least, among things existent, one cause is active, the other passive,[82] and that the active cause is the universal Mind, absolutely pure and unmixed, beyond virtue, beyond knowledge, and beyond the good itself and the beautiful itself; whereas the passive cause is in itself lifeless and motionless, but when moved, shaped, and quickened by Mind, it is transformed into the most perfect masterwork, this world. (*Op.* 7–9)

The Cause of Creation, and the Nature of Primordial Matter

Should one wish to search out the cause for the sake of which the universe was created, it seems to me that he would not miss the mark in saying what indeed one of the men of old did say,[83] that the Father and Creator is good; and for this reason he did not begrudge the excellence of his own nature to a substance[84] having of itself nothing lovely, though capable of becoming all things. For of itself it was without order, without quality, without soul, (without homogeneity), full of heterogeneity, discord, disharmony; but it admitted a turning and changing to the best, the contrary of all these, to order, quality, homogeneity, identity, concord, harmony, to all that is characteristic of the better Form.

Without counselor (for who else was there?), and making use of his own powers alone, God determined that he must, with lavish and rich boons, show kindness to that nature which without Divine bounty was incapable of obtaining anything good of itself. But not in accordance with the greatness of his own boons does he confer benefits—for these are uncircumscribed and without end—but according to the capacities of the recipients. For creation is unable in its nature to receive the good in the same way that it is the nature of God to confer it, since his powers exceed all bounds, whereas creation, being too feeble to take in their magnitude, would have given out, had not God weighed and appropriately measured out that which falls to the share of each. (*Op.* 21–23)[85]

God Divides Primordial Matter by Means of His All-Incising Logos

The Artificer took this substance and began to divide as follows. First he made two sections, the heavy and the light, separating the dense from the rare. He then again divided these two parts; the rare into air and fire, the dense into water and earth, and these visible elements he laid down in advance as foundations of the visible world. . . .

Thus did God sharpen his all-incising Logos and divide the formless and qualityless universal being, and the four elements of the world that had been separated off from it, and the animals and plants constituted from these. (*Her.* 134, 140)

God Alone Can Divide Things Equally with Absolute Precision

Since the text not only says "He divided" but also "He divided them in the middle," it is necessary to make mention, however briefly, of the matter of equal sections. That which is divided exactly in the middle produces equal sections. Now no man can divide anything into equal sections with precision, but one of the sections is inevitably too little or too large, if not by much, at any rate by a little, very likely eluding our perception, which naturally and habitually impinges on larger masses but is unable to grasp those indivisible and without parts. No created thing is found to produce equality measured by the impartial principle of truth. It seems, then, that it is God alone whose justice is precise and alone is able to "divide in the middle" things material and immaterial, so that no section is greater or less by even a hair's breadth, and is capable of sharing an equality absolute and consummate.[86] (*Her.* 141–143)

The Primordial Matter of Creation Is Unworthy of Praise

Now it was not the matter subjected to his creative activity, material inanimate, discordant, and dissoluble, and what is more in itself perishable, irregular, and unequal, that God praised,[87] but the works of his own art accomplished by a power unique, equal, and uniform, and through knowledge ever one and the same. And thus by the rule of proportion all things were held equal and similar to all else, in accordance with the principle of God's art and knowledge. (*Her.* 160)

There Was a Time When the World Was Not

Now to one who is determined to follow an authentic philosophy and lay claim to a piety guileless and pure, Moses teaches this truly admirable and divine command that he should not suppose any of the parts of the universe to be a sovereign deity. For the world has come to be, and its genesis is the beginning of its destruction, even if through the providence of God it be immortal, and there was a time when it was not.[88] But to say of God that he formerly was not, and that he came to be at a particular time and is not eternally existent, is sacrilege. (*Decal.* 58)

God Calculated for the Creation of the World Precisely Sufficient Matter

As to the quantity of the substance, on the assumption that it was truly created, the following is to be said. God calculated for the creation of the world precisely sufficient matter so that there be neither lack nor excess. For it were absurd if specialized craftsmen when fashioning an object, especially a costly one, weigh out sufficient material, he who invented numbers, measures, and equality in them had no concern for what was adequate. I will say indeed with all candor that the world needed neither less nor more substance for its construction, for otherwise it would have been neither perfect nor complete in all its parts, but since it was well created, it was brought to completion out of perfect substance. For it is a characteristic of a master craftsman before he begins any construction to see after sufficient material. A man, to be sure, even if superior to everyone in knowledge, since he is unable completely to escape the errors congenital to mortals, might perhaps be deceived with regard to the quantity of material needed when he executes his art, at times having to add to what is too little, at others to remove what is excessive. But he who is as it were the fountainhead of all knowledge would not lay down as a foundation anything lacking or excessive, since he employs measures elaborated with marvellous accuracy, all praiseworthy. (*Prov.* 2.50–51, Gr. fr., LCL 9.454–457)[89]

B. CREATION OF THE INTELLIGIBLE WORLD

The Intelligible World within the Divine Mind
Compared to a Blueprint within the Architect's Mind

For God, being God, judged in advance that a beautiful copy would never be produced except from a beautiful pattern and that no sense object would be irreproachable that was not modeled after an archetypal and intelligible idea. So when he willed to create this visible world, he first formed the intelligible world, so that he might employ a pattern completely Godlike and incorporeal for the production of the corporeal world, a more recent image of one that was older, which was to comprise as many sensible kinds as there were intelligible ones in the other.

To say or to suppose that that world composed of the ideas is in some place is improper; but how it was put together we shall know if we closely attend to some similitude taken from our own world. When a city is being founded to satisfy the great ambition of some king or ruler who pretends to absolute power, and magnificent in his pride further embellishes his good fortune, there comes forward now and then some trained architect who, after observing the mild climate and convenient location of the site, first maps out in his own mind virtually all the parts of the city that is to be brought to completion, temples, gymnasia, town halls, marketplaces, harbors, docks, lanes, wall constructions, the erection of houses as well as public buildings. Accordingly, after having received in his soul, as in wax, the impressions of each of these objects, he carries in his mind the image of an intelligible city. Then, after awakening these images through his innate power of memory, and imprinting their stamp even further, like a good craftsman keeping his eye on the model, he begins to build the city of stones and timber, adapting the corporeal objects to each of the incorporeal ideas.

Similarly must we think about God. When he was minded to found the Great City, he first conceived the forms of its parts, out of which he put together the intelligible world, and, using that as a model, he also brought to completion the sensible world. As, then, the city prefigured in the architect's mind held no place externally but was stamped in the soul of the artisan, so too the intelligible world could have no other location than the Divine Logos, which established the world order. For what other place could there be for his powers sufficient to receive and contain, I say not all, but any of them whatever unmixed.[90] (*Op.* 16–20)

The Intelligible World Is the Divine Logos in the Act of Creation

If one should wish to express it more baldly, he would say that the Intelligible World is nothing else than the Divine Logos already in the act of building the cosmos, for the intelligible city is nothing else than the reasoning of the architect already intent on founding the city. This is Moses' teaching, not mine; for in his description of man's creation in the sequel he explicitly acknowledges that he was molded after the image of God (Gen. 1:27). Now if the part is an image of an image, and the whole form, this entire sensible world since it is greater than the human image, is a copy of the divine image, it is clear that the archetypal seal, which we declare to be the intelligible world, would be the very Logos of God. (*Op.* 24–25)

Creation of the Intelligible World

First, then, the Creator made an incorporeal heaven and an invisible earth and the Form of air and void. The one he named "darkness," since air is by nature black; the other, "abyss," for the void is very deep and immense. Next came the incorporeal essence of water and pneuma (breath), and topping them all in the seventh place, that of light, which, in its turn incorporeal, was an intelligible pattern of the sun and all the luminous stars that were to take shape across the heavens. (*Op.* 29)

SELECTIONS

Creation of Incorporeal Ideas Deduced from Genesis 2:4–5

Concluding the creation narrative he says by way of summary:

> This is the book of the genesis of heaven and earth, when they came into being, on the day on which God made the heaven and the earth and every green shrub of the field before it appeared upon the earth, and all grass of the field before it sprang up. (Gen. 2:4–5)

Is he not manifestly setting before us the incorporeal and intelligible ideas that are the seals of the sensible objects of creation? For before the earth greened, young verdure itself existed in the nature of things, and before grass sprang up in the field, an invisible grass existed. We must suppose that prior also to each of all the other objects judged by the senses, there existed the more ancient forms and measures through which all things that come into being are shaped and measured, for even if he has not gone through all things severally but only collectively, taking thought as much as any for brevity, the few things said constitute nonetheless patterns for the whole of nature, which without an incorporeal model accomplishes nothing in the world of sense. (*Op*. 129–130)[91]

The Logos Used as an Instrument in Creating the World

Bezalel means, then, "in the shadow of God";[92] but God's shadow is his Logos, which he used as an instrument and thus created the world. This shadow and representation, as it were, is in turn the archetype of other things. For just as God is the Pattern of the Image, which was just named Shadow, so does the Image become the pattern of others, as Moses made clear at the beginning of the Law Code by saying, "And God made man after the Image of God" (Gen. 1:27); thus the Image had been modeled after God, but man after the Image, which had acquired the force of a pattern. (*LA* 3.96)[93]

God Had Intercourse with His Knowledge and Begat Created Being

We should at once rightly say that the Craftsman who made this universe was at the same time the father of what was begotten, while the mother was the knowledge of its creator. With his knowledge God had intercourse,[94] not in human fashion, and begat created being.[95] Knowledge received the divine seed and with birth-throes bearing perfect fruit bore the only beloved and sense-perceptible Son, this world.[96] Thus wisdom is represented by one of the divine chorus as speaking of herself in this manner: "God obtained me first of all his works and founded me before the ages" (Prov. 8:22). For all that has come to birth must inevitably be younger than the mother and nurse of the All. (*Ebr.* 30–31)

C. THE CREATION OF MAN

Man the Noblest of Things Earthborn

God, being minded to join together the beginning and end of created things as being most lovingly related, made heaven the beginning and man the end, the one the most perfect of imperishable objects of sense, the other the best of the earthborn and the perishable, a miniature heaven if one is to speak the truth. He carries impressed in his mind many starlike natural endowments through his arts and sciences and the glorious speculations attached to each of the virtues. For since the corruptible and the incorruptible are by nature contraries, God allotted the fairest of each kind to the beginning and the end, heaven, as has been said, to the beginning, and man to the end. (*Op.* 82)[97]

Man Is a Heavenly Growth

For God made man, alone of things on earth, a heavenly growth, while he fixed on the ground the heads of all others, for they all have their head bent downward;[98] but man's head he lifted upward, that he may have nourishment celestial and imperishable, not terrestrial and perishable. For this reason he removed the part of our body least capable of sensation as far as possible from our reasoning faculty and planted our feet firmly to the earth, but our senses, bodyguards of the mind, he banished to a distance furthest from the ground, and bound them to the circuits of air and heaven,[99] which are imperishable. (*Det.* 85)

SELECTIONS

Heavenly and Earthly Man

After this he says that "God fashioned man by taking[100] clay from the earth, and breathed into his face the breath of life" (Gen. 2:7). By this also he shows very clearly that there is an immense difference between the man now fashioned and the one created earlier after the image of God. For the molded man is sense-perceptible, partaking already of specific quality, framed of body and soul, man or woman, by nature mortal; whereas he that was after the image was an idea or genus or seal, intelligible, incorporeal, neither male nor female, imperishable by nature.[101]

As for the individual sense-perceptible man, his constitution is said to be a composite of earthly substance and of divine breath; for his body was made through the Artificer's taking clay and fashioning out of it a human shape, but the soul was formed from nothing created whatever, but from the Father and Ruler of all; for that which he breathed in was nothing other than a Divine breath that migrated hither from that blessed and blissful nature for the benefit of our race, so that even if it is mortal as to its visible portion, it may in respect of its invisible portion become immortal. One might therefore legitimately say that man is located on the frontier between mortal and immortal nature, having a part in each to the extent that is necessary, and that he was created at once mortal and immortal, mortal as to his body, but in respect of his mind immortal. (*Op.* 134–135)[102]

The First Man Excelled All Other Men,
and Succeeding Generations Have Been Gradually Degenerating

Such, I think, was the first man created in body and soul, excelling all the men that now are, and all who have preceded us. For our origin is from men, whereas God created him, and the more excellent the maker, that much better the work. For as that which is in its prime is always better than that whose prime is past, whether animal or plant or fruit or anything else in nature, so the man first fashioned was likely the flower of our entire race, while those who came after no longer attained a like prime, inasmuch as subsequent generations have taken on forms and faculties ever fainter.[103] This is something I have observed happening in the plastic arts and in painting: the copies fall short of the originals, and what is painted or molded from

103

the copies even more so, due to their great distance from the original. The magnet displays a similar effect, for the iron ring that touches it is held fast more strongly, but that which touches this one less so.[103a] A third clings to the second, and a fourth to the third, and a fifth to the fourth, and so on in a long series, all held together by one attractive force, though not in like manner, for those further separated from the starting pont are continually being loosened through the relaxation of the attractive force, which is no longer capable of exercising the same binding power. Mankind seems to have undergone something similar. Generation by generation the powers and qualities both of body and of soul that men receive are feebler. (*Op.* 140–141)

Man's "Fall"

But since nothing in creation is constant, and things mortal necessarily undergo changes and vicissitudes, the first man too had to reap some ill fortune. And woman becomes for him the source of blameworthy life. For as long as he was alone he was like the world and God in his solitariness, and received in his soul the distinctive impresses of the nature of each, not all but as many as the human constitution can contain. But when woman too has been fashioned, beholding a sister figure and a kindred form, he found the sight satisfying and approached and greeted her. She, seeing no creature resembling herself more than he, shines with joy and coyly returns his greeting. Love supervenes, matches and joins into one the divided halves, as it were, of a single creature, and establishes in each a desire for fellowship with the other with a view to the production of their like. This desire begat also bodily pleasure, which is the source of wrongs and lawless deeds, and on which account men exchange the immortal and happy life for one that is mortal and miserable. (*Op.* 151–152)[104]

Five Lessons of the Creation Narrative

By his narrative of the creation of the world of which we have spoken Moses teaches us among many other things five that are fairest and best of all. First, that the Deity is and subsists, with a view to the atheists, some of whom have vacillated and have entertained doubts concerning God's existence, while the more audacious have boldly declared that he does not exist at all, but that it is merely asserted by men who obscure the truth with mythical fabrications. Second, that God is one, with a view to the propounders of polytheism, who do not blush to transpose mob rule, that worst of evil polities, from earth to heaven. Third, as already said, that the world came into being, with a view to those who think that it is uncreated and eternal, thus assigning to God no advantage at all. Fourth, that the world too is one, inasmuch as its Creator is one, who made his work like himself in its uniqueness, who made use of the entire material for the creation of the whole; for it would not have been a whole had it not been brought together and framed from all of its parts.[105] For there are those who assume that there are many worlds, some even that they are infinite in number. It is they who in truth are themselves [infinitely] ignorant[106] of things that it is good to know. Fifth, that God takes thought for the universe. For that the Creator takes care for his creation is required by the laws and ordinances of nature, in accordance with which parents too take care of their children.[107]

He who has gradually learnt these things not so much through his hearing as through his intelligence, and has stamped in his soul these marvelous and greatly prized ideas, that God both is and subsists, and that he that really Is One, and that he has created the world and has created it one world, as was said, like himself in his uniqueness, and that he ever takes thought for his creation will lead a blessed and happy life, having been stamped by the teachings of piety and holiness. (*Op.* 170–172)

D. TIME AND ETERNITY

Since the World Is Sense-Perceptible, It Must Have Been Created

But the great Moses, believing the uncreated to be wholly other than that which is visible, since all that is sense-perceptible is subject to becoming and change, never abiding the same, assigned to the invisible and intelligible as its kindred attribute, eternity, but to the sense-perceptible he assigned "becoming" as its appropriate name. Since this world is both visible and perceptible, it must necessarily also be created. (*Op.* 12)

PHILO OF ALEXANDRIA

All Things Created Simultaneously

He says that in six days the world was created, not because its Creator was in need of a length of time for his work, for it is a reasonable assumption that God does all things simultaneously, not only commanding but also thinking. Six days are mentioned because there was need of order for the things coming into being. Order implies number, and of numbers, according to the laws of nature, the most appropriate for productivity is six,[108] for counting from one it is the first perfect number, being equal to the product of its factors (i.e., $1 \times 2 \times 3$), as well as made up of the sum of these (i.e., $1 + 2 + 3$), its half being three, its third two, its sixth one. It is, so to speak, by nature both male and female, and is put together from the product of both. For among existent things, the odd is male, and the even female. Now of odd numbers three is the origin, and of even numbers, two, and the product of these two is six. For it was requisite that the world, being the most perfect of all things created, be established in accordance with a perfect number, namely six; and, since it was to have in itself creations resulting through mating, should be formed after the model of a mixed number, the first odd-even combination, one that should contain the form both of the male that sows and of the female the receives the seed. (*Op.* 13–14)[109]

Time Did Not Exist Before the World Came into Being

He says that "in the beginning God created the heaven and the earth," taking "beginning," not, as some think, in a chronological sense, for time did not exist before the world, but came into being either with it or after it. For since time is a dimension[110] of the world's movement, and movement could not be prior to that which is moved, but must necessarily arrive either later or simultaneously with it, time too must necessarily be either coeval with or later than the world.[111] To dare proclaim it older is contrary to philosophical principle. But if "beginning" is not now taken chronologically, it would be likely that its numerical sense is indicated, so that "in the beginning he made" is equivalent to "he made the heaven first": for it is indeed reasonable for it to come into being first, being both best of created things and formed from the purest material, since it was destined to be the truly sacred dwelling of manifestly perceptible

106

gods.[112] For even if the Creator created all things simultaneously, order was no less characteristic of all that was beautifully created, for there is no beauty in disorder. Now order is a sequence and concatenation of things that precede and of things that follow, if not in the finished productions, at least in the designs of the planners; for it is thus that they can be arranged with precision and be unerring and without confusion. (*Op.* 26–28)[113]

God Never Ceases to Create

For God never ceases to create, but even as it is the property of fire to burn and of snow to cool, so it is the property of God to create: and even much more so, inasmuch as he is the source of action to all other things. Well, moreover, does Moses say "caused to rest" (Gen. 2:2), not "rested"; for he causes to rest that which appears to be creating, though actually ineffective, but himself never ceases creating. For this reason Moses adds "he caused to rest what he had begun" (Gen. 2:3). For whatever is fashioned by our arts, when finished stands still and stays put, but the products of divine skill, after being completed, move in turn;[114] for their endings are the beginnings of other things, as the end of day is the beginning of night, and the openings of a month or year must of course be regarded as limits of those expired; birth again is accomplished through other things' perishing, and destruction through new births, so that the saying is a true one:

Nothing born goes to ruin,
but element is separated from element
to produce another shape.[115] (*LA* 1.5–7)[116]

God's Word Is Deed

But the Divine Tutor outstrips even time, for not even when he created the universe did time cooperate with him, since time itself was called into existence along with the world. For God's creation was simultaneous with his speaking, allowing no interval between the two; or, to put into play a truer view, his word was deed. (*Sacr.* 65)[117]

With God All Is Timeless

The "new" (Lev. 2:14) is for the following reason. Those who fondly cling to the old-time days, grizzly and fabled, not having comprehended the swift and timeless power of God, it persuasively teaches to accept ideas new, flowering, and vigorous, so that, after having been bred on antique fables transmitted by a remote past, they may not entertain false notions, but rather receiving in full abundance from the ever ageless God new and fresh goods, learn to consider nothing ancient, nothing at all past, with God, but all becoming and existing timelessly. (*Sacr.* 76)

God's Life Is Eternity, the Archetype of Time,
Which May Be Called His Grandson

But God is the creator of time also, for he is the father of time's father, that is of the universe, whose motion he has made the origin of the former. Thus time holds in relation to God the position of grandson. For this world, inasmuch as it is sense-perceptible, is the younger son of God. The elder son, the intelligible world, he considered worthy of the birthright and intended it to remain by his side.[118] So this younger son, the sensible world, when set in motion, caused the nature of time to emerge brightly. Thus with God there is no future, since he has brought the boundaries of the ages under his own power. For God's life is not a time, but eternity, the archetype and pattern of time; and in eternity there is neither past nor future, but only present existence.[119] (*Deus* 31–32)

Heaven Is an Eternal Day, But the Earthly Life Is Sunk in Sleep

If one should be willing to peer into the interior of things, he will find heaven to be an eternal day, without night or any shadow, because it is unceasingly illumined by inextinguishable and pure beams of light. As much as among us those who are awake are superior to those asleep, so in the entire cosmos are the heavenly things superior to the earthly, for the former enjoy unsleeping wakefulness in virtue of operations unerring, infallible, and always steering a correct course, whereas the latter are mastered by sleep, and even if they momentarily awaken are dragged down again and fall asleep, because they can see nothing straightforwardly with their soul but wander and stumble about. For they are blinded by false opinions that compel them to dream, and lagging behind realities are incapable of apprehending anything firmly and securely. (*Jos.* 146–147)

God Is Eternally Creating the World

How else did God begin to create the world? Was it by taking the disorderly, erratic, and unblending movements of matter first and then fashioning the world in a beautiful manner? Rather the Creator fashioned it while always thinking. Yet God's thinking was not anterior to his creating, and there never was a time when God was not creating; the ideas have been with him ever since the beginning. For the will of God does not happen later because it is always with Him and because the natural movements never cease. So it is that He, always thinking, creates and gives beginning of being to sense-perceptible things, so that both should exist together: the ever-creating divine mind and the sense-perceptible things to which beginning of being is given. For it is impossible that that to which good befell through beneficence would have its benefits apart from a benefactor; the giver is the benefactor and the recipient the beneficiary. (*Prov.* 1.7)

E. COSMOLOGY

Perpetuity of the Species

But not only were the fruits nourishment for animals, but also a means of providing for the perpetual reproduction of their kind, holding within them the seed substances, in which the [seminal] principles[120] of all things lie hidden and indiscernible, becoming visibly manifest in the course of the seasonal cycle. For God willed that Nature should run a circular long-distance course,[121] rendering the species immortal, and giving them a share in eternity. For this reason he both led the beginning speedily toward the end, and made the end return to the beginning; for out of the plants comes the fruit, as an end out of a beginning, and out of the fruit again, holding the seed in itself, comes the plant, as a beginning out of an end. (*Op.* 43–44)

PHILO OF ALEXANDRIA

The Loving Interdependence of All Things
Reveals Nature's Perfection

For God has given all created things to all on loan, and has made no particular thing perfect, that it should have no need at all of another. Thus in striving to obtain what it needs, it must necessarily approach that which is capable of furnishing it, and that in turn must approach it, and both one another. For through this interchange and intercourse, even as a lyre is tuned through unlike notes, they were meant to come to fellowship and concord and make harmony, submitting to a universal give and take with a view to the consummation of the entire cosmos. Thus does love attract inanimate to animate, irrational to rational, trees to men, men to plants, wild to tame, and tame to wild, male to female, female to male; so too, in a word, land creatures to water creatures, water creatures to those of the air, and the latter to both [the former]; so again heaven to earth, earth to heaven, air to water, and water to pneuma [breath] again, intermediate natures to each other and those at the extremes, those at the extremes to the intermediate and to their own. Winter is in need of summer, summer of winter, spring of both, and autumn of spring; each needs each, and all, so to speak, are in dire need of all, so that the whole, of which these are the parts, might be a perfect work worthy of its creator, this world.[122] (*Cher.* 109–112)

The Principles of Cohesion, Growth, Soul, and Reason[123]

Among the various kinds of bodies, the Creator has bound some by means of cohesion, others by growth, others by soul, and others yet by rational soul.[124] Thus, in stones and timber that has been detached from its organic growth, he made cohesion a truly powerful bond. The latter is an air current returning to itself;[125] for it begins to extend itself from the center of the body to its boundaries, and when it has reached the outermost surface it bends back on its course till it arrives at the very place from which it first set out. This continuous double course[126] of cohesion is indestructible; and it is this the runners imitate at the triennial festivals in the public theaters of mankind and exhibit as a great and glorious feat, well worth the striving.

Growth God allotted to plants, constituting it a blend of many faculties, nutritive, transformative, and augmentative. . . .

SELECTIONS

Soul God made different from growth in three ways, through sensation, "impression," and impulse. For plants are without impulse and impression, and have no share in sense-perception, while animals participate in all three combined. Sensation, as the name itself indicates, is "a putting in,"[127] and introduces the appearances to the mind. For mind is an immense and all-receiving storehouse[128] in which all that comes through sight or hearing is placed and stored. (*Deus* 35–37, 41–43)[129]

Animal Skills Are Not Learned

Now for example, birds fly, aquatics swim, and terrestrials walk. Is this done by learning? Certainly not. Each of the above-mentioned creatures does it by its nature. Likewise bees make honeycombs by nature, not by learning. Spiders also make their fine work of lace spontaneously.[130] If one wishes to be dissuaded from wrong thinking about creatures, he should go to look at the trees and notice every intricate detail. These too have many aesthetic features but no skill in the arts.

Have you not seen the vine when it begins to bear fruit in the springtime?[131] First it covers the buds with leaves. Then, like a mother, it nurtures them gradually, makes them grow, and keeps changing the sour grapes to sweet grapes until the fruit is fully ripe. Has it been instructed in this care? Through its most amazing and wonderfully functioning nature, it not only bears essential fruit but also elegantly decorates its trunk with long layers of bark and twining sprays, and puts forth green leaves on its branches of various shapes. Its appearance is lustrous and of marvelous aspect. Its comeliness strongly appeals not only to the eyes but also to the olfactory sense; for it sends out a sweet odor of incense that fills the surrounding air with a pleasant and pervasive fragrance. (*Animal.* 78–79)

Animals Display Neither Fraudulence nor Wisdom

It is difficult to think that animals behave with great fraudulence and substantial wisdom. Certainly those who attest to such a wisdom do not realize that they themselves are utterly ignorant. And even if they have any understanding it is very insignificant, superficial, and dull. In regard to those who remain childlike, their grasp of knowledge is uncertain, wavering, and childish compared with the rational mind of the mature.

Even if the horse of Aristogiton was limping without having an injured leg, it was not cheating.[132] It only appeared to be cheating, since cheating is rational. Perhaps it had a protracted pain in its leg and was reminded to have a rest. Is not a quiet repose very often forgotten until such a time when its memory is rekindled?

Even the assertion of those who think that hounds track by making use of the fifth mode of syllogism[133] is to be dismissed. The same could be said of those who gather clams or any other thing that moves. That they seem to follow a definite pattern is only logical speculation on the part of those who have no sense of philosophy, not even in dreams. Then one has to say that all who are in search of something are making use of the fifth mode of syllogism! These and other similar assertions are delusive fallacies of those more accustomed to the plausibility and sophistry of matters than to the discipline of examining the truth.

We agree that there are some decent and good qualities that are applicable to animals and many other functions that help preserve and maintain their courage; these are observed by sight. There is certainty in everything perceived or discerned in all the various species. But surely animals have no share of reasoning ability, for reasoning ability extends itself to a multiplicity of abstract concepts in the mind's perception of God, the universe, laws, provincial practices, the state, state affairs, and numerous other things, none of which animals understand.

The horse lifts up its head and neighs, the deer and the hare are timid, the fox is crafty, and many others are attached and devoted to their offspring. But certainly keen insight of mind is not for every soul; rather, what has been designed and fashioned by nature was appropriately given to each as parts of body and soul, to each constituent its proper function toward its own perfection and toward that of the whole being. . . .

Never think that dogs, onagers, fawns, various species of monkeys, and all that perform marvelously in theatrical shows learn by reasoning. Very often the need for food stirs up suffering in creatures such as these. Every creature that has partaken of soul is subject to suffering, and it is through suffering hunger that they submit to rules that have been set.[134] (*Animal.* 82–86, 90)

SELECTIONS

To Elevate Animals to the Level of Man Is the Height of Injustice

Now what has been said about mental reasoning suffices; we must next consider the uttered. Although blackbirds, crows, parrots, and all the like can produce different kinds of utterances, they cannot produce an articulated voice in any manner whatever. Furthermore I think that the holes of wind instruments have a marked similarity, for certainly the powerful sounds they release are unintelligible, coarse, and not clearly explained. So also are the meaningless and insignificant sounds produced by the animals previously mentioned. These are not so much real expressions of conceptual words as they are chirps.

Take the trumpet, the lyre, and all kinds of musical instruments as common examples. When the air escapes through them, they emit powerful sounds that resemble the human voice. But these are unclear and do not convey distinct meaning. Anyone who wishes to consider the numerous and diverse expressions of sound will find it easy to form the same opinion. One may also prove positively that listeners differ one from another; it is not to be expected that all shall have the same impressions. These defective utterances are even unlike those of stammerers. Surely all who are not endowed with euphonious speech are full of darkness.

Let us now stop criticizing nature and committing sacrilege. To elevate animals to the level of the human race and to grant equality to unequals is the height of injustice. To ascribe serious self-restraint to indifferent and almost invisible creatures is to insult those whom nature has endowed with the best part. (*Animal.* 98–100)

Moses Confirms the Chaldeans' Doctrine of *Sympatheia* But Rejects Their Divinization of the World

The Chaldeans are reputed to have elaborated astronomy and the casting of nativities above all other people. They have established a harmony between the terrestrial and the superterrestrial, between things heavenly and earthly. Following as it were the laws of musical proportion,[135] they have revealed the perfect concord of the universe through the sympathetic communion of its parts with one another, which though spatially separated remain unparted in their kinship. These men surmised that this visible universe was the only thing in existence, either being itself God or containing God in itself as the soul of the whole.[136] Deifying Fate and Necessity, they filled human life with impiety by teaching that aside from phenomena there is no other cause of anything at all, but that the circuits of sun and moon and other stars assign to each being both good things and their opposites.

Moses, however, seems indeed to subscribe to the notion of the sympathetic communion of the world's parts, inasmuch as he declared the world to be one and created, for if it is created and one then it is likely that the same elemental substances have been laid down as a substratum for all created things in their several parts, on the principle that unified bodies hold together.[137] With their opinion concerning God, on the other hand, he is at variance, holding that neither the universe nor its soul is the primal God, any more than the stars or their circling motions are the primary causes of the things that happen to men. In his view, this entire universe is held together by invisible powers, which the Creator has projected from the ends of the earth to the bounds of heaven exercising forethought that what was well bound should not be loosened:[138] for the powers of the universe are bonds unbreakable. (*Mig.* 178–181)[139]

All Things Are Proportionately Equal,
and Man May Be Seen as a Microcosm

Virtually all things large and small throughout the world are proportionately equal.[140] Those who have precisely examined the facts of nature say that the four elements are proportionately equal, and that the whole world came into existence and thereafter abides forever through having been blended according to a proportion that assigned an equal measure to each of its parts. They tell us also that the four qualities in us, dry, wet, cold, and hot, have been blended and harmonized by proportional equality, and that we are nothing but a compound of the four powers blended in this manner.[141] If one were to tackle each item individually, he could go on at infinite length. For he would find on examination that the smallest animals are proportionately equal to the largest, as the swallow to the eagle, the red mullet to the whale, and the ant to the elephant. For their bodies, souls, emotions, pains, and pleasures, and also their affinities and aversions and all that animal nature is capable of, are virtually all alike when equalized by the rule of proportion. Some have thus made bold to assert that the tiny animal man is equal to the whole world, in view of the fact that each consists of body and rational soul, and thus they declared that man is a small world and alternatively the world a great man.[142] (*Her.* 152–155)

The Law of Opposites

After teaching us the lesson of equal division, Holy Scripture leads us on to the knowledge of the opposites, telling us that "He placed the sections facing opposite each other" (Gen. 15:10). For in truth virtually everything in the world is by nature opposite to something else. Let us begin with things primary. Hot is opposite to cold, dry to wet, light to heavy, darkness to light, night to day. . . .

Superbly, then, does the interpreter of nature's facts,[143] taking pity for our laziness and negligence, unstintingly teach us on every occasion, as he does here, that the placing of opposites to face one another refers not to things existing as wholes but as sections. For that which is formed of two opposites constitutes a single whole, by the division of which the opposites are known. Is not this the capital teaching that the Greeks say their great and illustrious Heraclitus placed at the fore of his philosophy and vaunted it as a new discovery? Actually it was an ancient discovery of Moses, that the opposites are formed from the same object, to which they are related as sections, as has been clearly indicated. (*Her.* 207–208, 213–214)[144]

The Music of the Spheres

For man is in receipt of a singular prerogative beyond all other animals, to worship the Existent, but heaven is ever making music, producing in accordance with its celestial motions the perfect harmony. If the sound of it chanced to reach our ears, there would arise irrepressible cravings, frenzied longings, ceaseless and insane passions, making us refrain from necessaries, and no longer take nourishment from food and drink through the throat in the manner of mortals, but as beings destined for immortality, from inspired strains of perfect music coming through our ears. To such strains, it is said, Moses was listening, when, having become disembodied, for forty days and as many nights he touched neither bread nor water at all.[145] (*Somn.* 1.35–36)

PHILO OF ALEXANDRIA

Eulogy of Cosmic Equality and Justice

As for justice itself, what poet or prose writer could worthily sing its praise, standing as it does superior to all eulogy and panegyric? Indeed one of its excellences, and that the greatest, its noble lineage, would be quite sufficient for its praise even if one were to pass over all the rest in silence. For Equality, as the meticulous inquirers into natural philosophy have handed down to us, is the mother of justice.[146] Now equality is light without shadow, an intelligible sun, to give it its true designation, for its opposite, Inequality, which includes that which exceeds and that which is exceeded, is the origin and source of darkness.[147] All things in heaven and earth have equality well arranged through unalterable laws and ordinances. For who is unaware that the relation of days to nights and nights to days is measured by the sun through the equality of proportionate intervals? The annual spring and autumnal equinoxes, so called from what has actually taken place, nature has made so plainly evident that even the most uncultured perceive the equal length in the days and nights. Again, are not the cycles of the moon as she runs her circular course from the conjunction to the full orb and from her consummation to the conjunction measured by equal intervals? The sum and sizes of her phases, waxing and waning, are identical, thus corresponding in both forms of quantity, number and magnitude. And as equality has received singular honor in heaven, the purest part of being, so has it also in its neighbor, the air. With the fourfold division of the year into what are called the annual seasons, the air naturally undergoes changes and vicissitudes, and in these changes and vicissitudes it exhibits an indescribable order in disorder. For divided by an equal number of months into winter, spring, summer, and autumn, three for each season, it fills out the year, which, as its very name[148] indicates, contains, as it is brought to its close, everything in itself, something it would not have been able to do if it had not submitted itself[149] to the annual seasons. But equality stretches down from the heavenly and upper regions to the terrestrial too. Its pure essence, which is akin to ether, it raises up on high, but its raylike nature. a derivative splendor, in sunlike fashion, it sends earthward. For all that strikes a false note in human life is the work of inequality, but all that maintains its fitting order is that of equality, which in universal being is most properly called the cosmic order, in cities democracy,[150] the best regulated and most excellent of constitutions, in bodies, health, and in souls, moral virtue. Inequality, on the other hand, is the cause of sicknesses and vices. Time will fail even one possessed of the longest life span if he should wish to detail all the praises of equality and her offspring justice, wherefore it seems to me preferable to be content with what has been said in order to stir the memory of the lovers of knowledge, and leave the rest to be inscribed in their souls, divine gems in the holiest of dwellings. (*Spec.* 4.230–238)

Triadic Division of the Universe

And most in accord with reality is the passage concerning the three measures (Gen. 18:6), for in reality all things are measured by three, having a beginning, middle, and end. . . . Hence, Homer's statement was not made simplistically (*Iliad* 15.189): "All things are divided into three." And the Pythagoreans assume that the triad among numbers and the right-angled triangle among figures are the foundation of the knowledge *(gnōsis)* [or "coming into being"—*genesis*] of all things. And so, one measure is that by which the incorporeal and intelligible world was constituted. And the second measure is that by which the perceptible heaven was established in the fifth (element) [sc. ether], attaining to a more wonderful and divine essence, unaltered and unchanged in comparison with these (things below), and remaining the same. And the third measure is the way in which sublunary things were made out of the four powers, earth, water, air, and fire, admitting generation and corruption. Now the measure of the incorporeal forms by which the intelligible world was constituted must be said to be the eldest of causes [sc. the Logos]. And (the cause) of the fifth, perceptible and circular essence, which the heaven has allotted to it, is the Creative power of the Existent One, for it has found an imperishable, pure, and unmixed blessing in obtaining an immortal and incorruptible portion. But the kingly (power) (is the cause) of sublunary things, those that (are subject to) change and alteration because they participate in generation and corruption.[151] (*QG* 4.8)

The Interchange of the Elements Indicates
a Single Underlying Substratum

Why does he say, "And the tabernacle shall be one"? (Exod. 26:6)
Someone may say, "But, Master Theologian, who does not know that many are not one, especially since you have already said, 'The

tabernacle shall be made of ten curtains' and not 'the tabernacles'?" May it not be, therefore, that the tabernacle's being "one" is a firmer seal indicating the unities of sublunary things? For even though earth is distinct from water, and water from air, and air from fire, and fire from each of these, nevertheless all are adapted to one determined form. For it is natural that the matter that was perfected out of so many things should be one, especially since the interchange of the elements with one another clearly demonstrates their common nature.[152] (*QE* 2.88)

The Sphericity of the World

The shape of the world, just like that of the universe, beloved, is through foresight made spherical because, in the first place, it is the most mobile shape of all. Moreover, this is most necessary lest, being slowed down, the world should fall into the vast void[153] and all its parts collapse into its center. Furthermore, only in this way could it maintain its inertia, bracing to the center of the two circles. The spherical shape is highly praised in Plato's *Timaeus* for its advantages,[154] and it is so fully described that there is no need for additional praise. (*Prov.* 2.56)

V. SOULS, ANGELS, AND DAEMONS

A. PREEXISTENCE AND INCARNATION OF SOULS

Descent of Souls Motivated by Satiety

Conversely Moses unreservedly approves those reptiles capable of leaping upward. Thus he says, "These you may eat of the flying reptiles which go on four legs, which have legs above their feet, so as to leap with them from the earth" (Lev. 11:21). These are symbols of the souls that, though rooted like reptiles to the terrestrial body, have the power, once purified, to haunt the heights, exchanging earth for heaven and corruption for immortality. We must accordingly believe that a heavy dose of sheer ill luck[155] has infected those souls that, nourished in air and the purest ether, migrated to earth, the region of mortality and evil, because they were unable to endure the satiety[156] of divine goods. (*Her.* 239–240)[157]

Descent of Souls Due to a Law of Necessity

Why does Abraham say, "I am an immigrant and sojourner among you"? (Gen. 23:4)

But does not every wise soul live like an immigrant and sojourner in this mortal body, after having for habitat and country the most pure substance of heaven, from which it migrates to this habitat by a compelling law? Perhaps this was in order that it might carefully inspect terrestrial things, that even these might not be without a share in wisdom to participate in the better life, or in order that it might be akin to created beings and not be continuously and completely happy? (*QG* 4.74)[158]

B. THE NATURE OF SOUL

Soul Divided into Eight Parts

But since, in accordance with a certain natural sympathy, earthly things depend on those of heaven, the principle of the number seven, having its origin from above, descended also to us and visited the race of mortals. To begin with, if we omit the ruling part, our soul is divided into seven parts, five senses, the organ of speech, and last the organ of generation.[159] All these, as in puppet shows, are drawn with strings by the ruling part, now at rest, now moving, each in its appropriate positions and movements. (*Op.* 117)

Tripartite Division of Soul

Our soul is tripartite, one part reasoning, a second spirited, a third desiderative. Some philosophers[160] have distinguished these parts from each other in regard to function only, some also in regard to their locations. These have gone on to allot to the reasoning part the region of the head, saying that, where the king is, there too are his bodyguards, and that the senses in the region of the head are the bodyguards of the mind,[161] so that the king must be there too, having obtained it, like a citadel in a city, for his dwelling. To the spirited part they allot the breast, since nature has fortified that part with the solidity and strength of continuous bones, as if arming a good soldier with coat of mail and shield for the repulse of his opponents. To the desiderative part they allot the region about the lower abdomen and the belly, for it is there that lust, irrational appetence, has its abode. (*LA* 3. 115)

The Illusory Self

I am composed of body and soul, I seem to have mind, reason, sense, yet I find none of them my own. For where was my body prior to my birth, and whither will it go when I have departed? Where are the various states produced by the life stages of an illusory self? Where is the newborn babe, the child, the boy, the pubescent, the stripling, the bearded youth, the lad, the full-grown man? Whence came the soul, whither will it go, how long will it be our mate? Can we tell its essential nature? When did we acquire it? Prior to our birth? But we were not then in existence. What of it after death? But then we who are embodied, compounds endowed with quality, shall be no more, but shall hasten to our rebirth, to be with the unbodied, without composition and without quality.[162] But now, inasmuch as we are alive, we are the dominated rather than the rulers, known rather than knowing. The soul knows us, though unknown by us, and imposes commands we are obliged to obey as servants their mistress. And when it will, it will transact its divorce in court[163] and depart, leaving our home desolate of life. If we press it to remain, it will dissolve our relationship. So subtle is its nature that it furnishes no handle to the body.[164] (*Cher.* 113–115)

The Substance of the Soul is Twofold

The term *soul* is used in two senses, both for the soul as a whole and for its ruling part, which strictly speaking is the soul's soul,[165] just as eye can mean either the whole orb or the most important part, that by which we see. Consequently, it was the view of the lawgiver that the substance of the soul also is twofold, blood being that of the soul as a whole, and the divine breath that of its most dominant part.

He thus says outright "the soul of every flesh is the blood" (Lev. 17:11). Well does he assign the flow of blood to the mass of the flesh, for they are a close fit. The substance of the mind, however, he did not attach to anything created, but introduced it as breathed on by God. For the Creator of all, he says, "blew into his face the breath of life, and man became a living soul" (Gen. 2:7), in the same manner that we are also told that he was formed after the image of his Creator (Gen. 1:27). There are thus two kinds of men, one that of those living by reason, the divine breath, the other of those who live by blood and the pleasure of the flesh. The latter is something molded of earth, the other is the faithful impress of the divine image. (*Her.* 55–57)[166]

C. IMMORTALITY OF THE SOUL

The Soul's True Life

He says further, "In the day that you eat of it, you shall die the death" (Gen. 2:17). And yet after they have eaten, not only do they not die, but they beget children and become for others the cause of life. What then is to be said? That death is twofold, one of men in general, the other of the soul in particular. The death of man is the separation of the soul from the body,[167] while the death of the soul is the destruction of virtue and the acquisition of vice. Therefore he says not only "die" but "die the death," indicating not the common death, but that special death truly so called, that of the soul becoming entombed in every sort of passion and vice. And this death is virtually in opposition to the other. The latter is a separation of components that had been combined, namely, body and soul, whereas the former, on the other hand, is an encounter of the two, in which the worse, the body, gains the mastery, and the better, the soul, is overmastered. But wherever Moses speaks of "dying the death," note that he means it in the sense of the penalty death, not that which comes by nature. Natural death is that in which soul is separated from body, the penalty death comes to be when the soul dies to the life of virtue,[168] and is alive only to that of wickedness. Heraclitus did well in following Moses' teaching on this point; for he says, "We live their death, and are dead to their life." He means that now, when we are living, the soul is dead and is entombed in the body as in a sepulchre; but should we die, the soul lives its proper life, released from the pernicious corpse to which it was bound, the body.[169] (*LA* 1.105–108)

The Fully Purified Soul Is Immortal

Having said so much with regard to these points too he adds, "but you shall depart to your fathers nourished with peace, in a goodly old age" (Gen. 15:15). So then we the imperfect are exposed to war and slavery, and scarcely find release from the terrors that threaten us. But the perfect race is subject neither to war nor to slavery, and is nourished in peace and absolutely secure freedom.

A fine lesson is given us when he represents the good man not as dying but departing, in order that the kind of soul that is fully purified be shown to be inextinguishable and immortal, destined to undergo a journey from hence to heaven, and not dissolution and corruption, which death appears to bring.

After "you shall depart" it is written "to thy fathers." What fathers is a matter worthy of inquiry. For Scripture could not mean those who had lived in the land of the Chaldeans, the only ones he regarded as kinsfolk, since at the word of the oracle he had moved away from all those of his blood. For it is written, "The Lord said to Abraham, 'go forth from your land and from your kinsfolk and from your father's house to the land that I will show you, and I will make you into a great nation'" (Gen. 12:1, 2). Was it reasonable that he who had been alienated from his own by the divine thoughtfulness should again be reconciled with these very same persons? Or that he who was destined to be chief of another nation and race be attached to a former one? God would not have graciously bestowed on him a fresh and in a way novel nation and race if he were not separating him completely from the old. For assuredly he is the chief of a people and a race, from whom there shot up as from a root the young sprout called Israel, which reflects on and contemplates all the facts of nature. So it has been expressly stated that "the old be cleared out from the face of the new" (Lev. 26:10). For what profit will they on whom new goods in abundance have rained down suddenly and unexpectedly still find in antiquarian lore and old, stale customs?

He does not then designate as "fathers" those from whom the soul has departed, those buried in the tombs of Chaldea, but, as some say, the sun, moon, and other stars to which it is held that all earthly things owe their birth or, as others think, the archetypal ideas, those intelligible and invisible models of things visible and sensible here, models to which, they say, the Sage's mind transfers its abode.

Others again have surmised that by "fathers" are meant the four principles and powers from which the world has been put together, earth, water, air and fire. For into these, they say, each thing that has come into being is duly resolved. Just as nouns and verbs and all other parts of speech are constituted out of the elements of the alphabet and are again resolved into those ultimate forms, just so is each of us composed of the four elements, borrowing small portions from each substance, and at determined periods of time he repays this debt,[170] rendering the dry to earth, the wet to water, the cold to air, and the warm to fire. These all concern the body, but the soul nature, which is intellectual and celestial, will come to the purest ether as to its father. For let it be granted that, as the ancients have it, there is a fifth substance, moving in a circle,[171] differing in its superiority from the four, out of which they thought the stars and the whole heaven came into being, and of which, it must consequently be assumed, the human mind too is a fragment. (*Her.* 275–283)

The True Hades Is the Life of the Bad

The mind that sees God and truly loves him, he "plants in" as a vine-branch of goodly quality, and he extends its roots to reach to eternity and gives it fecundity for the acquisition and enjoyment of virtue. That is why Moses prays as follows, "Bring them in and plant them in" (Exod. 15:17), that the divine saplings may not be for a day but long-lasting and immortal. The unjust and godless soul, on the other hand, he banishes from himself to the furthest bounds, and scatters them to the region of pleasures and lusts and injustices. That region is most appropriately called the region of the impious, but it is not the mythical one in Hades. For the true Hades is the life of the bad, a life fiendish, defiled by blood guilt, and liable to every curse. (*Cong.* 56–57)[172]

VI. THE DIVINE TRANSCENDENCE

A. TWO WAYS OF KNOWING GOD

The Teleological Argument

The ancient thinkers investigated how we first conceived of the Deity; then those reputed to be the best philosophers asserted that it was from the world and its parts and the powers subsisting in these that we obtained an apprehension of the First Cause.[173] Indeed, if one were to see a house carefully constructed with a gateway, colonnades, men's apartments, women's apartments, and the other buildings, he will get an idea of the artificer, for he will not believe that the house was completed without art and a craftsman; and similarly in the case of a city and a ship and every smaller or greater construction. Just so anyone coming into this world, as into an immense house or city, and beholding the sky circling round and comprehending every thing within it, and planets and fixed stars without any deviation moving in rhythmical harmony, useful to the whole, and earth that has been alloted the central place, with streams of water and air arrayed between, and in addition living creatures mortal and immortal, varieties of plants and fruits, will surely infer that these have not been fashioned without consummate art, but that the craftsman of this whole universe was and is God. Those who reason thus apprehend God by means of his shadow, perceiving the Artificer by means of his works. (*LA* 3.97–99)[174]

The Cosmological Argument Reveals God's Existence But Not His Essence

The calf, you see, is not constructed out of all the women's finery, but out of their earrings alone (Exod. 32:2), for the lawgiver is teaching us that no manufactured God is a God for sight and in reality, but for hearsay evidence and belief, and the hearsay of a woman at that, not a man's, for to entertain such nonsense is the work of a sinewless and truly effeminate soul. But the truly Existent can be perceived and known not only through the ears, but with the eyes of the understanding, from the dynamics of the cosmos, and from the continuous and ceaseless motion of his ineffable works. Wherefore in the great Song[175] it is said by God himself,[176] "See, see that I am" (Deut. 32:39), indicating that the truly Existent is apprehended through his activity[177] rather than by an exposition framed out of words. When we say that the Existent is visible, we are not using words in their literal sense, but it is an analogical usage of the word by which it is referred to each one of his powers. In the present passage he does not say, "See me," for it is impossible that the God who Is should be perceived at all by created being, but he says "See that I am," that is "Behold my Existence." For it suffices for man's reasoning to advance as far as to learn that the Cause of the universe is and subsists. To be eager to apply oneself further, so as to inquire about essence or quality in God, is folly primeval. Not even to Moses, the all-wise, did God grant this, despite his many entreaties, but an oracle was issued to him, "You will see that which is behind me, but my face you will not see" (Exod. 33:23). This meant that all that comes after God is within the good man's grasp, while he himself alone is incomprehensible, at least via a straight and direct approach (for through such an approach his nature would have been disclosed); but capable of being apprehended by the powers that follow and attend him; for these present not his essence but his existence from the things accomplished by him. (*Post.* 167–169)[178]

An Argument from Analogy: As There Is Mind in Man, So Is There in the Universe

While saying all this in refutation of the Chaldean opinion, Moses considers it necessary to resist those still Chaldaizing and recall them to the truth, and he begins his lesson thus: I am amazed at you gentlemen, that you have been suddenly lifted to such a height above the earth, and are hovering there, and, bobbing up above the lower atmosphere, are treading the ether, thinking to gain precise knowledge of the movement of the sun, the cycles of the moon, and the gloriously harmonious dances of the other constellations. For these are too high for your thoughts, inasmuch as their lot is one that is happier and more divine. Descend therefore from heaven, and having come down, do not investigate in turn earth and sea and rivers, and the various forms of plants and animals, but explore yourselves[179] and your

125

own nature only, establishing your abode with yourselves rather than elsewhere: for by examining the conditions of your own domicile, the part that is master in it, and that which is subject, the animate and the inanimate, the rational and the irrational, the immortal and the mortal, the better and the worse, you will straightway obtain a clear knowledge of God and of his works. For you will conclude that, as there is mind in you, so is there in the universe, and that as your mind has assumed the rule and mastery over everything in you, and has made each of the parts subject to itself, so too he that is invested with hegemony over all drives the chariot of the world[180] with the reins of absolute law and justice, exercising forethought not only for things more worthy of preference, but also for those that seem to us more obscure. (*Mig.* 184–186)[181]

Rising above the Ninth

The priests are expressly told to offer always the tenth of the ephah of fine flour (Lev. 6:20), for they have learned to rise above the ninth, the sense-perceptible world, the seeming deity,[182] and to worship him who is truly tenth and unique. For the world has obtained for its portion nine parts, eight in heaven, the sphere of fixed stars and the seven wanderers ever borne along in the same order, while earth with water and air make the ninth,[183] for the three are constituted a single family, subject to changes and transformations of every kind. The masses honor these nine parts and the world compacted of them, but the man of perfection honors him that is above the nine, the God who created them, the tenth. For transcending the entire divine oeuvre he is filled with yearning for its Artificer, ever anxious to become his suppliant and servant. For this reason the priest offers continuously a tenth to him who is tenth, unique and eternal. (*Congr.* 103–105)

The Direct Apprehension of God

There is a mind more perfect and more purified, which has been initiated into the great mysteries,[184] a mind that discovers the First Cause not from created things as one may learn of the abiding object from its shadow, but transcends creation and obtains a clear impression of the Uncreated, so as from him to apprehend both himself and his shadow, that is, the Logos and this world. This mind is Moses who says, "Manifest yourself to me, that I may see you clearly" (Exod. 33:13); "Would that you were not made manifest to me by means of heaven or earth or water or air or absolutely anything that belongs to creation, and would that I did not behold your form as in a mirror in aught else than in you, the Deity, for the impressions in created things are dissolved, but those in the Uncreated continue steadfast, secure and eternal." It was for this reason that God called Moses and spoke to him (Lev. 1:1). Bezalel too did he call, but not in the same manner. One receives the impression of God from the First Cause himself, the other perceived the Artificer, as from a shadow, from created things, by way of inference. (*LA* 3.100–102)[185]

The Human Soul Could Never Have Conceived of God, Had He Not Breathed into It

"Breathed into" (Gen. 2:7) is equivalent to "inspired" or "besouled" the soulless; for heaven forbid that we should be infected with such far-out nonsense as to think that God employs for inbreathing organs such as mouth or nostrils; for God is without every quality, not only without human form. Yet the expression indicates something that accords with reality. For three things are required, that which inbreathes, that which receives, that which is inbreathed: that which inbreathes is God, that which receives is the mind, that which is inbreathed is the (divine) breath. What, then, do we infer from these elements? A union of all three is produced, as God extends his power through the mediant breath to the subject. And to what purpose, save that we may obtain a conception of him? For how could the soul have conceived of God had he not infused it and taken hold of it as far as was possible? For the human mind would never have made bold to soar so high as to apprehend the nature of God had not God himself drawn it up to himself, so far as it was possible for the human mind to be drawn up, and imprinted it in accordance with the (divine) powers accessible to its reasoning. (*LA* 1.36–38)[186]

By Light, Light

After the self-taught, who enjoyed rich natural endowments, the third to reach perfection is the Man of Practice, who receives as his special reward the vision of God. For having applied himself to all aspects of human life and dealt with them in no offhand manner, and

127

having evaded no toil or danger on the chance that he might be able to track down the truth, which is well worth pursuing, he found among mortal kind a profound darkness on land, water, air, and ether. For the ether and the entire heaven presented to him the appearance of night, since the whole sensible realm lacks determination, and the indeterminate[187] is the brother of darkness and its kin. In his earlier period he kept the eye of his soul shut, but through unremitting struggles he laboriously began to open it and to part and throw off the obscuring mist. For an incorporeal beam purer than ether suddenly flashed over him and disclosed the intelligible world led by its charioteer. That charioteer, irradiated by a circle of undiluted light, was difficult to discern or to divine, for the eye was enfeebled by the sparkling lights. Yet in spite of the abundant light that flooded it, it held its own in its extraordinary yearning to behold the vision. The Father and Savior, perceiving his genuine longing and desire, felt pity, and lending strength to the penetration of his sight did not grudge him a vision of himself, to the extent that it was possible for created and mortal nature to contain it. Yet it was not a vision showing what he is, but only that he is. For the former, which is better than the good, more venerable than the monad, and purer than the unit, cannot be discerned by anyone else; for to him alone is it allowed to comprehend himself.

As for the fact that God exists, although the term subsistence is comprehensible, neither do all apprehend it, nor do they do so in the best manner. Some have denied the existence of the Godhead outright, while others vacillate and are at a loss, as though unable to say whether it exists or not. Others still, who acquired their notions about the existence of God through habit rather than reasoning, from those who brought them up, believe that their piety is on the right track, although they have stamped it with the mark of superstition. But if there have been some who have had the capacity through knowledge to form an image of the Creator and Ruler of all, they have, as the saying goes, advanced from down to up. Entering the world as into a well-ordered city they have beheld the earth firmly established with its mountains and plains, filled with sown crops and trees and fruits and all kinds of living creatures besides; and spread over it, seas and lakes and rivers both spring-fed and torrential; they have seen too the mild temperatures of air and breezes, the harmonious changes of the annual seasons, and topping them all the sun and the moon, the wandering and fixed stars, the entire heaven with its own host arranged in companies, a veritable universe revolving within the universe.[188] In their admiration and astonishment they arrived at a conception consistent with the phenomena, that surely all these beauties and such surpassing order did not come into being automatically, but through some world-building creator, and that there must be a providence; for it is a law of nature that a creator should take care of what has been produced.

Now these men, godlike and superior to the other classes, have, as I have said, advanced from down to up by a sort of heavenly ladder and by a reasonable argument inferred the Creator from his works. But if some have been capable of apprehending him through himself without the cooperation of any reasoning process to lead them to the sight, they must in truth be inscribed among the holy and genuine worshipers and friends of God. Of their number is he who in the Hebrew is called Israel, but in Greek the God-seer, who sees not the nature of God, for that, as I said, is impossible—but that he is. This knowledge he has gained from no other source, not from things terrestrial or celestial, nor from the elements or compounds mortal or immortal, but summoned by him alone who was pleased to reveal his own proper existence to the suppliant. How this means of approach has come about is worth looking at through the use of a similitude. Do we see the sense-perceptible sun by anything other than the sun, or the stars by any other than the stars, and in general is not light seen by light? Similarly, God too is his own splendor and is discerned through himself alone, without anything else assisting or being capable of assisting with a view to the perfect apprehension of his existence. They are but makers of inferences who strive to discern the Uncreated and Creator of all from his creation, acting similarly to those who search out the nature of the monad from the dyad, whereas observation of the dyad should begin with the monad, which is the source.[189] The pursuers of truth are they who form an image of God through God, light through light.[190] (*Praem.* 36–46)

B. THE NATURE OF GOD

God Loves to Give and Creates No Soul Barren of Good

God loves to give and freely bestows good things on all, even to the imperfect, inviting them to a partnership in virtue and a zeal for it, at the same time displaying his own superabundant wealth, and how it suffices even for those who will derive no great profit from it. This he shows most vividly in other cases too. For when he rains on the sea, and makes springs gush forth in the most desolate areas, and waters the poor, rough, and sterile soil, pouring on it rivers in flood, what else does he show than the exceeding greatness of his own wealth and goodness? This is the reason he created no soul barren of good,[191] even if its practice be impossible to some. (*LA* 1.34)

God Is the Soul of the Universe, But His Substance Is Unknowable

We must inquire why, when he gave names to all the other creatures, Adam did not give one to himself. What, then, are we to say? The mind that is in each of us can apprehend other objects, but is incapable of knowing itself. For just as the eye sees everything else, but does not see itself, so the mind too perceives everything else but does not apprehend itself. For let it say what it is and of what sort, breath or blood or fire or air or anything else, or only that it is a body or on the contrary incorporeal. Are they not then simple-minded who examine the nature of God's substance? For how should those who are ignorant of the substance of their own soul[191a] have a precise understanding of the soul of the universe? For we may conceive of God as the soul of the universe.[192] (*LA* 1.91)[193]

God's Nature Is Simple

That God is alone may also be taken in the sense that neither before creation was there anything with God, nor, after the universe had come into being, is anything placed in the same class with him; for he needs absolutely nothing. An even better interpretation is the following: God is alone and one, not a composite but a simple nature, whereas each one of us and all other created beings is a multiplicity. I, for example, am a multiplicity: soul and body. The soul has one part irrational, one part rational, the body has the warm and cold, heavy and light, dry and moist. But God is not a composite, comprised of many parts, but is unmixed with anything else. For whatever is added to God is either superior or inferior or equal to him, but there is nothing equal or superior to God. And no lesser thing is assimilated to him, otherwise he too will be lessened. But if he can be lessened, he will also be capable of corruption, something it is wrong to entertain even in thought. God is therefore in the category of the one and the monad, or rather the monad is in the category of the One God. For, like time, all number is subsequent to the universe, whereas God is prior to the universe and its Creator. (*LA* 2.2–3)

God Gives Time for Repentance

But in this point too observe the goodness of the Existent. The treasury of good things he opens, those of evil things he shuts tight. For it is God's property to hold out good things and to be ahead in bestowing them, but to be restrained in bringing on evil things.[194] But Moses, heightening God's gracious liberality, says that the treasuries of evils are shut tight not only at other times, but also when the soul is out of step with the ordered march of right reason, when it would have been deservedly deemed worthy of punishment. For he says that the treasuries of evil things[195] were sealed in the day of vengeance (Deut. 32:34), Sacred Scripture thus indicating that not even against the sinners will God proceed at once, but grants time for repentance,[196] and the healing and setting right of one's faultering step. (*LA* 3.105–106)

God Alone Keeps Festival

For God has assigned the feasts to himself, thereby establishing a principle indispensable for the disciples of philosophy. The principle is this. God alone truly keeps festival. He alone rejoices, and he alone has delight, and he alone makes merry; to him alone it is given to enjoy the peace without any mixture of war. He knows no grief or fear and has no share of ill, stands firm and free from pain, and is full of vigor and happiness unmixed. His nature is absolutely perfect, or rather he is himself the summit, end, and limit of happiness. He partakes of nothing outside of himself with a view to improvement, but has given a share of his own to all particular things from the fountain of beauty, himself. For the beautiful things in the world could never have been what they are if they had not been modeled after the truly beautiful archetype,[197] the Uncreated, the Blessed, the Imperishable. (*Cher.* 85–86)[198]

131

God's Rest Is Acting with Complete Ease

For this reason Moses frequently in his laws calls the Sabbath, which means "rest," God's Sabbath (Exod. 20:10, etc.), not man's, thus touching on a compelling point in the science of nature. In all that exists there is, truth to say, but one thing that rests, that is God. But rest he does not call inaction,[199] for the cause of all things is by its nature active, never ceasing to create things most beautiful. God's rest is rather an acting with complete ease, without toil or stress.[200] (*Cher.* 87)

God Is Everywhere and His Motion Is That of Pneumatic Tension

But if the Logos has outstripped all, much more is this true of the Speaker himself, as he testifies elsewhere saying: "Here I stand there before you" (Exod. 17:6). For he shows that his subsistence is before all created being, and that he who is here is also there and elsewhere and everywhere, since he has filled everything through and through and has left nothing empty of himself.[201] For he does not say, "I will stand here and there," but even now, when I am present here, I stand at the same time also there. My motion is not one involving change of place, so as to occupy one place while leaving another, but it is a tensional motion.[202] (*Sacr.* 67–68)

God Alone Has Veritable Being

Do you not see that Abraham, when he had "abandoned land and kin and his father's house" (Gen. 12:1), that is, the body, sense, and speech, begins to encounter the powers of the Existent?[203] For when he has withdrawn from his entire household, the Law says that "God appeared to him" (Gen. 12:7), showing that he clearly manifests himself to him who slips out of things mortal and bounds upward into the incorporeal soul of this body of ours. So Moses "takes his tent and pitches it outside the camp" (Exod. 33:7) and separates it far from the bodily encampment, in the expectation that only thus might he become a perfect suppliant and worshiper of God.

This tent he says is called the "Tent of Testimony," choosing his words with great care, to indicate that the Tent of the Existent actually exists, and is not merely so designated. For among the virtues, that of God truly is, really existing, since God alone has veritable being. This is why Moses will say of him as best he may,[204] "I am he that is" (Exod. 3:14), implying that things posterior to him have no real being,[205] but are believed to exist in imagination only. Moses' tent, however, which symbolically represents human virtue, is worthy of the designation but not of existence, inasmuch as it is a copy and representation of that divine virtue. (*Det.* 159–160)

The Nature of the Standing One Is Repose

But Abraham the wise, since he stands immobile, draws near to God the standing One; for it says "he was standing immobile before the Lord and he drew near and said" (Gen. 18:23–33). For only a truly unchanging soul has access to the unchanging God, and the soul so disposed stands truly close to the divine power.

But the oracle delivered to the all-wise Moses shows most plainly the firm steadfastness of the men of virtue. It runs thus: "But you, stand here with me" (Deut. 5:31). This oracle makes two points, one that the Existent who moves and turns all else is himself unmoved and unchanging; and second that he gives the man of virtue a share in his own nature, which is repose.[206] For just as crooked things are, I believe, made straight by a correct rule, so moving things are restrained and come to a halt by the force of him who stands. (*Post.* 27–28)[207]

God's Gifts Are Proportionate to the Capacities of the Recipients

Do you not see that even God does not utter oracles in keeping with the greatness of his own perfection, but always in accord with the capacity of those to be benefited? For who could have contained the force of the divine oracles, which are too great for any power of hearing? This seems to be indicated most truthfully by those who say to Moses: "You speak to us, and let not God speak to us, lest we die" (Exod. 20:19); for they recognized that they possess in themselves no worthy organ when God is framing laws for his congregation. Were he to exhibit his own wealth, not even the entire earth with the sea made into land could contain it, unless we suppose that rainfall and other cosmic phenomena occur according to fixed periods of time and not continuously, through some lack and scarcity of them, and not out of forethought for those in need of them, who would be harmed rather than benefited by an unbroken enjoyment of like gifts. Wherefore God always holds back on his first gifts before those who obtain them as their portion are satiated and wax insolent; and storing them up in turn gives others in their stead, with a third round to replace the second, and even new ones in place of the earlier, sometimes different, sometimes the same. For creation is never without a share of the gifts of God—for otherwise it would assuredly have perished—but it is incapable of bearing their full and abundant flow. On this account, wishing that we should profit from the gifts he grants, he measures out the things given in accordance with the strength of those who receive them. (*Post.* 143–145)[208]

Argument *a minori ad maius* for God's
Transcendence of All Material Existence

Now, when you have examined the whole of your individual dwelling [i.e., your body] with the greatest precision and have discerned the definition of each of its parts, rouse yourselves and seek that migration hence which heralds not death but immortality. You will perceive clear signs of this, even while trammeled by the bodily and sensible caverns. These signs will appear at times in deep sleep, for then the mind retires, and, withdrawing from the senses and all other bodily things, begins to communicate with itself,[209] focusing its view on truth as a mirror,[210] and washing away the imprints of all its sense images, it is inspired through dreams by absolutely true prophecies concerning the future. Or again it may be in a waking state; for when the mind is mastered by some philosophical speculation and is drawn to it, it follows this, but remains oblivious to all that concerns the bodily mass. And if the senses thwart the contemplation of the intelligible, those fond of such contemplation are concerned to eliminate their onset. They shut their eyes, plug their ears, and restrain the impulses derived from the other senses, and deem it right to spend their time in solitude and darkness, so that the eye of the soul, to whom God has given the power to perceive things intelligible, may not be obscured by any object of sense.

If in this manner you learn to effect a divorce from things mortal, you will also be taught concepts regarding the Uncreated. For surely you do not believe that while your mind, having stripped itself of body, sensation, speech, can apart from these see in their nakedness existing things, the Mind of the universe, God, is not outside all material nature, he who contains but is not contained, and has not sallied forth beyond it in thought alone, as a man, but also in his essential being, as befits God. For our mind has not created the body, but is the work of Another; and it is therefore contained in the body as in a vessel. But the Mind of all things has produced the universe, and that which has created is superior to the thing created, so that it could not be contained in its inferior, apart from the fact that it is not fitting that a father be included in his son, but rather that a son should continue to grow through the care of his father. (*Mig.* 189–193)

God Is Called Place

According to the third meaning [of the word *place*], God himself is called place[211] from the fact that he contains all, but is contained by nothing whatever, and that he is a place of refuge for all, and because he is his own space, having occupied himself and being contained in himself alone.[212] For as for me, I am not a place but in a place, and every existent likewise, for that which is contained is different from that which contains it, and the Godhead, being contained by nothing, is necessarily itself its own place. (*Somn.* 1.63)[213]

God Alone Is the True Peace

Know then, my friend, that God alone is the absolutely authentic and veritable peace, but the whole of created and perishable substance is one continuous war. For God is a being of free will, but [created] substance is governed by necessity. Whosoever then has the strength to forsake war and necessity, creation and perishing, and go over to the side of the uncreated, of the imperishable, of free will, of peace, may justly be said to be the dwelling place and city of God. (*Somn.* 2.253)[214]

God Employs the Weakest as the Instruments of His Punishment

Someone may perhaps inquire[215] why God punished the land [of Egypt] through such insignificant and negligible creatures, disregarding the use of bears and lions and leopards and the other kinds of wild beasts that feed on human flesh;[216] and, if not these, at least then the Egyptian asps, whose bites are such as to effect immediate death. If the inquirer really does not know, let him learn: first, God wished to admonish the inhabitants of the land rather than to destroy them, for had he wished to do away with them altogether he would not have used animals to assist him in the assault, but God-sent evils, famine and plague. And after this let him learn an additional lesson, one that is necessary throughout life. What is this? When men wage war, they pass in review the most powerful auxiliary forces to fight as their allies, and thus make up for their own weakness; but God, the highest and greatest power, needs no one. But if, somehow, he wills to use some as instruments of punishment, he chooses not the strongest and the greatest, of whose strength he takes no thought, but furnishes the slightest and the smallest with irresistible and invincible powers, and through them requites the evildoers, as he does in this case. For what is slighter than a gnat? Yet it had such great force that all Egypt gave up and was forced to cry out, "This is the finger of God"; for the hand of God not even the entire habitable world from one end to the other, or rather not even the whole universe, could stand against it. (*Mos.* 1.109–112)

God Continually Plays and Is Joyful

What is the game that Abimelech, looking through the window, saw Isaac playing with his wife? (Gen. 26:8b)

The literal meaning represents lawful commerce with one's wife. But as for the deeper meaning, it must denote that not every game is blameworthy but sometimes it is virtuous and praiseworthy, for it is a sign of the innocence and sincerity of the pure festiveness of the heart. For the age of playfulness is guileless and without cunning, whence[217] the noun "boy" was derived. And from this, in accordance with (our) understanding, the festive enjoyments of perfect men, which are worthy and virtuous, are called "game." And wicked and luxury-loving men have no share or part or taste of this at all but lead sorrowful and painful lives. The virtuous, however, happily enjoy (this) always, (as) men, when their souls are impressed on the mortal body, or when they are released and separated and removed at death, or else when they have never in any way been bound (to bodies). So also (do) the divine beings that the sacred word of Moses is wont to call "angels," and the stars. For these are, as it were, intelligible, marvelous and divine natures, having acquired eternal joy unmixed with sorrow. Similar is the universal and whole heaven and world since it is both a rational animal and a virtuous animal and philosophical by nature. And for this reason it is without sorrow or fear, and full of joy. Moreover, it is said that even the Father and Creator of all continually rejoices in his life and plays and is joyful, finding pleasure in accordance with the divine play and in joyfulness. And he has no need of anything, but with joy he delights in himself and in his powers and in the worlds made by him.[218] But in the system of invisible evidence these are measures of all incorporeal forms in the likeness and in the image of the invisible.

Rightly, therefore, and properly does the wise man, believing his end (to consist in) likeness to God, strive so far as possible to unite the created with the uncreated and the mortal with the immortal, and not to be deficient or wanting in gladness and joyfulness in his likeness. For this reason he plays this game of unchangeable and constant virtue with Rebecca, whose name is to be interpreted in the [Greek] language as "Constancy." This game and delight of the soul the wicked man does not know, since he has no marriage with wonderful pleasure. But the progressive man, as if looking from a window, sees it but not the whole of it and not the mingling of both alone. For this there is need of the especially sharp-sighted eyes of one accustomed (to seeing) from afar and of those who are accustomed to see. (*QG* 4.188)[219]

C. ANTHROPOMORPHISM AND ANTHROPOPATHISM

God Is Not Anthropomorphic

After all the rest, as has been said, Moses tells us that man was created after the image of God and after his likeness (Gen. 1:26). This is quite well put, for nothing earthborn resembles God more than man. Let no one, however, represent the likeness through the characteristics of body; for neither is God in human form, nor is the human body Godlike. The word *image* is used here with regard to the Mind, sovereign of the soul;[220] for it is after the pattern of that unique and universal Mind as an archetype that the mind in each individual was formed. It is in a way a god to him who carries it impressed in his mind; for the relationship the great Ruler bears to the world as a whole is precisely that which the human mind holds within man. It is invisible while itself seeing all things, and though apprehending the substances of others, its own substance is unknown. (*Op.* 69)[221]

PHILO OF ALEXANDRIA

We Find It Difficult to Escape the Thought
That God Is Anthropopathic

We are unable continuously to treasure in our souls the capital idea that is worthy of the Primal Cause, that "God is not as man" (Num. 23:19), in order to transcend all descriptions in human form. But possessing as our greatest share that which is mortal, we are incapable of conceiving anything independently of ourselves, and have not the strength to sidestep our own defects. We crawl into our mortal envelope like snails and like hedgehogs wind ourselves into a ball, and entertain ideas about the blessed and the imperishable identical to those about ourselves. We shun indeed in words the far-out notion that the Godhead is of human form, but in actual fact we incur the impiety that he possesses human passions. Hence in addition to hands and feet, entrances and exits, we invent for him enmities, aversions, estrangements, anger, parts, and passions unfitting the Cause. And of such too is the oath, an aid for our weakness. (*Sacr.* 94–96)[222]

Anthropomorphic Language Is for the Instruction of the Many

Having sufficiently clarified this point let us consider what follows. It reads thus: "I will blot out man whom I made from the face of the earth, from man to beast, from reptiles to the winged fowl of heaven, because I was wroth in that I made him" (Gen. 6:7). Again, some[223] on hearing these words, assume that the Existent feels wrath and anger, whereas he is not susceptible to any emotion at all. For anxiety is peculiar to human weakness, but neither the irrational emotions nor the parts and limbs of the body are at all appropriate to God.

Nonetheless, such expressions are used by the Lawgiver just so far as they furnish an elementary lesson, for the admonition of those who could not otherwise be brought to their senses. For among the laws that consist of commands and prohibitions, laws, that is, in the strict sense of the word, two ultimate summary statements are set forth concerning the First Cause, one that "God is not like a man" (Num. 23:19); the other that he is as a man. But though the former is guaranteed by absolutely secure criteria of truth, the latter is introduced for the instruction of the many. Wherefore it is also said of him, "like a man he shall discipline his son" (Deut. 8:5). Thus it is for discipline and admonition, not because God's nature is such, that this is said of him. Among men some are lovers of soul, some of the body. The companions of the soul, who are able to associate with intelligible and incorporeal natures, do not compare the Existent to any form of created thing. They have excluded him from every quality, for one of the things that pertains to his blessedness and supreme felicity is that his existence is apprehended as simple, without any other distinguishing characteristic; and thus they have allowed a representation of him only in respect of existence, not endowing him with any form. But those who have concluded a treaty and a truce with the body are unable to doff the garment of the flesh and see a nature uniquely simple and self-sufficient in itself, without admixture and composition. They therefore conceive of the universal Cause precisely as they do of themselves, not taking into account that while a being that comes into existence through the union of several faculties needs several parts to serve the needs of each, God being uncreated and bringing all the others into being had no need of anything belonging to things generated.

For what are we to think? If he makes use of bodily organs,[224] he has feet to go forward. But whither will he go, since he fills everything? To whom will he go, when none is his equal? And to what purpose? For it cannot be out of concern for his health as with us.[225] Hands too he must have both to receive and to give, yet he receives nothing from anyone, for aside from his lack of need, all possessions are his, and he gives by employing as minister of his gifts the Logos through which also he created the world.[226] Nor had he any need of eyes, through which no perception can take place without sensible light. But sensible light is a created thing, whereas God saw before creation, being himself his own light. What need is there to speak of the organs of nourishment? If he has them, he takes nourishment and after filling up he rests, and after resting he has need again, and the rest of what follows on this I will not discuss. These are the mythical inventions of the impious who theoretically represent the Deity as of human form, but in fact as having human emotions.

Why then does Moses speak of feet and hands, entrances and exits, with regard to the Uncreated, or of his arming to ward off his enemies? For he represents him as bearing a sword and using shafts and winds and devastating fire (roaring hurricane and thunderbolt the poets call them, using different expressions, and say they are the weapons of the Primal Cause). Why again does he speak of his jealousy, his wrath, his transports of anger and similar emotions, which he details and describes in human terms? But to those who make such inquiries he answers thus: "Sirs, he who seeks to frame the best laws must have one goal, to profit all those who come into contact with them. Those who have been favored with good natural endowments and a training in every respect unexceptionable, and thus find their later course through life a highway broad and straight, have truth as their traveling companion, and being initiated by her into the authentic mysteries of the Existent do not assign to him any of the traits of created being besides. These find most appropriate the principle found in the revealed oracles that "God is not as a man," but neither as the heaven or the universe.[227] For the latter are forms of a certain kind and are accessible to our senses, but God is not apprehensible even by the mind, except as to the fact alone that he is. For it is his existence we apprehend, but of the things outside of his existence nothing.

But those who are of a dull and obtuse nature, who have been ill-served in their early training,[228] incapable as they are of sharp vision, are in need of monitoring physicians who will devise the proper treatment for their present condition. For ill-bred and foolish slaves too are profited by a master who frightens them, since in dread of his threats and menaces they involuntarily accept rebuke through fear. Let all such learn the lies that will benefit them, if they are unable to become wise through truth. Thus the most esteemed physicians do not dare tell the truth to those dangerously ill in body,[229] since they know that they will thereby become more disheartened and their sickness will not be cured, whereas through the consolation of the opposite approach they will bear their present condition more lightly and the illness will abate.

For what sensible physician would say to his patient, "Sir, you will undergo surgery, cautery, amputation," even if he were likely to submit to these out of necessity. No one will speak in this way. For that patient, failing in advance in his resolve and contracting another malady, that of the soul, more painful than the earlier one of the body, will collapse in the face of the treatment, whereas if through the physician's deceit he expects the opposite, he will gladly, patiently endure everything, even if the healing process be most painful. Now since the lawgiver has become a supreme physician[230] for the morbid states and maladies of the soul, he set himself one task and goal, to excise the diseases of the mind, roots and all, so that nothing remain to bear the germ of incurable disease. In this way he hoped to be able to extirpate them by representing the Primal Cause as employing threats, showing displeasure and implacable anger, and also using weaponry for his assaults on the unrighteous. For only thus can the fool be chided. Accordingly it seems to me that with the two aforementioned principles, "God is as a man," and "God is not as a man," he has woven together two others closely akin and consistent with them, fear and love. For I note that all the exhortations to piety in the law refer either to love or fear of the Existent.[231] To those, then, who acknowledge no human part or emotion concerning the Existent, and honor him for his own sake alone, to love is most appropriate, but to fear is most suitable to the others. (*Deus* 51–69)[232]

D. THE *VIA NEGATIVA* AND THE *VIA EMINENTIAE*

No Assertions Can Be Made of God's Essence

Who is capable of asserting of the Primal Cause that it is incorporeal or corporeal, or that it possesses quality or is qualityless,[233] or, in general, who could make a firm statement concerning his essence or quality or state or movement? He alone will make dogmatic assertions regarding himself, since he alone has unerringly precise knowledge of his own nature. (*LA* 3.206)[234]

God Is Ineffable and Consequently Inconceivable and Incomprehensible

Do not however suppose that the Existent, which truly exists, is apprehended by any man; for we have in us no organ by which we may form an image of it, neither sense organ, for it is not sense-perceptible, nor mind. So Moses, the student of invisible nature—for the divine oracles say that he entered the darkness (Exod. 20:21), a figure intimating the invisible and incorporeal existence—searched everywhere and into everything and sought to see with distinct clarity the object of his great yearning and the only good. But finding nothing, not even an idea that resembled what he hoped for, in despair and learning from others, he flies for refuge to the object of his search itself and makes the following supplication: "Reveal yourself to me that I may see you clearly" (Exod. 33:13). And yet he does not attain his purpose, since the knowledge of things both material and immaterial that come after the Existent are considered a most ample gift for the best race among mortals. For we read: "You will see what is behind me, but my face will not be seen by you" (Exod. 33:23), meaning that all that comes after the Existent, both material and immaterial, is accessible to apprehension, even if it is not all already apprehended, but he alone by his very nature cannot be seen. And why is it astonishing if the Existent is inapprehensable to men when even the mind in each of us is unknown to us? For who has seen the true nature of the soul, whose obscurity has bred innumerable disputes among the sophists who propose opinions contrary to each other or even completely opposed in kind?[235]

It follows that not even a proper name can be given to the truly Existent. Observe that when the prophet earnestly inquires what he must answer those who ask about his name he says "I am he that is" (Exod. 3:14), which is equivalent to "My nature is to be, not to be spoken." But that humankind should not be in complete want of a designation for the Supremely Good, he allows them to use analogically, as though it were his proper name, the title of Lord God of the three natures, teaching, perfection, practice, whose recorded symbols are Abraham, Isaac, and Jacob. For this, he says, is "my name through the ages," inasmuch as it belongs to our time period, not to the precosmic, "and my memorial," not a name set beyond memory and thought, and again "for generations" (Exod. 3:15), not for beings ungenerated. For those who have entered the realm of mortal creation require the analogical use of the divine name, so that they may approach if not the facticity at least the name of the Supremely Good, and be ruled according to it. This is also shown by an oracle revealed as from the mouth of the Ruler of the universe that no proper name of him has been disclosed to anyone. "I appeared," he says, "to Abraham, Isaac, and Jacob, being their God, and my name of 'Lord' I did not reveal to them" (Exod. 6:3). For if the hyperbaton[236] is changed back to grammatical sequence, the meaning would be as follows: "My proper name I did not reveal to them," but only the one for analogical use, for the reasons already mentioned. So ineffable indeed is the Existent that not even the ministering powers tell us a proper name. Thus after the wrestling match that the Man of Practice fought in his quest for virtue, he says to the unseen master,[237] "Declare to me your name," and he said, "Why do you ask this my name?" (Gen. 32:29), and he does not disclose his personal and proper name. "Suffice it for you," he says, "to profit from my benediction, but as for names, those

142

symbols of created things, seek them not among imperishable natures." Do not, then, be thoroughly perplexed if you find the highest of all beings to be ineffable, when his Logos, too, cannot be expressed by us through his own name. And indeed if he is ineffable, he is also inconceivable and incomprehensible. (*Mut.* 7–15)[238]

The *Via Eminentiae*

The race is called in Hebrew[239] Israel, but if the name is translated into Greek, "seeing God."[240] This faculty seems to me the most prized of all possessions, both private and public. For if the sight of elders or teachers or rulers or parents rouses the beholders to respect, decency, and eagerness for a life of self-control, how great a support for virtue and nobility may we expect to find in souls that have transcended all things created and have been trained to behold the uncreated and divine, the primally Good[241] and Beautiful and Happy and Blessed, or, if the truth must be told, that which is better than the Good, more beautiful than the Beautiful, more blessed than Blessedness, more happy than Happiness itself, and anything there may be more perfect than the aforementioned? For reason[242] cannot attain to ascend to God, who is altogether impalpable but subsides and slips away unable to find the proper words to use as stepping-stones to disclose, I do not say the Existent, for not even if the whole heaven became an articulate voice would it find a supply of accurate and unerring words for that, but even his attendant[243] powers. (*Legat.* 4–6)[244]

VII. KNOWLEDGE AND PROPHECY

A. THEORY OF KNOWLEDGE

The Human Mind Is a Fragment of the Divine Logos

Every man, in respect of his mind, is intimately related to the divine Logos, being an imprint or fragment or effulgence of that blessed nature, but in the constitution of his body he is related to the entire world, for he is a blend of the same things, earth, water, air, and fire, each of the elements having contributed the share that falls to it to complete an entirely sufficient material that the Creator had to take in order to fashion this visible image. (*Op.* 146)[245]

The Mind Is God of the Irrational Soul

As the face is the ruling part of the body, so is the mind the ruling part of the soul: into this alone does God breathe, but he does not deign to do so with the other parts, the senses, speech, and the reproductive organ; for these are secondary in capacity. By what, then, did these also receive the life-breath? By the mind evidently. For the mind gives a share of what it has received from God to the irrational part of the soul, so that the mind was animated by God, but the irrational part by the mind. For the mind is, as it were, God of the irrational part, for which reason Scripture did not shrink from saying of Moses that he was "a God to Pharaoh" (Exod. 7:1).[246] For of the things that came into being some come into being by God's power and through his direct action,[247] while others come into being by God's power but not through his direct action. The things that are supremely good were made both by God and through his direct action; thus he will go on to say, "God planted a pleasure-ground" (Gen. 2:8): To these the mind belongs; but the irrational part came into being by God's power but not through his direct action, but through the rational element that rules and holds sway in the soul. (*LA* 1.39–41)

The Purification of the Irrational Soul

But the part of the soul that is pure and unmixed is the perfectly pure mind. This mind, inspired from above, when kept free from sickness and harm, is fitly restored in its entirety, after being resolved into its elemental state, as a holy libation[248] to him who inspired and maintained it free from all evil. The mixed kind is the senses, for which nature has created the proper mixing-bowls.[249] The eyes are the "bowls" of sight, the ears of hearing, the nostrils of the sense of smell, and the others have their fitting receptacles. Into these bowls the holy Logos pours of the blood, deeming it fit that our irrational part should be animated and become in a way rational, following the divine circuits of the mind, and keeping itself pure from the objects of sense, which hold out their deceitful allure. (*Her.* 184–185)[250]

SELECTIONS

The Ruling Faculty Transmits Its Powers to the Organs of Sense

Could not one say that each of the senses is watered from the mind as from a spring, and that it broadens and extends its powers like streams of water? Nobody of sound mind, at any rate, would say that eyes see, but mind by means of eyes, nor that ears hear, but mind by means of ears, nor that nostrils smell, but the ruling faculty by using them.

For this reason it is said in Genesis, "A fountain rose up out of the earth and watered all the face of the earth" (Gen. 2:6). For since nature allotted the face to the senses as the choicest part of the whole body, the fountain arising from the ruling faculty, dividing itself in many directions, sends up something like conduits as far as the face, and through them it transmits its powers to each of the sense organs.[251] (*Post.* 126–127)

Impression and Impulse

Impression is an imprint in the soul.[252] For the soul, like a ring or seal,[253] received the appropriate imprint of those things that each of the senses introduces. The mind like wax[254] receives the imprint and preserves it in sharp clarity, until forgetfuness, memory's antagonist, smooths away the imprint and renders it faint or completely obliterates it. But the object that has appeared, and made the impression at times renders the soul well disposed at other times the reverse.[255] This affection of the soul is called impulse, which has been defined as the initial movement of the soul. (*Deus* 43–44)

Two Kinds of Ignorance

There are two kinds of ignorance, one simple, total obtuseness, the other twofold, when a man is afflicted not only by a lack of knowledge, but also, led on by a false notion of his own wisdom, thinks he knows what he does not know at all. The first evil is a lesser one, for it is the cause of minor and perhaps involuntary errors; the second is the greater, for it engenders great wrongs, not only those that are involuntary but also those already premeditated.[256] (*Ebr.* 162–163)

PHILO OF ALEXANDRIA

The Tropes of Aenesidemus

He who takes pride in his power to deliberate or his competence to choose some things and avoid others should be reminded (of the true state of things) by means of the following. If from the same objects it were always the case that the same impressions were invariably to result it would perhaps be necessary that the two faculties of judgment established in us by nature, sense and mind, should be honored as unerring and incorruptible, and that we should not through doubt suspend judgment concerning anything but, putting our trust in single appearances, choose the one and abandon the other. But since we are variously affected by them, we can say nothing certain about anything, inasmuch as the appearance is unstable and subject to multifarious and manifold changes. Since the impression is unstable, the judgment we form of it must be unstable too. The reasons for this are many.[257] (*Ebr.* 169 –170)

Dissension among the So-Called Philosophers

As for myself, I am not astonished that the milling and motley multitude, an ignominious slave to usages and customs introduced at random, drilled from the very cradle[258] to obey them as masters and despots, beaten down in spirit and incapable of being vigorous and high-spirited,[259] should put their faith in traditions transmitted once for all, and leaving their minds unexercised, should express assent and denial without inquiry or examination. But I am astounded that the crowd of so-called philosophers,[260] who pretend to be seeking unerring clarity in things, are divided into battalions and companies and propound doctrines that are discordant and frequently opposed not on some single chance point, but on virtually all points great and small in which their investigations are involved. (*Ebr.* 198)

The Sophistic Disputes

The stumbling blocks that come from the soul's potential allies are such as we find in the dogmatic disputes of the sophists. For insofar as they incline toward one end, contemplation of the facts of nature, they may be said to be friends, but in that they are not of one mind in their specialized research they may be said to be engaged in intestine strife. Thus those who assert that the universe is uncreated

146

are at odds with those who propound the idea of its creation; those who say that it will be destroyed with those who assert that though by nature destructible, it will never be destroyed, since it is secured by an exceedingly powerful bond, the will of its Creator; those who maintain that nothing is, but that all things become, with those who hold the contrary opinion; those who expound in detail that man is the measure of all things with those who nullify the standards of sense and mind; and, in general, those who propose the view that everything is beyond our apprehension with those who affirm that many things can be cognized. And indeed sun and moon and the whole heaven, earth and air and water and virtually all that is constituted of them, have furnished their investigators with matter for contention and rivalry when they search out their essential natures and qualities, their changes and vicissitudes, their coming and ceasing to be. Although they do not treat the magnitudes and movements of the heavenly bodies as an incidental inquiry, they come to different opinions and arrive at no consensus, until the man who is both midwife and judge "takes his seat among them" (Gen. 15:11)[261] and observes the offspring of each soul, casts away all that are not worth rearing, but saves those that are fit and deems them worthy of proper care. Philosophical issues have become full of discord, because the credulous mind, proceeding by conjecture, flees from the truth. The difficulty in finding and tracking the truth has, in my view, produced these intellectual wranglings.[262] (*Her.* 246–248)

Sight Superior to Hearing and Devoid of Falseness

Hearing holds second rank to seeing, and sight is the portion of Israel, the genuine firstborn son, for Israel translated means "seeing God."[263] It is possible to hear the false and take it for true, for hearing is deceptive, but sight, by which existing things are truly apprehended, does not lie. (*Fug.* 208)[264]

Wisdom Is Limitless

Therefore the diggers say that they have found no water in this well (Gen. 26:32), since the ends of knowledge prove to be not only hard to find but completely beyond finding. That is why in letters and in geometry one person surpasses the other, since there is no way to set bounds to their extensions and amplifications. For what remains to be learned is always lurking about and attending us with greater force than what has already become for us acquired knowledge; so that the man who is assumed to have attained the very limits of knowledge is considered in the judgment of another to have come halfway, whereas in the tribunal of justice he appears to be just beginning. For "life is short," said someone, "and art is long";[265] and he best takes in its magnitude who probes it deeply and digs it like a well.

It is for this reason, so the story goes, that a grey-haired man of extreme age shed tears when dying, not in any cowardly fear of death, but out of his longing for education, and the fact that he is now first embarking on it when he takes his final leave of it.[266] The soul experiences its most vigorous flowering of knowledge when the body's prime is withering away through length of years. So it is a hard fate to be tripped up by the heels before one has attained one's prime and spent one's youth in the more accurate apprehension of things. This experience is common to all who love to learn, for whom new speculations rise up and shine forth on the old. Many of these does the soul, when not barren and unfruitful, bring forth; many does nature herself manifest to those of sharp-sighted intelligence, without any advance token. (*Somn.* 1.8–11)

The Nature of the Celestial Bodies Is Unknowable

All these we perceive, but heaven's nature is incomprehensible, since it has sent us no manifest token of itself. For what can we say? That it is solid crystal, as some have held? Or that it is absolutely pure fire? Or that it is a fifth substance, moving in a circle, having no part in the four elements? Again, we ask, has the fixed and outermost sphere upward depth, or is it nothing but a surface, without depth, similar to plane geometrical figures? Again, are the stars masses of earth full of fire? Some have said that they were glens and groves and fiery lumps of red-hot metal, men who are themselves deserving of a prison and mill-house, in which such instruments are found for punishment of the impious. Or are they a continuous, and, as one has said, "condensed" harmony, indissoluble compressions of ether? Are they animate and intelligent, or have they no share in intelligence and soul? Are their motions determined by deliberation or by necessity alone? And the moon, does it bring with it a light of its own or a borrowed light made to shine by the rays of the sun? Or is it neither of these by and in itself, but one produced from both, a mixture as it were of fire both its own and borrowed? All these and suchlike questions pertaining to heaven, that fourth and best cosmic substance, are obscure and beyond our comprehension, relying on conjecture and surmise, not on the solid reasoning of truth; so that one could confidently swear that no mortal will ever have the capacity to apprehend any of these things clearly. For this reason the fourth well, which was dry, was called "Oath," being the endless and utterly elusive inquiry into the fourth of the elements constituting the cosmos, heaven.[267] (*Somn.* 1.21–24)

The Nature of the Human Mind Is Unknowable

Is, then, the fourth element in ourselves, the ruling mind, comprehensible? By no means. For what do we consider its substance to be? Breath or blood or body in general? It is evidently not body, but must be said to be incorporeal. Is it a limit, or form, or number, or continuity, or harmony, or what among existing things? Does it penetrate at once from without at our birth? Or does the hot nature within us become exceedingly hard by means of the air enveloping it, like red-hot iron in the cold water of the smithy? For this reason too it seems to have been called soul, on account of this "cooling" process. Again, when we die, is it extinguished and does it perish along with our bodies, or survive for a long time, or is it completely imperishable? And where in the body[268] does the mind lie concealed? Has it been assigned a dwelling? Some have consecrated to it the head, the citadel within us, around which the senses stand watch, since they believe it reasonable that they be stationed nearby like bodyguards who watch over some mighty monarch. Others contend obstinately for their view that its image is carried in the heart. So it is always the fourth that is beyond comprehension. In the universe it is the heaven as opposed to the nature of air, earth, and water; in man it is mind over against the body, sense perception, and interpretive speech. (*Somn.* 1.30–33)[269]

The Corporeal World Is the Gateway to the Intelligible World

The world, which he named a "house,"[270] he also designated as a "gate of" the true "heaven" (Gen. 28:17). What is this? The intelligible world constituted of the Forms in him who was appointed in accordance with the divine profusion cannot be apprehended save through the analogy of this sensible and visible world. For neither is it possible to form an idea of any other incorporeal thing among existents except by taking one's start from corporeal objects. From their state of rest came the conception of place, from their motion, time, whereas points, lines, and superficies, in short, limits, from what covers their exterior like a garment. For it was by analogy with the sensible world that the intelligible world too was conceived; for the sensible is a sort of gate into the latter. For as those who wish to see our cities enter through gates, so all who wish to apprehend the invisible world are guided by the impression of the visible one. The world whose substance is intelligible apart from any sight whatever of shapes, but only by means of the Archetypal Form present in the world fashioned in accordance with the image beheld by him without shadow—that world will change its name, when all its walls and every gate have been removed so that no one will see it derivatively but behold its unchanging beauty by itself alone, through a sight ineffable and indescribable.[271] (*Somn.* 1.186–188)

The Human Soul Is Capable of Discovering
Only a Semblance of the Truth

Now, if trained in the doctrines of wisdom and self-control and every virtue, we had washed away the stains of the passions and soul disturbances, perhaps God would not have deemed it unworthy to instruct souls thoroughly purified and made luminously radiant in the knowledge of things celestial either through dreams or oracles or signs or wonders. But since we bear the impression of the indelible imprints of injustice and folly and the other vices, we must be content if through reasonable conjectures through our own devices we may discover some semblance of the truth. (*Aet.* 2)

B. *PISTIS:* TRUST IN GOD (OR THE CONFIDENT CONVICTION OF INTUITIVE REASON)[272]

It Is Best to Trust in God and Not in Insecure Conjectures

It is best then to trust in God and not in obscure reasonings and insecure conjectures: "Abraham put his trust in God, and was held righteous" (Gen. 15:6); and Moses holds the leadership since he is attested as being "faithful in all [of God's] house" (Num. 12:7). But if we mistakenly trust our private reasonings we shall construct and build the city of the mind that destroys the truth: for *Sihon* means "destroying." For this reason one who has had a dream finds on awakening that all the movement and exertions of the foolish men are dreams devoid of reality. Indeed, mind itself was found to be a dream. For to trust God is a true teaching, but to trust empty reasonings is a lie. An irrational impulse issues forth and roams about both from the reasonings and from the mind that destroys the truth; wherefore also he says, "There went forth a fire from Heshbon, a flame from the city of Sihon" (Num. 21:28). For it is truly[273] irrational to put trust in plausible reasonings or in a mind that destroys the truth. (*LA* 3.228–229)

Moses Seeks God in the Hope of Exchanging Doubt for an Absolutely Firm Conviction

These and other exhortatons like these does Moses address to others. But he himself yearns so unceasingly to see God and to be seen by him that he beseeches him to clearly reveal his own nature (Exod. 33:13), so hard to divine, so that, having already once had a share of unerring opinion, he might exchange unreliable doubt for an absolutely firm conviction. (*Post.* 13)[274]

To Trust in God Alone Is No Easy Thing

The words "Abraham put his trust in God" (Gen. 15:6) are necessarily added in praise of him who has thus reposed his trust. Yet perhaps someone might say, do you judge this worthy of praise? When it is God who speaks and promises, who would not pay attention, even if he were the most unjust and impious of mankind? To him we will answer, "Noble sir, do not without due inquiry deprive the Sage of his seemly praises, or attribute to the unworthy the most perfect of virtues, trust, or censure our knowledge of these matters. If you should be willing to make a deeper and less superficial inquiry, you will clearly recognize that to trust in God alone without taking anything else besides is no easy thing, by reason of our kinship with mortality, to which we are yoked, and which persuades us to maintain our trust in material goods, repute, rule, friends, health, bodily

151

strength, and many other things. To purge oneself of each of these, to distrust created being, which in itself is completely unworthy of trust, to trust only in God who alone is truly worthy of trust, is a task for a great and celestial understanding, no longer enticed by anything earthly. (*Her*. 90–93)[275]

Trust in God, Not in Physicians

This is an attribute of virtually all those who vacillate, even though they do not concede it in so many words. When anything befalls them that does not accord with their wish, inasmuch as they do not maintain a firm trust in God their Savior, they flee first to creaturely aid, to physicians, herbs, drug compounds, a strict regimen, and all the other aids employed by mortals. And if one say to them, "Flee, foolish ones, to the one and only physician of soul disorders and abandon the falsely designated help of created being,[276] subject to suffering," they laugh and mock, exclaiming, "by and by for that," so that, whatever might happen, they would not beseech the Deity for the prevention of the evils at hand. But when all human remedies are of no avail, and all things, even those that heal, are found to be harmful, then in their utter helplessness, despairing of all other aid, unwillingly and belatedly, the wretches barely flee to the only Savior, God. He, inasmuch as he knows that what is done under the constraint of necessity is invalid, does not in all cases follow his customary (mercy), but only when it may be used for good and with profit. (*Sacr*. 70–71)[277]

He Who Puts His Trust in God Alone Will Be Truly Blessed

Now he who has unerringly trusted in God has comprehended the treachery inherent in all else, all that is created and perishable, beginning with the two boastful elements within himself, reasoning and sense-perception. Each has allotted to it its own council chamber and tribunal, one for the inquiry into intelligible things, the other into visible things, one with truth, the other with opinion for its goal. The instability and vacillation of opinion is evident from the fact that it is based on likelihood and plausibilities, and every likeness by its seductive similarity falsifies the original. Reasoning, the ruler of sense perception, which believes that it has attached to itself the judgments of things intelligible that always abide the same, is found to be blemished on many counts. For when it tackles a vast number of particular things it becomes incapable, grows exhausted, and gives out like an athlete hurled down by superior strength. But he to whom it has been granted to gaze beyond and transcend all things, corporeal as well as incorporeal, and to stand fast and find support in God alone with firm reasoning and a conviction unswerving and absolutely secure, will be a truly happy and thrice blessed man. (*Praem.* 28–30)[278]

C. PROPHECY

The Prophet Has No Utterance of His Own,
and When the Divine Light Shines, the Human Light Sets

In every man of virtue it is the holy Logos that attests to his gift of prophecy. For the prophet utters nothing that is his own, but all his utterances are of alien derivation, the prompting of another. The wicked may not become God's interpreter, so that no bad man is properly speaking inspired of God. The name is fitting only for the wise, since he alone is a sounding instrument of God, whose chords are invisibly plucked and smitten by him. All, at any rate, who are recorded by Moses as just are introduced as possessed and prophesying.

Noah was just. Is he not also at once a prophet? Were not the prayers and the curses that he uttered with regard to later generations and that were confirmed by the reality of events prophesied by him under divine possession?

What of Isaac? What of Jacob? For they too are acknowledged as prophets by many other acts, but chiefly by their addresses to their children. For "Come together that I may announce what will befall you at the end of the days" (Gen. 49:1) were the words of one inspired. Apprehension of the future does not belong to men.

What of Moses? Is he not everywhere celebrated as a prophet? For it says, "If there should be among you a prophet of the Lord, I will be made known to him in a vision, but to Moses in plain appearance and not through riddles" (Num. 12:6, 8), and further, "Never again did there arise a prophet like Moses, whom the Lord knew face to face" (Deut. 34:10).

Admirably then does he indicate the inspired man when he says "about sunset there fell on him an ecstasy" (Gen. 15:12). "Sun" is his

153

symbolic figure for our mind. For what reasoning is in us, the sun is in the world, for both are bearers of light, one sending forth to the whole world a sensible light, the other bestowing on ourselves the intelligible rays of apprehension. For as long as the mind still casts its light all about us, pouring as it were a noonday radiance into the entire soul, we are self-contained, not possessed. But when it comes to its setting, naturally ecstasy and divine possession and madness fall on us. For when the divine light shines, the human light sets, and when the divine light sets, the human dawns and rises. This is what is wont to occur to the prophetic kind. Our mind is ejected at the arrival of the divine Spirit, but at the latter's removal, the mind reestablishes itself. For it is not meet that mortal cohabit with the immortal. It is on this account that the setting of reasoning and the darkness enveloping it produce ecstasy and inspired frenzy. (*Her.* 259–265)[279]

Three Kinds of Dreams

In describing the third kind of God-sent dreams we may suitably summon Moses as our ally, that, as he learned when he was ignorant, he may teach us too in our ignorance regarding their signs, by illuminating each. The third kind of dreams arises whenever the soul in sleep, moving of itself and agitating itself, becomes frenzied and, inspired, prophesies the future through its prescient power. The first category of dreams consisted in God's originating the movement and invisibly suggesting things obscure to us but well known to him; whereas the second category involved the concerted movement of our understanding with the soul of the universe and its being filled with inspired frenzy, through which it is permitted to foretell many coming events.[280]

For this reason, the hierophant revealed quite clearly and distinctly the appearances that belong to the first description, since God's intimations through these dreams were like clear oracles. Those that belong to the second description he interpreted neither with exceeding clarity nor with excessive obscurity. An illustration of these is the vision that appeared on the heavenly stairway. For this vision was indeed enigmatic, but the riddle was not unduly concealed from the sharp-sighted. The appearances of the third kind being more obscure than the former because of the depth and density of their riddling nature required the aid of oneirocritical knowledge. Hence all the dreams of this sort recorded by the lawgiver are interpreted by men expert in the aforementioned science. (*Somn.* 2.1–4)[281]

Prophetic Dreams

The nature of the liver is mercurial and exceedingly smooth and in virtue of its smoothness it functions like an exceedingly bright mirror.[282] Consequently, when the mind, withdrawing from its daytime cares, with the body relaxed in sleep and no sensation to obstruct its path, begins to concentrate itself and examine its thoughts by itself without contamination, it gazes on the liver as on a mirror, enjoying a pure contemplation of all things intelligible, and surveying the images to see whether there is any deformity in them, it avoids these and selects their opposites and thus, well pleased with all its representations, prophesies future events by means of dreams. (*Spec.* 1.219)

Two Types of Prophecy

We said above that there are four attributes that belong to the truly perfect ruler. He must have kingship, legislative skill, priesthood, and prophecy, so that through his legislative skill he may command what ought to be done and forbid what ought not to be done, through the priesthood conduct not only things human but things divine, and through prophecy reveal by inspiration what is inapprehensible through reasoning. I have discussed the first three and have shown that Moses was the best of kings, of legislators, and of high priests, and will now finally show that he was the most illustrious of prophets. Now I am not unaware that all the things written in the sacred books are oracles delivered through Moses; but I will discuss those that are more particularly his, after making the following preliminary remarks. Of the divine oracles, some are spoken by God himself with his prophet as interpreter, some were revealed through question and answer, others by Moses himself, when inspired and possessed and transported out of himself. The first kind are entirely and exclusively tokens of the divine virtues, graciousness and beneficence, by which he encourages all men to noble action, and especially the nation of his worshipers, for whom he opens up a road that leads to happiness. The second kind entails mixture and partnership: The prophet makes inquiry about the things for which he has been searching and God responds and instructs him. The third kind are attributed to the lawgiver himself: God has granted him a share of his own prognostic power, through which he will prophesy the future. Now, the first kind must be deferred,[283] for they are too great for human praise; scarcely indeed could heaven and the earth and the entire universe worthily sing their praises. Moreover, they are delivered as if through an interpreter, and interpretation and prophecy are two different things. The second kind I will at once attempt to describe, interweaving with it the third kind, in which that divine possession of the speaker is manifest, in virtue of which he is above all and in the strict sense considered a prophet. [284] (*Mos.* 2.187–191)[285]

The Decalogue: Prophecy through the Divine Voice

The ten words or oracles, in reality laws or ordinances, were revealed by the Father of All when the nation, men and women alike, were assembled together. Did he utter them himself in the guise of a voice? Perish the thought: may it never enter our mind, for God is not as a man in need of mouth, tongue, and windpipe.[286] It seems to me rather that God on that occasion performed a truly holy miracle, by commanding an invisible sound to be created in the air more marvelous than all instruments and fitted with perfect harmonies, not inanimate, nor yet composed of body and soul like a living creature, but a rational soul full of lucidity and clarity, which, shaping the air and heightening its tension and transforming it into flaming fire, sounded forth like breath through a trumpet an articulate voice so great that those farthest away seemed to hear it with the same distinctness as those nearby. For it is the nature of human voices when extended to the maximum to give out so that the apprehensions of those far off become indistinct, growing gradually fainter with every increase in extension, since the organs too are perishable. But the power of God breathing on the newly made voice stirred it up and caused it to blaze forth, and spreading it on every side, rendered its end more luminous than its beginning by inspiring in the souls of each another kind of hearing far superior to that through the ears. For that sense, being in a way sluggish, remains inert until struck by the air and put into motion, but the hearing of the mind inspired by God reaches out to make the first advance to meet the spoken words with the swiftest speed.[287] (*Decal.* 32–35)[288]

SELECTIONS

VIII. WORSHIP

It is Impossible to Honor God as He Deserves

For no one honors God in a manner worthy of him, but only as is just. If it is impossible to return to one's parents as many favors as one has received, for it is impossible to give birth to them in turn, how must it not be impossible to requite or to praise in accordance with his worth him who has framed the universe out of things non-existent? For in doing that he furnished us with every virtue. (*LA* 3.10)[289]

Man Can Offer God Nothing But a Loving Disposition

But it is wrong to say that religion, which is service of God, is able to supply that which will benefit the Deity; for he is benefited by nothing, inasmuch as he is in need of nothing, nor does anything exist capable of adding to his superiority in all things. On the contrary, he benefits all things continuously and unceasingly. So that when we say that religion is service of God,[290] we mean some such service as slaves render their masters when they are determined to perform without hesitation what they are bidden to do. But again there will be a difference; for the masters are in need of service, but God does not need it. It follows that, while to masters their slaves render services that will benefit them, to God men can offer nothing but a loving disposition toward their Lord. For they will find nothing to improve, everything their Lord has being perfect from the first, but they will greatly benefit themselves by taking care to be rendered intimates of God. (*Det.* 55–56)[291]

Prayer and Sacrifice Must Be Offered with a Pure Heart

Though wanting nothing, God bids us in the extravagance of his beneficence to our race to offer him what is his own. For if we train ourselves to show him gratitude and honor, we shall be clear of wrongdoing and purge away that which defiles our lives in word, thought, and deed.[292] For it is absurd that one should not be permitted to enter the temples without having first bathed and cleansed his body, yet should attempt to pray and sacrifice with his mind still stained and sullied. And yet the temples are made of stones and timber, inanimate matter, and in itself the body too is inanimate. But for all that, though inanimate it is not to touch things inanimate without being subject to lustrations and purificatory offerings; and shall one then dare with soul impure to approach the God who is perfectly pure, and that too without any intention of repenting? He who has deemed it right not only to refrain from any further evil but also to wash away the old may approach with joy, but let him who lacks these sentiments, since he is insusceptible of purification, keep far off. For he will never escape detection by him who sees into the recesses of the mind and tarries amid its inmost shrines. (*Deus* 7–9)[293]

Holiness Is Not So Much a Matter of Place as a State of Mind

At the present moment my ruling part is in substance in my body, but virtually in Italy or Sicily, when it is pondering on these countries, and in heaven, when it is contemplating heaven. Thus it frequently happens that individuals who are bodily in profane spots are in reality in most sacred ones, while, on the other hand, others who are in holy shrines are in thought profane, through its taking on inclinations toward evil and base impressions. (*LA* 1.62)[294]

"The Lord Shepherds Me, and I Shall Want Nothing"

Let therefore even the whole universe, that greatest and most perfect flock of the God who Is, say, "The Lord shepherds me, and I shall want nothing" (Ps. 23:1). Let each individual too say the same, not with the voice that flows through tongue and mouth, reaching over a brief stretch of air, but with that of the understanding that extends and touches the ends of the universe. For it is impossible that there should be any lack of due portion, when God is the ruler, whose wont it is to grant good things in fullness and perfection to all existing things. (*Agr.* 52–53)[295]

In Bringing Himself the Worshiper Brings the Best of Sacrifices

It is therefore necessary that those who are about to visit the temple for participation in sacrifice be brightened and cleansed in body, and prior to body in soul. For the soul is queen and mistress and superior in every respect inasmuch as it has been allotted a nature more divine. The things that cleanse the mind are wisdom and wisdom's teachings, which lead to the contemplation of the universe and its contents, and the sacred company of the remaining virtues and the noble and highly praiseworthy actions accompanying them. He, then, who is adorned with these may confidently come to the sanctuary as a place truly his own, the best of all dwelling places, to present himself as victim. But he in whose heart there lodge concealed covetousness and lusts for wrongful acts should remain still and keep hidden and restrain his shameless madness and excessive rashness where caution is profitable. For the holy place of the truly Existent is not to be trodden by the unholy.[296] To such a one I would say, "Noble sir, God does not rejoice in sacrifices even if one offer hecatombs, for all things are his possessions, but though he possesses he needs none of them, but he takes delight in a God-loving disposition and in men who practice holiness, and from these he gladly accepts barley ground and unground and the meanest gifts in preference to the costliest,[297] holding them to be the most precious." And indeed though they bring nothing else, in bringing themselves[298] they offer the best sacrifice, the truly perfect fullness of moral nobility, as they celebrate with hymns and thanksgivings their Benefactor and Savior, God, sometimes with the organs of speech, sometimes without tongue or mouth, when within the soul and in thought alone they render their recitals and outcries. These only one ear can apprehend, that of God, for human hearing cannot attain to a share in their perception. (*Spec.* 1.269–272)[299]

The True Altar of God Is the Thankful Soul of the Sage

The true altar of God is the thankful soul of the sage, compacted of perfect virtues unsevered and undivided,[300] for no part of virtue is useless. On this altar the sacred light is ever kindled and maintained unextinguished, and the light of thought is wisdom, just as on the contrary darkness of the soul is folly. For what sensible light is to the eyes with regard to the apprehension of bodies, knowledge is to reasoning in respect of the contemplation of things incorporeal and intelligible, and its light shines forever, never dimmed or extinguished. (*Spec.* 1.287–288)

PHILO OF ALEXANDRIA

Our Gratitude to God Can Be Expressed Only by Hymns of Praise
Rendered by the Mind Alone

Fitly does Moses speak of the fruit of education as being not only
"holy" but "for praise" (Lev. 19:24); for each of the virtues is a holy
matter, but thanksgiving is surpassingly so. Now it is impossible genuinely to render thanks to God by means of buildings, votive offerings, and sacrifices as most people believe, for not even the whole
world could be a sanctuary worthy of God's honor. It must rather be
rendered through hymns of praise, not those the resonant voice shall
sing but such as the invisible and perfectly pure mind reechoes and
intones. Indeed there is an ancient tale about, the invention of wise
men, handed down successively by memory, as is usual, to subsequent
generations, which has not eluded my ears, which are ever gluttons
for instruction. It goes as follows. When, they say, the Creator had
brought the whole world to completion, he inquired of one of his
spokesmen whether he missed anything that had not been created
among the things on earth or in the water or in the air above or in
heaven, the furthest element of the universe. His response was that
all was perfect and complete in every respect and that he was searching for one thing only, the word that would praise them, a word that
would not so much praise as announce the preeminence of all things,
even those that appear the most miniscule and insignificant, for the
mere description of the works of God was entirely sufficient praise
for them, since they were in need of no external supplementation for
their embellishment, but possessed in the inerrancy of truth their
most perfect encomium. When the father of the universe heard this,
he approved what had been said, and not long after the highly musical race of hymnodists appeared, sprung from one of his powers,
virgin Memory, whom the multitude, modifying the name, call
"Mnemosyne."[301]

So goes the myth of the ancients. In line with this, we say that
God's most fitting work is to show kindness, whereas that of creation
is to render thanks, since it is incapable of making a greater return
than this, for whatever else it may have wished to give in requital will
be found to be the personal property of the Creator, and not that of
creation, which brings it. Having learned, then, that in what pertains
to the honor due to God, one work alone is incumbent on us, namely
thanksgiving, let us pursue this always and everywhere through spoken words and elegant compositions. Let us never neglect to compose

encomia both in prose and poetry, so that with or without musical accompaniment, and with both forms of voice, to which speech and song have been assigned, both the Creator and the world be celebrated, the one, as someone has said, the best of causes, the other, the most perfect of things created. (*Plant.* 126–131)

Fear and Confidence in Facing God

The man of virtue enjoys such outspokenness that he has the courage not only to speak and cry out, but even to make protestation out of a sense of true conviction and genuine feeling. For take the words "if you will forgive them their sin, forgive; but if not, blot me out of the book which you have written" (Exod. 32:32); and "Did I conceive all this people, or did I bring them forth, that you say to me, 'take them to your bosom, as a nurse bears the suckling'?" (Num. 11:12); or, again, "Whence shall I get flesh to give to this people, seeing that they weep against me? Shall sheep and oxen be slaughtered, or all the fish of the sea be gathered together and suffice?" (Num. 11:13, 22). Or, "Lord, why have you afflicted this people and why have you sent me? And from the time I went to Pharaoh to speak in your name, he has afflicted the people, and you have not saved your people" (Exod. 5:22, 23). These words and such as these anyone would have feared to say even to one of the kings whose sovereignty is limited to a particular kingdom; yet he had the courage to declare them even before God. He arrived at this limit, not simply of daring but of approved daring, because all the wise are friends of God, and especially in the view of the truly holy legislator. Outspokenness is akin to friendship. For to whom should a man speak with frankness but to his friend? Most excellently, then, is Moses celebrated as the friend of God, so that all that was courageously and boldly ventured forth by him appears to have been put forward in friendship rather than out of willfulness. For rashness is characteristic of the willful, but bold confidence of the friend.

But observe, on the other hand, that confidence is blended with caution. For the words "What will you give me?" (Gen. 15:2) exhibit confidence, but "Master" indicates caution.... He who says, "Master, what will you give me?" virtually says the following: "I am not unaware of your surpassing power, I know the fearfulness of your lordship; I approach you in fear and trembling, and yet again I am confident. For it was you who made known to me that I should have no fear; you have 'given me an instructed tongue that I should know when to speak' (Isa. 50:4), my mouth that was sewed up you have unraveled, and having opened it you rendered it more articulate; you have taught me to say what should be said, confirming the oracle 'I will open[302] your mouth, and teach you what you shall speak' (Exod. 4:12). For who was I that you should give me a share in speech, that you should promise me a 'reward,' a more perfect good than 'grace' or 'gift.' Am I not a migrant from my country; was I not expelled from my kinsfolk; was I not alienated from my father's house? Do not all men call me disinherited, fugitive, desolate, disfranchised? You, Master, are my country, my kinsfolk, my paternal hearth, my franchise, my free speech, my great and glorious and inalienable wealth. Why then shall I not fearlessly speak my mind? Why shall I not make inquiry concerning that which I deem it right to learn something more? Yet I who assert my confidence concede in turn my feelings of terror and fear, though the fear and confidence do not wage irreconcilable war within me, as one might suppose, but constitute a harmonious blend. I feast insatiably on this blend, which has persuaded me to be neither outspoken without caution, nor cautious without speaking freely. For I have learned to measure my own nothingness and to gaze in wonderment at the exceeding perfection of your loving-kindness. And when I perceive that I am 'earth and ashes' or whatever is still more worthless, it is then that I have the courage to approach you, when I am humbled, relegated to dust, reduced to the elemental point which seems not even to exist."[303] (*Her.* 19–22, 24–29)

The World Offers Itself Daily to God in Ceaseless Gratitude

These four, of which the incense is compounded (Exod. 30:34–35), are, I believe, symbols of the elements out of which the entire world was brought to its completion. Moses is likening the oil of myrrh to water, the onycha to earth, the galbanum to air, and the clear frankincense to fire.... The harmoniously blended mixture of these elements proves to be that most venerable, perfect, and truly holy work, the world which, he thinks, should under the symbol of the incense render thanks to its Creator, so that while apparently it is the compound prepared by the perfumer's art that is burnt as incense, in reality it is the world fashioned by divine wisdom, which is brought as a burnt offering morning and evening. This is indeed a life fitting for the world, that it should give thanks to its Father and Creator continuously and without interruption, all but evaporating and returning to its elemental state, to indicate that it hoards nothing as treasure, but dedicates itself entire as a votive offering to God its begetter. (*Her.* 197, 199–200)[304]

God Discloses a Name to Man for the Sake of Prayer

For God is in need of no name; yet though he needed it not, he nevertheless graciously bestowed on mankind a designation of himself suited to them, so that men might find refuge in supplications and prayers and not be deprived of good hope. (*Abr.* 51)[305]

The Gracious God Who Assents to Prayers

But a king and lawgiver ought to have under his purview not only human but divine things, for without God's thoughtfulness, the affairs of kings and subjects cannot succeed. Wherefore one such as he needs the chief priesthood, so that with the aid of perfect rites and perfect knowledge of the service of God he may make petition on behalf of himself and those whom he rules, for aversion of evils and sharing of good, from the gracious One who assents to prayers. For surely he will bring prayers to perfect fulfillment, since he is kindly by nature and deems worthy of special privilege those who serve him genuinely. (*Mos.* 2.5)[306]

The Suppliants of God Are They Who Love the Virtuous Life

What Moses had himself he gave [to his people] at once; what he did not possess he supplicated God to grant them, knowing that though the fountains of his grace are ever-flowing they are not accessible to all, but only to suppliants. And suppliants are those who love the life of virtue, to whom it is permitted, since they are thirsty for wisdom, to draw from fountains that are truly holy. (*Virt.* 79)

IX. MYSTICISM

The Limit of Happiness Is the Presence of God

But it is something great that Abraham asks, namely that God shall not pass by nor remove to a distance and leave his soul desolate and empty (Gen. 18:3). For the limit of happiness is the presence of God, which completely fills the whole soul with his whole incorporeal and eternal light. And (the limit) of misery is (his) passing on the way, for immediately thereafter comes heavy and profound darkness, which possesses (the soul). Wherefore also the fratricide Cain says, "Great is the guilt of my punishment that you leave me" (Gen. 4:13),[307] indicating that there is no greater punishment for the soul than to be abandoned by God. Moreover, in another place Moses says, "Lest the Lord be removed from them,"[308] showing that for the soul to be separated from the contemplation of the Existent One is the most complete of evils. For these reasons he attempts to lead the people toward God, not (any men), for this is not possible, but god-loving souls that can (be led), when a heavenly love and desire have come on them and seized them. (*QG* 4.4)[309]

Make Your Soul a Shrine of God,
For the Beginning and End of Happiness Is to Be Able to See God

For the Savior is beneficent and kind, and he wishes to except the rational race from all living creatures. He therefore honors them with an even ampler gift, a great benefaction in which all kinds of good things are found, and he graciously grants his appearance, if only there be a suitable place, purified with holiness and every (kind of) purity. For if, O mind, you do not prepare yourself of yourself, excising desires, pleasures, griefs, fears, follies, injustices, and related evils, and do (not) change and adapt yourself to the vision of holiness, you will end your life in blindness, unable to see the intelligible sun. If, however, you are worthily initiated and can be consecrated to God and in a certain sense become an animate shrine of the Father, (then) instead of having closed eyes, you will see the First (Cause) and in wakefulness you will cease from the deep sleep in which you have been held. Then will appear to you that manifest One who causes incorporeal rays to shine for you, and grants visions of the unambiguous and indescribable things of nature and the abundant sources of other good things. For the beginning and end of happiness is to be able to see God. But this cannot happen to him who has not made his soul, as I said before, a sanctuary and altogether a shrine of God. (*QE* 2.51)[310]

What Worthier House Could Be Found for God than the Purified Soul?

What worthier house could be found for God in the realm of creation than a soul that is perfectly purified,[311] which holds that only the Noble is Good and ranks all others so accounted as but satellites and subjects? But God is said to dwell in a house not as in a place, for he contains all things and is contained by none, but in the sense of exercising special care and providence over that place. Care of the house is necessarily affixed to every householder. Let everyone indeed on whom God's loving goodness has fallen as rain pray that he may obtain the All-ruler as his occupant who shall exalt this paltry edifice, the mind, high above the earth and join it to the ends of heaven. (*Sobr.* 62–64)

The Quest for God Is Never Fruitless

The quest for God, best of all existing things, the Incomparable, the Cause of all, gladdens us the moment we embark on our search, and is never without issue, since by reason of his gracious nature he advances to meet us with his virgin graces,[312] and shows himself to those who long to see him, not as he is, for this is impossible, since even Moses "turned away his face, for he was afraid to look upon God" (Exod. 3:6) but so far as it was allowable that created nature should approach the inconceivable Power. (*Fug.* 141)[313]

The Mind Possessed by Divine Love

When the mind is possessed by divine love, when it exerts itself to reach the innermost shrine,[314] when it moves forward with all effort and zeal, under the impact of the divine inspiration it forgets everything else, forgets itself, and retains memory and attachment for him alone whose attendant and servant it is, to whom it dedicates the incense offering of hallowed and intelligible virtues. But when the inspiration is stilled and the intense longing subsides, it races back from the divine and becomes man and encounters the human interests that lay in wait for it in the outer court to snatch it away should it but venture forth from within. (*Somn.* 2.232)

The Wise Man's Insatiable Longing for the Divine

But (Scripture) shows that the character of the wise man is not quickly satisfied but is constant and hard to efface and hard to remove from the idea of that which is above the good and above the wise man and above the very best. And various conversations come together, one after the other, so that he never departs from the conversation of speech because of his insatiable and incessant desire and longing, by which the sovereign (mind) is drawn and seized; and it is led by the attractive force of sovereign existences. (*QG* 4.140)[315]

Those Called Upward

This is the reason those who are persistently insatiate of wisdom and knowledge are said in the Oracles to have been called upward; for it is right that those who have received the divine inbreathing should be called up to him. For when trees are pulled up root and branch by whirlwinds and hurricanes, and heavily freighted ships of giant tonnage are plucked from mid-ocean as though they were the lightest of objects, and lakes and rivers are borne aloft, and earth's hollows are emptied of their flood, which has been drawn up by tangled wind eddies of enormous force, it is strange if the mind, being a light substance, is not made buoyant and raised to the highest summit by the all-powerful divine Spirit whose nature is to vanquish all that exists below. And how much more so must this be the case with the mind of a genuine philosopher. For such a one does not sink downward by reason of weight toward objects dear to body and earth, from which he has ever labored hard to be separated and estranged. He is thus borne upward insatiably enamored of natures lofty, utterly holy and happy. That is why Moses, the steward and guardian of the mysteries of the Existent, will be one called above; for it is said in the book of Leviticus, "He called Moses up" (Lev. 1:1). One called up will Bezalel also be, who is held worthy of the second rank. For him too does God call up for the construction and overseeing of the sacred works (Exod. 31:2ff.). But Bezalel will bear away the secondary honors due to the call above, whereas Moses will carry off the primary ones. For the former fashions the shadows, as painters do, for whom there is no divine license to create anything animate. Bezalel, in effect, means "making in shadows." Moses, on the other hand, was assigned the task of producing not shadows but the very archetypes of things. For it is the wont of the Primal Cause, above all, to reveal the objects proper to each, to some in a clearer and more luminous vision as though in pure sunlight, to others more faintly as though in the shade. (*Plant.* 23–27)

Mind's Abandonment of Body, Sense Perception, and Speech

"And the Lord said to Abraham, Go forth from your native land and from your kindred and from your father's house, to the land that I will show you. I will make of you a great nation, and I will bless you; I will make your name great, and you shall be blessed. I will bless those who bless you, and those who curse you I will curse, and in you shall all the tribes of the earth be blessed" (Gen. 12:1–3).

Intent on purifying man's soul, God initially assigns it as its starting point for full salvation its migration out of three regions, body, sense perception, and speech. "Land" is a symbol of body, "kindred" of sense perception, "father's house" of speech. Why so? Because the body received its substance from the earth and is again resolved into earth. Moses testfies to this when he says, "Earth you are and to earth you shall return" (Gen. 3:19); for he also says that the body was clay compacted into human shape, and that which suffers dissolution must be dissolved into the elements that were originally bound together.[316] As for sense perception, it is akin and sister to understanding, the irrational to the rational, for both these are parts of one soul. And speech is our "father's house" because mind is our father, sowing its faculties in each of the parts of the body, and distributing to them their functions since it is endued with the care and guardianship of them all, and the house in which it dwells, removed from the rest of the household, is speech. For just as the hearth is the dwelling place of man, so is speech that of the mind. For in speech, as in its home, it is displayed arranging and ordering itself and all the conceptions it engenders. . . .

We have thus shown how "lord" represents body, "kindred" sense perception, and "father's house" speech. The words "Go forth from these" are not equivalent to "Disengage yourself from them in substance," since such a command would be a prescription of death.

The words are equal instead to "Make yourself a stranger to them in your mental disposition; cleave to none of them and stand above them all; they are your subjects, never treat them as sovereigns; you are a king, be trained to rule, not to be ruled, throughout your life be getting to know yourself, as Moses teaches on many occasions, saying 'Give heed to yourself' (Exod. 24:12), for so you will perceive those whom it is appropriate for you to obey and those whom it befits you to command."

Go forth, then, from the earthly matter that envelops you. Escape, man, from the abominable prison, your body, and from the pleasures and lusts that act as its jailers, with all your might and main; let go nothing that can injure them, and threaten them with a combined host.

Depart also from sense perception, your kin. For the moment you have made a loan of yourself to each of the senses and have become the alien property of those who have borrowed you, and the good thing that was your own you have lost. You are well aware, though all men should maintain their calm, how eyes lead you, and ears, and the whole crowd of your other kinsfolk, in the direction of their own lives. But if you desire to recover the loan of yourself and win your own property without separating or alienating any portion of it, you will lay claim to a happy life, ever enjoying the use and pleasure of goods that are not alien but are peculiarly your own.

Again, migrate also from speech, which Moses has called "your father's house," so that you may not be deceived by the beauties of words and expressions and be severed from the authentic beauty that lies in the matter disclosed. For it is absurd that shadow gain the advantage over objects, or a copy over originals. Verbal expression is like a shadow or copy, while the substance conveyed by verbal exposition resembles objects and originals. To these the man who aims at being rather than seeming ought to cling, while removing himself from the former.[317] (*Mig.* 1–4, 7–12)[318]

Recognition of Man's Nothingness

Among these is Abraham who gained much progress and improvement toward the acquisition of the highest knowledge: for when above all he knew himself, then above all did he despair of himself, in order that he might arrive at a precise knowledge of the truly Existent. And this is how it is: He who has profoundly comprehended himself, profoundly despairs[319] of himself, having perceived in advance the absolute nothingness of creating being. And the man who has despaired of himself knows the Existent. (*Somn.* 1.60)[320]

Departure from Self

Who then shall be the heir? Not the sort of reasoning that voluntarily abides in the prison of the body, but that which loosed from its bonds and liberated has come forth outside the walls, and if we may say so, abandoned its own self. For "he who shall come out of you," it says, "shall be your heir" (Gen. 15:4).

If then, my soul,[321] a yearning comes upon you to inherit the divine goods, abandon not only your land, that is, the body; your kinsfolk, that is, the senses; your father's house (Gen. 12:1), that is, speech, but escape also your own self and stand aside from yourself, like persons possessed and corybants seized by Bacchic frenzy and carried away by some kind of prophetic inspiration. For it is the mind that is filled with the Deity and no longer in itself, but is agitated and maddened by a heavenly passion, drawn by the truly Existent and attracted upward to it, preceded by truth, which removes all obstacles in its path so that it may advance on a level highway—such a mind has the inheritance. (*Her.* 68–70)[322]

Attachment to God

"The tribe of Levi," he says, "shall have no lot or portion among the children of Israel, for the Lord himself is their portion" (Deut. 10:9); and there is an utterance intoned by the oracles in the name of God that runs as follows: "I am your portion and inheritance" (Num. 18:20). For in truth the mind that has been utterly purified, and that renounces all things belonging to creation, knows and recognizes but One alone, the Uncreated, to whom it has drawn nigh, and by whom it has been taken as a partner. For who is able to say "God himself is alone to me," save one who clings to nothing that comes after him? And this is the Levite temper of mind, for the word means "He is to me (i.e., mine)," since different things are honored by different people, but by him alone is honor rendered to the highest and most excellent Cause of all things. (*Plant.* 63–64)[323]

Referring All Things to God

There are two minds, that of the universe, which is God, and the individual mind. He who flees from his own mind takes refuge with the Mind of all things. For he that abandons his own mind grants that that which pertains to the human mind is nothing, and attributes all things to God. On the other hand, he that flees from God affirms that He is the cause of nothing, but that he himself is the cause of all things that come into being. Many indeed say that all things in the world are borne along spontaneously, without anyone to guide them, and that the human mind by itself established arts, professions, laws, customs, rules of conduct within the state, individual and communal, regarding both men and irrational animals. But note, my soul, the difference between the two views; for the one abandons the particular, created, and mortal mind, and verily chooses as its patron the universal Mind, uncreated and imperishable; the other view, on the contrary, rejects God, and mistakenly calls in as its ally the mind, which is insufficient even to help itself. (*LA* 3.29–31)[324]

The Soul That Rests in God

The clearest evidence for the soul beloved of God is the psalm in which are contained the words "the barren has borne seven, but she that is multiple has languished in her offspring" (1 Sam. 2:5). And yet it is the mother of one child—Samuel—who is speaking. How then can she say that she has borne seven, unless, in full accord with reality, she believes the Monad to be identical with the hebdomad,[325] not only in arithmetical lore, but also in the harmony of the universe and in the thoughts of the virtuous soul? For Samuel who is appointed to God alone and associates with no one else at all possesses a nature in conformity with the One and the Monad, the truly Existent. But this state is that of the Seven, when a soul rests in God and toils no longer at any mortal task,[326] and has abandoned the Six,[327] which God has apportioned to those incapable of obtaining the first prize, but must necessarily lay claim to the second. (*Deus* 10–12)

Contemplation of God without Audible Speech

For in this way only could that which is best in ourselves become inclined to serve the Best of all Existents: if first the man were resolved into soul, his brother body and its endless lusts being severed and cut in two; if next the soul cast off, as I have said, that neighbor of our rational element, the irrational, which, like a torrent divided five ways through the channels of the senses, excites the onrush of the passions; if immediately thereafter reasoning sever and disperse that which seems to be closest to it, the uttered word, so that the thought within the mind may be left behind alone, bereft of body, bereft of sense perception, bereft of the utterance of resonant speech. For thus left behind, it will live a life in accord with such solitude, and will cleave in purity and without distraction to the Alone Existent.[328] (*Fug.* 91–92)

The Vision of the Logos

It is characteristic of those who serve the Existent that theirs are not the tasks of cupbearers or bakers or cooks or any other earthly tasks, nor do they mold or construct material things like brickwork, but in their reasonings ascend to the ethereal height, setting before them Moses, the genus beloved of God,[329] to lead the way. For then they shall behold the place,[330] which in reality is the Logos, where stands God the steadfast and unchanging, and also "what lies under his feet like the work of a brick[331] of sapphire, like the form of the firmament of the heaven" (Exod. 24:10), namely, the sensible world intimated through these words. For it is fitting for those who have entered into comradeship with knowledge to long to see the Existent, but if they are unable, to see at least his image, the truly holy Logos, and after the Logos its most perfect work in the realm of the sensible, this world. For philosophy was never anything but the earnest desire to see things precisely as they are. (*Conf.* 95–97)[332]

Extending the Soul to the Bounds of the All

Next, she [Hannah] denies that she has taken wine or intoxicating drink, exulting in the fact that her entire life was one of continuing sobriety (1 Sam. 1:15). For truly it was a great and wondrous feat to enjoy a reasoning that is wide ranging, free, and pure, inebriated by no passion. The result of this is that the mind that has been filled with the unmixed wine of sobriety becomes a libation in its whole being, a libation poured out to God. What else was signified by the words, "I will pour out my soul before the Lord" but "I will conse-

171

crate it all to him, I will undo all the shackles that bound it securely, which the empty cares of mortal life had fastened upon it; I will carry it abroad, extend and diffuse it, so that it shall touch the bounds of the All, and hasten to that loveliest and most glorious of visions, the vision of the Uncreated."[333] (*Ebr.* 151–152)[334]

The Mind Enjoys Timeless Contact with the Entire Universe

For the mind, alone of all our endowments, being swiftest of all things, outstrips and outdistances the time in which it seems to be found, and by virtue of invisible faculties enjoys timeless contact with both the whole and its parts,[335] and with their respective causes. And having already come not only as far as the ends of earth and sea but of air and sky also, not even there did it come to a halt, holding the world to constitute a narrow boundary for its continuous and unceasing course, and eager to advance beyond, and apprehend if possible the nature of God, which except for its bare existence is inapprehensible. For how was it likely that the human mind being so tiny, hemmed in by such puny masses[336] as brain or heart, should be able to contain such an immense magnitude of sky and universe, had it not been an inseparable portion of that divine and blessed soul? For nothing is severed or detached from the divine, but only extended.[337] When the mind, therefore, that has received its share in the perfection of the whole conceives of the universe, it stretches out as widely as the bounds of the whole, for its force is susceptible of attraction. (*Det.* 89–90)[338]

Meeting with the Logos Sudden and Unexpected

It is extraordinarily apt that he [Abraham] does not say that he came to the place, but that he met with a place (Gen. 18:33); for coming is a matter of choice, but meeting is often without one's volition, and this is so in order that the divine Logos, manifesting itself suddenly as a fellow-traveler to a desolate soul, might tender it an unexpected joy, greater than hope. "For Moses too leads the people forth to meet God" (Exod. 19:17), knowing full well that he comes invisibly to the souls that long to converse with him. (*Somn.* 1.71)[339]

SELECTIONS

Sober Intoxication

Again, when soaring upward the mind has spied the atmosphere and its changes, it is borne yet higher to the ether and the celestial revolution, and is carried around with the dances of the planets and fixed stars, in accordance with the laws of perfect music, following the love of wisdom that guides it. When it has transcended all sensible substance,[340] at that point it longs for the intelligible, and on beholding in that realm beauties beyond measure, the patterns and originals of the sensible things in the world below it is possessed by a sober intoxication[341] like those seized with Corybantic frenzy, and is inspired, filled by another sort of longing and a more fitting desire. Escorted by this to the uppermost vault of things intelligible, it seems to be on its way to the Great King himself; but while it keenly strives to see him, pure and untempered rays of concentrated light stream forth like a flood, so that through its flashing bursts, the eye of the understanding spins with dizziness.[342] (*Op.* 70–71)[343]

The Soul That Sees God Enjoys Equipoise and Tranquillity

Note what is said about wise Abraham, that he was "standing in front of God" (Gen. 18:22), for when is it likely that a mind should stand and no longer sway as on a balance except when it is opposite God, seeing and being seen? For its equilibrium derives from two sources; from seeing the Incomparable, because it is not then drawn in a contrary direction by things similar to itself; from being seen, because the mind that the Ruler judges worthy to come within his sight he assigns for the best alone, namely for himself.

To Moses, too, the following oracle was delivered: "But as for you, stand here with me" (Deut. 5:31), from which one may adduce both points mentioned above, the unwavering character of the man of virtue and the absolute firmness of the Existent. For he who draws near to God is made akin to the Existent, and in accordance with his immutability becomes self-standing. Moreover, the mind that has found rest has clearly recognized how great a good tranquillity is, and astounded at its beauty has grasped that it is either God's portion alone or of that nature which lies midway between mortal and immortal kind. (*Somn.* 2.226–228)

173

Souls That Cleave to God Become Virgins Again

But as for the deeper meaning, such souls as love themselves honor the mind as a husband and as a father—as a husband perhaps because it sows in them the powers of the senses by which the sense-perceptible object is attained and seized; and (they honor it) as a father because it is thought to be the parent of disciplines and arts. But those who are free of self-love and hasten to God draw near as to a highly concerned and caring father. And as the male sows the seeds of good thoughts and intentions and words and deeds, and (as) it happens customarily among humans that the opposite thing comes about, for when a male comes in contact with a female he makes the virgin as a woman, so when souls cleave[344] to God, from being women they become virgins, throwing off the womanly corruptions that are (found) in sense perception and passion. Morover, they follow after and pursue the genuine and unmated virgin, the veritable wisdom of God. And so rightly do such minds become widows and are orphaned of mortal things and acquire for themselves and have as husband the right law of nature, with which they live. And (they have) the same (as) father to tell them with greater concern, as though (they were) his sons, what they ought to do (*QE* 2.3)

X. PROVIDENCE, THEODICY AND MIRACLES

A. PROVIDENCE

Nothing Is Uncertain or Future to God, Who Takes Forethought for All Things

For a mere man it is impossible to foresee the occurrences of future events or the sentiments of others, but to God as in pure sunlight[345] all things are manifest. For having reached into the recesses of the soul, what is invisible to others is clearly discernible to him. He employs his characteristic virtues of forethought and foreknowledge, and allows nothing to act independently or escape his comprehension. For not even concerning future events is he susceptible of uncertainty, since nothing is uncertain or future to God. It is evident that the parent must have knowledge of his offspring, the craftsman of the objects fashioned[346] by him, the steward of the things managed by him. But God is truly the father and craftsman and steward of all things celestial and cosmic. (*Deus* 29–30)[347]

Those Who Deny Creation Eliminate Providence

Those who declare that this world is uncreated are unaware that they have undercut that which is most beneficial and indispensable for piety, namely providence. For reason persuades us that what has been created should be cared for by its Father and Creator. It is a father's aim in regard to his offspring and a craftsman's in regard to what was fashioned by him to preserve them, and by every means to repulse all that is noxious and harmful, whereas all that is profitable and advantageous he desires to provide for them in every possible way; but there is no affinity whatever between what was not created and one who did not create it. It is a worthless and baneful doctrine, establishing anarchy in this cosmos as in a city without overseer, arbitrator, or judge, by whom it is right that all things be administered and governed. (*Op.* 9–11)

The Fortunes of Empire

If you do not wish to examine the fortunes of individual men, consider the vicissitudes, both for better and for worse, of whole regions and nations.[348] Greece was once in full flower, but the Macedonians took away its power. Macedonia flourished in its turn, but when it was divided into portions it grew feeble until it was utterly extinguished. Before the Macedonians the affairs of the Persians enjoyed success, but a single day destroyed their great and mighty empire, and now Parthians, once their subjects, rule over Persians who were but lately their masters. Egypt once exhibited great splendor for a very long time, yet its immense success passed away like a cloud. What of the Ethiopians, what of Carthage, and the parts toward Libya? What of the kings of Pontus? What of Europe and Asia, and in short the whole civilized world?[349] Is it not tossed up and down and driven wildly like ships at sea, subject now to favorable, now to contrary winds?

For the divine Logos that most men call fortune runs a circular course.[350] Accordingly, in its perpetual flux it makes distribution city by city, nation by nation, country by country, giving to these what belonged to others, and to all what belonged to all, and exchanging only from time to time the possessions of each, so that the whole world should like one city maintain the best of constitutions, democracy.[351] (*Deus* 173–176)[352]

God Employs the Elements for the Punishment of the Impious

Ten were the punishments brought upon the land [of Egypt]—a perfect number for the chastisement of those who brought error to perfection. The chastisement differed from the usual, for the elements of the universe, earth, water, air, and fire, carried out the attack. God deemed it right that the elements through which the world was brought to perfection should destroy the land of the impious, to show the might of the sovereignty he exercises, inasmuch as the same elements that, with an eye toward their preservation, he shaped for the creation of the universe, he also applied to the destruction of the impious whenever he so wished. He distributes the punishments by assigning the three belonging to the denser elements, from which our bodily qualities were produced, to the brother of Moses; an equal number, belonging to air and fire, the two most productive of life, he assigns to Moses alone; one, the seventh, he commits to both in common; and the other three, which complete the ten, he entrusts to himself.[353] (*Mos.* 1.96–97)

B. THEODICY

Creation of Man's Irrational Soul Assigned to the Powers, So That Man's Evil Acts May Not Be Ascribed to God

One might rightly raise the question what reason there could possibly be that he ascribed the creation of man alone not to one creator, as in the case of the rest, but, as it were, to several. For he introduces the Father of the Universe speaking as follows: "Let us make man after our image and likeness." Could he, I would ask, to whom all things are subject, be in need of anyone whatever? Or could it be that when he created the heaven and the earth and the sea, he required the cooperation of no one, yet was unable by his own power alone, without the assistance of others, to frame a creature so puny and perishable as man? The absolutely true cause of this is perforce known to God alone, but the cause that through likely conjecture appears plausible and reasonable I ought not to conceal. It is this. Among existing things some partake neither of virtue nor of vice, like plants and irrational animals; the one because they are inanimate and provided with a nature deprived of sense impressions, the other because from them mind and reason have been excised: for mind and reason may be regarded as the abode of vice and virtue, whose nature it is to dwell in them. Others in turn partake of virtue alone, having no share whatever in vice. Such are the stars; for these are said to be living creatures, but living creatures endowed with mind, or better yet each of them is a mind in itself, completely virtuous and insusceptible of any evil. Others are of mixed nature, as man, who is prone to contraries, wisdom and folly, self-control and wantonness, courage and cowardice, justice and injustice, and in short to good and evil, noble and base, virtue and vice. Now it was most fitting for God the universal Father to create those virtuous beings by himself alone, because of their kinship to him. To create those that are indifferent was not alien to him, since they have no share in the vice he hates. To create those of mixed nature was in one respect fitting, in another unfitting; fitting in virtue of the better form blended in them, alien because of the contrary and lesser form. For this reason it is at the creation of man alone that we are told by Moses that God said, "Let us make," which indicates the enlistment of others as assistants. It is to the end that God, the universal Ruler, may claim credit for a man's blameless plans and deeds when he acts in accord with right reason, while others of his subordinates lay claim to those of a contrary sort. For it was necessary that the Father be blameless of evil toward his offspring, and vice and vicious activities are an evil thing.[354] (*Op.* 72–75)[355]

God Chastises Not Directly,
But By Means of His Regent or Punitive Power

I have not detailed all this, however, in order to exhibit the novel and stupendous calamities wrought by God, but in my desire to make another point. The Scriptures tell us that of the three who appeared to the Sage [Abraham] in the guise of men two only arrived in the land subsequently obliterated in order to destroy its inhabitants, but the third did not deem it right to come. That one, in my view, was the truly Existent, who held that it was fitting that he be present to bestow good things by his own agency, but should turn over the execution of the opposite to his powers alone acting in his service, so that he might be considered the cause of good only, but not directly the cause of anything evil. Those kings who imitate the divine nature appear to me to act in this way, offering boons by themselves, but establishing punishments by means of others. But since of the two powers one is beneficent and the other punitive it was natural that each make its appearance in the land of the Sodomites, for of the five finest cities situated there four were to be burnt, but one was to be left unaffected, safe from all evil. It was necessary that the destruction take place by means of the Punitive Power, but the preservation by means of the Beneficent Power. Yet since the portion preserved did not possess virtues that were complete and perfect, while it was benefited by a power of the Existent, it was considered unworthy of receiving a direct vision of him. (*Abr.* 142–146)[356]

God Bestows the Principal Boons,
But the Secondary Ones Are Given by His Angels

Now those of whom we have been speaking pray to be nourished by the Logos of God. But Jacob, transcending even the Logos, says he is nourished by God himself. He speaks as follows: "The God to whom my fathers Abraham and Isaac were well pleasing, the God who nourishes me from my youth to this day, the Angel who redeemed me from all ills, bless these boys" (Gen. 48:15–16). How appropriate is his mode of expression! He considers God as the one who nourishes him, not his Logos; but the Angel, who is the Logos, as healer of ills. These words are fully in accord with reality. It is his view that He that Is should himself in his own person grant the principal boons, while his Angels and logoi give the secondary ones; and secondary are those that comprise release from ills. For this reason, I think, God grants health in its simplest sense, namely, that which is preceded by no illness in our bodies, by himself alone, but health that comes through escape from illness he bestows through medical art, ascribing to knowledge and practitioner the appearance of healing, although in reality it is he himself that heals both by these means and without them. It is the same with regard to the soul. The good things, the nourishment, God bestows by his own agency, but those that comprise release from ills through his Angels and logoi. (*LA* 3.177–178)[357]

The Treasuries of Evil Are in Ourselves

Accordingly no premeditated wrong committed with secret hostility and with guile may rightly be imputed to God, but rather to ourselves. For it is in ourselves, as I have indicated, that the treasuries of evil are located; with God are those of good only. Whosoever, therefore, takes refuge, that is, blames not himself but God for his sins,[358] let him be punished, by being deprived of the refuge uniquely reserved for the delivery and safety of suppliants, namely the altar. And rightly so. For the altar is filled with unblemished victims, that is souls innocent and purified; and it is a blemish that can hardly, if at all, be remedied, to declare that God is the cause also of evil. All men of such character are keenly concerned with love of self rather than love of God. Let them depart from the holy precincts, in order that, defiled and unpurified as they are, they may not behold even from afar the holy flame of the soul inextinguishably kindled and offered up to God in the entirety of its plenary power. (*Fug.* 79–81)[359]

Even That Which Is Unpleasant to Man
Serves the Preservation of the All

Joy is in fact the best and noblest of the rational emotions, by which the soul is thoroughly filled with cheerfulness, rejoicing in the Father and Creator of all, rejoicing also in all his actions, which are devoid of malice even when not conducive to his own pleasure, since they occur for a noble end and for the preservation of all things. For it is like the case of a physician who, in the course of grave and serious diseases, sometimes removes parts of the body while aiming at the health of the rest, and the pilot who, at the onset of a storm, jettisons cargo in his concern for the safety of those sailing with him. No blame attaches either to the physician for the disabling or to the pilot for the loss of cargo, but to the contrary, both are praised for looking to what is profitable rather than what is pleasant, and for having acted correctly. In the same way we must always hold universal nature in admiration and be content with every cosmic transaction, free as it is from voluntary malice, inquiring not whether anything has occurred that is unpleasant to us, but whether the universe is being guided and piloted safely like a well-ordered state. (*Praem.* 32–34)[360]

The Inferior Creation Necessary
in Order to Manifest the Superior One

Note that it is not the Lord who slays Er, but God. For it is not insofar as he rules and governs by the absolute power of his sovereignty that he destroys the body but insofar as he exercises Goodness and Kindness (for God is the name of the Goodness of the Primal Cause), so that you may know that he had made the inanimate things also not by exercising Authority but Goodness, through which he also made the animate creatures. For it was necessary with a view to the manifestation of the superior beings that there should be in existence an inferior creation also, by means of the same power, the Goodness of the Primal Cause.[361] (*LA* 3.73)

A Temporary Tyranny Is Not Without Its Uses

Furthermore, my friend, do not hold a temporary tyranny to be without its uses. For neither is punishment useless, and the infliction of penalties is either most profitable to the good or at least not less than profitable.[362] For this reason punishment is employed in all correctly drawn up laws, and those who drew them up are praised, for what the tyrant is to the people, that punishment is to the law. When, therefore, states are gripped by a dearth and scarcity of virtue, and overflowing folly abounds, God, desiring to sluice off the onrush of wickedness like the stream of a torrent, gives strength and power to men naturally fit to rule in order to purify our race. For vice cannot be purged without the presence of a savage soul. And just as states maintain public executions for the punishment of murderers, traitors, and temple robbers, not that they approve of the mentality of these persons, but taking account of the usefulness of their service, so the Guardian of the great city, this world, sets up tyrants like public executioners over the cities he sees swelling with violence, injustice, impiety, and all the other evils, in order that they may finally come to a halt and abate. Then too God deems it right to top it all by punishing the instruments of his purge as capital offenders, inasmuch as they served him with a soul encrusted with impurity and ruthless. For just as the force of fire after consuming the fuel supplied to it finally encroaches on itself,[363] in the same manner those who have seized dominion over the masses when they have destroyed the cities and depopulated them pay the penalty for all their deeds with their own destruction. And why should we wonder that God exorcises the evil that has spread through cities and countries and nations by having recourse to tyrants? For often without employing other ministers he accomplishes this by himself alone by bringing famine or pestilence or earthquake and all the other divine visitations whereby vast throngs of people perish daily, and a large portion of the world is devastated out of his concern for virtue. (*Prov.* 2.31–32 [37–41])

God's Providence Is Limited

When Providence is said to govern the universe, it does not mean that God is the cause of everything; certainly not of evil, of that which lies outside the course of nature, or of any of those things that are not at all beneficial. He is no more responsible than the councilmen, the rulers, and the judges of a virtuous city said to be governed by law.[364] They praise and honor those who are good, and reprimand and punish those who are evil as well as all who deviate from the commonly accepted order. Violence, rapine, and the like are not caused by the law but by the lawlessness of the inhabitants. The same may be said of the governing of the universe by Providence. It is not that God is responsible for everything; nay, the attributes of His nature are altogether good and benevolent. On the contrary, the unruly nature of matter and that of vice is a product of deviation and not caused by God. (*Prov.* 2.82)

Natural Evils Are Only Secondary Effects
of the Primary Works of Nature

Quakes, pestilences, thunderbolts, and similar phenomena are said to be divine visitations, though in reality they are nothing of the kind. For God is in no way the cause of evil, but these things are engendered by changes in the elements. They are not primary works of nature but consequent to her necessary works, and attendant on the Primary.[365] If persons of a more refined character share in the harm they cause, the blame must not be laid at the door of the divine administration, for in the first place it does not follow that if persons are considered good by us they really are so, for God's standards are more precise than all those employed by the human mind. Second, the divine forethought is content to oversee the most essential aspects of worldly affairs, just as in kingdoms and military commands there is a preoccupation with cities and masses of troops and not with some insignificant or obscure chance individual.[366] Some claim that just as at the execution of tyrants it is customary to slay their kinsfolk too, so that wrongdoings may be held in check by the magnitude of the punishment, similarly it is also normal in the course of pestilential diseases that some of the guiltless should perish so that in the future others learn to be self-controlled. Aside from this, it is inevitable that persons brought into a contaminated atmosphere contract the sickness, just as in a storm those aboard ship share the danger equally. (*Prov.* 2.102 [53–55])

The Usefulness of Venomous Reptiles

As for reptiles, the venomous species have not come into being by providential design but as a secondary effect, as I have already said above. For they are quickened when their inherent moisture grows warmer. Some are brought to life by putrefaction, as, for instance, worms by the putrefaction in food, and lice by that in perspiration. But all those that have their birth out of their proper substance by a seminal and primary natural process are reasonably ascribed to providence. Concerning the latter, too, I have heard two theories I should not wish to conceal, to the effect that they have been created for the benefit of man. One of them was as follows. Some have said that the venomous animals cooperate in many medicinal cures, and those who practice the medical art methodically by employing them scientifically where necessary have an abundance of antidotes to provide an unexpected cure for those critically ill.[367] And to this day we may see those who undertake the practice of medicine without indifference or carelessness making use of every one of these creatures in their primary preparation of medicinal compounds. The other theory belongs, as is fitting, not to medicine but to philosophy. It affirms that these creatures were prepared by God for the punishment of the errant just as generals and rulers have their whips and swords, and for this reason, while quiescent the rest of the time, they are stirred up to violence against the condemned, whom nature in her incorruptible tribunal has sentenced to death.[368] (*Prov.* 2.104 [59–61])

182

SELECTIONS

Greece May Be Relatively Poor Agriculturally But Intellectually It Is Exceedingly Rich

Greece must not be accused[369] of being a poor and unproductive land, for it too has deep soil. If the land of the barbarians surpasses it in fruitfulness, it holds the advantage to be sure in nourishment but is in turn inferior in the people it nourishes, for whose sake the nourishment is produced. For Greece alone truly produces men, she who gives birth to a heavenly plant[370] and a divine offshoot, perfect reasoning closely akin to scientific knowledge. The cause of this is that the mind is naturally sharpened by the subtlety of the air.[371] Wherefore Heraclitus[372] is on target when he says, "Where the land is dry the soul is wisest and best." One may find proof of this from the fact that the sober and frugal possess superior intelligence, while those who constantly gorge themselves with food and drink are most lacking in wisdom, since their reasoning is drowned by what comes in. It is for this reason that in the land of the barbarians, shoots and trunks grow very large due to their good nurture and the animals there are among the most prolific, but of intelligence it is most unproductive, because the uninterrupted and continual exhalations from the earth and water overpower it and prevent it from being quickened[373] by the air that is its source. (*Prov.* 2.109–110 [66–67]).

Why the Philosophers Were Not Inspired by the Muses

PHILO: You, who love wisdom, are still unaware that through such words you have charged the whole human race with folly. It certainly is not as you say. The fame of Hesiod and Homer has indeed reached the uttermost parts of the world, by virtue of the hidden meanings of their words. Many historians from their time on have admired them, and there are those who admire them down to our day. Even if there are instances where both seem to have erred, one should not blame them for these, but should praise them for the many things they expressed accurately, by which they became helpful in the conduct of life.[374] Similarly, it is fair to praise the cosmos without looking at the bad things on earth: gnats, ants, fleas, and the like; instead, one should contemplate the nature of the sky, the course of the sun, the waxing of the moon, the breadth of the sea, the flow of rivers, the vicissitudes of climate, the annual succession of the seasons, the birth

183

of animals, the peculiar features of plants, the bearing of fruit, and numerous other things each of which is performed with divine skill and surpassing beauty. Moreover, what you mentioned a short while ago is also not the case. There is nothing spoken blasphemously of gods. There is, however, a symbolic significance to physics, the mystery of which it is improper to reveal to those uninitiated. I would have demonstrated to you by way of example some structures showing how it is possible to establish a certain meaning according to rules. In accordance with these rules, however, it is forbidden to reveal mysteries to those not admitted into them.

What has been fabulously told about Hephaestus associates him with fire, that about Hera with the nature of air,[375] that about Hermes with the Logos,[376] and those about others with their respective realms following the theological method. And those poets whom you, a would-be praiser, were accusing a short while ago were only praising the Deity in a most appropriate way. Unless you accept the rules for allegorical meanings, you will be ranked with those who are very childish, who, because of their ignorance, will bypass an icon on wood by Apelles for a letter on a mite, admiring that which is worthy of disdain and rejecting that which is worthy of full acceptance.

Now, why is it that Empedocles, Parmenides, Xenophanes, and a host of their followers did not receive the inspiration of the Muses while theologizing? Because, noble sir, it is not for man to become god and somehow appropriate everything to himself; he is still human, belonging to the mortal race, a kin to error and fault. He should at least desire finally to attain the good things, without reaching to grab what does not lie within his natural constitution. It might have been better for them and for philosophy had they abandoned poetry and devoted themselves to dialectic and dialogue. This is what Plato, the greatest of all, did. When he devoted himself to poetry,[377] his ambitions were not fully realized. Consequently, he turned toward that direction whence nature was calling him and recorded the questions and answers of Socrates, the early Pythagorean philosophy, and the rest of his dialogues, the beauty and magnanimity of which surpass the grandeur of poetry. He also went on to reprimand those who attempt to write something without possessing poetical talent, saying:

> He who without divine madness comes to the door of the
> Muses, asserting that he will be a competent poet by art, is

unaccomplished, and the poetry (of the sane man) vanishes before that of the inspired madmen [*Phaedrus* 245A]. (*Prov.* 2.42–43)

C. MIRACLES

All Things Are Possible to God

When Moses heard these complaints, he pardoned them, but remembered the divine oracles, and having separated his mind and his speech, he simultaneously petitioned God secretly with the one to save them from their irremediable misfortunes, and with the other he encouraged and comforted those who were clamoring against him. "Do not lose heart," he said, "God's manner of defense is not like that of men. Why are you quick to trust in that alone which is probable and plausible? The God who brings aid has no need of armament. It is his special property to find a way where there is none. What is impossible to all of created being is possible to him alone,[378] ready to his hand." (*Mos.* 1.173–174)

Sweetening of the Bitter Waters

But God sent forth in advance his gracious power, and, opening the unsleeping eye of the suppliant's soul, showed him a tree, which he ordered him to lift up and cast into the springs. This may have been a tree formed by nature to exert a power hitherto[379] unknown, or possibly was created then for the first time for the use it was destined to serve. When the order was executed, the springs grew sweet and were changed into drinkable water, so that no one could even discern whether they were ever bitter, since no trace or residue remained to remind one of their former foulness. (*Mos.* 1.185–186)[380]

Trust in Moses Rather Than in What Is Probable and Plausible

Moses, thus rebuked, was not so much annoyed with the slanders brought against him as with the inconstancy of their judgment. For after experiencing innumerable events beyond their expectations and outside the ordinary course of things, they ought not to have been guided by anything probable or plausible,[381] but should have put their trust in him, since they had received the clearest proofs of his truthfulness in all things. (*Mos.* 1.196)

The Major Miracles Are Nature's Familiar and Unceasing Wonders

If anyone disbelieves these things, he neither knows God nor has ever sought to know him; for if he had he would instantly have perceived, and that with a firm apprehension, that these incredibly strange events are but child's play to God. He need but direct his gaze at things truly magnificent and deserving of his earnest concern, the creation of heaven and the revolutions of the planets and the fixed stars, the irradiation of light from the sun by day and from the moon by night, the establishment of the earth in the very center of the universe, the vast expanses of continents and islands and the innumerable species of animals and plants, and in addition the effusion of seas, the rushing waters of rivers, spring-fed and torrential, the streams of everflowing fountains, some gushing cold, others warm water, atmospheric changes of all kinds, the demarcations of the annual seasons and other beauties innumerable. Life would fail the man who wished to describe the particular parts or rather any one of the major divisions of the universe, even if he were endowed with length of life beyond that of all other men. But these things, though truly wondrous, are despised because they are familiar, whereas those that are unfamiliar, however insignificant they may be, through our love of novelty, we regard with amazement, yielding to exotic impressions.[382] (*Mos.* 1.212–213)

The Miracle of the Manna

Inspired and possessed, Moses utters the following words of prophecy: To mortals there is given the deep-soiled plain, which they cut into furrows and plough, and sow, and perform all the other tasks of husbandry, thus providing the annual fruits so as to enjoy an abundance of the necessaries of life. But God has subject to him not one portion of the universe but the whole world and its parts, to minister[383] as slaves to their master for every service that he wishes. He has now then decided that the air shall produce food instead of water,[384] for the earth too often brings rain. For what is the river of Egypt, annually rising like the flood-tide in its sallies when it waters the fields, but a downpour falling like a shower from below?[385] (*Mos.* 1.201–202)

A Prodigy of Nature

At that time, it is said, there occurred a great prodigy of nature that no one remembers ever having happened before. A cloud shaped like a huge pillar went before the multitude, by day radiating a sun-like brightness, but at night a flamelike blaze, so that they should not stray on their journey but follow the path of an inerrant guide. Perhaps indeed it was one of the subordinates of the great King, an unseen angel, a guide showing the way enveloped in the cloud, whom it is not permitted to see with the eyes of the body.[386] (*Mos.* 1.165–166)

XI. ETHICAL THEORY

A. FREEDOM AND DETERMINISM

The Mind's Passivity

The question may be asked, "Why, in view of the fact that to imitate God's acts is an act of piety, am I forbidden to plant a grove beside the altar, whereas God plants a pleasure ground?" For it says, "You shall not plant for yourself a grove; you shall not make for yourself any wood beside the altar of the Lord your God" (Deut. 16:21). What then are we to say? That it is fitting for God to plant and build virtues in the soul, but that mind is self-loving and godless which deems itself equal to God and supposes itself active though proven to be passive. When God sows and plants noble qualities in the soul, the mind that says "It is I that plant" is guilty of impiety. (*LA* 1.48–49)[387]

A Man's State of Mind Depends on God

"God cast," he says, "a trance upon Adam, and he slept" (Gen. 2.21). Quite correctly so: for the mind's trance and turning is its sleep, and it falls into a trance when it ceases to be occupied with the objects that belong to it; and when it is not active with these, it is asleep. Rightly does he say that he falls into a trance, that is, he is changed, not by himself, but by God who casts it on him, brings it on, and dispatches it. For if the change depended on us, I should make use of it whenever I wished, and when I had no such preference I should then continue unchanged. But as it is, the change is actually repugnant to me, and often, when wishing to conceive something proper, I am flooded with streams of improper thoughts; and conversely when taking up the notion of something base, I have cleansed myself of it with the water of wholesome reflection,[388] God having through his grace poured into my soul a sweet draught instead of the bitter one. (*LA* 2.31–32)

It is Characteristic of God to Act, But of Created Being to Suffer

What more hostile foe could there be for the soul than one who in his boastfulness claims for himself what is proper to God? For to act is the property of God, something which may not be ascribed to created beings, whereas it is the property of creation to suffer. He who recognizes this in advance as something fitting and necessary will readily endure what befalls him, however grievous it may be, but he who considers it an alien thing will be oppressed by an endless burden and suffer the penalty of Sisyphus, unable even to raise his head, subject to all the horrors that assault and torment him, and aggravating each of them through a spirit of submissive compliance, the malady of an ignoble and cowardly soul. Rather ought he to endure and put up face-to-face resistance, fortifying and steeling his resolution by his patience and endurance, the most forceful of virtues. (*Cher.* 77–78)

Rolling With the Punches of Fate

There are two modes of being clipped; one is characterized by reciprocity amid resistance,[389] the other by yielding submissively. A sheep or a hide or a "fleece" exerts no activity of its own but is passively clipped by another, but man cooperates, assumes a special position, and adapts himself, thus blending the active with the passive. It is the same with receiving blows. One kind is that which befalls an offending slave who is worthy of stripes or a free man who is stretched on the wheel for his knavery, or any of the inanimate things, such as stones, wood, gold, silver and whatever materials are beaten out or divided in a forge. The other kind is that which occurs to an athlete in the course of a boxing match or pancratium for the sake of the victor's crown. He shakes off the blows raining on him with either hand, and turning his neck this way and that, he guards against blows, or often he moves on tiptoe and raises himself to his full height, or, contrariwise tightening and constricting himself, he compels his adversary to launch his hands into empty space and engage in virtual shadowboxing. But the slave or the metal lies subdued and unresponsive, ready to suffer all that the one who handles it is minded to do.

This state of being we should never admit into our bodies, much less into our souls, but rather that condition which is characterized by reciprocity, for mortal kind must inevitably suffer. Let us not like effeminate men, invertebrate and unstrung, succumbing before the first shot is fired, our psychic energies drained, sink in utter exhaustion. Invigorated instead by the firm tension of our minds, let us have the strength to lighten and alleviate the onset of the impending terrors. (*Cher.* 79–82)

All Belongs to God Who Ultimately Takes Back His Own

Is my mind my own possession? That conjecturer of falsehoods, that producer of delusion, the deranged, the fatuous, and in frenzy, melancholy, and extreme senility revealed as witless. Is my expression my own possession, or my organs of speech? A slight malady is sufficient cause to incapacitate the tongue and sew up the mouth of the most eloquent, and the expectation of some horror terrifies vast throngs and renders them speechless. I am not even master of my senses, but more likely their slave, following wherever they lead, to colors, shapes, sounds, scents, flavors, and the other bodily things.

All this, I believe, has made it evident that we make use of the possessions of another, that neither glory, nor riches, nor honors, nor offices, nor all that relates to body or soul are our own, not even life itself. And if we recognize that we have them on loan we shall attend to them as God's possessions, assuming from the first that it is the master's custom to reclaim his own when he wishes. We shall thus lighten our distress at their removal.[390] But as it is, the masses believe all things to be their own and become violently disturbed at the absence or lack of anything. (*Cher.* 116–118)[391]

Guarding the Trust of Soul, Sense, and Speech by Dedicating Them to God

He [Abraham] is confident that he will be the inheritor of wisdom; he seeks only to know the way in which this will come about (Gen. 15:8). That it will come about, he has fully and firmly grasped by reason of the divine promises. Bestowing praise, then, on his yearning to learn, his teacher begins his exposition with an elementary introduction, in which the first and most essential words are "take for me" (Gen. 15:9). A brief phrase, but broad in significance for it reveals a great deal.

First it says, "You have no good of your own, but whatever you believe you have, Another has provided." Whence we infer that all things are the possession of him who gives, not of creation the beggar, which stretches out her hand to take. Second, "Even if you take, take not for yourself, but account what has been given as a loan on deposit and return it to him who entrusted and leased it to you, thus fitly and justly exchanging an ancient favor with a later one and repaying him who paid you in advance." For countless many are they who deny the sacred trusts and in their immeasurable greed consume as their own what belongs to Another. But you, my friend, try with all your might not merely to guard unharmed and unadulterated what you have received, but deem it worthy also of the utmost care, in order that he who entrusted it to you may find nothing to blame in your guardianship of it. Now the Creator of life has placed in your trust soul, speech, and sense, which are symbolically called in Sacred Scripture heifer, ram, and goat (Gen. 15:9). Some through self-love straightaway appropriate these, others store them up for restitution at the most opportune moment. The number of those who appropriate the trust is past counting, for which of us does not assert that soul and sense and speech are all his own possessions, thinking that to perceive, to speak, to apprehend, repose with him alone. But small is the number of those who truly guard the trust as something holy and inviolate. These have dedicated to God the triple offering of soul, sense, and speech, for they took them all not for themselves but for God; so that they naturally acknowledge that on him depend the activities of each, the reflections of the mind, the expressions of language, the impressions of sense. (*Her.* 101–108)[392]

Beginnings and Ends Belong to God

And as the beginnings are God's, so too are the ends. Moses testifies to this when he commands to set aside and promise the end to the Lord (Num. 31:28ff.). What happens in the world testifies to it too. How is that? The beginning of the plant is the seed, its end the fruit, and both are the work of nature, not of husbandry. Again in science, the beginning, as has been shown, is nature, but its limit is not within the purview of man. For no one is perfect in any of his pursuits, but perfections and consummations truly belong to One alone. And so it remains for us to be tossed about on the frontier between beginning and end, learning, teaching, tilling, and performing with the sweat of our brow, as it were, every other labor, so that creation too appears to be achieving something. More clearly indeed does Moses acknowledge that beginnings and ends belong to God when he says concerning the creation of the world, "In the beginning he made" (Gen. 1:1), and further on, "God finished the heaven and the earth" (Gen. 2:1–2). (*Her.* 120–122)[393]

It Is God Who Sows, but the Fruit of His Sowing
He Bestows as a Gift

The explanation of the mystery must then begin in this wise. Man and woman, the human male and female, in compliance with nature, join in sexual intimacy for the procreation of children. But virtues that are productive of innumerable perfections may not have mortal man for their lot, yet if they receive not the seed of generation from another they will never of themselves conceive. Who is it then who sows in them the good except the Father of things existent, the God who is unbegotten and is the begetter of all? It is he then who sows, but the fruit of his sowing, which is characteristically his, he presents as a gift. For God engenders nothing for himself, inasmuch as he is in need of nothing, but all for him who begs to receive.

I will furnish as trustworthy surety for my words Moses, the holiest of men. For he represents Sarah as conceiving at the time when God visited her in her solitude (Gen. 21:1), but she brings forth now

191

not to the Author of her visitation, but to him who yearns for wisdom, whose name is Abraham. His teaching is even clearer when he says in regard to Leah that God opened her womb (Gen. 29:31). Now to open the womb belongs to the husband, but when she conceived she brought forth not to God (for he alone is competent and absolutely self-sufficient for himself), but to him who submits to toil on behalf of the good, Jacob. Virtue thus receives the divine seed from the Primal Cause, but brings forth to one of her own lovers, who is preferred above all her wooers. Again Isaac the all-wise supplicated God, and through the power of him who was thus supplicated, Rebecca, who is Steadfastness, became pregnant (Gen. 25:21). And without supplication or entreaty did Moses, when he took Zipporah, the winged and lofty virtue, find her pregnant through no mortal act (Exod. 2:22). (*Cher.* 43–47).

Moses Banishes the Champions of Mind from the Holy Congregation

The champions of mind ascribe to it the leadership and sovereignty of human affairs, and affirm that it is capable of preserving the past through memory, to firmly apprehend the present, and to envisage and calculate the future by means of probable conjecture. It is mind[394] that sowed and planted the deep and fertile soil of mountain and plain, having invented agriculture so useful for life. It was mind that constructed a ship and by inventions of indescribable ingenuity converted the land-creature man into one that floats,[395] opened up on the sea branching lanes serving as highways to the harbors and coves of the different cities, and made the inhabitants of the mainland and the islanders known to one another, who would never have met if a vessel had not been built.[396] It is mind that discovered the mechanical and the so-called finer arts. It is mind that contrived and augmented and brought to their consummation letters and numbers and music and the whole cycle of school studies. It was mind too that gave birth to philosophy, the supreme good, and through each of its parts benefited human life, the logical to produce precision of expression, the ethical for the improvement of character, the physical to give knowledge of heaven and the universe. And they recount a multitude of other encomia in honor of the mind referring to what has already been mentioned, which they heap up and accumulate, but with which it is not now the time to trouble ourselves. (*Spec.* 1.334–336)

192

SELECTIONS

God Has Created Some Souls Faulty and Others Excellent

And if you examine the matter, my friend, you will find that God has created in the soul some natures that are censurable and blameworthy of themselves, and others in every way virtuous and praiseworthy, as is the case with plants and animals. Note that among the plants the Creator has made some for cultivation, useful and salutary, whereas others he has made wild and harmful and the causes of disease and destruction, and likewise with animals. (*LA* 3.75–76)

God Knows the Nature of His Handiwork while Yet in the Womb

Again, of Jacob and Esau while yet in the womb, God declares that the one is a ruler, leader, and master, but that Esau is a subject and a slave. For God, the Creator of life, knows well the pieces of his own workmanship before he has carved and consummated them, and the faculties they will enjoy at a later time, in brief their deeds and experiences. (*LA* 3.88)

Man Is God's Instrument

Leave these particular structures and contemplate the greatest of houses or cities, this universe. You will find that its cause is God, by whom it has come into being, its material the four elements, from which it was blended, its instrument the Logos of God, through which it was constructed, and the final cause of its fashioning is the goodness of the Craftsman. This discrimination of causes is made by truth lovers who long for true and sound knowledge. But those who assert that they possess something through God assume the Cause, that is the Creator, to be the instrument, and the instrument, that is the human mind, to be the cause.

Right reason would also censure Joseph when he said that *through* God would the clear meaning of the dreams be discovered (Gen. 40:8). He ought to have said that by him as cause the explanation and precise meaning of things obscure would fittingly take place. For we are the instruments,[397] now tensed now slackened, through which particular actions take place; and it is the Artificer who effects the percussion of both our bodily and psychic powers, he by whom all things are moved. (*Cher.* 127–128)

193

PHILO OF ALEXANDRIA

The Human Mind Alone Was Deemed Worthy of Freedom by God

For it is the mind alone that the Father who begat it deemed worthy of freedom, and loosening the bonds of necessity, allowed it to range free,[398] and of that power of volition which constitutes his most intimate and fitting possession presented it with such a portion as it was capable of receiving.[399] For the other living creatures in whose souls the mind, the element earmarked for liberty, has no place have been handed over to the service of man, as slaves to a master. But man who is possessed of spontaneous and self-determined judgment[400] and performs for the most part activities deliberately chosen is rightly blamed[401] for what he does with premeditation, praised when he acts correctly of his own will. In the others, the plants and animals, no praise is due if they are fruitful, nor blame if they fail to be productive: for they acquire their movements and changes in either direction through no deliberate choice or volition of their own. But the soul of man alone has received from God the faculty of voluntary movement, and in this way especially is assimilated to him, and thus being liberated, as far as possible, from that hard and grievous mistress Necessity may suitably be charged with guilt, in that it does not honor its Liberator. And therefore it will in all justice pay the inexorable penalty reserved for ungrateful freedmen.[402] (*Deus* 47–48)[403]

God Pulls the Strings of the Puppet Senses

"Dwell with him, child," says Rebecca, not forever, but "for a few days" (Gen. 27:44). This means, "Examine closely the country of the senses; know yourself and the parts of which you are constituted, what each one is, and for what it was made, and how it is its nature to function, and who it is, invisible, who invisibly sets the puppets in motion and pulls their strings,[404] whether it be the mind within you or the Mind of the Universe." (*Fug.* 46)[405]

Diseases of the Body Inconsequential If the Soul Is Healthy

Bodily diseases, provided the soul is healthy, do very little damage.[406] And the health of the soul consists in the proper blend of its faculties, spiritedness, lust, and reason, with the reason prevailing and reining in both the others like restive horses.[407] The distinctive name of this health is self-control, since it effects the preservation[408]

194

of one of our powers, that of wise thinking. For often when that power runs the risk of being overwhelmed by the tide of the passions, it prevents it from sinking below and draws it up and raises it aloft, vitalizing it and quickening it, and giving it a kind of immortality. (*Virt.* 13–14)

Astral Fatalism Rejected

(77) It is simply convenient for a man not to admit that there is a providence that does everything. Departing from sound thinking, from that personal freedom which is from her,[409] he admires the absence of Providence more than Providence. For he lets go the bit that Providence has fastened to his teeth, being impatient to receive from her a life of perfect wisdom. He ascribes all her acts to birth and chance, and maintains that nature itself throughout this whole universe is managed by the stars.[410]

(78) To me, these sophistical endeavors seem to be neither enlightened nor illuminating, but acts of great injustice and deceptions artfully designed to mislead whoever wishes to deprive himself of personal freedom; moreover, they are ostensible grounds for those who wish to find pretexts boldly to commit some related acts of injustice. . . .

(79) We ought to know before every activity, if we do not err in this, whether man's self-conduct is decisive or whether everything is to be ascribed to powers of nativity. We shall examine this with a very candid question: Would it be fair for city magistrates to pass the death sentence on evildoers had the evil they have committed not been in their power but due to the shifting of the stars in the position of aggression, which would not allow them to control their own lives when compelled by the tyrannical power of the stars?

(80) What kind of justice will that be, which hands over to punishment those who sin against their will, who have committed their acts involuntarily, having no control over their conduct? Which law can condemn a soul when it is not in control of the will that affects the choice of evil acts? How can a soul at the time of birth oppose being conducted against its will? . . .

(81) If the powers of nativity war against the will of everyone, how would one censure the man who is forcibly drawn to evil by celestial stars? Not even God himself would be able to enforce a law, for that person would have this to say even to God: "Release my soul

from the powers of nativity and I will observe the law." Which patricide and matricide would be justly condemned if he were led by stars to kill his parents against his will? Or who would be able to censure this adulterous woman who was forced by stars into illicit union? . . .

(82) Now, if everything is dispensed at birth, then laws, piety, justice, and the verdicts of judges should be abrogated, since man's will is not free when he does what has been predestined for him. For when the power of self-conduct is denied and every act is attributed to powers of nativity, there will be no glory in virtue, no besetment of sin, no courage, no sagacity to speak of—everything being done involuntarily. The prison sentences by judges would seem to be in vain, the courthouses and tribunals unfair. For why should we ever condemn to death someone whose offense is not of his own doing? And would not holding the wicked in chains be unnecessary when they are held unto wickedness by the firm chains of the supernal powers of nativity?

(83) But since judges can quell the wickedness of evildoers through fear, the powers of nativity cannot rule over all. For when evildoers are fearful of torments, they choose a humble and peaceful life, being terrified by the fear of death. . . . They are capable of determining their own conduct by turning in the direction each of them wishes; for, in essence, freedom is the ability to do whatever one wills.

(84) Did not also the Jews choose on their own the law of circumcision? This they did not forsake afterwards but transmitted it to their children. Neither powers of nativity nor cycles of stars could force them to do away with it, since the laws govern their minds and not the powers of nativity. Moreover, they cease from work on the seventh day, which they call the Sabbath, and abstain from meats and other things not allowed by the law. It could not be said that they are all under the self-same powers of nativity, under whose forceful compulsion they do that which God has commanded to Moses. Now, since Jews bear offspring at various moments, hours, and days, and their life-style, discipline, and teachings of the law are alike, how could it be said that all men are subject to powers of nativity?

(86) What powers of nativity taught the Egyptians to devote themselves to a defiled form of worship? Does Egypt alone have such stars so that only the Egyptians would have such a custom? Since their births occur on various days and hours, why would they not

conduct themselves differently? Yet those with different days and hours happen to have similar conduct and actions. Did they receive the same amount of wisdom again and again at the same time?

(87) When sudden defeat shatters a city during a war, do I have to say that all were under the powers of nativity?[411] And when a pestilence that is not destined for all strikes someone, how does it happen that a countless multitude is plagued at the same time? Where is the unerring designation of the powers of nativity? And who is able to apprehend the fixation of man's birth, the obscurity of insemination? For the time when childbirth is determined—the precise moment required by those who are called astrologers—cannot be stated accurately. Yet those who claim to be astrologers rely on this evidence. They even claim to determine from the latter stages of birth the time of the first insemination. . . .[412]

(88) In order that the free reason for each individual may not fall under the bondage of the powers of nativity, it is necessary to consider these things and to instruct with virtuous words, regarding instruction to be good. Also, considering with a diligent spirit the findings of our quest, we should not allow the movements of the stars to haunt mankind. Now, the so-called zodiacal circle itself is derived from Providence, as we implied in the preceding discussions. Providence awes by means of these stars; these created beings do her biddings, these recipients which take the cause of their genesis from another. Providence is the cause of all in all. She is the one of whom existence and being are born; in fact, those that are created acknowledge the Creator.[413] (*Prov.* 1.77–84, 86–88)[414]

B. NATURAL LAW

The World Is in Harmony with the Law and the Law with the World

Among other lawgivers, some have drawn up a code naked and unembellished[415] of that which is held right among their people, while others, enveloping their thought with a mass of superfluous bombast, have befuddled the masses by cloaking the truth behind a mask of mythical fictions. But Moses, bypassing both these approaches, the one as unreflective, unpainstaking, and unphilosophical, the other as mendacious and full of jugglery, made the exordium to his laws most beautiful and most majestic. He did not preface his work by abruptly stating what ought or ought not to be done, and, on the other hand, in view of the necessity of molding in advance the minds of those who were to live under the laws, he refrained from fabricating myths or assenting to those framed by others. His exordium is, as I have said, most admirable, since it encompassed the creation of the world, in order to indicate that the world and the Law are in mutual accord, and that a man who is law abiding is thereby immediately constituted a world citizen,[416] guiding his actions aright according to nature's intent, in conformity with which the entire universe is administered. (*Op.* 1–3)[417]

Living According to Nature, the Wise Man's Actions Are Nothing but the Words of God

We are told next that "Abraham went forth as the Lord had spoken to him" (Gen. 12:4). This is the end celebrated by the best philosophers, to live in agreement with nature; and it is attained whenever the mind, having entered on the path of virtue, treads the track of right reason and follows God, mindful of his ordinances, and always and everywhere confirming them all both by word and deed. For "he went forth as the Lord spoke to him": The meaning of this is that as God speaks—and he speaks in a manner most admirable and praiseworthy—so the man of virtue does everything, blamelessly making straight his life-path, so that the actions of the sage differ in no way from the Divine words. Elsewhere, in any case, he says "Abraham" did[418] "all my law" (Gen. 26:5): "law" being evidently nothing else than the Divine Logos commanding what we ought to do and forbidding what we should not do, as Moses attests to by saying "he received a law from his words" (Deut. 33:3f.). If, then, the law is a Divine Logos, and the man of virtue does the law, then surely he does the Logos, so that, as I said, the Divine logoi are the wise man's actions. (*Mig.* 127–130)

The Patriarchs Were Living Laws

Since it is necessary to examine the laws in a regular and consistent sequence, we shall postpone the particular laws, which are, so to speak, copies,[419] and examine first those that are more general and are, as it were, models of these copies. These are such men as lived nobly and blamelessly, whose virtues stand durably recorded in the most Holy Scriptures, not only with the object of praising them, but also for the sake of exhorting their readers and leading them to a like zeal; for these men have been animate and rational laws, and Moses has exalted them for two reasons. First, he wished to show that the laws laid down are not inconsistent with nature; second, that it is no laborious task to live in accordance with the established laws, since the early generations before any of the particular laws were written down at all lived according to the unwritten law with complete ease, so that one might fittingly say that the enacted laws are nothing else than memorials of the life of the ancients, detailing in antiquarian style the words and deeds they adopted. For they were not pupils or disciples of others, nor were they instructed by tutors what to say or do: They were self-taught and were laws unto themselves, and clinging fondly to conformity with nature, and assuming nature itself to be, as indeed it is, the most venerable of statutes, their whole life was well ordered. They never committed any blameworthy action voluntarily, and with regard to their chance errors they loudly implored God and propitiated him with prayers and supplications so as to secure participation in a perfect life successful in both spheres of action, both the premeditated and the involuntary. (*Abr.* 2–6)[420]

The World Is a Megalopolis with a Single Law

After the literal interpretation it is fitting that we add the underlying meaning, for roughly all or most of the lawbook is an allegory. The type of character here under discussion is called by the Hebrews "Joseph," but by the Greeks "addition of a lord," a most accurate designation and quite appropriate for the thing being indicated, for polity as found among the various peoples is an addition to nature,[421] which possesses a universal lordship. For this world is the Megalopolis or "great city,"[422] and it enjoys a single polity and single law, and this is the Logos of nature, enjoining what should be done and forbidding what should not be done. But your local cities are unlimited in number and live under diverse polities and laws by no means identical, for different cities have different customs and usages that are extra inventions and additions. The cause of this is the absence of mingling and community not only of Greeks with barbarians or barbarians with Greeks but also within each individual group, among elements of the same stock. And then, it seems, they dream up causes for this that are unjustifiable, such as undesirable seasons, infertility, poverty of soil, the lay of the land, whether it is maritime or inland or whether it is on an island or on the mainland and the like. Of the true cause they are silent, and that is their greed and mutual distrust, on which account they are unsatisfied with the laws of nature, and bestow the name of law on that which appears to be of common benefit to like-minded masses of people. Particular polities are therefore reasonably regarded rather as additions to the single polity of nature, for the laws of the various states are additions to the right reason of nature, and the politician is an addition to the man who lives according to nature. (*Jos.* 28–31)

The Lifelong Festival of Those Who Follow Nature

The law records that every day is a festival,[423] accommodating itself to the blameless life, that of men[424] who follow nature and her ordinances. And if only the vices had not prevailed and lorded it over our reflections concerning what is profitable and ejected them from each of our souls—if instead the forces of the virtues had remained altogether invincible, the time from birth to death would be one continuous feast, and houses and cities enjoying security and peace would, in all tranquillity, have been full of every good thing. As it is, the excesses and mutual attacks that men and women alike contrive against themselves and each other have cut off the continuity of this cheerful contentment. (*Spec.* 2.42–43)

Those Who Mate with Women of Proven Sterility
Are the Enemies of Nature

They too must be reproached who plough a hard and stony land. And who should they be but those who unite with barren women? For on the prowl for licentious pleasure, like the most lustful of men they destroy the generative seeds with deliberate intent.[425] For what other reason do they have such women plighted to them? It cannot be in the hope of offspring, a hope they know must inevitably fail of accomplishment; it can only be through exceeding frenzy and an incontinence that is incurable. Those who marry maidens in ignorance at the time of their fitness or unfitness for successful delivery of children, and, when they learn much later on through their childlessness that they are barren, do not send them away, deserve our pardon, for they are vanquished by the imperious constraint of intimacy and are incapable of dissolving the ancient love charms imprinted in their souls through long companionship.[426] But those who woo women whose sterility has already been proved with other husbands, and do but copulate like pigs or goats, ought to be recorded in the lists of the impious as adversaries of God. For while God in his love for all living things and for mankind is painstakingly diligent to effect the preservation and permanence of all species, those who in the very sowing contrive to extinguish the seed are confessedly the enemies of nature. (*Spec.* 3.34–36)[427]

Those Who Practice Infanticide
Overthrow the Ordinances of Nature

Read this law, you good and highly prized parents, and hide your faces for shame, you who are ever athirst for the blood of your children, who wickedly lie in wait for those newly brought forth with a view to exposing them,[428] you implacable enemies of the whole human race. To whom will you show favor, you the murderers of your own children, who do your part to lay waste cities and begin the destruction with your closest kin, who overthrow the ordinances of nature and destroy all that she constructs, who in the brutality of your savage and ferocious souls fortify destruction against generation and death against life? Do you not see that our legislator, who excels in every way, was diligent to provide that not even the offspring of irrational animals should be separated from their mother so long as they are being suckled? Even more for your sake, good friends, was this rule made, in order that, if not by nature then at least through instruction, you may learn love of him. Nature furnished such abundance in the most suitable places, where those who are in need may easily enjoy it, while the lawgiver, exercising great forethought, keeps watch that none thwart the bountiful and salutary gifts of God. (*Virt.* 131–133)

Right Reason Is an Infallible Law
Imprinted on the Mind by Nature

Right reason is an infallible law imprinted not by this or that individual, the perishable work of a mortal, nor on papyrus or stone slabs, a thing inanimate on materials inanimate,[429] but by immortal

201

nature on the immortal mind, never to perish.[430] One may accordingly be astonished at the short-sightedness of those who fail to discern
the evident characteristics of things, and declare that the laws of Solon and Lycurgus, inasmuch as they govern and rule the citizens who
obey their authority, are all-sufficient to secure liberty for Athens
and Sparta, the greatest of republics, but that right reason, the fountainhead of all other law, is incapable of imparting liberty to the wise
who obey all that it prescribes or forbids. (*Prob.* 46–47)

C. CONSCIENCE

The "Man" Dwelling in the Human Soul Is the Real Man

Some say that the proper name of the man who found Joseph
wandering on the plain has not been indicated (Gen. 37:15), and in
this they are themselves in a way in error through their inability to
see clearly the right path of things. For had they not suffered the in-
capacitation of the eye of their soul, they would have recognized that
the most characteristic and most accurate name of the true man is
simply "man," the most appropriate designation of a mind possessing
reason and articulate expression. This "man" dwelling in the soul of
each of us is found now as ruler and king, now as judge and umpire
of life's contests. Sometimes he plays the role of witness or accuser,
and convicts us invisibly from within, not allowing us even to open
our mouth, but seizing and curbing it with the reins of conscience he
checks the tongue's self-willed and rebellious course. This cross-ex-
aminer inquired of the soul when he saw it wandering, "What are
you seeking?" (Gen. 37:15). (*Det.* 22–24)[431]

The Scrutinizer Enters Us like a Pure Beam of Light

So long, indeed, as the divine Logos has not come into our soul
as into some home, all its acts are free from guilt, for the guardian
or father or teacher or whatever else we must call the priest, by
whom alone it can be admonished and made wise, is far away. We
must pardon those who err through ignorance, since they are inexperienced in what ought to be done. For they do not even apprehend
their deeds as errors, and there are times when they believe that their
greatest stumblings constitute virtuous actions. But when the Scru-
tinizer, the true priest, enters us like a light beam[432] utterly pure, we

then discover the tainted intentions stored up in our soul and the guilty and censurable actions to which we put our hands in ignorance of what is to our benefit. (*Deus* 134–135)[433]

Even the Most Wicked Suffer Pangs of Conscience

For all, however wicked, receive conceptions to the effect that their unjust acts will not escape God's notice and that they cannot completely evade the penalty. For how do they know that they will be scattered? They do clearly say "Before we are dispersed" (Gen. 11:4). But it is the conscience within that convicts them and pricks them in spite of their vehement pursuit of godlessness, thus inducing them all unwilling to concede that all human affairs are overseen by a superior essence and that awaiting them is justice, an impartial avenger, who detests the unjust actions of the impious and the arguments that advocate them. (*Conf.* 120–121)

The Logos Enters the Soul and Extracts a Confession of Wickedness

What is the meaning of the words "God went in to Abimelech in his sleep at night, and said, Behold, you shall die because of the woman whom you did take, and she is living with a man"? (Gen. 20:3).

The literal meaning is clearly signified. But as for the deeper meaning, it presents something like the following. The foolish man who violently insists that he possesses virtue is convicted by the divine Logos, which enters his soul and examines and searches him to confess that this is the possession of another man and not his. And most excellently is it written, "in his sleep at night." For the foolish soul spends its life carefully shut up in the darkness and night and deep sleep, and it has no part at all in wakefulness. (*QG* 4.62)

D. THE ROAD TO WISDOM

The Three Constituents of Natural Ability

The man whom God receives, he deems worthy of three qualities, which constitute being naturally well endowed, quickness of mind, persistence, power of memory. Quickness of mind is his place-ment in the garden, persistence is his practice of noble deeds, the power of memory his guarding and keeping in mind of the holy pre-cepts. But the "molded" mind neither recalls nor performs that which is noble, but is only quick to apprehend it. Accordingly, after being placed in the garden, he presently runs off and is cast out. (*LA* 1.55)

Let Us Make Our Souls a Fit Dwelling for God

Since he invisibly enters this region that constitutes the soul, let us render that place as beautiful as we may, to be a fit dwelling of God. Otherwise he will remove unnoticed into some other home, which appears to him to have been better constructed. For if when we are about to entertain kings, we make our own houses brighter, neglecting no adornment, but use all freely and abundantly, having as our aim that their lodging be most pleasant and possess the dignity that befits them, what sort of house must be prepared for God, the King of Kings, the Ruler of all, who in his gentleness and his love for man has deigned to visit created being and descend from the extrem-ities of heaven to the uttermost bounds of the earth in order to exhibit his goodness to our race? Shall it be of stone or wood? Perish the thought, its very utterance is defiling. For not even if the entire earth, undergoing a sudden change, should turn to gold or something more precious than gold, and all be then expended on the arts of craftsmen in the construction of colonnades, porticos, chambers, vestibules, and temples, would there be a place for his feet to tread. One home alone is worthy, a soul fit to receive him. If we were to say, then, that the invisible soul is the earthly dwelling of the invisible God, we should be speaking justly and rightly.

And in order that the house be firm and exceedingly beautiful, let natural excellence and instruction be laid down as its foundations, and let virtues and noble actions be erected on them, and let its finery be the acquisition of the preliminary learning of the schools. For from natural excellence come quickness of mind, tenacity, and mem-ory; from instruction, readiness to learn and diligence. They are like roots of a tree that is going to bring forth cultivated fruits, and with-out them it is impossible for the mind to be brought to perfection. From the virtues and accompanying good actions come the solidity and stability of a secure structure, and one who is determined to separate and banish the soul from the good grows exhausted in the face of such resolute force. From the study of the preliminary school learning come the things that serve as ornaments of the soul, attached to it as to a home.

For as stuccos, paintings, tablets, and arrangements of precious stones, with which not only walls but also pavements are adorned, as well as many other like things, contribute nothing to the strength of the building but only procure pleasure for its occupants, so does the school learning adorn the entire house of the soul. Grammar or literature investigates poetic composition and pursues the study of the achievements of old. Geometry gives us proportional equality and also heals by means of fine music with its rhythm, meter, and melody all that within us is unrhythmical, disproportionate, and dissonant. Rhetoric scrutinizes that which is particularly forceful in each subject, and adapting to it the expression befitting it, provides us with vehemence, strong expressions of emotion, and, contrariwise, relaxation and pleasure, and withal fluency and skillful ease in use of tongue and organs of speech.

If such a dwelling be constructed amid our mortal race, all human affairs will be filled with high hopes, in expectation of the descent of the divine powers. They will come bringing with them laws and ordinances from heaven for the purposes of sanctification and purification, in accordance with their father's bidding. Then enjoying a common life and board with virtue-loving souls, they sow within them the happy lineage, just as they gave to wise Abraham in return for their lodging with him that most perfect boon, Isaac. The purified mind rejoices in nothing more than in confessing that it has for its master the Ruler of all. For to be the slave of God is man's highest boast, more precious not only than liberty, but than wealth and office and all that mortal kind embraces. (*Cher.* 98–105)[434]

When God Induces Self-Taught Wisdom,
Knowledge That Comes from Teaching Must Be Terminated

It is undoubtedly profitable, if not for the acquisition of perfect virtue, at least for the life of civic virtue, to nurture the mind on ancient and primeval notions and investigate the hoary tradition of noble deeds that historians and the whole clan of poets have handed down as a memorial to their own and future generations. But when unforeseen and unhoped for, a sudden beam of self-taught wisdom has shone on us, when it has opened the closed eye of the soul and made us seers rather than hearers of knowledge, and set within our minds the swiftest of senses, sight, in place of the more sluggish sense of hearing, then it is to no purpose to further exercise the ear with words.[435] And so we read, "You shall eat the old and very old,[436] but also bring forth the old to make room for the new" (Lev. 26:10), which signifies the following. We must not disown any learning made venerable through time, but attempt to read the writings of the sages and to attend to the maxims and narratives of those who treat of antiquities and ever fondly inquire about the men and deeds of old, for it is exceedingly pleasant to be ignorant of nothing. But when God brings forth young shoots of self-taught wisdom in the soul, we must immediately terminate and destroy the knowledge that comes from teaching, which even of itself retires and slips out of sight. God's pupil, disciple, or apprentice, or whatever those who label things ought to call him, can no longer suffer the guidance of men. (*Sacr.* 78–79)

It Is a Grievous Task to Oppose Nature,
But Labor on Behalf of Virtue Is Always Beneficial

Knowling full well that without toil and care we may not obtain male offspring, Moses says next: "All that opens the womb of an ass, you shall exchange for a sheep" (Exod. 13:13). This is equivalent to saying exchange all toil for progress. For the ass is the symbol of toil—for he is a patient beast—and the sheep of progress, as the very name indicates.[437] Come then to the practice of the arts and professions and whatever else can be taught not disdainfully or frivolously but with full attentiveness, with your mind prepared steadfastly to submit to every form of drudgery, and endeavor not to be bound by fruitless toil, but to bring your labor to its most brilliant realization and obtain progress and improvement. For toil is to be borne for the sake of progress. But if, after all, though you submit to laborious drudgery, your nature does not improve in the least but opposes the advances resulting from progress, turn aside from it and remain undisturbed. It is a grievous task to oppose nature. And for this reason he adds "if you do not exchange it, you shall redeem it" (Exod. 13:13): that is, if you cannot gain progress in exchange for your labor, abandon the labor as well, for the word "redeem" suggests such a mean-

ing, namely to liberate your soul from a care that is endless and
fruitless.

But these words do not concern the virtues but only the intermediate arts and any necessary ones that are exercised for the care of
the body and the abundance of external goods. For labor undertaken
on behalf of perfect goods and virtues, even if it fail of its end, is of
itself sufficient to benefit from the first those exercised in it, whereas
those things that lie outside virtue, if their object is not reached, are
entirely profitless. It is just as it is with animals; if you remove the
head, all else is lost. And the head of actions is their end. They live
as long as the head is in some way accommodated, but if you wish to
cut it off or amputate it, they die. So athletes who cannot carry off
the prize of victory, but are always defeated, should retire. Merchants
or shipowners who experience continuous disasters at sea should
change their occupation and remain undisturbed. Those who have
pursued the intermediate arts, but because of their unmalleable nature have been incapable of absorbing any knowledge, deserve praise
if they lay them aside. For these things are not practiced for the sake
of the exercise, but for the object at which they aim. If then nature
stands in the way of better progress, let us not vainly resist her, but
if she cooperates with us, let us render homage to God with the first-
lings and honors that are the ransom of our souls, for they deliver it
from brutal masters and vindicate its freedom. (*Sacr.* 112–117)[438]

Jacob Prays That the Nation of Reason
Should Possess Natural Excellence

All oral instruction and learning is built on a nature receptive of
education as on a foundation layed down in advance; if nature is not
there to begin with all is useless. For those who are not naturally gift-
ed would seem to differ not at all from an oak or mute stone, since
nothing can adhere or fit into them, but all glances off and rebounds
as from a solid substance. As for the souls of the naturally endowed,
one can see them as duly tempered like smooth wax, neither too solid
nor too soft, readily receiving all that is heard and seen, itself taking
on perfect impressions of the forms which are clear copies preserved
by memory. It was thus necessary for him [Jacob] to pray that the nation of reason should possess natural excellence free from disease and
death (Deut. 33:6). For the life of virtue, which is life in its truest
form, is shared by few, and these are not of the common herd, none

of whom have a part in the true life, but only those, if there are such, to whom it is granted to flee human concerns and to live to God alone. (*Mut.* 211–213)[439]

Philosophy or God's Word Is the Royal Road to the Divine

Moses thinks that one should incline neither to the right nor to the left nor to any part of earthly Edom at all, but to pass by along the middle road, which he most properly calls the royal road (Num. 20:17); for since God is the first and sole King of the universe, the road leading to him, being a King's road, is also rightly called royal. This road you must hold to be philosophy, not that which is pursued by the contemporary crowd of Sophists, who having practiced the arts of speech in opposition to the truth called their sophistry wisdom, assigning a divine title to a miserable work. It is rather the philosophy that the ancient band of devotees achieved with great effort, turning aside from the bland charms of pleasure, elegantly and rigorously engaged in the study of the good.

This royal road then, which we have said to be true and authentic philosophy, is called by the Law the utterance and word of God.[440] For it is written, "You shall not turn away from the word which I command you this day to the right or to the left" (Deut. 28:14). Thus it is clearly demonstrated that the word of God is identical with the royal road, if, namely, he exhorts us to turn away neither from the word of God nor the royal way, as being synonymous, but with upright mind to advance on the straightforward path, a central roadway. (*Post.* 101–102)[441]

Knowledge Is Infinite

For the wealth of God's wisdom is unbounded and puts forth new shoots after the old so as never to cease growing young again and be flourishing. Wherefore all who imagine that they have arrived at the limit of any science are utterly simpleminded; for that which appeared to be near is very distant from its end, for no one was ever born who attained perfection in any subject of study, but so far falls short of it as a very young lad just beginning to learn compared with a master already grown grey both as to his age and his art. (*Post.* 151–152)

SELECTIONS

Similes Employed in the Threefold Division of Philosophy

We are told that the ancients likened philosophical discussion with its threefold division[442] to a field, comparing the part dealing with nature to trees and plants; the ethical part to fruits, for the sake of which the plants exist; and the logical division to an encircling fence. For just as the encompassing wall protects the fruit and plants in the field, holding off those wishing mischievously to steal in for the sake of pillage, in the same manner, the logical part of philosophy is the surest safeguard of those other two parts, the ethical and the physical. For when it explains doubtful and ambiguous expressions and dissolves arguments founded on ingenious quibbles, and employing absolutely lucid expression and indubitable demonstrations destroys seductive guile, that greatest snare of the soul and so noxious to it, it renders the mind like smooth wax ready to receive impressions flawless and trustworthy from the natural and moral sciences. (*Agr.* 14–16)[443]

The Perfect Man and the Man Making Progress

Moses then describes the perfect man as neither God nor man, but as I have already said, on the frontier between uncreated and perishable being. The man who is advancing, on the other hand, he places between the living and the dead, calling those living who cohabit with wisdom, and dead those who rejoice in folly, for it is said of Aaron that "he stood between the dead and the living, and the destruction abated" (Num. 16:48). For the man who is advancing is counted neither among those dead to the life of virtue, since he possesses a desire and zeal for the noble, nor among those who live in supreme and perfect happiness, for he still falls short of the consummation, but touches on both. And therefore he properly adds the words "the destruction abated," not "ceased." For with the perfect the things that crush and break down and shatter the soul do cease, but among those making progress they diminish, being as it were merely checked and constricted. (*Somn.* 2.234–236)

Different Stages of Moral Development

It beseems all these, the beginners, those advancing, and those who have attained perfection, to live without rivalry and not to en-

209

gage in war with the sophists, who are in constant and bickering disarray in their attempt to adulterate the truth, for the truth is dear to
peace, and peace is hostile to them. If unprofessional laymen engage
in this contest with seasoned warriors, they will be utterly vanquished; the beginner, through lack of experience, the man who is advancing, because he is imperfect, the man who has attained
perfection, bacause he is still unpracticed in virtue. Just as plaster
must firmly set and acquire solidity, so must the souls of those who
have been perfected become more firmly etablished, strengthened by
continuous practice and uninterrupted exercise. Those who have not
attained these qualities are said by the philosophers to be sages un-
conscious of their wisdom.[444] For they say that it is impossible for
those who have pushed on to the edge of wisdom and have just first
come into contact with its borders to be conscious of their own per-
fecting, that both cannot occur at the same time, the arrival at the
goal and the apprehension of the arrival, but that ignorance must
form a frontier between the two, not that ignorance which is far removed from knowledge, but that which is close by and next door to
it. It will, then, be the task of him who possesses apprehension and
understanding and is fully aware of his own powers to war with the
strife-loving cohort of sophists; for there is every expectation that
such a one will achieve victory. But for him whose vision is veiled by
the darkness of ignorance, the light of knowledge being as yet incapable of shining forth, it is safe to remain at home, that is, not to come
forward to the contest concerning things he has not thoroughly apprehended, but to be tranquil and calm. (*Agr.* 159–162)[445]

Many On the Verge of Attaining Piety
Are Suddenly Thrust Backward

There are others who, hoisting every sail of piety, have endeavored to make a swift voyage, and to put in at her harbor, and then,
when they were not far off, but on the verge of bringing their ship
to port, a sudden squall has burst upon them, and swelling the sails
of their forward-moving vessel, has thrust it into reverse, shearing
away much of the gear that assists in maintaining good navigation.
No one would blame these men for being still at sea, for their tardi-
ness was involuntary and occurred though they were making all
haste. Who, then, resembles these men, but he who vowed the so-
called "great vow"? [446] For he says: "If someone die suddenly beside

him, the head of his vow shall straightway be defiled, and he shall shave it." Then, after a few more words, he adds, "The former days shall be void, because the head of his vow was defiled" (Num. 6:9, 12). The involuntary nature of the soul's turning is shown by both of the words used, "sudden" and "straightway," for deliberate errors require time for planning the where and when and how of their accomplishment, whereas unintentional errors swoop down on us suddenly, thoughtlessly, and, if one may say so, timelessly. For it is difficult for those who, like runners, start on the path to piety to maintain a straight course without stumbling and without pausing for breath; for innumerable are the hindrances that impede all created being. The first requirement, then, which is the one and only thing that constitutes acting well, is never to lay hold of any deliberate wrongdoing and to have the strength to thrust aside the enormous host of voluntary offenses;[447] the second, not to linger in the practice of many involuntary offenses, nor to do so over a long period of time.

Admirably did he say that the days of the involuntary turning were void, not only because to err is void of reason, but also because it is impossible to give an account of involuntary errors. It is rare, then, if God grant anyone to run life's course from beginning to end without slackening or slipping, and to fly over either sort of transgressions, voluntary and involuntary, with a violent impetus of the swiftest velocity. (*Agr.* 174–180)

Listening with the Soul

There are indeed some for whom it is fitting to hear but not to speak, in whose regard it is said, "Be silent and hear" (Deut. 27:9). An excellent precept! For ignorance is exceedingly rash and garrulous; and its first remedy is silence, the second to give its attention to those who present something worth hearing. Yet let no one hold that this is the sole significance of the words "be silent and hear"; they prescribe something else of greater importance. They exhort us not only to be silent with the tongue and to hear with the ears, but to experience both of these also with the soul. For many who come to hear a discourse have not come with their minds, but wander abroad recounting to themselves innumerable thoughts on innumerable subjects, on their families, outsiders, matters private and public, which it would be sensible for them momentarily to forget. All these, so to speak, are successively enumerated, and because of the great murmur within they are unable to listen to the speaker. The latter discourses as in an audience not of humans, but of lifeless statues, who have ears but no hearing within them. (*Her.* 10–12)

Three Kinds of Life

There are three sorts of life, one God-directed, another creation-directed, another lying between these two, a mixture of both. The God-directed life has never come down to us, nor is it concerned with bodily constraints. The creation-directed life has not ascended at all nor has sought to ascend, but lurks in the recesses of Hades[448] and rejoices in a life that is no life. The mixed life is that which, frequently drawn by a higher order, is inspired and possessed, but often drawn in a contrary direction turns round in its track. (*Her.* 45–46).[449]

Preliminary Mating with Wisdom's Handmaiden, the Learning of the Schools

"Sarah the wife of Abraham was not bearing him children. Now she had an Egyptian maidservant named Hagar. And Sarah said to Abraham, 'Behold the Lord has closed me that I should not bear. Go in unto my maid that you may beget children from her' " (Gen. 16:1, 2). Sarah's name translated signifies "my sovereignty," and the wisdom in me, the self-control in me, the individual justice and each of the other virtues that belong only to me, are my sovereignty alone.[450] That sovereignty has charge over me and rules me who have resolved to obey her, since she is by nature a queen.

This power Moses quite paradoxically represents both as barren and as exceedingly prolific, since he acknowledges that from her was produced the most populous of nations. For virtue is truly sterile in respect of all that is bad, whereas she is so prolific of the virtues as not to require the art of midwifery, for she bears before the midwife comes. Animals and plants bear the fruit proper to them only after long intervals, once or twice at most in the year, in accordance with the number established for each by nature and harmonized with the annual seasons. But virtue, knowing no such intervals, ever bears unceasingly and uninterruptedly, without time pause,[451] not infants, to be sure, but good words, blameless plans, and praiseworthy acts.[452]

But as wealth that one cannot use does not benefit its possessor, so it is with wisdom's fertility, if she does not bear offspring that is profitable for ourselves. Some she judges quite worthy of living with her, but others do not appear to her to have attained the maturity[453] to submit to her commendable and moderate domesticity. To these she permits the execution of the preliminaries[454] of marriage and affords the hope of celebrating the full marriage rite in the future.

So Sarah, the virtue ruling my soul, engendered, but did not engender for me. For in my youthfulness I was not yet able to receive her offspring, wisdom, justice, piety, because of the multitude of bastard children whom empty imaginings had borne to me. The nurture of these, the constant pains and ceaseless cares, compelled me to neglect the genuinely true citizens. It is well then to pray that virtue may not only engender (she is prolific even without our prayer), but also may engender for ourselves, so that we may share in what she sows and produces and be truly happy. For she customarily engenders for God alone, thankfully rendering the first fruits of the goods she has obtained to him who, as Moses says, opens the ever virgin womb (Gen. 29:31).[455]

Thus, too, the candelabrum, the archetypal pattern of its later copy, gives light from one part only, namely that which is directed toward God. For being seventh and situated in the middle of six branches, divided two ways into triads that guard it on either side, it sends its rays upward toward the Existent,[456] considering its light too bright for mortal sight to impinge on it (Exod. 25:37, 31).

For this reason Moses does not say that Sarah did not engender, but only that she did not engender for some particular person. For we are not yet capable of receiving the seed of virtue unless we have first mated with her handmaiden, and the handmaiden of wisdom is the general culture gained through the preliminary learning of the schools. For just as in houses there are outer entrances in front of the apartment doors, and in cities suburbs through which we are able to proceed into the interior part, so the school course precedes virtue; the former is a route that leads to the latter.

We must understand that great themes require great introductions,[457] and the greatest of all themes is virtue, for it is concerned with the greatest of materials, the entire life of man.[458] It is thus natural that it will employ no minor preludes, but grammar, geometry, astronomy,[459] rhetoric, music, and all the other branches of intellectual theory. These are symbolized by Hagar, the handmaid of Sarah, as we shall show. For Sarah, we are told, said to Abraham: "Behold the Lord has closed me that I should not bear, go in unto my maid

that you may beget children from her." We must exclude from the
present discussion bodily unions or intercourse having pleasure as its
object. The union in question is a mating of mind with virtue, a mind
desirous of having children by her, and if it is unable to do so immediately, it is instructed to be betrothed to her handmaid, the intermediate education. (*Congr.* 1–12)[460]

The Encyclical Studies

Grammar teaches us the accounts of both poets and prose writers
and produces intelligence and vast knowledge.[461] It will teach us also
to despise all that our empty imaginings falsely invent, through the
misadventures that heroes and demigods who are celebrated by them
are said to have experienced.[462] Music will charm away the unrhyth-
mic by its rhythm, the disharmonic by its harmony, the out of tune
and unmelodious by its melody, and thus bring concord out of discord.[463] Geometry will implant in the soul that loves to learn the
seeds of equality and proportion, and by the subtlety of its sequential
speculations will produce a zeal for justice.[464] Rhetoric, sharpening
the mind[465] for speculation and exercising and welding thought to
expression, will render man truly rational, thus cultivating the peculiar and remarkable gift that nature has not bestowed on any other
living creature. Dialectic, the sister and twin,[466] as some have said, of
Rhetoric, by distinguishing true arguments from false and refuting
plausible[467] sophistries, will heal that great disease of the soul, deceit.

It is profitable then to associate with these and similar disciplines
and train in them in a preliminary way; for perhaps, yea perhaps, as
it has happened with many, we shall through the vassals be made acquainted with the sovereign virtues. Similarly consider that the encyclical studies with the subject matter belonging to each of them are
prepared as childhood nourishment[468] for the soul, whereas the perfect and proper food for those who are truly men are the virtues.
(*Congr.* 15–19)[469]

The Word-Huckstering Skeptics

Now it belongs to the best of races, Israel, to see the best, the truly Existent, for Israel means seeing God. The kind that aims at the
second place sees the second, the sense-perceptible heaven, and the
harmonious order of stars within it, with their truly musical orbital

motion. Third are the skeptics, who do not apply themselves to the best things in nature, whether sensible or intelligible, but are engrossed with petty quibbles and wrangling over trifles. With them swells the concubine Reuma, who "sees something," even if the most minute, for they are incapable of going in quest of the better things by which they might bring profit to their lives. As in the practice of medicine, the so-called word therapy is far removed from yielding benefit to the sick, for diseases are treated by drugs and surgery and regimen, but not by words;[470] so too in philosophy there are those who are merely word hucksters and word hunters,[471] who have no wish nor make it their business to cure their life brimming with infirmities, but from earliest youth to extreme old age do not blush to contend obstinately and battle over syllables, as if happiness depended on the unlimited and ineffectual overelaboration of words and expressions, and not on improving one's character, the fountainhead of human life,[472] by banishing the vices beyond its borders and establishing the virtues there instead. (*Congr.* 51–53)[473]

Imitating Life Models Rather Than Words

It is characteristic of the learner that he listens to a voice and to words, for by these alone is he taught, but he who acquires the good through practice and not through teaching pays attention not to what is said but to those who say it, and imitates their life in its succession of blameless actions. Thus it is said in the case of Jacob, when he is sent to marry one of his kin, "Jacob hearkened to his father and mother, and journeyed to Mesopotamia" (Gen. 28:7), not to their voice or words, for the practicer must be the imitator of a life, not the hearer of words, since the latter is characteristic of one who is being instructed, the former of the one who struggles through to the end. Thus through this text, too, we may grasp the difference between a learner and a practicer, the one being ruled in accordance with the speaker, the other by his words. (*Congr.* 69–70)[474]

Philosophy Must Be the Bondmaid of Wisdom

Enticed by the love charms of the handmaids, some have spurned the mistress, Philosophy, and have grown old,[475] either in the company of poems or among geometrical figures, or among the blendings of chromatic genera,[476] or among innumerable other things, and have been unable to soar upward to obtain the true-born wife. For each art has its refinements, its powers of attraction, and some lured[477] by these remain with them and forget their compacts with Philosophy. But he who abides by the agreements made provides all sorts of things from every source to please her. Rightly then did Holy Writ say in admiration of Abraham's fidelity that even then was Sarah his wife when, to please her, he wedded the handmaid. And indeed just as the school learning contributes to the acquisition of philosophy, so does philosophy to the attaining of wisdom. For philosophy is the pursuit of wisdom, and wisdom is the science of things divine and human and their causes.[478] Therefore just as the encyclical culture is the bondmaid[479] of philosophy, so is philosophy the maid of wisdom. Now philosophy teaches us the control of the belly and the parts below it, and control also of the tongue. These powers of control, it is said, are to be chosen for their own sake, but they will assume a more august aspect if pursued for the sake of honoring God and pleasing him. We must therefore keep the sovereign lady in mind, when we are about to woo her handmaids, and let us be called their husbands, but let her be our wife in actuality, and not merely in name. (*Congr.* 77–80)

The Six Cities of Refuge Represent the Logos and Its Two Constitutive Polar Principles with Their Various Subdivisions Serving the Different Levels of Human Capacity

These are the reasons on which account those who have committed involuntary homicide take refuge in the cities of the Temple wardens alone. We must next indicate what those cities are, and why they are six in number. Perhaps, then, the most venerable, most secure, and best metropolis, which is not just a city, is the Divine Logos, and to take refuge first in it is most advantageous. The other five, colonies as it were, are powers of Him who Speaks, their leader being Creative Power, in accordance with which he who creates via the Logos fashioned the world; second is the Regent Power, in accordance with which its Creator rules that which has come into being; third is the Gracious Power, through which the Craftsman has compassion and pity on his own work; fourth [is the Legislative Power, through which he enjoins what must be done; and fifth][480] that part of the Legislative Power by which he forbids those things that ought not be done.

SELECTIONS

Admirable and well fortified are these cities, excellent refuges for souls deserving to be ever safe: kind and benevolent is the ordinance, capable of providing encouragement and strength for achieving confidence. What could better exhibit the ungrudging abundance of these beneficent powers that exist by reason of the differences among those who have become subject to involuntary changes and are characterized by varying degrees of strength and weakness? The man who is capable of running swiftly it urges to direct all his powers without pausing for breath toward the supreme divine Logos, who is the fountain of wisdom,[481] in order that he may draw from its stream and find, in exchange for death, the prize of eternal life. One who is not as speedy it directs to the power that Moses designates as God, since by it the universe was established[482] and ordered: for one who has grasped that the universe has come into being acquires a great good, the knowledge of its Creator, which persuades the creature forthwith to love him who has begotten it. One less zealous it incites to take refuge with the Regent Power, for through fear of the sovereign, the subject is admonished by his chastening force, where a father's good will has no such effect on the child.[483] For him who does not succeed in arriving at the ends just mentioned, because he considers them too distant, other goals have been fixed nearer by of powers that are indispensable—the Gracious Power, the power that enjoins what ought to be done, and that which forbids what ought not to be done.[484] For he who has assumed that the Divinity is not inexorable but kindly, by reason of the gentleness of his nature, even if he should at first sin later repents in the hope of amnesty; and he who has grasped the notion that God is Lawgiver will by obeying all his commandments be truly happy, while the last will gain a last place of refuge, the averting of ills, even if he obtain no share of principal goods.[485]

These are the six cities, which Moses calls "cities of refuge" (Num. 35:12), five of which have been modeled and have their symbolic representations in the sanctuary: command and prohibition are represented by the Laws placed in the ark; the Gracious Power, by the cover of the ark, which is called the Mercy-seat;[486] the Creative and Regent Powers by the winged Cherubim set upon it. The divine Logos, situated high above these, has not received visible form since it resembles no object of sense but is itself an image of God, the most senior of all things intelligible, set[487] nearest, with no interval between, to the alone truly Existent. For it is said: "I will talk with you

217

from above the Mercy-seat, between the two Cherubim" (Exod. 25:21), indicating that while the Logos is the charioteer of the Powers, he who talks is mounted upon the universe.

He, then, who is free from even involuntary change—voluntary is out of the question—having God himself as his portion (Deut. 10:9) will dwell in him alone; whereas those who without premeditation and against their will have experienced failures will have the refuges mentioned above, so exuberantly and richly bestowed.

Among the cities of refuge, three are beyond the Jordan, far removed from our race. Which are these? The Logos of the Ruler and his Creative and his Regent Power: for heaven and the entire universe have a share in them. But those that adjoin us and are in contact with the mortal race of men, who alone have error as their lot, are the three on this side of the Jordan, the Gracious Power, the power that commands the things to be done, and that which forbids those not to be done; for these already touch us directly. For what need is there of prohibition for those who are not about to do wrong? What need of command for those whose nature precludes failure? And what need of the Gracious Power for those who are not going to err at all? But our race is in need of these powers by reason of its natural inclination both to voluntary and involuntary errors. (*Fug.* 94–105)[488]

Complete Virtue Is Impossible for Man

Infinite indeed are the defilements that sully the soul, which are impossible to wash or purge away completely. For there necessarily remain blemishes congenital to every mortal being, which may well be abated but cannot be completely destroyed. Should we then seek in the confused jumble of life one who is perfectly just or wise or self-controlled or generally good? Be satisfied if you find one who is not unjust, not foolish, not licentious, not cowardly, not entirely evil. We must be content with the overthrow of vices; the complete possession of virtue is impossible for man as we know him. With good reason then did He say, "Be blameless" (Gen. 17:1), for he takes freedom from error and blame to be a great advantage for achieving a happy life. (*Mut.* 49–51)[489]

Lifelong Virtue Is Impossible

But one may perhaps say: why, having once attained conviction, did [Abraham] admit any trace or shadow or breath of distrust at all?

218

He who raises this objection seems to me to wish nothing else than to represent the created as the uncreated, the mortal as immortal, the perishable as imperishable, and, if one may say so, man as God. For he as much as says that the conviction that is man's portion should be so firm as to differ in no way from that of the Existent, which is perfect and complete in every way. For Moses says in the Greater Song, "God is faithful and there is no injustice in him" (Deut. 32:4). It is a mark of great ignorance to believe that the human soul can contain the unwavering, absolutely steadfast excellences of God. We ought to be content to be able to possess the images of these, which to a very large extent fall short of their archetypes. And perhaps this is naturally so, for the excellences of God are inevitably unmixed, since God is not a compound, but a simple nature, whereas those of man are mixed, since we, too, are mixtures, with divine and human blended in us and harmonized in accordance with the proportions of perfect music, and what is constituted of a plurality of elements is subject to countervailing natural forces drawing it to each of these elements. Happy is he to whom it has been granted to incline toward the better and more godlike portion for the greater part of his life. For it is impossible to do so throughout the whole of his life, for at times the rival mortal burden turns the balance, and lying in wait watches for the right moment amid the indispositions of reason to forcibly counter it. (*Mut.* 181–185)

The Self-Taught

Learn then, soul, that Sarah too, namely virtue, "shall bear you a son" (Gen. 17:19), not only Hagar, the intermediate instruction. For Hagar's offspring receives teaching but Sarah's is completely self-taught. And do not be astonished that God, who produces all good things, has produced this kind too, rare indeed on earth, but innumerable in heaven. You may learn this from the other elements of which man is constituted. Do eyes see by virtue of instruction, do nostrils learn to smell, do the hands touch or feet advance at the command or exhortation of tutors? As for our impulses and impressions, the primary motions and conditions of the soul, have they come into being through teaching? Has our mind learned how to think and apprehend by attending the class of some master? All these, freed from instruction, employ a spontaneous nature for their proper activities. Why then do you still wonder that God showers down virtue without

219

toil or fatigue, in need of no special care, but perfect and complete from the first? (*Mut.* 255–258)[490]

The Nature of the Self-Taught Is New and Higher Than Our Reasoning

Having said this much about the third head also, let us go on to the fourth and last of those proposed, in which although there is no "seeking," "finding" is wont to come forth to meet us. In this category every wise man is placed who is spontaneously self-taught; for he is improved not through investigations, exercises, and toils, but the moment he is born he finds wisdom ready-made, showered down from heaven above, and this he sucks in undiluted and is feasted and is continuously drunk with the sober drunkenness that comes with right reason. This is he whom the oracles call "Isaac," whom the soul did not conceive at one time, and give birth to at another, for it says, "she conceived and gave birth" (Gen. 12:2), as though instantaneously. For he that was thus born was not a man, but a most pure thought, beautiful by nature rather than by cultivation. For this reason, she that gave birth to it is said "to have abandoned the ways of women" (Gen. 18:11), the customary, conjectural, and human ways. For the self-taught kind is new, superior to reasoning, and truly divine, taking shape not through human design but through God-inspired frenzy.[491] Are you not aware that Hebrew women need no midwives for their delivery, but "give birth," as Moses says, "before the midwives arrive" (Exod. 1:19), that is, before modes of inquiry, arts, sciences, with the cooperation of nature alone? (*Fug.* 166–168)

The Healing Power of Reason

For reason lifts up the spirit of our race, oppressed as it is by a most grievous fate. Even, then, as the kindliness, intimacy, and courtesy of friends have often healed those oppressed by sorrows or fears or some other ills, so not often but always is it evil-averting reason that alone repels the most grievous burden imposed on us by the constraints of the body to which we are bound or by the unforeseen mishaps that swoop down on us from without. For reason is our friend, familiar, intimate, companion, bound to, or rather joined and united with us by an invisible and indissoluble glue. For this reason it both predicts what will be useful and, when something undesirable has occurred, stands by to offer unsolicited aid, bringing not only one of two forms of assistance, that of the adviser who does not act or that of the silent confederate, but both of these. For the power that it deploys does not work by half measures, but is complete in every direction, and if it fails in its intended effort or in its execution, it resorts to its third mode of aid, consolation. For as wounds are healed by medicinal preparations, so are the disorders of the soul healed by reason,[492] of which the lawgiver says it must be returned "before the setting of the sun" (Exod. 22:26), which means before the setting of the exceedingly brilliant rays of God, the greatest and absolutely manifest, which, in his compassion, he dispatches from heaven into the mind of man. (*Somn.* 1.110–112)

Souls Still Attached to the Body Take God's Image for the Original

To the souls that are disembodied and in his service it is natural that God should reveal himself as he is, conversing with them as friend with friends; but to souls that are still in a body he gives himself the appearance of angels, not altering his own nature for he is unchangeable, but implanting in those who form an impression of him a semblance of another form so that they take the image to be not a copy but that original form itself. (*Somn.* 1.232)[493]

Abraham, Isaac, and Jacob Represent
Teaching, Nature, and Practice

These words do indeed appear to refer to holy men, but they are also indications of a nature less apparent but vastly superior to that of sensible objects. For Holy Writ seems to be investigating soul types, all of them virtuous, one that aims at the good through teaching, one through nature, and one through practice.[494] The first one, called Abraham, is the symbol of virtue acquired through teaching; the second, Isaac, of natural virtue; the third, Jacob, of virtue got through practice. But we must not fail to recognize that each of the three lays claim to the three qualities, but received his name from that which greatly predominated in him; for teaching cannot be consummated without nature or practice, nor is nature capable of reaching its end without learning or practice, nor practice either unless there was the prior foundation of nature and teaching. Very appropriately, then, did Moses link the connection of these three, nominally men, but in reality, as I have said, virtues—teaching, nature, practice. (*Abr.* 52–54)[495]

Abraham Transcends His Chaldean Belief in the World as God

The migrations disclosed by the literal sense of Scripture are made by a man of wisdom, but according to the laws of allegory by a virtue-loving soul in search of the true God. For the Chaldeans, who especially cultivated astronomy and ascribed everything to the movements of the stars, assumed that cosmic phenomena are regulated by forces contained in numbers and mathematical proportions. They exalted visible existence and took no account of the intelligible and invisible. But while exploring the order controlling these numbers in accordance with the revolutions of the sun, moon, and other planets and fixed stars and the changes of the annual seasons and the affinity of celestial with earthly phenomena, they took the world itself to be God, thus impiously comparing the created to its Creator. Nourished by this doctrine and "Chaldaizing" over a long period of time, Abraham opened his soul's eye as though after profound sleep, and beginning to see the pure beam instead of the deep darkness, he followed the light and observed what he had not beheld before, a charioteer and pilot in control of the world and securely guiding his own work, and exercising care and leadership over it and all such parts of it as are worthy of the divine concern. To fix the vision revealed to him more firmly in his mind, the Holy Word directly says to him: "Friend, great things are often recognized by models on a reduced scale, and by looking at them the observer enlarges his view to an infinite extent. Dismiss, then, those who explore the heavens and the science of Chaldea,[496] and depart for a short time from the greatest of cities, this world, to the lesser, in virtue of which you will be better able to apprehend the overseer of the Universe." (*Abr.* 68–71)[497]

The Triple Vision of the One and Three
Classes of Human Dispositions

So much for the literal explanation; we must now begin the allegorical. Spoken words are symbols of that which is apprehended by the intellect alone. When, then, as at high noon, the soul is fully illuminated and, entirely filled with intelligible light, it is rendered shadowless by the rays of light diffused all around it, it perceives a

222

triple vision of a single object, one representing it as it really is, the other two like two shadows reflected from it. This is something that occurs also for those living in the sensible light; whether standing or moving, objects often cast two shadows simultaneously. No one, however, should suppose that the shadow can properly be referred to God. It is only an analogical use of words in order to afford a clearer view of the fact being set forth, for the truth is not so. Rather, as anyone who stands closest to the truth would say, in the central position is the Father of the Universe, who in Holy Scriptures is properly called the Existent One, and on either side of him are the senior powers that are nearest to him, the Creative and the Regent. The Creative is designated God, since through it he established and ordered the universe; the Regent is called Lord, for it is right that the Creator should rule and hold sway over what he has brought into being. The central Being, then, attended by each of his powers, presents to the mind that has vision the appearance, now of one, now of three: of one when perfectly purified and transcending not only the multitude of numbers but even the dyad, neighbor to the unit, it hastens to the form that is unmixed and uncombined, and is in itself in need of nothing whatever; of three, when as yet uninitiated into the greater mysteries,[498] it still celebrates the lesser ones, and is unable to apprehend the Existent by itself alone and apart from anything else, but only through its actions, either creative or ruling. This is, as they say, a "second best voyage";[499] yet it shares in a view that is no less dear to God. But the former mode has not merely a share, it is itself the God-beloved view, or rather it is truth, more venerable than any point of view, more precious than any act of thinking.

We must, however, support what is being set forth, in a more familiar manner. There are three classes of human dispositions, each of which has allotted to it one of the aforementioned visions. To the best is given the middle vision, that of the truly Existent; to the next best, the vision on the right, the Beneficent, whose name is God; to the third, the vision on the left, the Ruling, called Lord. Dispositions of the best kind worship the one who exists by himself alone, independent of anyone, and are not diverted toward anything else, since they are singularly directed to the honoring of the One. Of the other two, one is introduced and commended to the Father by the Beneficent, the other by the Regent Power.

My meaning is something as follows: Men, when they perceive anyone approaching them under the pretext of friendship in quest of advantages, eye them suspiciously and turn away, fearing their false flattery and blandishments as most pernicious. But God, who is insusceptible of harm, gladly invites all who choose to honor him under any form whatever, deeming no one to be deserving of contemptuous dismissal. Indeed, to all whose souls have ears, he all but openly renders these oracular words: "My first prizes are laid up for those who serve me for myself alone, the second for those who do so for their own sakes, either in hope of obtaining good things or expecting release from punishments, since though their worship is mercenary and not disinterested, it is nonetheless enclosed within the divine precincts and does not stray without. But the prizes in store for those who serve me for myself will be those of friendship; to those whose motive is advantage, they indicate not friendship, but that I do not consider them as aliens. For I accept both him who wishes to share my Beneficent Power in order to participate in its boons and him who through fear propitiates my Ruling and Sovereign Authority to avoid punishment. For I am well aware that not only will they not become worse, but they will be improved through their continuous worship and practice of a piety pure and unalloyed. For however varied are the dispositions through which are produced their impulses to please me, no charge is to be brought against them, for they have one end and aim, to serve me.[500] (*Abr.* 119–130)

Speech and Thought Should Never Be Detached from Actions

Yet reason is of no advantage, in spite of its solemn pronouncements of the noble and virtuous, unless accompanied by actions in conformity with it. Accordingly Moses attached the breast-piece to the ephod so that it should not come loose (Exod. 28:28), judging that speech and thought should never be detached from actions. For the shoulder is made by him the symbol of deeds and activity. (*Mos.* 2.130)[501]

The Sabbath Is a Time for the Study of Philosophy

For it was customary always, as circumstances permitted, and primarily on the Seventh Day, as I have explained above, to pursue philosophy, the ruler expounding and teaching what ought to be said and done, while the people advanced in virtue and were improved both in character and life-style. From that time on it is still the practice of the Jews today to pursue their ancestral philosophy every seventh day, dedicating that time to the theoretical study of the truths of nature. For what are our places of prayer in the different cities but schools of wisdom, courage, self-control, and justice, and also of piety, holiness, and every virtue, by which duties to God and men are perceived and correctly performed? (*Mos.* 2.215–216)[502]

Parents Praised for Providing Their Children with Gymnastic Training and Instruction in the School Studies

Who could be more readily called benefactors than parents in relation to their children, having brought them out of nonexistence, and then held them worthy of nurture, and later of education both of body and soul, so that they may have not only life, but a good life? They have benefited the body through gymnastic training, with a view to its vigor and good condition, and lissomeness of bodily movement and posture marked by rhythm and propriety. They have done the same for the soul through letters, arithmetic, geometry, music, and philosophy as a whole, which raises aloft the mind installed within a mortal body and escorts it to heaven and displays to it the blessed and happy natures that dwell there, and produces in it a passionate longing for the unchanging and harmonious order that in obedience to their commander they never abandon. (*Spec.* 2.229–230)

Becoming Male

For progress is indeed nothing else than the giving up of the female gender by changing into the male, since the female gender is material, passive, corporeal, and sense-perceptible, while the male is active, rational, incorporeal, and more akin to mind and thought. (*QE* 1.8)[503]

E.   VIRTUE AND VICE

The Four Virtues

"A river issues from Eden to water the garden, and there it is separated into four heads; the name of the one is Pheison; this is that which circles about the whole land of Evilat, there where the gold is;

225

and the gold of that land is good; and there is the ruby and the emerald. And the name of the second river is Geon; this skirts all the land of Ethiopia. And the third river is Tigris" (Gen. 2:10–14). By these rivers he wishes to indicate the particular virtues. These are four in number,[504] wisdom, self-control, courage, justice. The largest river, of which the four are effluences, is generic virtue, which we have called "goodness." The four effluences are the virtues of the same number. Generic virtue takes its beginning from Eden, the wisdom of God, which is full of joy, brightness and delight, exulting in and priding itself only on God its Father;[505] but the four specific virtues derive from the generic virtue, which like a river irrigates the right conduct of each of them with the abundant flow of noble actions. (*LA* 1.63–64)[506]

Pleasure Is Intrinsically Evil

"And the Lord God said to the serpent, 'Because you did this accursed are you from among all cattle and from among all the beasts of the earth. On your breast[507] and your belly shall you go, and earth shall you eat all the days of your life. And I will put enmity between you and the woman, and between your offspring and her offspring. He shall watch for your head, and you shall watch for his heel' " (Gen. 3:14ff.). Why does he curse the snake without listening to his defense, though commanding elsewhere, as is reasonable, that the two parties to a controversy "should stand forth" (Deut. 19:17) and that credibility not be granted in advance to one of them? You see, indeed, that God did not place advance credence in Adam as against his wife, but gives her an occasion to defend herself, when he inquires, "What is this you have done?" (Gen. 3:13), and she confesses that she blundered because of the deceit of the subtle serpentlike pleasure. What, then, prevented God, when the woman said "the serpent deceived me," from inquiring of the serpent whether he deceived her, instead of cursing him unjudged and without allowing a defense? We must accordingly say that sense perception belongs to things neither good nor bad, but is an intermediate thing and common to wise man and fool alike, and when found in a fool it is bad, when found in a virtuous man, good. Reasonably then, since its nature is not in itself evil, but vacillating, it inclines to either side, both good and evil, it is not condemned before it has confessed that it followed evil. But the serpent, pleasure, is of itself evil, and is therefore not found at all in a good man, the bad man enjoying it all to himself. Most appropriately, then, does God impose the curse without allowing her a defense, since she contains no seed of virtue but always and everywhere is found culpable and abominable.[508](*LA* 3.65–68)

Pleasure Is the Foundation of All the Irrational Emotions

Why, then, does pleasure appear to be worse than the other passions? Because it is more or less at the bottom of them all, like a kind of beginning and foundation.[509] Lust comes into being through love of pleasure; pain comes with its removal; fear again is engendered through anxiety at its absence. It is clear, then, that all the passions are rooted in pleasure, and these might perhaps never have arisen at all if the groundwork for their production, pleasure, were not laid down in advance. (*LA* 3.113)[510]

Virtue for Virtue's Sake

But the man of virtue acquires day for the sake of day, and light for the sake of light, and the beautiful for the sake of the beautiful alone, not for the sake of anything else. And this is why he adds "that I may test them, to see whether they will walk in my law or not" (Exod. 16:4); for this is the divine law, to prize excellence for its own sake.[511] Right reason, therefore, tests all practicers as one does coinage, to see whether they have been sullied, in that they refer the soul's good to something external, or whether, as men of excellence, they distinguish and maintain this good within the mind alone. Such men prove to be nourished not with earthly things but with celestial forms of knowledge. (*LA* 3.167–168)[512]

External Goods Unessential for the Good Life

For strictly speaking it is impossible to rejoice either over the abundance of goods or possessions or brilliance of reputation, or generally over anything external, since they are inanimate and unstable and are of themselves subject to ruin. It is the same with strength and vigor and other bodily advantages, things we share with the basest of men and that frequently bring inexorable destruction on those who possess them. Since, then, genuine and authentic joy is found in the goods of the soul alone, it is in himself that every wise man rejoices and not in the things surrounding him; for the things that are in himself are excellences of mind, in which it is worth taking pride, but the things surrounding him are either bodily comfort or the abundance of external things, of which one must not boast. (*Det.* 136–137)[513]

The Importance of External Goods

When will [the truly happy life] come about? When prosperous external conditions bring abundance and high reputation, favorable bodily conditions bring wealth and strength, and favorable conditions of soul bring the enjoyment of virtues. For each part is in need of its own guards.[514] The body is guarded by good repute and unstinted abundance of wealth, the soul by the complete and perfect health of the body, the mind by the speculative theory of the sciences. (*Her.* 285–286)[515]

The Triple Perfection of Spiritual, Corporeal, and External Goods

Why does (Scripture) say, "On that day He made a covenant with Abraham, saying, To thy seed will I give this land from the river of Egypt to the great river Euphrates"? (Gen. 15:18)

The literal meaning is that it describes the boundaries of the region between the two rivers, that of Egypt and the Euphrates, for anciently the land and the river were homonymously called "Egypt." A witness to this is the poet,[516] who says, "At the river of Egypt stay the ships which you steer from both sides." But as for the deeper meaning, it indicates felicity, which is the culmination of the three goods: the spiritual, the bodily, and those which are external. This (doctrine) was praised by some of the philosophers who came afterward, (such as) Aristotle and the Peripatetics. Moreover, this is said to have been also the legislation of Pythagoras. For Egypt is the symbol of the bodily and external goods, while the Euphrates (is the symbol) of the spiritual, for through them veritable and true joy comes into being, having as its source wisdom and every virtue. And the boundaries rightly take their beginning from Egypt and they end at the Euphrates. For in the end it is difficult to attain those things that pertain to the soul; but first one must proceed through the bodily and external goods, health and keenness of sense and beauty and strength, which are wont to flourish and grow and be attained in youth. And

228

similarly those things that pertain to profitable business and piloting and agriculture and trade. All such things are proper to youth; especially those things that have been rightly mentioned. (*QG* 3.16)

He That Is Despondent Is Not a Man

For what could be more fitting for one who is truly a man than a hope and expectation of obtaining good things from the God who alone is bountiful? This is, truth to tell, the only origin of men in the strict sense, since those who do not set their hope on God have no share in a rational nature, Accordingly, having first said of Enos, "This man hoped to invoke the name of God," he adds expressly, "This is the book of the lineage of men" (Gen. 5:1). These are weighty words, for it is thereby inscribed in the book of God that man alone is hopeful, so that contrariwise, he who is despondent is not a man. (*Det.* 138–139)

Those Who Perform Any Action without the Assent of Their Judgment Do Not Achieve Righteousness

Now the Law says that "some went up with violence into the hill country, and the Amorite who inhabited those hills came out and wounded them, as the bees might do, and chased them from Seir to Hormah" (Deut. 1:43, 44). For inevitably those who are naturally unsuited for the acquisition of the arts, who use force and laboriously cultivate them, not only fail to achieve their end but also incur disgrace. Those, too, who perform any other required action unwillingly, without the assent of their judgment,[517] but by doing violence to their volition, do not act correctly, but are wounded and pursued by their conscience. Would you say that they who restore deposits of little value because they are hunting for the spoliation of larger game [518] are men of outstanding good faith when at the very moment of restoration they have done great violence to their natural bad faith, which never ceases to prick them? (*Deus* 99–101)

Mortal Goods Must Not Be Avoided through Indifference or Inexperience of Them

What profit is there in passing by all the mortal goods of mortal beings if we pass them by not under the impetus of right reason, but as some do through hesitation or indifference or inexperience of them?[519] For they are not all everywhere held in honor; but some honor these, others those. Accordingly, in his desire to prove that it is under the impetus of right reason that we should grow disdainful of the things mentioned, he adds to the words "I will pass by" these others "through your land." For this he knew was the most essential of all, that though we found ourselves amidst all the abundant materials that constitute the apparent goods, we should not be caught in any of the nets thrown in our path by each of them, but like fire, to have the strength with a single charge to break in twain their continuous and unceasing onrush. (*Deus* 152–153)

Unholy Athletic Contests Contrasted with the Holy Contest for Virtue

Yield, then, to others the prizes in these unholy contests, but wreathe your own head with those of the truly holy ones. And deem not holy those contests that the states celebrate in their triennial festivals, and have built for them theaters to hold many myriads of men; for in these the first prizes are carried off either by one who has thrown his opponent and has stretched him either on his back or prone on the ground, or the man who can box or combine boxing with wrestling, and abstain from no act of outrage or injustice. Some, with considerable force, sharpen and harden an iron-filled thong,[520] put it around both hands, and cut up the heads and faces of their opponents, and, when they succeed in bringing their blows to bear, they break the rest of their limbs, and then lay claim to prizes and victory crowns for their pitiless savagery. As for the other contests, of runners or of those who enter the pentathlon, what person of sound mind would not laugh at them for having practiced to jump as far as possible, and measuring the distances and vying for fleetness of foot? And yet not only one of the larger animals, a gazelle or a stag, but even a puppy or young hare among the smaller ones will, without hurrying much, outstrip them when running at full clip and without pausing for breath. None of these contests is truly sacred, and even if all men testify to it, they would inevitably be convicted of bearing false witness against themselves. For it was the admirers of these contests who established the laws against violent men, and the penalties for assault, and assigned judges to pass judgment concerning each of these. How then is it reasonable that the very same persons become indignant at assaults committed in private and have ordained inexorable penalties for them, but for those who have done so publicly, at festive assemblies and in theaters, they have established by law crowns and victory announcements and other rewards? ... The Olympic contest alone can rightly be called sacred, not the one the inhabitants of Elis administer, but the one that aims at the acquisition of divine and truly Olympian virtues.[521] (*Agr.* 113–119)

Youth and Age Reckoned Not Chronologically
But in Accordance with the Presence or Absence of Virtue

In many passages of the Law, indeed, Moses calls those who are advanced in age "young" and contrariwise, those who have not yet grown old he designated "elders," looking not to whether one's years are many or few, or whether a period of time is short or long, but to the faculties of the soul whose movements are good or bad. He thus calls Ishmael, who had already lived for a period of almost twenty years, a child in comparison with Isaac who was full-grown in virtue. For when Abraham sent Hagar and Ishmael away from his house, it says, "He took bread loaves and a skin of water and gave them to Hagar and put also the child on her shoulder," and again "she cast the child down under a single pine," and "I will not see the death of the child" (Gen. 21:14–16). And yet Ishmael was circumcised at the age of thirteen years, before the birth of Isaac, and when the latter at about the age of seven ceased to be nourished on milk, he is banished with his mother, because he, the bastard, played on an equal footing with the true-born. And yet, although already a young man, he is called a child, the sophist thus being compared to the sage. For wisdom is the allotment of Isaac and sophistry that of Ishmael as we shall show in a special treatise, when we delineate the character of each of them. For the infant bears exactly the same relation to the full-grown man as the sophist does to the sage, or the encyclical studies to the sciences that deal with virtues. (*Sob.* 7–9) [522]

The Simple and Unmixed Nature

Admirable and precise is Moses' designation of the soul of the bad man as "mixed": for it is brought together and collected and is truly a miscellany formed of multiple rival opinions, one in number, but myriad in its variety. For this reason, in addition to "mixed" it is also called a "multitude" (Exod. 12:38); for he whose view is concentrated on one object alone is simple and unmixed and truly smooth, but he who sets for himself many life-goals is manifold, mixed, and truly rough. It is for this reason that the oracles represent Jacob, who practices nobility, as smooth, but Esau, who exercised himself in the most shameful things, as hairy[523] (Gen. 27:11). (*Mig.* 152–153)[524]

How to Control Anger

What, then, is the advice of Patience? It is one absolutely wonderful and highly prized. If ever, she says, you see the passion of wrath and anger stirred up and brutalized in yourself or anyone else, a passion bred by our irrational and untamed nature, do not by provoking it further render it all the more savage, for its bites may be incurable, but cool down its seething and excessively hot nature and soften it, for if it should become tame and manageable, it will cause little damage. What, then, is the way to tame and soften it? Adapt and transform yourself in outward appearance and follow initially whatever it wishes, and not opposing it in any way, profess to share its likes and dislikes. In this way it will be rendered propitious. When it has thus been soothed, drop the pretense, and no longer expecting to suffer any evil at its hands, you will easily return to your proper concerns. (*Mig.* 210–211)

The Four Passions

It is well to hear what the predictions were that were thus said to Abraham. First, that God does not grant the lover of virtue to dwell in the body as in a homeland, but only permits him to sojourn there as in a foreign country. For "knowing you shall know," he says, "that your seed will be sojourners in a land not their own" (Gen. 15:3). But every fool regards his bodily estate as natural, and trains himself to dwell there, not to sojourn in it.

This is one teaching. Another is that the earthly things that bring on the soul slavery, ill treatment, and terrible humiliation, to use his own terms,[525] are "not our own." For the bodily passions are truly bastards and aliens to the understanding, engendered by the flesh in which they are rooted.

And the slavery lasts "four hundred years" (Gen. 15:13), corresponding to the powers of the four passions.[526] When pleasure rules, thought is lifted upward and inflated, raised up by inane levity. When desire is master, a longing arises for what is absent and suspends the soul on unfulfilled hope as on a noose. For the soul is ever thirsty, but is unable to drink, undergoing the torments of Tantalus. Under the dominance of grief it contracts and constricts,[527] like trees that shed their leaves and dry up. When fear has made itself monarch no one deems it right to stand fast but takes to flight, expecting in this way alone to be saved. For while desire exercises an attractive force and compels us to pursue the object of our desire even though it fly away from us, fear, on the other hand, creates a sense of estrangement and removes and separates us far from the appearance [that frightens us]. (*Her.* 267–270)

Never Even Entertain a Wicked Thought

Why then, there should be three modes of purification, it is worth exploring. Faulty and correct actions fall roughly into three categories, thought, words, and deeds. For this reason, in his Exhortations, Moses, when teaching that the acquisition of the good is neither impossible nor difficult to pursue, says "You need not fly up to heaven nor go to the ends of the earth and sea to lay hold of it; but it is near, very near." Thereupon he shows it in a manner virtually visible to the eye: "Every work," he says, "is in your mouth, and in your heart, and in your hands" (Deut. 30:12ff.), which symbolically signifies in your words, designs, and deeds. For good designs, good words, and good deeds constitute human happiness, just as their opposites make up unhappiness, since right and faulty action are located in the same three places, heart, mouth, and hand. For indeed some plan quite reasonably and speak what is best, and do what ought to be done. Of the three, harboring faulty designs is the least serious, the most serious being the perpetration of wrong, and standing midway between the two is saying what we ought not to say. Yet the least serious proves to be the most difficult to extricate ourselves from, for it is a hard thing to still the soul's turnings. Sooner might one stay a rushing torrent than their uncontrollable flood. For numberless are the preoccupations of the mind and they press on one another like a mighty swell and sweep and churn up and violently overturn its entire being.[528]

This then is the best and most perfect mode of purification, never even to entertain a wicked thought, but to live as a fellow citizen in peace and compliance of the law under the guidance of justice. The second best is not to err in words, either by lying or perjury or deceit or trickery or false accusations, and in general to unleash for the destruction of others the mouth and tongue, which it were better to bridle and bind with bonds unbreakable. (*Mut.* 236–240)

Caution Is the Better Part of Valor

Surely then such men have lost their wits and have gone berserk who eagerly display untimely candor, and at times dare to oppose kings and tyrants in words and deeds. They do not perceive that not only do they have their necks under the yoke like cattle, but that they are so bound with their whole bodies and souls, their helpless wives, children, parents, and the extensive kinship and association of friends and relatives, and that he who holds the reins can with perfect ease spur, drive on, or hold back and restrain, and arrange whatever pleases him, small or great. And therefore they are branded and scourged and mutilated and undergo the ensemble of all the tortures pitiless cruelty can inflict short of death, and to top it all they are lead away to their slaughter.

These are the wages of untimely candor, which in the view of sensible judges is not candor at all; rather they are the gifts of[529] foolishness, folly, and incurable melancholia. What say you? Who, if he sees a storm at its height, a violent headwind, a roaring hurricane, and a surging sea, sets sail and puts out to sea when he ought to remain in harbor? What pilot or skipper was ever so inebriated and in such a fit of drunkenness as to wish to sail with all these dangers swooping down on him, with the net result that the ship, waterlogged by the sea pouring in from above, is swallowed up crew and all? For he who wishes to have a danger-free voyage can always wait for a fair wind that is favorable and smooth. (*Somn.* 2.83–86)

Ask Not What the Universe Can Do for You . . .

But we say that the lover of confused zeal, irrational contention, and vainglory is ever puffed up by folly, and claims to transcend not only men but also the natural world, and thinks that all things have come into being for his sake, and that it is necessary for each of them, earth, water, air, and sky, to pay their tribute to him as king. And so

234

great is the stupidity to which he is subject that he has not the strength to infer what even an unintelligent child could understand, that no artificer ever fashions the whole for the sake of the part, but the part for the sake of the whole, and that man is a part of the all, so that since he has come into being for the completion of the universe, it would be right for him to make his contribution to it. But some people are so filled with nonsense that they are annoyed if the universe does not follow their wishes.[530] (*Somn.* 2.115)

Moderations of the Passions

When Abraham had lost his lifelong companion, such as described in our discourse and revealed in the oracles, like an athlete he prevailed over the grief that was already besetting him and preparing to tangle with his soul. He strengthened and emboldened the natural antagonist of passion, reason, which he had employed as his counselor throughout his life, and at that point in particular deemed worthy of obedience, since it advised what was best and profitable. Its advice was that he should neither fret beyond measure as at an entirely novel and unprecedented misfortune, nor show a complete lack of emotion, as though nothing distressing had occurred, but choose the mean rather that the extremes and try to moderate his passions, not feel annoyance at nature for recovering the debt due her, but quietly and gently lighten what had befallen him.[531] (*Abr.* 256–257)

Learning a Lesson from the Animals

To them I should rightly say: "Beasts ought to become tame through contact with men." [532] I have often observed lions, bears, and panthers become tame, not only with regard to those who feed them, in gratitude for the provision of their necessaries, but also in regard to everyone else, by virtue, it seems to me, of their resemblance to the former. It is always well for the inferior to follow the superior in the expectation of improvement. But in the present case, I shall be compelled to say the contrary of this: "You men should imitate some of the beasts." These know and have been taught to benefit their benefactors in turn. Watchdogs protect and die in defense of their masters, when some danger suddenly overtakes them. Sheep dogs, they say, fight for their flocks, holding out until they are either victorious or die, in order to maintain the herdsmen unharmed. Is it not, then, the shame of shames that in the matter of returning favors a man should be discomfited by a dog, the most civilized of creatures by the most brazen of beasts? (*Decal.* 113–115)

Soul Defects Are Much More Serious Than Bodily Defects

Even natural pleasure is frequently greatly to blame when one's enjoyment of it is immoderate and insatiable, as, for instance, people who are exceedingly gluttonous, even though they do not partake of forbidden foods, and men who are passionate wiith their wives and are mad for sex, and lustfully associate not with the wives of others, but with their own. But the blame lies in most cases with the body rather than with the soul, since the body contains a large amount of fire, which on exhausting the fuel fed it soon seeks another supply, and it further contains a great deal of moisture, whose violent stream is channeled through the genitalia, creating in them itchings, irritations, and titillations without end.

But they who are mad for the wives of others, sometimes those of their relations and friends, who live to outrage their neighbors, who seek to adulterate whole clans with vast populations, to reverse their nuptial aspirations and render their hopes of offspring fruitless—these are incurably diseased in soul and must be punished with death as the common enemies of the whole human race, so that they may not, while living in a state of amnesty, destroy more homes and become the instructors of others who are anxious to emulate the evils of their ways. (*Spec.* 3.9–11)[533]

F. PHILANTHROPIA

All Have Equal Rights of Kinship
Since They Are the Children of One Common Mother

For if the Uncreated, the Incorruptible, the Eternal, who needs nothing and is the Creator of all, the Benefactor and King of kings and God of gods, could not brook to disdain even the humblest, but deemed it right to feast him sumptuously on holy oracles and ordinances, as if he were going to feast him alone and for him alone prepare the banquet to exhilarate a soul instructed in the secret rites and admitted for initiation into the great mysteries, how is it seemly for me, a mortal, to bear my neck high, be puffed-up and act haughtily toward my peers, who though their fortunes be unequal, enjoy an equal and like kinship, since they can lay claim to the one common mother of mankind, Nature? Therefore, even were I to take in tow the dominion of earth and sea, I will make myself accessible and affable to the poorest, to the least distinguished, to those deprived of the help of kin, to those orphaned of both their parents, to wives biding their widowhood, and older folks who have either never had children at all or have lost, through an early death, those whom they have begotten. Since I am a man, I shall not deem it right to admit pretentiousness and theatrical solemnity, but shall remain within nature's ambit, and not overstep her limits. I shall accustom my mind to entertain human feeling, not only because of the inscrutable reversals of the affairs of both the prosperous and the unfortunate, but also because it is fitting that even if good fortune should remain firmly unchanged, a man ought not be oblivious of what he is. It is for this reason, as it seems to me, that [God] wished to proffer the oracles in the singular form, and deliver them as though to a single person.[534] (*Decal.* 41–43)[535]

Man's Reason Makes Him Most Akin to God and Is the Bond Leading to Human Harmony

The second commandment is not to commit murder. For Nature, who has begotten man, the most civilized of animals, to be gregarious and sociable, has invited him to a life of concord and fellowship by endowing him with reason, which leads to a harmonious blend of characteristics. He who commits murder should be fully aware that he is subverting the laws and statutes of nature so excellently enacted for the benefit of all. He should also further realize that he is guilty of sacrilege, since he has spoiled the holiest of God's possessions.[536] For what votive offering is more august or hallowed than a man? Gold and silver and precious stones and other exceedingly costly substances serve as lifeless ornaments of buildings that are equally lifeless. But man, the best of living creatures, in virtue of the superior element in him, the soul, is most akin to heaven,[537] the purest element of existence and, as most would have it, also the Father of the world, inasmuch as he is in receipt of a mind that is a closer likeness than anything else on earth of the eternal and blessed Form. (*Decal.* 132–134)[538]

PHILO OF ALEXANDRIA

If God, Who Needs Nothing, Cares for Man, How Much More Should Man, Who Possesses Nothing That Is His Own?

For if the Creator and Maker of the universe, who is in need of nothing that he has produced, has regard not to his own immense might and sovereignty but to your weakness, and grants you a share of his gracious power, supplying the deficiencies that are yours, what is it fitting for you to do in behalf of men who are natural kin, and sprang from the same elements, you who have brought nothing into the world, not even yourself? For naked you came, noble sir, and naked will you again depart,[539] and the span between your birth and death is a loan to you from God. During this time span what is more appropriate for you to do than to cultivate fellowship, concord, equality, humanity, and the rest of the virtues, and to jettison the inequitable, unjust, and irreconcilable viciousness, which renders man, the most civilized of animals, into one wild and savage? (*Spec.* 1.294–295)

Sabbath-Rest for Servants Rooted in the Concept of Equality

But it seems that Moses added the other injunctions because of the less obedient who pay little attention to his commandments, and required not only free men to cease from work on the Sabbath, but allowed the same to menservants and handmaids, proclaiming to them security and virtual freedom after every six days, in order to teach both master and servant an admirable lesson. The masters must become accustomed to work with their own hands, not waiting for the services and ministrations of their household slaves,[540] so that if any adverse circumstance should prevail in the course of the vicissitudes of human affairs, they may not through inexperience of personal labor be distressed from the start and renounce the tasks enjoined on them, but use the different parts of their body with greater agility and act with vigor and ease. The servants, on the other hand, should not despair of higher hopes, but, possessing in the relaxation that comes after every six days an ember or spark of freedom, look for their complete release if they remain true and loyal to their masters. From the occasional submission of free men to perform the services of slaves and the possibility for the slaves to share in a sense of security, the result will be that human life will advance toward the highest perfection of virtue, when both the seemingly illustrious and the

238

obscurer sort remember equality and repay each other a necessary debt.

But it is not to the servants alone that the Law has granted the Sabbath rest, but also to the cattle. The servants are indeed free by nature,[541] for no man is naturally a slave, but the irrational animals have been made ready for the need and service of men and rank as slaves.[542] (*Spec.* 2.66–69)[543]

The Benevolent Humanity of the Mosaic Law

With these considerations in view, the expounder of the laws proclaimed a rest for the land and restrained the husbandman from his work after every six-year period. But he introduced this regulation not only for the reason just mentioned but also because of his customary humanity, which he thinks fit to interweave into every part of his legislation, thereby impressing on the readers of Sacred Scripture sociable and kindly character traits. For he commands them not to shut off any field during the seventh year. All vineyards and olive yards are to be left open and similarly other properties, whether of sown crops, or trees, so that the poor may freely use the wild-growing fruits as much, if not more so, than the proprietors.[544] Thus, on the one hand, he did not allow the masters to till their fields with the aim of sparing them the distress, that having provided the expenditure they yet receive no profits in return, and, on the other hand, he thought fit that the needy should for that period of time at any rate enjoy as their own what seemed to belong to others, thus delivering them from any beggarly mien and the reproaches attached to mendicants. Is it not proper that we cherish laws filled with such gentleness, by which the rich are instructed to distribute and share what they have and the poor are exhorted not to be haunting the homes of the affluent on every occasion under the necessity of amending their indigence, but at times also to derive profit from the fruits that, as I have said, grow wild, and which they can regard as their own? (*Spec.* 2.104–107)[545]

In Showing Kindness, Man Imitates God

For what one of the ancients aptly remarked is true, that in nothing does human behavior more nearly resemble God than in showing kindness.[546] For what greater good could there be for the created than to imitate God the eternal? Let not the rich man, then, heap up an abundance of gold and silver and accumulate it in his home, but let him bring it forth publicly so that he may alleviate the austere way of life of the needy with this cheerful distributions of benefits. If he is held in high esteem, let him not raise himself up on pride and boastful insolence, but honor equality and allow free expression to men of little distinction. If he enjoys bodily vigor, let him be the support of the weaker and not as men do in gymnastic contests beat down the less powerful, but aspire to share his own strength with those who of themselves collapse in exhaustion. All who have drawn from wisdom's fountains drive away envy beyond the borders of the mind and, without being exhorted, spontaneously set to work to benefit their neighbors and pour into their souls via the ears the streams of their reflections in order to afford them an equal share in their knowledge.[547] And when they see young folk naturally well endowed like thriving fine-bred plants, they rejoice to think that they have found heirs to that spiritual wealth which is the only true wealth. They take them in charge and cultivate their souls with principles and doctrines until, after being fully assimilated, they bear the fruit of noble living. (*Spec.* 4.73–75)

G. THE WISE MAN AND HIS GOAL OF APATHEIA/EUPATHEIA

Moses Practices Absolute Freedom from Passion,
But Aaron Only Moderation of Passion

For God assigned to the wise man the best portion, the capacity to cut out the passions. Notice how the perfect man always exercises an absolute freedom from passion. But Aaron, who is gradually advancing, second in rank, practices moderation, as I have said; for he is as yet incapable of cutting out the breast and the spirited element, but he brings to bear on it the guidance of reason with its firmly attached virtues, and this is the oracle on which is Manifestation and Truth.

But Scripture will set out the difference more clearly by means of the following words: "The breast of the offering placed [on the altar], and the shoulder of the part removed, I have taken from the Israelites from the sacrifices of your salvation, and have given them to Aaron and his sons" (Lev. 7:34). Note that these are incapable of taking the breast by itself, but must take it with the shoulder, whereas Moses takes it without the shoulder. Why so? Because he, being perfect, entertains no petty[548] or mean thoughts, nor any desire to moderate his passions, but out of the abundance of his soul he cuts away all the passions throughout; while the others rush into battle against the passions with meager resources and on an insignificant scale, but soon become reconciled and conclude a truce with them, offering conciliatory words, that these like a charioteer may bridle their excessive impetus. Moreover, the shoulder is a symbol of toil and stress, and such is the attendant and minister of holy things, since he is given to exercise and toil. But the man on whom God bestows his perfect goods in superabundance is free from toil. He who acquires virtue through toil is found to fall short of the perfection of Moses, who received it effortlessly and easily from God. For just as toiling itself falls short of the effortless achievement and is inferior to it, so does the imperfect fall short of the perfect and learning of that which is self-taught. This is why Aaron takes the breast with the shoulder, but Moses without the shoulder. (*LA* 3.131–135)

Moses Cuts Away the Desiderative and Spirited Elements

But some, exceeding all measure, have indulged not only what comes under the head of desire, but also its sister passion, vehement emotion, wishing to rekindle the entire irrational portion of the soul, and thus destroy the mind. For that which was said literally of the serpent is in reality a truly divine oracle that applies to every passion-loving man: "On your breast and your belly shall you go" (Gen. 3:14); for vehement emotion is located in the breast, and desire in the belly. The fool advances by means of both vehement emotion and desire without intermission, after ejecting mind, its charioteer and leader. The man of opposite character has excised[549] vehement emotion and desire, and has signed up the Divine Logos as his pilot, even as Moses, most beloved of God, who, when offering the whole burnt sacrifices of the soul, "will wash out the belly" (Lev. 8:21), that is, will cleanse away every form of desire, but "the breast from the ram of consecration he will remove" (Lev. 8:2). This undoubtedly signifies the warlike spirited element in its entirety, which is removed so that the better portion of the soul that is left, the rational element, may employ its truly free and noble-minded impulses toward all things beautiful, with nothing tugging at it any longer and diverting it. (*Mig.* 66–67)[550]

Moses Rejects All Forms of Pleasure

Similarly, we shall now find Moses, the perfect sage, purging away and shaking off pleasures, but the man gradually advancing not so treating every form of pleasure, but admitting the kind that is simple and inevitable, while declining what is superfluous and extravagant by way of delicacies.[551] For in regard to Moses, Scripture expresses itself as follows: "And he washed with water both the belly and the feet of the whole burnt-offering" (Lev. 9:14). This is very well put; for the wise man consecrates his whole soul as being worthy to be brought before God because it is free from voluntary or involuntary blemish;[552] and, being in this condition, he washes out and purges away and cleanses the entire belly with its own and its subjacent pleasures, not just a part; indeed he is so contemptuous of it that he does not even admit necessary food and drink, nourished as he is by the contemplation of things divine. And therefore it is also attested of him elsewhere: "For forty days he ate no bread and drank no water" (Exod. 34:28), when he was on the holy mountain and listened to the oracles of God as he ordained the Law (*LA* 3.140–142)

Moses, the Divine Loan to Earthlings, Is Appointed as God to the Bodily Region with Its Ruling Mind

Some there are whom God has advanced even higher, and has rendered them capable of soaring above every species and genus, and set them down beside himself. Such is Moses to whom he says: "As for you, stand here with me" (Deut. 5:31). When Moses, then, was on the verge of death, he neither "leaves" nor "is added" like the former, since he is insusceptible of either addition or taking away. But "by the Word" of the Primal Cause he is translated (Deut. 34:5), that "Word" through which also the whole universe was fashioned. Thus you may learn that God regards the Wise Man of equal honor with the universe, for it is through the same Logos, by which he created the universe, that he draws the perfect man from earthly affairs to himself.

242

SELECTIONS

And even when he gave him as a loan to earthlings and allowed him to consort with them, he did not attach to him the ordinary excellence of rulers and kings, under the guidance of which he could rule the passions of the soul with main force, but appointed him as god,[553] and proclaimed the entire region of the bodily with its ruling mind as his subjects and slaves. "For I give you," he says, "as god to Pharaoh" (Exod. 7:1); but God does not suffer addition or diminution, being fully equal to himself. And therefore it is said that no one knows his grave (Deut. 34:6), for who would be capable of perceiving the migration of a perfect soul to the Existent? Not even the soul undergoing it, in my opinion, knows of its improvement, since at that juncture it is God-possessed. For God does not consult with one receiving benefits concerning the favors he is about to bestow, but ordinarily extends his kindness in abundance to him who does not anticipate it. (*Sacr.* 8–10)

The Paradoxical Nature of the Wise Man

For wisdom is rather God's friend than his servant. And therefore he says clearly of Abraham, "Shall I conceal anything from Abraham my friend?"[554] (Gen. 18:17). Now, he who possesses this portion has advanced beyond the limits of human happiness. He alone is nobly born, for he has enrolled God as his father and has become by adoption his only son, not merely rich, but exceedingly rich, living luxuriously amid good things only, abundant and genuine, unaged by time, ever renewing their prime; not merely of high repute, but glorious, for he reaps the praise that is never counterfeited by flattery, but confirmed by truth; sole kin, for he has received from the All-ruler the unchallenged might of universal sovereignty; sole freeman, for he is released from the most troublesome of mistresses, empty opinion, whom, in view of her excessive pride, God the liberator has deposed from her citadel.[555] (*Sob.* 55–57)

The Righteous Man Is the Foundation of Mankind

Further there have been instances of a household or a city or a country or nations and regions of the earth[556] enjoying great prosperity through a single individual's showing concern for nobility of character. This has been especially the case with one on whom God has bestowed, in addition to a good disposition, irresistible power, just as he gives to the musician and every craftsman the instruments for his music or art and to fire logs as its fuel. For in reality the righteous man is the support of humankind. All that he has he brings forth publicly and gives abundantly for the benefit of those who will use them. What he does not find in his own possession, he asks of God, the sole possessor of all riches; and God opens his heavenly treasury and showers forth his goods in a flood, like rain and snow, so that all the receptacles of the earth are filled to overflowing. These gifts it is God's custom to bestow, since he does not turn away from the word that supplicates him; for it is said elsewhere, after Moses had beseeched him, "I am gracious to them in accordance with your word" (Num. 14:20); and this is apparently equivalent to "In you shall all the tribes of the earth be blessed." . . .

Let us pray then that, like a pillar[557] in a house, the righteous mind within the soul, and in mankind the righteous man, may endure for the healing of our maladies; for as long as he is hale and healthy, we need not despair of our hopes for complete salvation, for our Savior God, I believe, holds out his perfectly all-healing remedy, his Gracious Power, and entrusts it to his suppliant and worshiper to use for the deliverance of those who are sick, applying it as an emollient for those soul-wounds that follies and injustices and the rest of the jagged horde of vices have cut open. (*Mig.* 120–124)[558]

The Sage's Soul Is a Replica of Heaven

For he wishes to represent the sage's soul as a replica of heaven, or if one may speak hyperbolically, a heaven on earth, containing within itself, as does the ether, pure forms of being, ordered movements, harmonious circuits, divine revolutions, beams of virtues utterly starlike and dazzling.[559] And if it be impossible to reckon the number of the sensible stars, how much more so is that true of those that are intelligible? For in my view as much as one faculty of judgment is better or worse than another, since mind is better than sense and sense duller than reasoning, so far do the objects they judge differ; and thus do things intelligible vastly exceed in number things sensible. The eyes of the body are but the smallest part of the eye of the soul. That is like the sun; the others are like candles, accustomed to being lighted and extinguished. (*Her.* 88–89)

SELECTIONS

The Wise Man Enjoys the Pure Peace of the Soul

The man that is nurtured on these teachings enjoys the peace that is endless, released from unabating toils. Peace does not differ from Seven according to the Lawgiver: for on the Seventh Day creation lays aside its seeming[560] activity and rests. Fittingly, then, when taken symbolically, is it said, "And the sabbath of the land shall be food for you" (Lev. 25:6); for rest in God is the only nourishment and enjoyment, since it secures the greatest good, the peace unmarred by war. For the peace that reigns in the cities is mixed with internecine war; but the peace of the soul is free from all discord. (*Fug.* 173–174)[561]

The Wise Man Exists, but Is Concealed from Us Who Are Evil

This kind of person is rare and hardly to be found,[562] but it is not impossible that he should exist. This is shown by the oracle revealed concerning Enoch: "Enoch was well pleasing to God and was not found" (Gen. 5:24), for where could one search and find this good thing, what seas should he cross, what islands, what continents should he visit? Shall he find it among the Greeks or barbarians? Are there not even today among the devotees of philosophy some who say that wisdom is nonexistent, since the wise man no longer exists? No one, in their view, from the beginning of man's creation up to our present life, has been held to be completely blameless, for it is impossible for one bound in a mortal body to be absolutely happy. Whether these statements are correct we will investigate at the opportune moment. For the present we will follow the oracle and say that wisdom is indeed something existent, and so too the lover of wisdom, the wise man, but though he exists he is concealed[563] from us who are evil, for good is unwilling to associate with bad. Therefore it is said that "he was not found," this type of character that was well pleasing to God, undoubtedly in the sense that although actually existing he was hidden and shunned our company; for he is also said to have been "translated" (ibid.), that is to have removed and made the migration from the mortal life to the immortal. (*Mut.* 34–38)

The Sage's Kin Are His Virtues

So greatly does Moses glorify the lover of virtue that when he traces his lineage he does not, as he usually does in the case of others,

245

make a catalogue of his grandfathers, or great-grandfathers, or ancestors in the male or female line, but of certain virtues, thus all but
openly proclaiming that the sage has no other home, kin, and country
save virtues and virtuous actions; "for these," he says, "are the generations of Noah. Noah, a just man, perfect in his generation, was
well-pleasing to God."[564] (*Abr.* 31)

The Sage Who Follows God Enjoys the Rational Emotion of Joy

The one who was to be sacrificed is called in Chaldean Isaac, but
when translated into Greek, Laughter. But laughter here is not taken
as the laughter that arises in the body when we are engaged in play,
but the rational emotion[565] of the understanding, joy. This the wise
man is said to dutifully sacrifice to God, thus showing through a symbol that rejoicing is most appropriate to God alone. For mankind is
troubled and very fearful of evils either present or expected, so that
men are vexed by things unpalatable that are at hand or agitated by
the disturbing fear of those that are yet to come. But the nature of
God is without grief or fear and free from all passion, and alone partakes of perfect happiness and bliss. To the temper of mind that has
made this true acknowledgment, God, in his goodness and benevolence, having driven away envy from his presence, returns the gift according to the measure of the recipient's capacity. And he virtually
delivers the following oracle: "The entire gamut of joy and the act of
rejoicing I know well is the possession of none other save me alone,
the Father of All. Yet, though in possession of this good, I do not begrudge its use by those who are worthy and who should be worthy
except one who should follow me and my will, for he will be least disturbed and fearful if he advances along this road, which is inaccessi-
ble to passion and vice, but well traveled by rational emotions and
virtues."

Let no one assume, however, that joy descends from heaven to
earth undiluted and free from any admixture of grief. It is rather a
mixture of both, though the better component is predominant, just as
light too in heaven is pure and without any admixture of darkness,
but in the sublunary regions it appears with an admixture of dusky
air. This was the reason, it seems to me, that Sarah, who is named
after virtue, first laughs and then denies her laughter in response to
her questioner. She feared lest she usurp the joy that belongs to no
created being but to God alone. Holy Writ therefore encourages her

246

and says: "Have no care; you did indeed laugh and you have a share in joy." For the Father did not permit the human race to be born amid griefs and pains and irremediable burdens, but mixed with them something of the better nature, and judged it right that the soul should at times enjoy calm and fair weather. As for the soul of the wise, he willed that it should pass the greater part of its life in the joy and cheer of the spectacles offered by the universe. (*Abr.* 201–207)[566]

The Wise Are Superb Observers of Nature and Rise Superior to the Blows of Fortune

All who practice wisdom, either among the Greeks or the barbarians, and live a blameless and irreproachable life, choosing neither to be wronged nor to retaliate a wrong, avoid the gatherings of busybodies and censure the places they frequent, law courts, council chambers, markets, assemblies, and generally any company or concourse of rash individuals. Striving for a life free of war and peaceful, they are superb observers of nature and all that it contains, investigating earth, sea, air, and heaven and the beings within them, and roaming in their thoughts with the circuiting moon and sun and the other stars fixed on the earth, they give wings to their souls, so that treading the ether they may fully inspect the powers residing in it, as behooves those who have become cosmopolitans, and have recognized the world to be a city whose citizens are the associates of wisdom, registered as such by virtue, to whom is entrusted the governing of the universal commonwealth. Filled with nobility and accustomed to having no regard for bodily or external ills, practiced in showing utter indifference to things indifferent,[567] schooled against the pleasures and lusts, ever applying themselves generally to stand above the passions, taught to exert all their strength to destroy the bastion built up by the latter, unbowed by fortune's assaults through advance calculations of its onsets, since the heaviest adversities are lightened by anticipation,[568] when the mind no longer finds anything novel in the events and apprehends them but dully as if they were *déjà vu* and stale. Such men naturally rejoice in virtue and make their whole life a feast. These indeed constitute but a small number, an ember of wisdom smoldering within the cities, that virtue may not be completely extinguished and disappear from our race. But if men everywhere shared the view of these few and became what nature intended them to be, all of them blameless, guiltless, lovers of wisdom, rejoicing in moral excellence for its own sake, and considering it the only good, and all the other goods but slaves and vassals subject to their rule, the cities would brim with happiness, free from all that causes grief and fear, and full of what produces joys and rational emotions, so that no season be wanting in cheerful living and the whole cycle of the year be a feast. (*Spec.* 2.44–48)

The Wise Man Is Equal in Worth to a Complete Nation

For when word and thought, design and act, are at one, life is praiseworthy and perfect,[569] but when these are at odds with one another, it is imperfect and blameworthy. If one does not lose sight of this harmony, he will be well pleasing to God, becoming at once God loving and God beloved. It was thus in full accordance with what has been said that this oracle was given: "You have today chosen God to be God to you, and the Lord has chosen you today to be a people to him" Deut. 26:17–18). Splendid is this reciprocation of choice, when man hastens to serve the Existent, and God wins that suppliant over forthwith and anticipates the will of him who genuinely and authentically comes to do him service. And that true servant and suppliant, though but one in number, is virtually what God's own choice makes him,[570] the whole people, equal in worth to a whole nation. And indeed this is naturally the case. In a ship the pilot is of equal weight to all the crew, and in an army the general is equal in weight to all the soldiers, since if he is destroyed the result is defeat, as surely as if the entire force had fallen, from its youngest recruits to its oldest veterans. In the same way the wise man can vie in worth with a whole nation, fortified by the impregnable wall of godliness. (*Virt.* 184–186)

A Sorites or Chain Syllogism Proving That the Wise Man Alone Is Free[571]

For some only with great difficulty, under the impact of an unbroken series of demonstrations, perceive this point. Thus the following argument is right on the mark: He who in every way acts wisely does all things well; he who does all things well does all things correctly; he who does all things correctly also acts unerringly, blamelessly, faultlessly, irreproachably, and with impunity, and therefore will have the power to do everything, and to live as he wishes, and he who has this power is free. (*Prob.* 58–59)

The Wise Are Not Inexistent, as Evidenced by the Seven Greek Sages, the Magi, the Gymnosophists, and the Essenes

It is for this reason that land and sea are full of the rich, the celebrated, and those devoted to pleasures, whereas of the wise, the just, and the virtuous, the number is small. But this small body though scanty is not nonexistent. This is attested by Greece and the world outside Greece. In Greece there flourished those appropriately[572] designated as the seven wise men, and both before and after these, we may reasonably assume, others were in their full flower, but the memory of the more ancient ones has disappeared through the lapse of long periods of time, and as for the more recent ones, it has grown faint through the prevailing negligence of their contemporaries.

In the outside world, in which deeds are held in higher esteem,[573] we find large groups of highly accomplished men. Among the Persians there is the class of the Magi, who investigate the workings of nature in order to discover the truth, and silently, through exceptionally clear visions, receive and transmit the revelation of divine virtues.[574] In India there is the order of the Gymnosophists,[575] who cultivate ethical as well as physical philosophy and make the whole of their lives an exhibition of virtue.

Palestinian Syria, too, has not been unproductive of moral excellence, a land occupied by no negligible portion of the populous Jewish nation. Some among them, more than four thousand in number, are called Essenes.[576] Their name, in my opinion, though the form of the Greek is imprecise, is derived from the word ὁσιότης (Holiness), since they have become in the highest degree servants of God, not by sacrificing animals, but by deeming it right to render their minds holy. To begin with, these people live in villages and avoid the cities because of the inveterate lawlessness of their inhabitants, for they know that association with them would result in an incurable attack on their souls, like a disease that comes from a noxious atmosphere.[577] Some of them till the land, while other pursue crafts that contribute to peace and so benefit themselves and their neighbors. They do not store up gold and silver or acquire large parcels of land out of a desire for revenues, but provide what is needed for life's necessities. For though, virtually alone among all people, they have become money-

249

less and propertyless through studied action rather than through a lack of good fortune, they are considered exceedingly rich, since they judge frugality and easy contentment to be, as is indeed the case, an abundance of wealth. You would not find among them a single manufacturer of arrows, javelins, daggers, helmets, breastplate or shield, nor in general any armorer or maker of engines, or anyone pursuing a war-involved project, nor indeed any of the peaceful kind that easily slip into vice, for knowledge of commerce either wholesale or retail or marine is beyond their wildest dreams, since they banish every occasion for cupidity. There is not a single slave among them, but all are free, exchanging services with one another, and they condemn the slave masters not merely as unjust men who outrage the principle of equality, but as impious individuals who abrogate the law of nature, who has begotten and reared all men alike like a mother, and made them genuine brothers, not just nominally but in actual reality. This kinship has been confounded by a designing and spreading cupidity, which has wrought alienation instead of affinity and hatred instead of friendship.

In the realm of philosophy they abandon the logical part to word hunters as inessential for the acquisition of virtue, and the physical to star-gazing visionaries as beyond the scope of human nature, but make an exception of the part that treats philosophically of the existence of God and the birth of the universe. But the ethical part they carefully elaborate, utilizing as trainers their ancestral laws, which the human mind could not possibly have conceived without divine inspiration.

In these laws they are instructed at all times, but expecially on every seventh day. For the Seventh Day is held holy, and on it they refrain from all other work and proceed to sacred spots they call synagogues. There they sit arranged according to their ages, the young below the elders, with the proper decorum and with attentive ears. Then one takes up the books and reads aloud and another among the more practiced comes forward and explicates what is not understood. The greater part of their philosophical study is conveyed via symbols following an antique mode.[578] They are trained to piety, holiness, justice, domestic and civic conduct, knowledge of what is truly good, evil, or indifferent, how to choose what they ought, and avoid the opposite, employing as their three definitive criteria love of God, love of virtue, love of men. Of their love of God they furnish innumerable examples: a continuous and unbroken purity their whole life through, rejection of oaths, truthfulness, their belief that the Deity is the cause of all good things and nothing bad. Illustrative of their love of virtue is their freedom from the love of money, reputation, or pleasure, their self-mastery and endurance, and, again, their frugality, simplicity, easy contentment, lack of arrogance, lawfulness, steadfastness, and all similar qualities; illustrative of their love of men is their goodwill, sense of equality, and their spirit of fellowship that beggars description, though some brief remarks about it will not be inopportune. First, then, no one's house is his own in the sense of not being shared by all, for in addition to the fact that they dwell together in communes it is open to men of like zeal from the outside to visit them.

Furthermore, they all have a single treasury and common expenditures; their clothes are held in common and also their food, inasmuch as they maintain a public mess. Such sharing of a common roof, life, and board will not be found elsewhere to be more firmly established in fact. And perhaps this is naturally so. For all that they receive in salary for the day's work they do not keep as their private possession but throw it into the common stock and make it available for those who wish to make use of its benefit. The sick are not neglected because they are incapable of providing anything, since what is required for their nursing is held in readiness in the common stock, so that they can spend with complete security from abundant stores. The elders enjoy the respect and care that real[579] children bestow on their parents, and they are fully and abundantly provided for in their old age by countless hands and minds.

Such are the athletes of virtue produced by a philosophy free from the useless pedantry of Greek terminology, which sets forth laudable actions as its practice exercises, and through which the liberty that is never subject to slavery is firmly extablished. Here is the proof. Many sovereigns have arisen to power over the country on various occasions, diverse in nature and in conduct. Some were eager to carry the day in the practice of the wild savagery of beasts, omitting no form of cruelty. They slaughtered their subjects en masse, or like cooks carved them piecemeal limb by limb while yet alive, and did not cease until they endured the same misfortunes at the hands of justice, who oversees human affairs. Others transformed this wild frenzy into another kind of viciousness. They pursued an indescribable bitterness, while speaking calmly, though under the outward show of their milder language they exhibited their exceedingly wrathful character. They fawned like venomous hounds, but were the cause of ir-remediable ills and left behind them in city after city the unforgettable sufferings of their victims as memorials of their impiety and hatred of men. Yet none of these, neither the most savage-hearted nor the most profoundly treacherous, were capable of accusing the society of Essenes or holy ones here described. No match for the excellence of these people, they all treated them as men independent and free by nature, celebrating their common meals and their ineffable sense of fellowship, which is the clearest indication of a perfect and supremely happy life. (*Prob.* 72–91)

The Four Rational Emotions

Why does (Scripture) say, "Every reptile that lives shall be to you for food" (Gen. 9:3)?

The nature of reptiles is twofold. One is poisonous, and the other is tame. Poisonous are those serpents that in place of feet use the belly and breast to crawl along; and tame are those that have legs above their feet. This is the literal meaning. But as for the deeper meaning, the passions resemble unclean reptiles, while rational emotions (resemble) clean (reptiles). For alongside the passion of Pleasure there is Joy. And alongside Desire there is Will. And alongside Grief there is Compunction. And alongside Fear there is Caution. Thus these passions threaten souls with death and murder, whereas rational emotions are truly living, as he himself has shown in allegorizing, and are the causes of life for those who possess them. (*QG.* 2.57)

The Wise Man Will Sometimes Act in a Seemingly Vicious Manner

Why does she put a skin of goats on his arms and on his neck? (Gen. 27:16).

The literal meaning is clear and apparent, (namely) that it was for the sake of being unknown and that (his father) might not understand and that when he was in his presence he might not seem to be who he (really) was but might seem to be the brother who was absent. And she threw the skins of goats over his arms and naked neck because the latter (Esau) was hairy. But as for the deeper meaning, the arms and the back of the neck are stronger than all of man's (other) limbs, and they are smooth. And the wise man is gleaming and naked to the truth; and just as in the case of the other virtues, so also does he in pure fashion exhibit and practice and pursue courage. And if it sometimes happens that he conceals this and makes it hairy because of the necessity of the occasion, and uses economy, he still remains in the same state and does not retreat from his original purpose, but because of involuntary occurrences he changes to another kind of form, as in a theater, for the benefit of the spectators. For this is just what physicians are accustomed to do, for they change the foods of ill persons, and their places (of residence) and the ways (of living) they had before their illness. And the physician who is skilled in worldly matters does foolish things for a time (but) wisely, and unlasciviously and moderately does lecherous things, and bravely does cowardly things, and righteously does unrighteous things. And sometimes he will speak falsehoods, not being a liar, and he will deceive, not being a deceiver, and he will insult, not being an insulter.[580] (*QG* 4.204)

H. *ASCETICISM*

The Soul Is Entombed in the Body as in a Sepulchre

Wherever Moses says "to die the death," observe that he means death as a penalty, not that which comes about naturally. Natural death is that in which soul is separated from body, whereas the penalty death takes place when the soul dies to the life of virtue, and is alive only to that of wickedness. Excellent too is the saying of Heraclitus, who on this point followed Moses' teaching, for he says: "We live their death, and are dead to their life." His intent is that now, when we are alive, the soul is dead, and is buried in the body as in a sepulchre; but if we should die, the soul lives its own life and is delivered from the body, the pernicious corpse to which it is bound.[581] (*LA* 1.107–108)

Pleasure Is Indispensable, but the Man of Virtue Does Not Use It as a Perfect Good

Created being must make use of pleasure, but the base will use it as a perfect good, the man of virtue only as a necessity, for apart from pleasure nothing in mortal kind comes into being. Again, the base individual adjudges the acquisition of wealth a most perfect good, the man of virtue only as necessary and useful. It is natural then that God wishes to see and learn how the mind invites and receives each of these, whether as good, or as indifferent, or as bad but at all events serviceable. (*LA* 2.17)[582]

The God-loving Soul Strips Itself of the Body

The God-loving soul, having stripped itself of the body and the objects dear to the body, and having fled far away from these, acquires fixity, firmness and stability in the perfect precepts of virtue. It is therefore attested to by God that it loves what is noble; "for," says he, "it was called the tent of witness." He passes over in silence who it is that calls it so, in order that the soul may be roused and consider who it is that bears testimony to virtue-loving minds. For this reason the high priest shall not enter the Holy of Holies in his robe (Lev. 16:1ff.), but having doffed the vesture of opinions and impressions of the soul, and having left it behind for those who love externals and esteem semblance above reality, shall enter naked without colors and sounds, to pour as a libation the soul-blood and offer as incense the whole mind to God our savior and benefactor. (*LA* 2.55–56)[583]

The Body Is Wicked and a Plotter against the Soul

For this reason, in the matter of Er too, without evident cause, God knows him to be wicked and slays him (Gen. 38:7). For he is not unaware that the body, our "leathery" bulk (Er means "leathery") is wicked and a plotter against the soul, and is even a cadaver, and always dead. For you must not imagine that each of us is anything but a corpse-bearer, the soul rousing and effortlessly bearing the body, which is of itself a corpse.[584] And note, if you will, the soul's great vigor. The most robust athlete would not have the strength to carry his own statue for a short while, but the soul, sometimes for as long as one hundred years, easily carries the statue of the human being without tiring; for it is not now that God slays Er, but from the very first he made the body a corpse. By nature, as I have said, it is wicked and a plotter against the soul, but this is not apparent to all, but to God alone and anyone who is dear to God; for it says that "Er was wicked before the Lord." For when the mind is concerned with lofty matters and is initiated into the mysteries of the Lord, it judges the body to be wicked and hostile; but when it withdraws from the investigation of things divine, it deems it friendly to itself, its kin and brother, for it has recourse to what is dear to the body. On this account there is a difference between the soul of an athlete and the soul of a philosopher. For the athlete refers all to the good health of the body, and, body-lover that he is, would abandon the soul itself for its sake; but the philosopher, being in love with the nobility that lives in himself, cares for the soul, and disregards that which is in reality a corpse, the body, with the sole aim that the best part of him, his soul, may not be wronged by an evil thing, the cadaver to which it is bound. (*LA* 3.69–72)[585]

No Two Things So Utterly Antagonistic as Knowledge and Pleasure of the Flesh

This way, you must know, is wisdom. For reason, guided along that straight and broad highway, reaches its goal, and that goal is the recognition and knowledge of God. Every comrade of the flesh hates, attacks, and seeks to destroy this path. For no two things are so utterly antagonistic as knowledge and pleasure of the flesh. (*Deus* 143)[586]

God Abhors All Counterfeit Approaches

But Joseph, though he fancied that he had made progress, is found wandering; for he says, "a man found him wandering in the plain" (Gen. 37:15), showing that it is not toil by itself that is good, but toil accompanied by art. For just as it is fitting not to practice music unmusically or grammar ungrammatically, or, to put it in a word, any art without art or with bad art, but to pursue each art artfully, so neither is it proper to practice wisdom with cunning or self-control with niggardliness, or courage with rashness, or piety in a superstitious way, or any other knowledge concerning virtue in an ignorant manner;[587] for these are all admittedly dead ends. Wherefore there is also a law laid down "to pursue justice justly" (Deut. 16:20), so that we may seek justice and every virtue by means of acts that are akin to it, but not those that are contrary to it. If you then observe anyone not accepting food or drink at the proper time, or declining baths and unguents, or neglecting his clothing, or lying on the ground and living in miserable lodgings, and then on this basis sim-

255

ulating self-control, pity his error and show him the true method of self-control; for all these practices are ineffectual and wearisome labors, ruining body and soul by starving and other maltreatments. A man may undergo holy lustrations and purifications, defiling his understanding while cleansing his body; he may again through an abundance of wealth establish a temple with munificent expenditures on supplies; he may sacrifice hecatombs and slaughter oxen continuously; he may adorn the sanctuary with costly votive offerings, bringing forth abundant material and craftsmanship more priceless than silver and gold; yet will he not be inscribed among the pious. For this man too has strayed from the path leading to piety, holding it to be cultic ritual instead of holiness, and offering gifts to him who is unbribable and will not accept such things, and flattering him who cannot be flattered, who welcomes authentic worship, but rejects counterfeit forms. Authentic worship is that of a soul bringing plain truth as its only sacrifice; counterfeit are all exhibitions made by means of external abundance. (*Det.* 17–21)

Better to Be Made a Eunuch Than to Be Mad after Illicit Unions

Accordingly it seems that those not completely lacking instruction would choose to be blinded rather than see unfitting things. and become deaf rather than listen to harmful words, and have their tongues cut out so as not to utter what may not be disclosed.[588] They say, for example, that certain wise men, while being tortured on the wheel to get them to divulge secrets, have bitten off their tongues,[589] and so contrived in turn a worse torture for their torturers, who were unable to learn what they desired to know. It is better to be made a eunuch than to be mad after illicit unions. All these things, inasmuch as they plunge the soul into irremediable disasters, would rightly incur the severest punishment and retribution. (*Det.* 175–176)

Enslavement to Spectacles and Musical Performances

For what other reason do we imagine that the theaters all over the world are filled daily with innumerable multitudes? The people who are slaves to musical performances and spectacles, allowing ears and eyes to be borne about unbridled; honoring lutists and the singers that accompany them, and every form of unmanly and effeminate music; favoring dancers and other actors, be ause they execute and hold effeminate poses and movements; applauding the incessant warfare on the stage without a thought for their own improvement or that of the community, but, wretches that they are, overturning through eyes and ears their own life. (*Agr.* 35)

The Nature of Wisdom Is Not Somber and Severe But Full of Joy and Gladness

We must further note that the nature of wisdom is not somber and severe, constricted by anxiety and gloom, but on the contrary cheerful and serene, full of joy and gladness, conditions that often induce a man to sport and jest not untastefully. Such sportiveness is in harmony with a sense of earnest dignity, like the harmony in a lyre attuned to the blending of a single melody through a series of answering notes.

According to Moses, at any rate, holiest of men, sport and laughter are the end of wisdom, not the kind indulged in by all children who are lacking in reason, but that which is found among those already grey-headed not only in respect of age but of sage counsel. Note that he says of the man who drew from the well of knowledge, hearing from no other, learning from no other, and self-accomplished, not that he had a share in laughter, but that he was laughter itself. This man is Isaac, whose name means laughter and for whom it is appropriate to sport with "endurance," whom the Hebrews call Rebecca. (*Plant.* 167–168)[590]

Those Guided by Empty Opinions Are Unable to Resist External Goods

I am amazed at the candor of the soul that, in dialoguing[591] with itself, confesses that it is unable to rise up against apparent goods, but is astonished at each of them and honors them and all but prefers them to herself. For which of us stands up to riches? Who prepares himself to wrestle with glory? Who among those still in the company of empty opinions despises honor of office? Not a single one. So long as none of these things is with us, we talk big, like companions of frugal contentment, which secures the life that is completely self-sufficient and righteous, and befitting the free and nobly born. But when there begins to blow on us the hope of any of the things mentioned, or even but a slight breeze of such hope, we are unmasked, we immediately yield and give way and are incapable of making a stand or offering resistance. Betrayed by the senses so dear to us, we abandon all alliance with the soul, and we desert, no longer in secret but openly. And perhaps naturally so. For feminine ways still prevail among us, and we are incapable as yet of washing them away, and flee to the men's quarters, as we are told was the case with the virtue-loving mind, named Sarah.

For she is represented by the oracles as "having left all the things of women" (Gen. 18:11), when she was on the verge of travail and about to beget the self-taught kind, named Isaac. She is said, too, to be without a mother, and to have inherited her kinship on the father's side alone and not on the mother's, thus having no part in female lineage. For it is said somewhere, "She is in truth my sister, my father's daughter though not my mother's" (Gen. 20:12). She is not born of sensible matter, ever taking shape and being dissolved and called mother or foster mother or nurse of created things by those in whom first the shoot of wisdom grew;[592] but she is born of the Father and Cause of all things. Transcending the entire world of bodily forms, and exulting in the joy that is in God, she will turn into an object of laughter the cares of men that are concerned with the affairs of war or peace. (*Ebr.* 56–62)

The Contaminating Effect of Overexposure to the Passions

There is nothing astonishing in his urging the mind subjected to the control of irrational passion not to give in, not to be swept away by the impetus of that passion's violence, but to exert every effort to stand its ground, and should it be unable to do so, even to flee. For an alternate plan for attaining safety for those who are unable to defend themselves is flight; since he who was a fighter by nature and had never become the slave of passions, but was constantly struggling with each of them, is not permitted to continue his wrestlings to the end, lest by his uninterrupted meeting with them he take on a serious blemish. For many have already become imitators of their antagonists' vice, as others, on the contrary, have imitated their virtue.[593] For this reason a divine oracle was revealed to him as follows: "Return to the land of your father and your kindred, and I will be with you" (Gen. 31:3); that is, "You have become a perfect athlete, and have been deemed worthy of the reward of prizes and crowns with Virtue presiding and holding out to you the palms of victory; make an end now of your love of contentiousness, so that you may not be forever toiling, but have the capacity to benefit from your efforts. This you will never find if you remain here, dwelling still among the objects of sense, and spending your time amid corporeal qualities, whose leader is Laban, for his name means quality. You must become a migrant to your father's land, that of the holy Logos, which is, in a way, father of those who are exercised with it: and that land is Wisdom, excellent abode of virtue-loving souls. In this country you will find the kind that is self-taught and self-instructed, that has no share in milklike baby food,[594] that has been prevented by a divine oracle from going down into Egypt (Gen. 26:2) and from meeting with the enticing pleasures of the flesh. That kind is called Isaac." (*Mig.* 26–29)

The Practical Comes before the Contemplative Life

We read that "Rebecca said to Jacob, 'Behold Esau your brother is threatening to kill you. Now, then, my child, listen to my voice and arise and flee to my brother Laban to Harran, and live with him for some days, until the wrath and anger of your brother turn away, and he forget what you have done to him: and I will send and fetch you from there' " (Gen. 27:42–45). For there are good grounds for fearing lest the worse part of the soul lie in wait from a position of ambush or even openly prepare for combat and overturn and overthrow the better part. And this is excellent advice given by Rebecca, judicious Patience. Whenever, she says, you see the base individual gushing with hostility against virtue and holding in high esteem things it ought to disregard, wealth, reputation, pleasure, and praising the practice of injustice as the instrumentality of each of these (for it is especially the wicked who amass silver and gold and attain fame), do not turn forthwith in the opposite direction and pursue penury, unaffectedness, and a severe and solitary mode of life; for you will only provoke your antagonist and stimulate a more grievous foe against you.

Consider, then, by what actions you may escape his maneuverings. Adapt yourself, not to his practices, but to the objects themselves that produce them—honors, offices, silver, gold, possessions, different colors and forms, beautiful objects. And whenever you encounter these, engrave, like a good artisan, as excellent a form as possible on the material substances, and accomplish a work worthy of praise. You are well aware that when a layman takes over a vessel capable of rescue, he overturns it, whereas a skilled pilot often saves one that is on the point of going down; and how ailing folk through the inexperience of those tending them fall into a precarious bodily condition, while others through experienced attendants escape even perilous disease. There is no need to elaborate. At all time, what is executed with skill convicts what is done without it, and the true praise of the one is the unerring condemnation of the other.

If, then, you wish to confound the worthless man of wealth, do not renounce abundance of possessions.[595] He, wretch that he is, will plainly appear either as servile and slavish in spirit, or petty usurer and skinflint, or, on the contrary, a frenetic profligate, ever ready to squander away funds and gorge himself, an exeedingly lavish patron of courtesans, pimps, panders, and every debauched crowd. But you will furnish loans to needy friends, will offer gifts to your country, you will help parents without means to marry off their daughters and provide them with a most ample dowry; you will all but place your private possessions into a common till and invite all deserving of favor to take their share.

Similarly, when someone is wild after fame and is boastful, if you wish to cast reproach on the poor wretch, do not turn away from the plaudits of the crowd if it is open to you to receive honor, and you will thus trip up the poor braggart in his arrogant stride. He will abuse his renown to insult and dishonor others better than himself, and will elevate above them men of lesser stature. You, on the other hand, will share your glory with all who are worthy, and provide security for the good, and improve the worse by your admonitions.

And if you go to sumptuous banquets where the wine is drunk unmixed, go confidently; for you will put the intemperate man to shame by your courteous behavior. He will fall on his paunch and open his insatiable appetites before he opens his mouth, take his fill in an unseemly manner, suck in his neighbor's food, and devour everything without a blush; and when he is satiated with food, he will as the poets say "drink with wide-open maw,"[596] and become an object for jeering laughter by the spectators. But you, in the absence of constraint, will practice moderation; and should you somehow be constrained to enjoy a wider range of pleasures, you will place the constraint under the rule of reason, and never transform pleasure into disgust, but, if I may say so, get soberly drunk.

Truth would therefore rightly blame those who without careful inquiry abandon the occupations of a citizen's life, and say that they have conceived a contempt for reputation and pleasure. For their contempt is feigned; their slovenliness, their sullen countenance, their severe and squalid life-style, are put forward as baits to give the impression of their being lovers of orderliness, self-control, and endurance. But they are unable to deceive the more precise observers whose glance is pentrating and who are not misled by appearance. For they reject this as the masking of other sentiments, and clearly see the precise nature of the things stored up within, and if they are beautiful they admire them, but if ugly , they mock and loathe them for their hypocrisy.

To such men, then, let us say: Do you strive after the life that is unsocial and unshared, solitary and alone? What demonstration did you make before this of community virtues?[597] Do you reject moneymaking? When engaged in commerce, were you willing to deal justly? You pretend to have no concern for the pleasure of the belly and the parts below it, but when you had abundant material for indulging in these, did you practice moderation? Do you disdain popular repute? Well, when you held positions of honor, did you practice a lack of affectation? You ridicule political activity, without perhaps perceiving its utility.

First, then, practice and apply yourselves in the affairs of both private and public life; and when by means of the sister virtues, household management and statesmanship, you have become statesmen and managers, make your migration, amidst this state of luxury, to a different and better way of life. For before the contemplative life it is well to struggle through the practical life, as a sort of prelude to a more perfect contest. You will thus escape the imputation of hesitancy and laziness.

So it was that the Levites were charged to perform their temple service until the age of fifty (Num. 4:3ff.), but, when released from their practical ministry, to observe and contemplate all things; receiving as a prize for their success in the active life a different way of life that delights in knowledge and speculation alone.

Moreover, it is essential that those who deem it right to lay claim to the obligations toward God should first fulfill those toward men; for it is sheer naiveté to assume that you will attain to the greater when you are unable to surmount the lesser. Learn then first the virtue applicable to man, so that you may also be involved with that applicable to God. (*Fug.* 23–38)[598]

PHILO OF ALEXANDRIA

We Must Take Flight from Earth to Heaven and Become Like God as Far as Possible

Now, it was absolutely essential that different regions be assigned to different things, heaven to a good thing, the earthly parts to an evil thing. The good is upward-mounting, and should it ever come to us, through the bounty of its Father, it rightly hastens to reverse its path; but the evil thing remains here, far removed from the Divine Choir,[599] making mortal life its prowling ground, and unable to die away and leave the human race. This sentiment was splendidly expressed by a man of distinction, one of those admired for their wisdom, when he said in his *Theaetetus:* "Evils cannot cease to exist, for there must ever be something opposed to the good; nor can they be established among the gods, but they haunt mortal nature and this region here. That is why we must attempt to take flight from here to there as swiftly as we can; flight means becoming like God as far as possible, and to become like God is to become just and intelligently devout."[600] (*Fug.* 62–63)

Disembodied Minds

Lusty and vigorous athletes are they who have fortified the servile body against the soul. Wan, wasted, and dessicated skeletons, so to speak, are those devoted to training, who have consigned their bodily vigor to their psychic force, and, truth to tell, have been resolved into one form, that of the soul, and become disembodied minds. The earthly element is naturally destroyed and dissolved when the mind in its totality chooses to be well pleasing to God. (*Mut.* 33)

The Wise Man Loves Solitude

The man of virtue, on the other hand, having become a devotee of the quiet life, withdraws and loves solitude, resolved to be unnoticed by the many, not through misanthropy, for he is, if anyone is, a lover of men, but through having rejected vice, which is welcomed by the multitude, who rejoice at what calls for mourning and are grieved at what it is well to be glad. For this reason he mostly remains cooped up at home and hardly steps out of doors, or else because of the continuous wave of visitors he leaves town and spends his time at an out-of-the-way farm, finding greater pleasure in having as his companions the cream of the human race, whose bodies time has dissolved but the flame of whose virtues has been quickened by the writings they have left behind in prose or verse, by which the soul is naturally improved. (*Abr.* 22–23)[601]

The Mind Frequenting the Heights Scoffs at Earthly Things

Such is the nature of the mind of those who have tasted holiness: It has learned to gaze upward and frequent the heights, and as it ever haunts the upper atmosphere and closely examines the divine loveliness, it scoffs at earthly things, considering them to be mere child's play, whereas those above it regards as objects of truly serious concern.[602] (*Mos.* 1.190)

Virtue Must Be Practiced in Both the Divine and the Human Spheres

After the ordinances dealing with the Sabbath, he gives the fifth commandment concerning the honor due to parents. He placed it on the borderline between the two sets of five, for it is the last of the first set, in which the most sacred commandments are enjoined, and it adjoins the second set, which contains the duties of man to man. The reason, I think, is the following. The nature of parents appears to be on the borderline between immortal and mortal being, the mortal because of their kinship with men and other animals in regard to the perishability of their body; the immortal because their power of generation assimilates them to God, the generator of the All.

Some indeed have heretofore attached themselves to one portion of the commandments while appearing to neglect the other. They have taken their fill of the pure wine of piety and, completely renouncing all other affairs, devoted their personal lives entirely to the service of God. Others, surmising that there is no good outside one's duties to men, have espoused nothing but companionship with their fellows. In their desire for solidarity they provide the good things of life for all to use equally and deem it right to alleviate their straitened conditions as far as possible. These may be justly called lovers of men, the former lovers of God. Both are incomplete in virtue, for only they who are highly esteemed in both spheres have it entire. But those who are neither counted among men by rejoicing with them at goods shared and grieving with them at their opposite nor hold fast to piety and holiness would seem to have been changed into the nature of beasts. Among the latter the palm of savagery will be borne away by those who pay no regard to parents and are thus enemies of both categories of the law, those concerning God and those concerning man. (*Decal.* 106–110)[603]

Body and Soul Should Relieve Each Other

But since we consist of body and soul, Moses assigned to the body its appropriate tasks and the soul what belongs to it, and endeavored that the two should wait on one another for relief. Thus while the body is working, the soul has a brief respite, but when the body is resting, the soul is hard at work, and so the best forms of life, the theoretical and the practical, successively give place and exchange roles with each other. The practical life has the number six allotted for ministering to the body, and the theoretical has seven for knowledge and perfection of the mind. (*Spec.* 2.64)

The Middle Path

Moses approved neither of austere training like the Spartan legislator nor of delicate living, like him who instructed the Ionians and Sybarites concerning dainty and luxurious practices. Instead he opened a middle path between the two. He relaxed the vehemence of the first, and tightened the laxity of the second, and as on a musical instrument blended the excessively high and low notes at either end of the scale with the middle chord, with a view to a life harmonious and impeccably concordant. He therefore meticulously and carefully set up rules as to what food ought or ought not to be used. (*Spec.* 4. 102)[604]

No One Is in Want, for the Best Things in Life Are Free

Poverty has vanquished multitudes, who like exhausted athletes have fallen to the ground softened by unmanliness. Yet in the judgment of truth not a one is in want, since he has as his supplier the indestructible wealth of nature;[605] the air, the first, the most essential and uninterrupted source of nurture, which is inhaled continuously night and day; then the abundant fountains and the everflowing streams of rivers fed not only by winter rain and snow but also by springs to provide us with drink; then for our food the productivity of all kinds of crops and different species of trees, which ever yield their annual fruit. Of these goods no one is deprived, but everyone everywhere enjoys them in superabundance. But if some, taking no account of nature's wealth, pursue that of hollow opinion, supporting themselves on something blind rather than seeing, and using defective guidance, they must inevitably fall. (*Virt.* 6–7)

The Wise Man Must Be Prepared to Abandon Country and Friends

If a man has truly come to despise pleasures and desires and resolves in all sincerity to stand above the passions, he must prepare for a migration, fleeing without turning backward home, country, kin, and friends.[606] For intimacy has an attractive force. We may fear lest in remaining he may be taken captive, cut off by the many love-charms enveloping him, whose representations will once more awaken base pursuits long stilled and create fresh memories of what it were well to have forgotten. Many have been made wiser through migration abroad and have been cured of their mad and frenzied cravings when sight can no longer supply to passion the images of pleasure. For through dissociation, it must inevitably be treading on empty space, since the source of the stimulus is no longer present. (*Praem.* 17–19)

The Use of Wine Is Superfluous

Why did the righteous man first plant a vineyard? (Gen. 9.20)

It was proper (for him) to fall into perplexity where he should find a plant after the flood, since all those things which were on the earth had wasted away and perished. But what was said a little earlier seemed to be true, (namely) that the earth was dried up at the spring season, and since spring is when plants blossom, it was therefore expected that both vines and vine-shoots would be found that could flourish, and that they would be gathered by the righteous man. But it must be shown why he first planted a vineyard and not wheat and barley, since some fruits are necessary and it is impossible to live without them, while others are the material of superfluous luxury. Now those which are necessary to life and beneficial, yet produced without co-operation, he consecrated and set apart for God; but su-

perfluous things (were assigned) to man, for the use of wine is superfluous and not necessary. And so, in the same way that God Himself
with His own hand caused fountains of potable water to flow out
without human co-operation, so also He gave wheat and barley. For
both forms of nourishment, food as well as drink, He alone by Himself bestowed (on man). But those (foods) which are for a life of luxury He did not keep for Himself nor grudge that they should fall to
man's possession. (*QG* 2.67)[607]

Mind Cannot Endure Unrelieved Tension and Requires Relaxation

What is the meaning of "The Lord went away as He ceased to
speak with Abraham. And Abraham returned to his place" (Gen.
18:33)?

The one who is begotten and brought into being is not wont to
be God-possessed always, but when he has been divinely inspired for
some time he then goes and returns to himself. For it is impossible
for the soul to remain permanently in the body when nothing slip-
pery or no obstacle strikes its feet. But it is necessary that the most
pure and luminous mind should be mixed with the mortal (element)
for necessary uses. This is what is indicated by the heavenly ladder,
(where) not only an ascent but also a descent of the angels is mentioned. And this is what is said of the prophet, (namely) his descent
and ascent reveal the swift turning and change of his thoughts. And
thought and change altogether bear a resemblance to those who practice continence for athletic well-being, whom their trainers teach
skillfully not in order to do violence to the body but that it may be
able to endure exhausting labors easily and not be worn down and afflicted by continuous and frequent labors. This too is what musicians
carefully observe in respect of their instruments, when they loosen
the strings lest they snap through unrelieved tension. For these reasons nature too has adjusted the voices of living creatures to sing not
with only one intensity but with all kinds of variation, becoming lax
and tense (in turn). And so, just as music is by its laws adapted not
only to distinct and increased intensities but also to medium ones and
to relaxations, so too is it with the mind. For when it is wholly intent
on pleasing the Father and becomes God-possessed, it is rightly said
to be fortunate. And when it ceases to be frenzied, after its enthusiasm it returns to itself and reflects on its own affairs and what is
proper to it. For piety and love of man are related virtues. And these

the wise man uses and observes, taking care to be reverent as a suppliant. While God stays, he remains there, and when He departs, he too departs. And the Father takes his departure because of his providential care and consideration for our race, knowing that it is by nature shackled and involved in its needs. Wherefore he saw fit to retire and be alone, for not everything is to be done by the sons in the sight of the Father. (*QG* 4.29)

Three Ways of Life

There are three ways of life, which are well known: the contemplative, the active, and the pleasurable. Great and excellent is the contemplative; slight and unbeautiful is the pleasurable; small and not small is the middle one, which touches on, and adheres to, both of them. It is small because of its proximity to pleasure; but it is great because of its nearness and also its kinship to contemplation. (*QG* 4.47)[608]

XII. MOSES AND THE LAW

Moses' Fame as Lawgiver Is Known Far and Wide, But the Man Himself Is Known to Few

I intend to record the life of Moses, whom some consider the lawgiver of the Jews, others as the interpreter of the Holy Laws, a man who is in every respect the greatest and most perfect, and whom it is my wish to make known to those who deserve not to be uninformed of him. For while the fame of the laws he left behind has traveled throughout the inhabited world and reached the ends of the earth, the man himself as he was in reality is known to few. This was due to the unwillingness of Greek men of letters to consider him worthy of mention, probably through envy[609] and also the disagreement of his laws in many instances with those ordained by the legislators of the various states. (*Mos.* 1.1–2)

Moses Taught by an International Team of Scholars

Teachers arrived forthwith from various places, some unbidden from the bordering areas and the Egyptian provinces, others summoned from Greece under promise of great bounty. But he soon outstripped their capacities, for his happy natural gifts anticipated their instruction, so that it seemed to be a case of recollection rather than of learning, and he himself even further devised conundrums for them. For great natures open up new spheres of knowledge, and just as bodies that are wholesome and agile in every part release their trainers from care so that they need pay them little or no attention, and just as vigorous and healthy trees that improve of themselves release the husbandmen, in the same way the naturally endowed soul goes forward in advance to meet its instruction, and derives more profit from itself than from its teachers, and having grasped some first principles of knowledge rushes forward, as the saying goes, like the horse to the meadow.[610] Arithmetic, geometry, the theory of rhythm, harmony, and meter, and the entire field of music as exhibited by the use of instruments or in the accounts of more specialized manuals and expositions, were transmitted to him by learned Egyptians.[611] They further instructed him in the philosophy conveyed through symbols, which they display in the so-called holy characters [hieroglyphs] and through the approbation accorded animals, to which they even pay divine honors. Greeks taught him the rest of the encyclical studies, and savants from the bordering countries taught him Assyrian letters and the Chaldean science of the heavenly bodies. The latter he also acquired from the Egyptians, who especially pursue astronomy. And when he had learned with precision from either nation both that on which they agree and that on which they disagree, avoiding polemics and strife, he sought the truth, since his mind was incapable of accepting anything false, as is the wont of sectarians, who maintain the doctrines proposed, whatever they happen to be, without examining whether they are trustworthy, thus acting exactly as hired lawyers who have no concern for justice. (*Mos.* 1.21–24)

Was the Mind in Moses Human or Divine or a Blend of Both?

Naturally, then, his disciples and everyone else were astonished, struck with amazement as at a novel spectacle, and investigated the nature of the mind that dwelt enshrined like an image in his body,[612] whether it was human or divine or a blend of both, since it contained nothing resembling the multitude, transcending them and exalted to a more splendid height. For he accorded to his belly nothing beyond the necessary tributes assessed by nature, and as for the pleasures below it, except for the begetting of lawful children, he did not even keep them in mind. He became to an extraordinary degree a practicer of frugal contentment and held the luxurious life in unparalleled mockery, for he longed to live to the soul alone and not the body. He displayed the principles of his philosophy through his daily actions. He spoke his mind and acted in accordance with his words with a view to harmony between speech and life,[613] so that his life should prove to be like his speech and his speech like his life, producing harmony as on a musical instrument. (*Mos.* 1.27–29)

Moses Was Master of the Elements and Entered into the Darkness Where God Was

And so, as he had fully renounced pelf, and the riches that are inflated among men, God rewarded him by giving him instead the greatest and most perfect wealth. That is the wealth of the whole earth and seas and rivers and all the other elements and compounds. For, since God deemed him worthy to appear as a partner in his own sphere, he gave over to him the entire world as a fitting possession for his heir. Therefore, each element obeyed him as its master, changed its properties, and submitted to his commands. And perhaps this is nothing marvellous, for if, as the proverb goes, friends' possessions are common,[614] and the prophet is called the friend of God,[615] it follows that he would also share God's possessions, so far as it is needful. For, since God possesses all things, he needs nothing, whereas the good man strictly possesses nothing, not even himself, but receives a share of the divine treasures to the extent that he is capable. And perhaps this is naturally the case. For he is a world citizen, for which reason he is not registered in any city of the inhabited world, rightly so, since he has received not some parcel of land but the world entire as his portion. Again, did he not enjoy a greater fellowship, that of the Father and Creator of the All, since he was deemed worthy of the selfsame designation? For he was named god and king of the whole nation, and is said to have entered into the darkness where God was,[616] namely into the unseen, invisible, incorporeal, and archetypal essence of existing things, thus beholding what may not be seen by mortal nature. For bringing himself and his own life into public view like a picture excellently wrought, he has set before us an admirable and godlike work as a model for those willing to copy

269

it. Happy are they who impress or strive to impress that image on their souls. For it were best that the mind should bear the perfect form of virtue, but if that is unattainable, let it at least have the indubitable desire to possess that form. (*Mos.* 1.155–159)

Proof That Moses Was the Best of Lawgivers and That His Laws Truly Come from God

That Moses himself was the best of all lawgivers everywhere, either among the Greeks or the barbarians, and that his laws are the most excellent and truly come from God, since they neglect nothing that is necessary, the following is the clearest proof. If anyone examines the legal usages of other peoples he will find that they have been shaken by innumerable causes—wars, tyrannies, or other undesirable events that befall them by the stroke of fortune's revolutions. Frequently, luxury, flowing to excess through unstinting supplies and superfluities, has destroyed the laws, since the multitudes are unable to bear "an excess of good things,"[617] but grow insolent through satiety, and insolence is the antagonist of Law. But Moses' laws alone, firm, unshaken, unswerving, stamped as it were by the seals of nature herself, remain solid from the day they were first enacted to now, and there is hope that they will remain for all future ages as though immortal, so long as the sun and the moon and the entire heaven and universe exist.[618] In any case, though the nation has experienced so many changes both by way of success and the reverse, nothing, not even the smallest part of his ordinances, has been disturbed; since all have clearly accorded high honor to their venerable and godlike character. (*Mos.* 2.12–15)

Almost Every Nation Has Come to Approve and Honor Our Laws

But this is not yet the marvel of it, though it may rightly be thought a great matter in itself, that the laws should have been firmly observed through all time. More wonderful, I believe, is the fact that not only the Jews but all other peoples and particularly those who have taken greater stock of virtue have grown devout to the point of approving and honoring our laws. In this they have obtained a singular honor, which belongs to no other code. The following is the proof. Among the Greek and barbarian states, there is virtually none that honors the institutions of any other. Indeed, scarcely does any state hold fast lastingly to its own, as it adapts them to meet the vicissitudes of times and circumstances. The Athenians censure the customs and legal usages of the Lacedaemonians, and the Lacedaemonians those of the Athenians; nor, in the barbarian sphere, do the Egyptians observe the laws of the Scythians nor the Scythians those of the Egyptians—nor, to put it briefly, the Asiatics those of Europeans, nor the Europeans those of the Asiatics. Virtually all people from the rising of the sun to its setting, every country, nation, and state are hostile to foreign institutions and believe that they increase the approbation of their own by showing disdain for those of others. This is not the case with ours. They draw the attention and win over all, barbarians, Greeks, mainlanders and islanders, nations east and west, Europe, Asia, the entire inhabited world from end to end.[619] (*Mos.* 2.17–20)

The Septuagint Version Is Divinely Inspired

Sitting here in concealment with none present save the natural elements, earth, water, air, heaven, the mystery of whose genesis they were on the verge of expounding first, for the creation account constitutes the beginning of the laws, they became as it were possessed and interpreted the divine word without each of them employing different expressions, but all employing precisely the same words and phrases, as though dictated[620] to each by an invisible prompter. Yet who does not know that every language, and Greek in particular, abounds in terms, and that the same notion can be variously rendered by paraphrasing and rewording, and suiting the diction to the occasion? This is something they say did not happen with this code of law, but the Greek words used corresponded exactly to the Chaldean, perfectly adapted to the things signified. For just as in geometry and dialectic, as I see it, the matters signified do not permit variety of expression, but what was first set down remains unaltered, similarly these writers, as it appears, discovered the expressions that coincide with the matter, and that alone or best of all would render forcefully and distinctly what was meant. The clearest proof of this is that, if the Chaldeans have learned Greek, or Greeks Chaldean, and read both versions, the Chaldean and its translation, they marvel at them and respect them as sisters, or rather one and the same, both in matter and words, and designate the authors not as translators but as prophets and hierophants, to whom it was granted in the purity of their thought to match their steps with the purest of spirits, the spirit of Moses. (*Mos.* 2.37–40)

The Israelite Image of Moses

So great was their admiration for that man, whoever he was who gave them the laws, that whatever received his approval received theirs too. So whether what he told them was a product of his own reasoning or was learnt from a divine being, they referred it all to God, and though many years have passed, exactly how many I cannot say, but at any rate more than two thousand, they have not altered even a single word of what had been written by him but would endure to die ten thousand deaths sooner than be persuaded of what is contrary to his laws and customs. (*Hypoth.* 6.8)

Moses' Calling Above Is a Second Birth Better Than the First

Why is the mountain covered with a cloud for six days, and Moses called above on the Seventh Day (Exod. 24:16b)?

The even number, six, he apportioned both to the creation of the world and to the election of the contemplative nation, wishing to show first of all that he created both the world and the nation elected for virtue. And in the second place, because he wishes the nation to be ordered and arrayed in the same manner as the whole world so that, as in the latter, it may have a fitting order in accord with the right law and canon of the unchanging placeless and unmoving nature of God. But the calling above of the prophet is a second birth[621] better than the first. For the latter is mixed with a body and had corruptible parents, while the former is an unmixed and simple soul of the sovereign, being changed from a productive to an unproductive form, which has no mother but only a father, who is (the Father) of all. Wherefore the calling above or, as we have said, the divine birth happened to come about for him in accordance with the ever-virginal nature of the hebdomad. For he is called on the Seventh Day, in this (respect) differing from the earthborn first molded man, for the latter came into being from the earth and with a body, while the former (came) from the ether and without a body. Wherefore the most appropriate number, six was assigned to the earthborn man, while to the one differently born (was assigned) the higher nature of the hebdo-mad. (*QE* 2.46)

The Vestments of the High Priest
Are a Representation of the World

Such were the vestments of the High Priest. But I must not omit mention of its meaning and that of its parts. The ensemble is a repro-duction and imitation of the world, and its elements correspond to each of its parts. We must begin with the full-length robe. This gar-ment is all violet, and thus a representation of the air; for the air is naturally black and after a fashion a robe reaching to the feet, since it stretches down from the sublunary regions to the ends of the earth, spread out on every side. It is for this reason that the garment, too, spreads out around the whole body from the breast to the feet. At the ankles there hang from it pomegranates, flower-work, and bells. The flower-work is a symbol of the earth, for it is from it that all things flower and germinate; the pomegranates represent the water, aptly so called from their flowing juice; while the bells represent the concor-dant harmony of these two, for neither is earth without water or wa-ter without earthy material sufficient for generation, but only the union and blending of both . . . .

As for the ephod, reason founded on plausible conjecture will represent it as a symbol of the heaven. For first, the two rounded em-erald stones on the shoulder blades signify, as some think, those stars that govern day and night, namely the sun and moon, or as might be said with a closer approach to the truth, each of the hemispheres of the sky. For, like the two stones, the hemisphere above the earth and that below it are equal to each other, and it is the nature of neither to diminish and increase as does the moon. Additional testimony is furnished by their color, for the appearance of the entire heaven yields a visual impression like that of the emerald. Six names, too, were necessarily engraved on each of the stones, since each of the hemispheres also divides the zodiac into two and intercepts six of the signs. . . .

It is with good reason that the oracular breast-piece is doubled, for reason is twofold both in the universe and in human nature. In the universe there is that reason which deals with the incorporeal and archetypal ideas, from which the intelligible world is brought into be-ing, and that which deals with visible objects, which are copies and

273

representations of those ideas out of which the sensible world was produced. In man the one is interior, the other in the form of utterance. The former is like a spring, while that which is voiced flows forth from it. (*Mos.* 2.117–119, 122–123,127)[622]

When the High Priest Enters the Sanctuary
the Whole Universe Enters with Him

Arrayed in this manner the high priest sets out to perform the cultic services, so that when he enters to offer the ancestral prayers and sacrifices the whole universe may enter with him, thanks to the representations[623] of it that he brings with him, the full-length robe a copy of the air, the pomegranate of water, the flower-work of earth, the scarlet of fire, the ephod of heaven, the rounded emeralds on the shoulder-tops in the form of two hemispheres with the six engravings on each of them, the twelve stones in four rows of threes on the breast an image of the zodiac, the oracular breast-piece an image of that Reason which holds together and administers all things. For it was essential for the man who was consecrated to the Father of the world to employ his Son[624] whose excellence is consummate as his intercessor, that sins may be forgotten and good things profusely abound. Perhaps, too, he is providing advance instruction to the servant of God that he ought to try from beginning to end to be worthy at least of the world, if not of the world's Creator. Since he is garbed in its representation, he ought forthwith to carry its pattern impressed in his mind, and so become himself transformed in a manner of speaking from a man into the nature of the world; and, if one may say so— and in speaking of truth it is right to speak unerringly—be himself a world in miniature. (*Mos.* 2.133–135)

Why the Laws Were Promulgated in the Desert and not in the City

To those who raise the question why Moses promulgated his laws not in the cities but in the heart of the desert, we may say first that most cities are full of countless evils, both impious acts toward God and injustices between man and man.[625] For there is nothing that has not been adulterated, the genuine surpassed by the spurious, the true by the specious, which is intrinsically false though it throws off plausible impressions that delude. It is in the cities, then, that

274

there is produced that most insidious of all things, vanity,[626] marveled at and worshiped by some who magnify hollow opinions by means of gold crowns and purple robes and multitudes of servants and carriages, on which these so-called blissful and happy people are borne aloft, sometimes yoking together mules or horses, sometimes even men, who bear the heavy burden of the litters about their necks, yet are oppressed in soul rather than body through an excess of arrogance. Vanity is also the architect of many other evils, boastfulness, haughtiness, inequality, and these are the sources of wars, both foreign and civil, suffering no place to remain at rest whether public or private, whether on sea or on land.

But why need we mention offenses between man and man? For through vanity, divine things too are held of little account, though they are thought to obtain the highest honors. But what honor can there be if truth is absent, truth honorable both in name and function, since indeed falsehood is, on the contrary, naturally dishonorable? This contempt for things divine is manifest to those of more acute vision. For men have by means of painting and sculpture[627] fashioned innumerable forms and surrounded them besides with shrines and temples and after erecting altars have assigned celestial and divine honors to idols of stone and wood and suchlike images, all of them lifeless. . . .

He had also a second thought[628] in mind. He who is about to receive the holy laws must purify his soul and cleanse away the deeply ingrained strains contracted through contact with the motley city rabble. But this cannot come about otherwise than by dwelling apart, and not immediately but only long afterwards, until the marks imprinted on him by his old transgressions have gradually grown faint, run off and disappeared. . . .

A third reason is the following. Just as they who set out on a long journey do not begin to furnish sails, rudders, and tillers when they have embarked and set sail from the harbor, but prepare for themselves each of the items contributing toward the voyage while still remaining on shore, in the same manner Moses did not deem it right that they should take their land allotments and settle in the cities and then seek out laws under which to enjoy a form of government, but should first prepare for themselves the norms of a political regime and be trained in those practices thanks to which communities are securely governed, and then settle down to make immediate use of the provisions of justice in harmony and fellowship and distributing to each his due.

Some also allege a fourth reason, which is not out of harmony with the truth but is in close correspondence with it. Since it was necessary to breed in their minds the conviction that the laws were not human inventions but quite evidently divine oracles, he led the nation far away from the cities into the heart of the desert, barren not only of cultivated fruits but also of water suitable for drinking. His thought was that if after lacking the necessaries of life and expecting to perish through hunger and thirst they suddenly found an abundance of useful things spontaneously produced, with the heaven raining down the nourishment called manna, and a production of quail from the air to add relish to their food, and with bitter water turning sweet for drinking and springs gushing forth from the flinty rock, they should no longer wonder whether the laws were divine oracles, since they had obtained the clearest touchstone of the truth in the supplies they had received in their need contrary to all expectation. For he who gave abundance of life's necessaries also granted the resources for the good life; for living they needed food and drink, which they found without making any preparations, whereas for good living they required laws and ordinances through which they would improve their souls. (*Decal.* 2–7, 10–11, 14–17)

Why Did God Address the Ten Oracles as to One Individual?

But one may appropriately raise the difficulty why, when so many thousands were gathered in one spot, he deemed it right to address each of his ten oracles not as to several persons but as to one,[629] "You shall not commit adultery, You shall not murder, You shall not steal," and similarly with the rest. We must answer first that he wishes to teach the readers of the Sacred Scriptures a most excellent lesson, that each single individual in himself, when he is law-abiding and obedient to God, is equal in value to a whole nation, even the most populous, or rather to all nations, and if we may go still further, even to the whole world.[630] For this reason, in another passage, in praising a certain just man, he says, "I am your God." Now, he was also the God of the universe, but he meant that subjects stationed in the same rank and giving a like satisfaction to their commander have an equal part in favor and honor. (*Decal.* 36–38)

SELECTIONS

Why the Ten Commandments Lay Down No Penalties

Next let us give the reason why he revealed the ten words or laws in the form of simple commands and prohibitions without laying down any penalty, as is the custom of legislators, against future transgressors. He was God, and thus naturally a good Lord, the cause of good only, and of nothing evil. He therefore regarded it most appropriate to his nature to issue his preserving commandments free from any admixture or share of punishment, that men might choose the best, not involuntarily and taking senseless fear for their counselor,[631] but of deliberate purpose and by virtue of intelligent reasoning. He therefore thought it right not to deliver his ordinances conjoined with punishment, though he did not grant immunity to evildoers, but knew that Justice his assessor,[632] the overseer of human affairs, will not remain inactive inasmuch as she is by nature a hater of evil, but will assume as her inborn task the requital of those who err. For it is fitting for the servants and lieutenants of God that like generals engaged in war they should employ their weapons against the deserters who abandon the ranks of justice. But it belongs to the Great King that the general security of the universe should be ascribed to him who protects the peace and everywhere continually supplies richly and abundantly the good things of peace to all. For in truth God is the Prince[633] of Peace, while his subalterns are the leaders in war. (*Decal.* 176–178)

Four Reasons Given for the Rite of Circumcision

The general categories of the special laws, the so-called Ten Commandments, have been carefully investigated in the preceding treatise. Following the sequence of our work, we must now examine the particular ordinances. I shall begin with that which is an object of derision among many people.[634] The circumcision of the genital organs is held in ridicule, though it is most zealously practiced by many other nations, epecially by the Egyptians, a people that appears to be populous, ancient, and philosophical in the highest degree.[635] It would therefore be proper to let go of the childish banter and investigate more wisely and seriously the causes thanks to which this custom has prevailed, and not hastily pass judgment on the recklessness of great nations. They should reflect that it is unnatural[636] that so many thousands in every generation undergo cutting, and mutilate their own bodies and those of their nearest kin while suffering severe pains, and that there are many conditions that impel them to maintain and discharge a practice introduced by the ancients. The principal reasons are four in number.

The first is that it secures release from the severe and virtually incurable malady of the foreskin called carbuncle, which, I believe, gets its name from the fact that it involves a chronic inflammation and which is more prone to befall those who retain the foreskin. Second, it furthers the cleanliness of the whole body as befits the consecrated order,[637] wherefore the Egyptian priests go even further and have their bodies shaved. For some impurities that ought to be purged collect gradually and retract in the hair and foreskin. Third, it assures the resemblance of the circumcised member to the heart. For as both are prepared for generation, the cardial *pneuma* for the generation of thought, the productive organ for living creatures, the earliest men deemed it right to assimilate the manifest and visible member through which sensible things are naturally engendered to the unseen and superior member, by which intelligible things are produced. The fourth and most essential reason is its predisposition to give fecundity, for it is said that the sperm has free passage without being scattered or flowing into the folds of the foreskin, and consequently the circumcised nations appear to be the most prolific and most populous.

These are the explanations that have reached us from the antiquarian studies of inspired men who researched the Mosaic Writings with the utmost care. As for myself, in addition to what has been said, I believe that circumcision is a symbol of two things that are particularly essential. One is the excision of pleasures that bewitch the mind. For since among the love-lures of pleasure the prize is carried off by the union of man and woman, the legislators thought it right to dock the organ that serves such intercourse, thus intimating that circumcision signifies the excision of excessive and superfluous pleasure, not of one pleasure alone, but through the one that is most violent also of all the others.[638]

The other reason is that a man should know himself and expel from his soul the grievous malady of conceit. For there are some who boast of their ability to fashion, like good sculptors, the fairest of creatures, man, and, puffed up with pride, have deified themselves, ignoring the true Cause of all created things, though they could find a corrective for their delusion in their acquaintances. For many men among them are sterile and many women barren, whose relations are without issue and who grow old childless. This evil opinion must therefore be excised from the mind together with all others that are not God-loving. (*Spec.* 1.1–11)[639]

The True Temple of God Is the Whole Universe

The highest and true temple of God is, we must believe, the whole universe,[640] having for its sanctuary the holiest part of all existence, namely heaven, for its votive offerings the stars, for its priests the angels, who are servitors of his powers, unbodied souls, not mixtures of rational and irrational nature as ours are, but with the irrational eliminated, completely mind, pure intelligences, in the likeness of the monad. The other temple is made by hand; for it was fitting not to inhibit the impulses of men who pay their tribute to piety and wish by means of sacrifices to express their thanks for the good things that befall them or to ask for pardon and forgiveness for errors committed. But he provided that there should not be temples built either in many places or many in the same place, judging that since God is one, there should also be only one temple.[641] (*Spec.* 1.66–67)

Unlike the Cities, the Jewish People Pay Their Dues with Indescribable Joy and Eagerness

From all this it is evident that the Law attaches to the priests the dignity and honor of royalty. As to sovereigns assuredly he commands that tribute should be given from every part of a man's property, but the manner of giving is in complete contrast to the way in which the cities make their contributions to their rulers. These pay under compulsion, painfully, and in a state of groaning, regarding the tax collectors as public scourges. They allege various excuses on different occasions, and pay out the appointed dues and tributes in disregard of the time limits prescribed. But those of our nation make their contributions at each of the annual seasons joyfully and cheerfully, anticipating the demand and shortening the time limits, in the belief that they are not giving but receiving. They do so with worshipful praise and thankfulness, men and women alike, with spontaneous zeal and readiness, and an eagerness that beggars description. (*Spec.* 1.142–144)

The Female Nature

Marketplaces, council chambers, law courts, confraternities, and meetings of vast crowds, life under the open air with its words and actions, befit men both in war and in peace. For women, on the other hand, the domestic life that abides within is appropriate, the maidens taking as their interior boundary the middle door, whereas those who have attained to full womanhood take the outer door.[642] For the nature of communities is twofold, the greater and the smaller; the greater we call cities and the smaller households.[643] As to the management of both forms, men have obtained that of the greater, which bears the name of statesmanship, whereas women have obtained that of the smaller, which goes under the name of household management. [644] A woman, then, should not meddle in matters external to the household, but should seek seclusion. She ought not to be found in the thoroughfares under the eyes of other men like a streetwalker, except when she must go to the temple,[645] and even then she should take care not to go when the market is full, but when most people have gone home, and so like a freeborn lady of true breeding quietly offer her oblations and prayers for the aversion of evil and the enjoyment of goods. That women, under the pretext of affording dutiful aid, should dare to sally forth against men reviling one another and locked in combat is most reprehensible and shameless. Even in wars, expeditions, and dangers threatening the entire community, the law does not deem it right for them to be found, having in view what is proper, which it was minded to maintain unaltered always and everywhere, considering it to be in itself a higher good than victory, freedom, and every form of success. If indeed a woman, learning that her husband is a victim of outrage, is overcome by the love induced by her conjugal attachment and is compelled by the momentary passion to rush forward, she must not in her boldness turn masculine beyond the bounds of nature,[646] but remain within the limits in which women may render aid. For it would be dreadful if any woman in her wish to rescue her husband from outrage should outrage herself displaying her own life as full of disgrace and heavy reproaches attributable to her incurable effrontery. Shall a woman, then, rant in the marketplace and utter some indecent expression or other? Should she not flee at the sound of another's foul language, while stopping up her ears? As it is, some go so far as not only to hurl abuse and contumely through endless talk, women[647] amidst a throng of men, but even apply their hands that were trained for weaving and spinning and not for blows and outrage like those of pancratiasts and boxers.

And though all else could be tolerated, this is hard to take, if a woman becomes so emboldened as to take hold of the genitals of her adversary. She is not to be spared insofar as she appears to be doing this in aid of her husband. She must be restrained from her excessive boldness by paying a penalty through which, though she wish to repeat the offense, she will be incapable of doing so, and those others of her sex who are more reckless will grow moderate through fear. And the penalty shall consist in the cutting off of the hand that handled what it was forbidden to touch.[648] The organizers of the gymnastic contests also deserve praise for banning women from the spectacle[649] in order that they may not be present when men are stripping themselves naked, nor debase the coin of modesty by disregarding the statutes of Nature, which she has ordained for each segment of our race. For neither is it proper for men to be present when women are disrobing but each of the sexes should turn aside from viewing the nakedness of the other and thus follow nature's intent. Surely, then, if their use of sight is reprehensible, their application of hands is far more blameworthy. For the eyes often take liberties and force us to see what we do not wish to see, but the hands are ranked among the parts that are subject to us and obediently minister to our orders.

This is the reason commonly given by many, but I have heard another from inspired men who assume that most of the texts of the Law are outward symbols of things hidden, expressing the inexpressible.[650] It goes as follows: The soul, like the family, has a male element in the male line and a female in the female line. The male soul attaches itself to God alone as the Father and Creator of the universe and Cause of all things. The female is devoted to what comes into being and perishes; it extends its power like a hand to take hold blindly of the fortuitous and welcomes the world of created being with all its innumerable changes and vicissitudes, instead of the unchangeable, blessed, and thrice happy divine nature. Naturally then is it clearly stated in a symbol to cut off the hand that had seized the testicles,[651] not in the sense that the body be mutilated by being deprived of a most essential member, but to excise the godless thoughts that employ as their foundation all that comes into being through birth; for the "testicles" are symbols of sowing and birth. Following the logical sequence of nature, I will add this too. The monad is the image of the first cause, the dyad that of passive and divisible matter. Therefore one who honors and welcomes the dyad before the monad[652] should not be unaware that he is approving of matter rather than of God. It is for this reason that the Law deemed it right to cut off this impulse of the soul as if it were a hand, for there is no greater impiety than to attribute to the passive principle the efficacy of the active one. (*Spec.* 3.169–180)

Greek Legislators Have Copied from the Tables of Moses

But ears, as one of the ancients[653] has pointedly remarked, are less reliable than eyes; they do not light on the facts but are diverted by words, which interpret the facts not always in accordance with the truth. And therefore certain legislators among the Greeks,[654] copying from the perfectly holy tables of Moses, seemed to have arranged things well in prohibiting the giving of hearsay evidence, with the idea that one must judge what one has seen to be trustworthy, but what one has heard as not entirely certain. (*Spec.* 4.60–61)

The Symbolism of the Dietary Laws

It might perhaps be assumed to be just that all wild beasts that feed on human flesh should suffer from men the same treatment they inflict on them. But Moses is of the opinion that we should abstain from the enjoyment of these, even though they provide a most pleasant and delectable feast, since he was considering what was appropriate for a civilized soul. For though it is fitting for the perpetrators of such acts to suffer the like, it is not proper for the sufferers to retaliate, lest they become brutalized unawares by the savage passion of anger. So cautious is he in this regard that, wishing to have full scope[655] to restrain the impulse for the food just mentioned, he also strictly forbade the use of the other carnivores, distinguishing the herbivores as constituting gentle herds, since they are naturally tame and live on the gentle fruits the earth produces and do not engage in scheming against others. They are ten in number:[656] the calf, the lamb, the kid, the deer, the gazelle, the buffalo, the wild goat, the pygarg, the antelope, and the giraffe. For since he always held fast to the science of arithmology, which he acutely perceived to be of the greatest import in all that exists, he never legislated any law, great or samll, without including and as it were adjusting to his enactments the appropriate

282

number. But of all the numbers from the monad and up, ten is the most perfect, and, as Moses says, most holy and sacred, and with it he marks the kinds of clean animals whose use he wished to assign to the members of his commonwealth.

He subjoins a general test and verification of the ten species of animals, employing two signs, the parted hoof and the chewing of the cud.[657] Animals lacking both or one of these are unclean. Now both these signs are symbols of the methods of teaching and learning most conducive to knowledge, by which the better is distinguished from the worse with a view to avoiding confusion. For just as the ruminant animal after chewing up the food fixes it in the gullet, again after a while draws it up and masticates it and then transfers it to the belly, in like manner the student, after receiving from the teacher through his ears the principles and intuitions of wisdom, prolongs the learning process, since he cannot straightway apprehend and grasp them with acumen, till by repeating in his memory through constant exercises, which function like the glue of conceptions, he firmly stamps their impression in his soul. But there appears to be no advantage in having a firm apprehension of ideas unless there is in addition a discrimination and distinction between them with a view to our choosing what we ought and avoiding their opposites, of which the parted hoof is the symbol. For the path of life is twofold, one branch leading to vice, the other to virtue, and we must turn away from the one and never abandon the other. For this reason all animals that are either solid-hoofed or many-hoofed[658] are unclean, the former because they hint at the notion that the good and the bad have one and the same nature, like concave and convex or an uphill and downhill road; the latter because they display before our lives many roads or rather dead ends, to deceive us, for with a multitude of roads it is no easy matter to perceive the best and most efficacious path.

After establishing these rules concerning the land animals he proceeds to describe those water creatures that are clean for eating. These too he marks by two distinguishing characteristics, fins and scales; all that have neither or only one he dismisses and rejects. The reason for this must be pointedly stated. Those species that lack both or one of these marks are swept away by the strong current, unable to withstand the force of its impetus; those who possess both divert it, frontally oppose it, and eagerly exercise themselves against the antagonist with an invincible zeal and audacity. When pushed they push back, when pursued they turn and attack, in straitened circumstances they open up wide pathways for easy escape. These two kinds of fish are symbolic, the first of a pleasure-loving soul, the latter of one that yearns for endurance and self-control. For the road that leads to pleasure is downhill and very easy, and causes one to glide rather than walk, whereas the one that leads to self-control is uphill, wearisome indeed, but exceedingly profitable.[659] The one carries us down and causes us to sink by driving us headlong, till it spits us out at the farthest edge; the other leads the unwearying heavenward and makes them immortal, since they have had strength to endure its roughness and virtual impassibility.

Following the same notion he declares that all the reptiles that do not have feet but[660] crawl by trailing along on their belly, or are four-legged and many-footed, are unclean for eating. [661] Here again, by reptiles he is intimating those who are devoted to their bellies and take their fill like a cormorant, paying to the wretched stomach unceasing tributes of strong drink, pastries, fish, and in general all the dainties produced with every kind of dish crafted by cooks and confectioners, whereby they rekindle and rouse the insatiable and unquenchable desires. By the four-legged and many-footed he means the sorry slaves not of one passion, namely desire, but of all. For these are generically four in number, though there are innumerable species, and while the tyranny of one is grievous, the tyranny of many is undoubtedly most oppressive and unbearable. Creeping things that have legs above their feet, so that they can leap from the ground, he classifies among the clean, as the species of grasshoppers and the so-called snake-fighter; [662] and here again by means of symbols he investigates the characteristics and dispositions of a rational soul. For the gravitation of the body, by its natural weight,[663] drags down the small-minded, strangling and constricting them with the multitude of the fleshly elements. Happy are they to whom it is granted to exert force with superior strength against the weight of its attractive force, taught by the rules of correct instruction to leap upward from the earth and earth-hugging things into the ether and the circuits of heaven, the sight of which is enviable and highly prized by those who come to it willingly and not at haphazard. (*Spec.* 4.103–115)

Moses Disapproves of Hunting

Skillful hunters who know how to shoot their prey with unerring aim that rarely misses and vaunt their success in the chase, particularly when they divide the portions of their quarry with fellow huntsmen as well as with the hounds, are praised by most legislators among Greeks and barbarians, not only for their courage, but also for their liberality of character. But the author of the holy commonwealth might rightly blame them, since for the reasons stated he forbade the enjoyment of animal carcasses outright, whether they perished naturally or were torn by wild beasts. If anyone of those given to training becomes a lover of gymnastic exercises as well as a lover of the hunt, because he assumes that it constitutes practice and a preliminary contest for war[664] and dangers inherent in facing enemies, he should when successful in the chase throw the seized prey to feast the hounds as a wage or prize for their boldness and unexceptionable aid. He himself should not touch them, thus learning beforehand from the example of irrational animals the sentiments he ought to entertain concerning enemies, with whom one should do battle not for unjust gain in imitation of plunderers, but in self-defense, either on account of injuries already suffered or those he expects to suffer in the future. (*Spec.* 4.120–121)

The Maintenance of Ancient Customs

Another precept of comon utility is "You shall not shift your neighbor's landmarks, set up by previous generations" (Deut. 19:14). Now this law, as it appears, was not framed merely for the allotments and boundaries of land with a view to the removal of greed but also for the maintenance of ancient customs.[665] For customs are unwritten laws,[666] the ordinances of men of old,[667] not engraved on slabs of stone or papyrus rolls consumed by moths, but on the souls of those who share in the same commonwealth. For children ought to inherit, aside from property, the paternal customs in which they were reared and have lived with from their very cradle, and not hold them in disdain because they have been handed down without being put into writing. For he who obeys the written laws may not rightly be praised, since he is admonished by constraint and fear of punishment, but he who is true to the unwritten deserves to be lauded, since he displays a virtue freely willed.[668] (*Spec.* 4.149–150)

Three Categories of Mosaic Oracles

The oracles delivered by Moses prove to be of three kinds. The first is concerned with the creation of the world, the second with history, the third with legislation. The creation account has been admirably and marvelously rendered in its entirety, beginning with the genesis of Heaven and leaving off with the fashioning of man. For Heaven is the most perfect of things incorruptible, as man of things mortal. For the Creator fashioned the world weaving in its creation immortal with mortal, the one created for rule, the other as subject and to come into being also in the future.[669] (*Praem.* 1)[670]

Zeno Drew from the Jewish Law Book

Zeno seems to have drawn this conception, as from a fountain, from the Jewish law book, where we hear of two brothers, one self-controlled, the other licentious, how their common father took pity for the one who had not attained to virtue and prayed that he should be a slave to his brother.[671] He took slavery, which appears to be the worst of evils, to be a perfect good for the fool, for his loss of independent choice would prevent him from erring with impunity, and his character would be improved under the authority set above him. (*Prob.* 57)[672]

XIII. UNIVERSALISM AND PARTICULARISM

A. ISRAEL

God Will Not Let Israel Receive the Death-Blow

Every created thing must necessarily undergo change, for this is its property, even as that of God is to be unchangeable. But while some, after being changed, remain that way until they are completely destroyed, others do so only to the extent of suffering what is characteristic of the mortal condition, and these straightway recover. For this reason Moses says, "He will not allow the Destroyer to enter your homes to smite" (Exod. 12:23); for he does allow the Destroyer (destruction being the soul's change) to enter into the soul, in order to indicate what is characteristic of created being; but God will not permit the offspring of "the seeing" Israel to be so changed as to be mortally stricken, but will force him to rise and emerge as from the depths and recover. (*LA* 2.33–34)[673]

SELECTIONS

In Israel, a Whole Nation Has Attained to Wisdom

But in the school of Moses it is not one man alone who may boast that he has learnt the rudiments[674] of wisdom, but an entire nation, vast in number. And we have the following proof. The soul of every one of his disciples has made bold to say to the king of apparent goods, the earthly Edom (for truly all seeming goods are earthly), "I will now pass by through your land" (Num. 20:17). What an extraordinary and magnificent promise![675] Will you be able, tell me, to pass over, go by, and speed past[676] the earthly goods of appearance and opinion? And will nothing, then, forcefully check and stay your forward impetus? Will you gaze at all the brimming treasuries of wealth in turn, yet abandon them and avert your eyes? Will you transcend the honors of high lineage, both paternal and maternal, or the nobility of birth celebrated by the multitude? And what of glory, for which men would give all in exchange, will you leave it behind and treat it as something absolutely valueless? Will you pass by bodily health, acuteness of perception, beauty highly prized, irresistible strength, and whatever else serves as the decor of our soul's house, or tomb,[677] or whatever name it must be given, so as to rank none of these in the province of the good? These are the highly venturesome acts of a celestial and heavenly soul that has abandoned the earth's environs and has been drawn up to live with divine natures. For when filled with the contemplation of the authentic and incorruptible goods, it naturally renounces those that are ephemeral and spurious. (*Deus* 148–151).

Israel, the Race That Sees the Truly Existent

To see the best, the truly Existent, belongs to the best of races, Israel, for Israel means seeing God.[678] The race that strives for second place sees the second best, the sensible heaven, and the harmonious order of the stars within it with its truly all-musical choral dance. (*Congr.* 51)

Israel's Despoiling of Egypt but a Bare Wage for Their Service

The Hebrews, thus driven and chased, and conscious of their own high lineage, undertook a daring act of a kind that was natural to freemen mindful of their being the object of unjust plotting. For

287

they took out with them much spoil, part of which they carried on their own persons, and part laden on beasts of burden. And they did this not out of love of money, or as one might say by way of accusation out of lust for the property of others. How could they? First, they were but acquiring a bare wage for the labors performed during their entire period of service; second, they were paying them back, not on an equivalent but on a lesser scale, for the suffering incurred through enslavement.[679] For how is property loss comparable to deprivation of liberty, for which sensible men are willing to give up not only their substance but their life? In either case, they acted correctly, either by receiving in a time of peace a salary of which they were deprived by the unwillingness of those who long refused to pay what was due,[680] or, as in wartime, considering it right to carry off their enemies' goods under the law of the victors. For the Egyptians began with unjust acts of violence, by reducing guests and suppliants to slavery like captives,[681] as I said before. The Hebrews, when the occasion presented itself, avenged themselves without armed preparation, shielded and protected by justice. (*Mos.* 1.140–142)

Israel, Whose Proper Portion Is the Ethereal Region, Is Victorious Over Its Opponents

But when they were about to engage in battle, Moses' hands were affected in the most marvelous way. They became very light and very heavy in turn, and whenever they became light and were raised on high, his own forces were strong and fighting courageously enjoyed brilliant success, but whenever his hands grew heavy, their adversaries prevailed. God thus indicated by means of symbols that the proper portion of the one party was the earth and lowest regions of the universe, of the other, the holiest region, the ether; and that, just as heaven rules in the universe and is superior to earth, so this nation will prevail over its opponents in war. (*Mos.* 1.217)

The Nations Will Ultimately Honor Israel's Laws Alone

Thus the laws are shown to be eagerly desired and highly prized by all, both plain people and rulers alike, and that in spite of the lack of success of our nation over a long period of time. It is natural that what belongs to those who are not in full vigor be in some way under a shadow. But if there should be some beginning toward a brighter condition, how great an improvement is likely to result! Each nation, I believe, would abandon its own ways, and bidding farewell to its ancestral customs, would turn to honoring our laws alone. For when the luster shed by our law is accompanied by national success, it will obscure the light of the others as the risen sun obscures the stars. (*Mos.* 2.43)

The Jewish High Priest Offers Prayers on Behalf of the Entire Human Race

There is also a third symbol in the holy vestments, which we must not pass over in silence. The priests of other nations are accustomed to offer prayer and sacrifices for their kinsmen and friends and fellow citizens only, but the High Priest of the Jews offers prayers and thanks not only on behalf of the entire human race but also for the parts of nature—earth, water, air, fire. For he holds the world to be, as it in truth is, his country,[682] and in its behalf he is accustomed to propitiate the Ruler with supplications and entreaties, imploring him to give his creature a share in his own equitable and merciful nature. (*Spec.* 1.97)[683]

The Israelites Are in the Truest Sense Men

Yet out of the whole human race he chose for their merit those who are truly men.[684] He judged them worthy of every care,[685] and called them to the service of himself, the everflowing fountain of things excellent, from which he also showers down the other virtues and pours them forth for enjoyment that confers the highest benefits, a drink bestowing immortality more than or as much as nectar. (*Spec.* 1.303)[686]

The Jewish Nation Corrected Mankind's Error of Idolatry

But if he exists, whom all Greeks and barbarians alike are at one in acknowledging,[687] the supreme Father of gods and men and Creator of the whole universe, whose nature, though invisible and inscrutable not only by the eye but by the mind, every student of science and other branches of philosophy longs to investigate and neglects nothing that may lead to its discovery and service—then all men ought to have attached themselves to him, and not to have in-

289

troduced new gods as through stage machinery to participate in equal honors. When they slipped into error concerning this most essential point, the Jewish nation, to put it precisely, corrected the fault of all the others.[688] They transcended all created things because they were created and perishable by nature, and chose the service of the Uncreated and Eternal alone, first because of its excellence, second because it is advantageous to be dedicated and attached to the elder rather than to the younger, to the ruler rather than to the subject, to the creator rather than to the creatures. And therefore I am astounded that some dare to accuse of inhumanity the nation that has shown such an extravagant sense of fellowship and goodwill to all men everywhere, that it has discharged its prayers and festivals and firstfruit offerings on behalf of the human race in general, and has served the truly existent God in its own name as well as in the name of those others who have evaded the service incumbent upon them. (*Spec.* 2.165–167)

The Jewish Race Is an Orphan

The whole Jewish race is, in a sense, in the relationship of an orphan in comparison with all the nations all about them. They, whenever misfortunes that are not divinely inflicted befall them, are through their international relations not without the resources of allies acting in concert with them. But the Jewish nation has none to come to its aid, since it lives under extraordinary laws that are necessarily solemn inasmuch as they encourage them to reach the summit of virtue. But solemnity is austere, and from austerity the great mass of men turn aside because of their approval of pleasure. Nevertheless as Moses tells us the Ruler of the Universe, to whom this people is allotted, takes pity and compassion on its orphaned and desolate condition, because out of the entire human race it was assigned as a kind of firstfruits to the Creator and Father. And the cause of this was the highly prized acts of justice and virtue of the founders of the race, which endure like immortal plants, bearing fruit ever fresh, salutary, and in every way profitable for their descendants, even though they themselves err, provided their errors are curable and not totally incorrigible.[689]

Yet let no one consider high lineage a perfect good and proceed to neglect noble actions, but reflect that greater anger is incurred by one who, though of noble parentage, nevertheless brings shame on those who begot him through the viciousness of his character; for possessing his own models of excellence to copy and yet taking no impressions of it for the sound reformation of his life, he is culpable. (*Spec.* 4.179–182)

Who Can Accuse Israel of Misanthropy
When They Extend Fair Treatment Even to Irrational Animals?

Moses, going yet beyond them, extended fair treatment even as far as irrational animals, so that by practicing on creatures of a different kind we may exercise humanity to an exceeding degree in our relations with our congeners, refraining from mutual vexations, and not storing up personal goods but bringing them forth publicly for all everywhere, as for kinsmen and brothers by nature. Let the clever defamers then continue to reproach the nation with misanthropy and charge the laws with recommending unsociable and inhuman practices, when these laws so manifestly grant a share of compassion even to animal herds, and our people from earliest youth through the guidance of the law transpose every indocility of soul into a gentler mode. (*Virt.* 140–141)

The Jewish Nation Stands above Other Nations,
as the Head above the Body

If then there happen to be one such man in a city, he will be superior to the city; if one such city, it will be superior to the surrounding country; one such nation, it will stand above all nations, as the head above the body, to be conspicuous, not for its own glory but rather for the benefit of the beholders. For the uninterrupted impressions of noble models imprint similar images in souls that are not completely toughened and hardened. (*Praem.* 114)

Jews Prefer Death Rather Than Allow
Even the Slightest of Their Traditions to Be Destroyed

For it was the Jews alone whom Gaius eyed suspiciously, because they alone deliberately opposed him and had been taught from the very cradle, as it were, by their parents, tutors, and instructors, and even more so by their holy laws and also the unwritten customs, to acknowledge one God who is the Father and Creator of the world. For all the others, men, women, cities, nations, countries, regions of the earth, I can almost say the whole inhabited world, although they lamented what was happening, flattered him nonetheless and glorified him beyond all measure and increased his vanity. Some too even introduced into Italy the barbarian custom of prostrating themselves,[690] thus debasing the nobility of Roman freedom. One nation alone set apart, that of the Jews, was suspected of intending opposition, since it was wont to undergo death as if it were immortality in order not to suffer the abrogation of any of its ancestral traditions, even the slightest,[691] since as with structures, with the removal of one part from below, the parts that still seem to be firmly standing are loosened and fall in ruins and collapse into the void thus formed. But the change being effected was no petty one, but the greatest of all that exists, namely the seeming transformation of the created and corruptible nature of man into the uncreated and incorruptible nature of deity, which our nation judged to be the most grievous sacrilege, for sooner could God change into man than man into God. This is not to speak of the acceptance of the other supreme evils of infidelity and ingratitude to the Benefactor of the whole world, who by his own might bestows an exceeding abundance of goods upon every part of the All. (*Legat.* 115–118)

The Jews Bear the Images of Their Laws
Imprinted within Their Souls

For all men observe their own customs, but this is particularly true of the Jewish nation. Taking the laws to be divinely revealed oracles, and having been instructed in this doctrine from their earliest youth, they bear the image of the commandments imprinted in their souls. Moreover, as they contemplate their clear forms and shapes their thoughts are ever full of amazement. Those foreigners who hold them in honor they welcome no less than their own countrymen, whereas those who abolish or mock them they hate as their fiercest enemies. And they feel such holy awe at each of the commandments that they would never accept all that men deem good fortune or happiness, call it what you will, in exchange for transgressing even the slightest of them. (*Legat.* 210–211)

SELECTIONS

The Chosen Race Is a Likeness of the World and Its Law Is a Likeness of the Laws of the World

In the second place, this world is a great city and is a legal one. And it is necessary for it to use the best law of state. And it is fitting that it should have a worthy author of law and legislator, since among men God appointed the contemplative race in the same manner (as the Law) for the world. And rightly does he legislate for this race, also prescribing (its Law) as a law for the world, for the chosen race is a likeness of the world, and its Law (is a likeness of the laws) of the world. (*QE* 2.42)

The Contemplative Nation Shall Blossom like the Lily

Wherefore some prophet says that the contemplative nation shall blossom like the lily,[692] indicating that it does not enjoy prosperity at the same time (as other nations) but that at the time when others have passed their prime, (Israel) begins (to flower) without the things it ought to have as inducements, for its flowering without water, when the sun is flaming, is not to be compared with what is usual. (*QE* 2.76)

B. PROSELYTES

Proselytes Should Be Honored

These he calls "proselytes," or newly arrived, because, in their disregard for mythical fictions while holding fast to pure truth, they have come forward to join the new and God-loving commonwealth. Thus while granting equal privileges to all incomers and as many favors as to the native-born, he exhorts the old aristocracy to honor them not only with external respect but with special friendship and exceptional goodwill. And surely with good reason; they have abandoned, he says, their country, their friends, and their kin for the sake of virtue and religion. Let them not be without a share in other cities, kin, and friends, and let there be places of refuge reserved for those coming of their own accord to piety. For the most effectual love charm, the indissoluble bond of the goodwill that unites us, is the honor we render the one God. (*Spec.* 1.51–52)[693]

PHILO OF ALEXANDRIA

Common Citizenship Rests on Virtue

The condition of the alien excludes any kind of partnership, unless through preeminent virtue one converts this too into a tie of kinship, for generally citizenship is founded on virtues and laws that teach that the Noble alone is Good. (*Spec.* 2.73)

Proselytes Automatically Acquire All the Virtues

And it is admirable and profitable to desert pointblank to virtue, and abandon vice, that insidious mistress. At the same time it necessarily follows, as in the sunlight the shadow follows the body, that with the rendering of honor to the God who Is, the entire fellowship of the virtues must follow in its wake. The proselytes become straightway self-controlled, continent, modest, gentle, kind, humane, reverent, just, generous, lovers of truth, superior to the seductions of money and pleasure. (*Virt.* 181–182)

God Espouses the Virtue That Springs from Lowly Birth

The proselyte raised aloft by his good fortune will be admired on all sides, marveled at and held blessed on two counts of highest excellence, that he voluntarily came over to the camp of God and that he has won a most appropriate prize, a secure place in heaven, which one may not describe, while the nobly sired who has debased the coinage of his high lineage will be dragged below and carried deep down into Tartarus itself and profound darkness. Thus may all men seeing these examples grow wise and learn that God espouses the virtue that springs from lowly birth, that he dismisses the roots but accepts the full-grown shoot, because through cultivation it has been converted to fruitfulness. (*Praem.* 152)

C. THE MESSIANIC AGE

Concord and Fellowship between Nations Will One Day Become Facts of Life

This is what our most holy prophet through the whole of his legislation wishes to establish, concord, fellowship, unanimity, harmony of character traits, through which houses, cities, nations, countries,

294

and the entire human race may arrive at supreme happiness. Hitherto these have been nothing but prayers, but they will, I am persuaded, become absolute facts, if God, even as he grants annual fruits, provide a fecundity of virtue. May we, who virtually from earliest youth have carried with us a longing for them, not be deprived of them. (*Virt.* 119–120)

The Savage Beasts Will Become Tame and War Will Finally Cease

Would that this good might illumine our lives and that we might be able to see that day in which savage beasts become tame. But well in advance of this the wild beasts within the soul must be tamed, and a greater boon than this cannot be found.[694] For is it not foolish to assume that we shall escape the damage wrought by the beasts without when we are constantly honing those within us into dire ferocity? We need not therefore abandon hope that when the wild beasts of the soul are tamed, the animals will become so too. Then I believe that bears and lions and panthers and the animals of India, elephants and tigers, and all others whose vigor and power are invincible, will change their solitary and lonely life for one of togetherness and little by little in imitation of the gregarious animals grow tamer when within the sight of men. They will no longer be provoked as heretofore, but will be awestruck and wary of him as their natural lord and master, while others will grow gentle in emulation of the docility and affection for the master, like little Maltese lapdogs who fawn with their tails, which they cheerfully wag. Then too the species of scorpions and serpents and other reptiles will find their venom idling. The Egyptian river too bears man-devouring creatures, the so-called crocodiles and hippopotamuses in close proximity[695] to the country's inhabitants, and the seas too carry many species of troublesome animals. Among all these the man of virtue will stand sacrosanct and inviolate, since God has honored virtue and has bestowed on it the prize of not being liable to attack.

Thus the war that is in time and nature anterior will be abolished through the pacification and taming of the wild beasts. The later one that came about by studied intent through greed will easily be brought to an end, since men, I believe, will be disconcerted if they should prove to be more savage than the irrational animals, after having eluded damage and injury from them. For it will naturally appear absolutely disgraceful that while venom-spraying and man-devouring brutes, savage and unsociable, have become converted to peace and gently disposed, man, an animal naturally gentle, akin to fellowship and concord, should breathe implacable murder against those of his own kind. (*Praem.* 88–92)

The Qualities of the Ultimate Sovereignty of God's Holy Ones

For "a man shall come forth,"[696] says the oracle, who will command an armed host and make war and subdue great and populous nations, because God has sent him the Succor befitting the devout, namely undaunted courage of soul and overpowering bodily strength, either of which is fearsome to the enemy, but joined together are completely irresistible. Some of the enemy, he says, will be unworthy to be defeated by men; against them he will array swarms of wasps[697] to bring upon them shameful destruction, while fighting in the defense of his holy ones. The latter will obtain not only a secure and bloodless victory in war but also incontestable sovereignty for the benefit of their subjects, which will accrue from their goodwill or fear or respect. For the holy ones practice three supreme virtues that contribute to government safe from subversion, namely, dignity, severity, and benevolence, through which the aforementioned feelings are produced. For dignity fashions respect, severity, fear, benevolence goodwill, and these when harmoniously blended in the soul cause subjects to be obedient to their rulers. (*Praem.* 95–97)

Those Who Possess the True Heavenly Wealth Will Have Also Earthly Riches in Abundance

Those who strive after the above-mentioned wealth, who embrace the gifts of nature and not those of empty imaginings, who practice frugality and self-control, will obtain also in vast profusion the wealth of sumptuous fare without effort. For it will rush in on them as most suited to receive it and as reverend men who know how properly to use it, and will gladly shun intercourse with licentious and violent men, in order not to minister to those who live to harm their neighbor and disregard those who serve the common good. For there is a divine oracle[698] that on those who keep the sacred ordinances Heaven will shower timely rains, and the earth will bear a crop of every sort of fruit, the plain of sown grain, the hill country of fruit trees, and no season will be left empty of some form of beneficence, but through the uninterrupted succession of divine gifts "the harvest will overtake the vintage, and the vintage the seed time" (Lev. 26:5). For those for whom the true wealth lies stored up in Heaven through the practice[699] of wisdom and godliness there is also an abundance of earthly goods,[700] their storehouses ever filled through the providence and care of God, because the impulses of their minds and the enterprises of their hands are not hindered in the successful accomplishment of what they ever zealously pursue. (*Praem.* 100–101, 104)

The Day of Redemption

If, however, they accept these chastisements as a warning rather than as aiming at their destruction, if feeling shame they undergo a complete change of heart, and reproach themselves for their errant ways, and make confession and acknowledgment of all their errors,[701] first within themselves with a mind purified so that their conscience is truthful and undisguised, second with their tongues for the improvement of their auditors, then they will obtain the favor of the God who saves and is propitious, who has furnished mankind with that singular and preeminent gift of kinship with his own Logos, from which as from an archetype the human mind came into being. For even if they should be at the ends of the earth, enslaved to those enemies who led them away captive, in one day as if by a prearranged signal they will be liberated, since their conversion in a body to virtue will strike their masters with amazement, and ashamed to rule over their superiors they will set them free. When they have obtained this unexpected freedom, those who were but shortly before scattered in Greece and in foreign parts over islands and continents will arise and hasten with one impulse from every side to the one assigned place, guided by a vision divine and superhuman, invisible to others, but manifest only to those being safely restored. Three intercessors they have for their reconciliation with the Father. One is the fairness and kindness of him who is invoked, who ever prefers pardon to punishment. The second is the holiness of the founders of the race because with souls released from their bodies they exhibit a service to their Ruler unfeigned and nakedly simple and are wont to make on behalf of their sons and daughters supplications that are not ineffectual since the Father grants them the privilege that their prayers should be heard.[702] The third is that through which above all the favor of the two already mentioned comes forward to meet them in advance, namely the improvement of those being drawn on to the conclusion of truce pacts, who with difficulty have been able to come out of a dead-end back on the road, whose goal is no other than to be pleasing to God, as sons to their father. At their arrival, the cities that but shortly before lay in ruins will be rebuilt, the desolate country will be inhabited, and the land rendered barren will change to fruitfulness; the successes of their fathers and progenitors will be considered negligible in view of the abundant riches at their disposal, which flowing from the graciousness of God as from an ever-flowing fountain will procure copious wealth for each individual and to all in common, proof against envy.

There will suddenly be a reversal of all things. God will turn the curses against the enemies who exulted over the nation's failures and jeered and railed at them, in the belief that they themselves would have an indestructible heritage of good fortune, which they hoped to leave to their children and descendants in succession, thinking that they would always see their opponents in a steady and fixed state of ill fortune that would be stored up for the future generations. In their folly they did not understand that they enjoyed their short-lived brilliance not on their own account but for the admonition of others, for whom, in view of their abolition of their ancestral institutions, a salutary remedy was found in grief, in their being greatly pained at the good fortune of their enemies.

Those then who were not utterly ruined after bewailing and groaning over their own rout will turn full circle and wend their way back to their ancestral prosperity. But these enemies who have laughed at their lamentations, resolved to celebrate their unlucky days as public festivals, made merry on their occasions for mourning, and generally were happy at the unhappiness of others will, when they begin to receive the wages of their cruelty, find that they wronged not the obscure and inconsequential but men of patrician lineage retaining the sparks of their noble birth, from which when rekindled the glory but shortly before quenched shines forth. For just as when tree trunks are cut away, as long as the roots are not removed, new shoots burgeon forth by which the old stumps are eclipsed, in the same way if in souls a slight germ of the qualities that promote virtue be left, though the rest have been removed, nonetheless from that tiny seed spring up the most precious and most beautiful things in human existence, by which cities abound once more with men and nations increase greatly in population. (*Praem.* 165–172)

NOTES

INTRODUCTION

1. See Y. Gutman, *The Beginnings of Jewish Hellenistic Literature* (Jerusalem, 1958–1963) 2 v. (Hebrew); M. Hengel, *Judaism and Hellenism* (Philadelphia, 1974), 1.83–175; B. Z. Wacholder, *Eupolemus: A Study of Judaeo-Greek Literature* (Cincinnati and New York, 1974); S. Lieberman, *Hellenism in Jewish Palestine* (New York, 1950).

2. See M. Alexandre, "La Culture Profane Chez Philon," *PAL*, pp. 105–130.

3. See E. G. Turner, "Tiberius Julius Alexander," *JRS* 44 (1954): 54–64. Cf. J. Schwarz, "Note sur la famille de Philon d'Alexandrie," *Mélanges Isidore Levy. Annuaire de l'Institut de philologie et d'histoire orientales et slaves. Université libre de Bruxelles* 13 (1953): 591–602; idem, "L'Égypte de Philon," *PAL*, pp. 35–45; and S. S. Foster, "A Note on the 'Note' of J. Schwarz," *SP* 4 (1976–1977): 25–32.

4. See V. Nikiprowetzky, *Le commentaire de l'écriture chez Philon d'Alexandrie* (Leiden, 1977), pp. 170–261.

5. W. Theiler, *Untersuchungen zur antiken Literatur* (Berlin, 1970), pp. 484–501; Dillon, pp. 139–83.

6. See Nikiprowetzky pp. 50–96.

7. For the chronology of Philo's writings, see Turner (cited in n. 3 above); A. Terian, "The Implications of Philo's Dialogues on [sic] his Exegetical Works," *SBL Seminar Papers* (Missoula, 1978), 1.181–90; Nikiprowetzky pp. 192–235; L. Massebieau, "Le Classement des oeuvres de Philon," *Bibliothèque de l'Ecole des Hautes Etudes, Sciences Religieuses* 1 (1889): 1–91; L. Cohn, "Einteilung und Chronologie der Schriften Philos," *Philologus*, Suppl. Bd. 7, 3 (1899): 389–435; L. Massebieau and E. Bréhier, "Essai sur la Chronologie de la vie et des oeuvres de Philon," *RHR* 53 (1906): 25–64.

8. See Ps-Aristeas 144–55, 161–70, 306; M. Hadas, *Aristeas to Philocrates* (New York, 1951); N. Walter, *Der Thoraausleger Aristobulos*, TV 86 (Berlin, 1964).

9. For further identifications of this sort, See D. Winston, "The Iranian Component in the Bible, Apocrypha, and Qumran," *HR* 5:2 (1966): 183–85, 213–16.

10. For a detailed account of Greek allegory, see J. Pépin, *Mythe et Allégorie* (Paris, 1976); idem, "Remarques sur la théorie de l'exégèse allégorique chez Philon," *PAL*, pp. 131–67. For Philonic allegory, see I. Christiansen, *Die Technik der allegorischen Auslegungswissenschaft bei Philo von Alexandrien* (Tübingen, 1969); R. M. Grant, *The Letter and the Spirit* (New York, 1957); R. G. Hammerton-Kelly, "Some Techniques of Composition in Philo's Allegorical Commentary with Special Reference to *De Agricultura*," in *Jews, Greeks and Christians, Essays in Honor of W. D. Davies*, ed. R. G. Hamerton-Kelly and R. Scroggs (Leiden, 1976), pp. 45–56.

NOTES

11. An analogy to Philo's allegorical interpretation of Scripture is Plutarch's allegorizing of Egyptian mythology in his *On Isis and Osiris.*

12. Cf. *Mos.* 1.4; *Spec.* 1.8, 3.178; *Abr.* 99; *Jos.* 151. See R. A. Culpepper, *The Johanine School* (Missoula, 1975), pp. 204–12.

13. This series contains the following treatises: *On the Creation of the World; Concerning Abraham; On Joseph; Life of Moses; On the Decalogue; On the Special Laws; On the Virtues; On Rewards and Punishments.* There is a likelihood that Philo also wrote treatises on Isaac (cf. *Sobr.* 9) and Jacob, which have been lost. Philo also refers to a special treatise on numbers, which we no longer have. For literature see n. 7 above.

14. In addition to Philo's exegetical works, we have a series of miscellaneous apologetic writings. These include the *Hypothetica* or *Apologia Pro Judaeis,* which survives only in two Greek extracts quoted by Eusebius. The first extract contains a rationalistic version of the Exodus, a eulogistic account of Moses, and a summary of the Mosaic constitution, contrasting its severity with the laxity of Gentile law, while the second describes the Essenes. Two further apologetic works are *Against Flaccus,* and *The Embassy to Gaius.* Finally, there are the philosophical treatises, including *That Every Good Man Is Free* (a sequel to an earlier treatise, whose theme was that "every bad man is a slave," but which has not survived), *On the Eternity of the World, On Providence* (except for several lengthy Greek fragments, preserved only in Armenian), and *Alexander or On Whether Brute Animals Possess Reason* (preserved only in Armenian, and called in Latin *De Animalibus*). The latter two works are in dialogue form. There is a German translation of *On Providence* by L. Früchtel, in *Philo von Alexandria, Die Werke in Deutscher Übersetzung,* ed. L. Cohn et al. (Berlin, 1964) 7.267–382; and a French translation by M. Hadas-Lebel, Lyon 35 (Paris, 1973). For the *De Animalibus,* see A. Terian's forthcoming translation and commentary to be published by the Philo Institute. The selections from the *De Animalibus* translated in this volume are the contribution of Professor A. Terian.

The brief fragment called by the Armenian excerptors *De Deo, On God* (preserved only in Armenian and printed in J. B. Aucher's *Philonis Judaei Paralipomena Armena translata* [Venice, 1826], pp. 613–19) is an exegesis of Genesis 18, and apparently belongs to *Philo's Allegory of the Law.* Adler sought to place it at the head of one of the lost books of the *De Somniis,* and M. Harl has found it to be authentically Philonic. See M. Adler, "Das philonische Fragment *De Deo,*" *MGWJ* 80 (1936): 163–70; and M. Harl, "Cosmologie grecque et Représentations juives dans l'Oeuvre de Philon d'Alexandrie," *PAL,* pp. 189–203. For a German translation of *De Deo,* see F. Siegert, *Drei hellenistischjüdische Predigten* (Tübingen 1980). Siegert believes that the author was probably not Philo, but someone who was a student of his writings.

15. Part one of this section is a condensed and somewhat modified version of D. Winston, "Philo's Theory of Cosmogony," chapter 8 in *Religious*

NOTES

Syncretism in Antiquity, ed. B. A. Pearson (Missoula, 1975). Part two reproduces D. Winston, "Philo's Theory of Eternal Creation," *AAJR Jubilee Volume* (forthcoming).

16. Cf. *QG* 4.160: "... the wicked man, as the first-born in general, is related to passive matter, which gives birth like a mother ... for the forms without a mother are from the Cause alone, which not ineptly might be said to be the mother of created Things." *Cher.* 125: "For the genesis of anything many elements must converge, the 'by which' (τὸ ὑφ' οὗ), the 'from which' (τὸ ἐξ οὗ) ..., the 'through which' (τὸ δι' ο ὗ), the 'for which'" (τὸ δι' ὅ) 127: "You will find that its (the universe's) cause is God, by whom it has come into being, its material the four elements, from which it was compounded, its instrument the Logos of God, through which it was constructed, and the final cause of the construction is the goodness of the architect." For the distinctions between active and passive within existing things, see Aristotle, *Phys.* 8.4.255a, 12–15; 254b, 27–33; *Gen. et Cor.* 2.9.335b, 29–31; *SVF* 1.85; Wolfson 1.296.

17. If we gather up all the attributes Philo applies to preexistent matter, we get the following list of negatives or implied negatives: ἄκοσμον, ἄτακτον, ἄψυχος, ἀκίνητος, ἄποιος, ἄμορφος, ἀσχημάτιστον, ἀτύπωτον, ἀνόμοιος, ἄπειρος; full of ἑτεροιότης, ἀναρμοστία, ἀσυμφωνία, σκότος, ἐρίζουσαν, πάσχουσα, παθητή, πλημμελές, πεφυρμένη, διαλυτήν, φθαρτήν, χείρων.

18. See D. Winston, "The Book of Wisdom's Theory of Cosmogony," *HR* 11 (1971): 186, n. 5. See also Lilla, pp. 193–96.

19. Cf. *Spec.* 1.30. To make the analogy more precise we should perhaps fill in the apparent lacuna in our text from a Platonic passage (*Rep.* 509 B–C), which Philo may very well have had in mind. We should then understand the passage as follows: Just as the sun (not only) makes hidden things visible, (but also provides for their generation), so, too, God not only made things visible but, acting the creator rather than a mere artificer, provided for the very generation of things that did not exist before. See Cohen-Yashar, *"Al Ba'ayat ha-Beriah yesh me-'Ayin"*, Annual of Bar-Ilan Univer. 4–5 (1967): 60–66; H. F. Weiss, Untersuchungen zur Kosmologie des hellenistischen u. palästinischen Judentums (Berlin, 1966), pp. 55–58. For the phrase ἃ πρότερον οὐκ ἦν, cf. Plato, *Soph.* 265 BC; Philo, *Jos.* 126; *Deus* 119; *Virt.* 130; for κτίστης, cf. Wisd. 1:14: ἔκτισεν γὰρ εἰς τὸ εἶναι τὰ πάντα. Equally ambiguous is the expression μὴ ὄν in *Op.* 81; *LA* 3.10; *Her.* 36. Drummond, on the other hand, believes that the reference here may be to God's creation of the intelligible forms prior to his formation of the sensible world (1.303–04).

20. For a detailed analysis of the creation sequence, see V. Nikiprowetzky, "Problèmes du Récit de la Création chez Philon d'Alexandrie," *REJ* 124 (1965): 271–306; for the generic heavenly man and the generic earthly man, see Baer, pp. 14–44. According to Baer's interpretation of the Philonic

303

texts, Gen. 1:27a refers not to the idea of man but to empirical man's rational soul. *Op.* 36–128 refers to the creation of the generic sense-perceptible world, beginning with heaven and ending with man. Because man is a composite, consisting of both a heavenly and an earthly part, in the case of man God first forms the genus of empirical man (the αἰσθητὸς καὶ ἐπὶ μέρους ἄνθρωπος).

21. For ἐπίτασις and ἄνεσις, cf. Wisd. 16:24, and my commentary ad loc. For a detailed source study see E. K. Goodenough, "A Neo-Pythagorean Source in Philo Judaeus," *Yale Class. Studies* 3 (1932): 117–64. A Pythagorean treatise called Περὶ ἀντικειμένων, and ascribed to Archytas by Simplicius, gives a detailed list of the opposites. Goodenough believes that the term λόγος τομεύς is a derivation from Pythagorean logic, which either Philo or his source raised from a logical term to a cosmic principle.

22. Very likely Philo, unlike Plato, was unwilling explicitly to ascribe even an irrational motion to preexistent matter (although some of his other adjectives imply it), since even such a disordered but autonomous motion would appear to compromise God's sovereign power. For the "pluralist" Plato this posed no problem, although it does seem to contradict his doctrine that soul is ultimately the cause of all motion. It should be noted, however, that some scholars have plausibly suggested that the precosmic chaos of the *Timaeus* could only have been meant by Plato to be taken as a symbol of the disordered motions of "matter," which are indirectly caused by the soul. See H. Cherniss, "The Sources of Evil according to Plato," in *Plato, A Collection of Critical Essays*, ed. G. Vlastos (New York, 1971), pp. 244–58; and L. Tarán, "The Creation Myth in Plato's Timaeus," in *Essays in Ancient Greek Philosophy*, ed. J. P. Anton and G. L. Kustas (New York, 1971), pp. 372–407, esp. 384–88.

23. See F. M. Cornford, *Plato's Cosmology* (New York, 1957), pp. 193–94.

24. Unlike Plato, who is a pluralist, Philo the monotheist is unwilling to allow even for a self-existing void, and so makes its pattern an eternal idea within the divine mind. In Plato's conception of matter, the self-existing Receptacle is its most stable and permanent constituent: "It must be called always the same, for it never departs at all from its own character" (*Tim.* 50B–C). Cf. F. Cornford: "Here as elsewhere the Receptacle does not owe its existence to the Demiurge but is represented as a given factor limiting his operation by necessary conditions" (cited n. 23), p. 193.

25. Among those scholars who have accepted Wolfson's interpretation are the following: G. Lindeskog, *Studien zum neutestamentlichen Schöpfungsgedanken* (1952), p. 154, n. 3; R. M. Grant, *Miracle and Natural Law in Graeco-Roman and Early Christian Thought* (Amsterdam, 1952), p. 141; C. de Vogel, *Greek Philosophy* (Leiden, 1964), 3.356, n. 5; R. Arnaldez Lyon 1.30.

26. See D. Winston (cited in n. 18).

27. Cf. Plotinus's theory of matter (2.4; 3.6. Plotinus compares matter to a mirror, and the "beings" that are in it to the images in a mirror [3.6.7.22–

NOTES

23]: εἴδωλα ἐν εἰδώλῳ ἀτεχνῶς, ὡς ἐν κατόπτρῳ τὸ ἀλλαχοῦ ἱδρυμένον, ἀλλαχοῦ φανταζόμενον).

28. Cf. K. Borman, *Die Ideen und Logoslehre Philons von Alexandrien* (Inaugural, Diss., Universität Köln, 1955), pp. 42–44.

29. The first and second incongruences could indeed be removed if we were to push Philo's doctrine of simultaneous, timeless creation to its logical conclusion. Philo would then be saying that God created the Forms, together with copies of the Forms (following for the moment Wolfson's interpretation), which though indeterminate could be rendered determinate, and that he simultaneously did so render them. Just as Saint Augustine could logically argue that God created a *nihil aliquid*, i.e., something that though unformed could be formed, and that he simultaneously did form it, meaning thereby that formless matter never existed as such, so did Philo mean to say by his formula that indeterminate forms never existed as such. (It is unclear from Wolfson's account of this matter whether he would subscribe to the above interpretation.) In any case, it is the third incongruence that is the most drastic, and that if allowed to stand would indicate the virtual collapse of Philo's attempt to Platonize his biblical understanding of creation.

30. *Encyclopedia of Philosophy*, ed. Paul Edwards (New York, 1967) 6.152.

31. "Nothing in fact is so foolish," says Philo, "as to raise the question whether the world is destroyed into nonexistence. More to the point is whether it suffers change from its orderly arrangement, with either varied forms of its elements and compounds dissolved into one and the same form, or reduced to total confusion when all is crushed and broken down" (*Aet.* 6).

32. Cf. *Prov.* 2.109 [66]. See H. Leisegang, "Philo's Schrift über die Ewigkeit der Welt," *Philologus* 92 (1937): 156–76.

33. Grant (cited n. 10), p. 141; de Vogel and R. Arnaldez (cited n. 25).

34. χώρα could also refer to an interval partly occupied by body and partly unoccupied. Cf. Lilla, p. 194, n. 3.

35. The following Platonists interpreted Plato's *Timaeus* analytically: Xenocrates, Speusippus, Crantor and his followers, Eudorus of Alexandria, Taurus, Albinus, Apuleius. See A. E. Taylor, *A Commentary on Plato's Timaeus* (Oxford, 1928), pp. 67–69; J. Pépin, *Théologie Cosmique* (Paris, 1964), pp. 38–43, 86–94; C. Baeumker, "Die Ewigkeit der Welt bei Plato," *Philosophische Monatshefte* 23 (1887): 513–29; A. J. Festugière, *Études de Philosophie Greque* (Paris, 1971), pp. 487–506; G. S. Claghorn, *Aristotle's Criticism of Plato's Timaeus* (The Hague, 1954), pp. 84–98; Dillon, p. 7.

According to the second century Platonist Severus, although the cosmos had no temporal origin, it is still periodically destroyed and renewed (Proclus *In Plat. Tim.* 1.289.7–13). See Pépin, p. 94; P. Merlan, in *Cambridge History of Later Greek and Early Medieval Philosophy* (Cambridge, 1967), pp. 78–79; Dillon, p. 263.

36. Merlan has pointed out that disagreement started early among the

NOTES

Platonists as to whether the two higher principles should have absolutely equal status (*Cambridge History*, p. 17). Hermodorus asserted that according to Plato, the Indefinite Dyad or Matter should not be called a first principle, and later Eudorus of Alexandria posits a supranoetic One above the Monad and Dyad. See Festugière, 4.308–10; Merlan, p. 81. On the nature of Speusippus's One, see P. Merlan, *From Platonism to Neoplatonism* (The Hague, 1960), pp. 96–140; H. J. Krämer, *Der Ursprung der Geistmetaphysik* (Amsterdam, 1967), pp. 207–18, 351–58; H. Happ, *Hyle* (Berlin, 1971), pp. 208–41; Dillon, pp. 12–18.

37. Philo could have endorsed the formulation of Crantor and his followers (if we follow Proclus's version, *In Plat. Tim.* 85a, rather than that of Plutarch, *Anim. Procr.* 1.1012D), but he probably preferred not to associate his position with that of the Platonists who coordinated the principle of matter with the One. Moreover, while Eudorus's concept of the One was very close to that of Philo, he not only seems to have employed the ἀγένητος formula, which Philo disliked (Plutarch ib.3.1013B), but very likely (under Neopythagorean influence) conceived of the One as emanating both the Monad and the Dyad, a notion Philo would certainly have rejected (Simplicius *In Phys.* 181, 10ff., Diels; Alex. Aphr. *In Met.* 988a10–11, Hayduck).

38. See now Aucher's Latin translation from the Armenian reprinted with a French translation, introduction and notes by M. Hadas-Lebel (Paris, 1973); P. Wendland, *Philo's Schrift über die Vorsehung* (Berlin, 1892); W. Bousset, *Jüdisch-Christlicher Schulbetrieb in Alexandria und Rom* (Göttingen, 1915), pp. 137ff.; M. Pohlenz, *Kleine Schriften* (Hildesheim, 1965), pp. 305–83, esp. 313–24; H. Leisegang, "Philo," in *PW* 20:1, col. 8–11; Lilla, p. 197, n. 2. Bousset finds *Prov.* 1.7–8 hopelessly contradictory ("Kurz, hier sind vollendete Widersprüche. Und nach allem, was wir von Philos schriftstellerischer Eigenart kennen, tun wir ihm kein Unrecht, wenn wir annehmen, dass er in 7–8 eine Ausführung, in welcher die platonische Annahme einer worweltlichen Materie vom Standpunkt der Behauptung der Ewigkeit der Welt aus abgelehnt wurde, gedankenlos und sinnlos in einem Zusammenhang hat stehen lassen, der eine entgegengesetzte Orientierung zeigt" [p. 146]). I believe, however, that in spite of the stylistic gaucherie of these passages (undoubtedly due to the Armenian translator), it is possible to extract from them a consistent Philonic doctrine. (Wendland, p. 184, thought these passages constituted a lost section of Philo's *De Aeternitate Mundi*, and although Bousset was unwilling to go that far, he was inclined to accept Wendland's suggestion that in this section of the *De Providentia* Philo was attempting to fulfill his promise at the end of *Aet.* 150.)

39. Cf. *Aet.* 14: τινὲς δὲ οἴονται σοφιζόμενοι κατὰ Πλάτωνα γενητὸν λέγεσθαι τὸν κόσμον.

40. Cf. *Op.* 7: τοῦ δὲ θεοῦ πολλὴν ἀπραξίαν ἀνάγνως κατεψεύσαντο; *Aet.* 83: "Moreover if all things are as they say consumed in the con-

flagration, what will God be doing during that time? Will he do nothing at all? ... But if all things are annihilated, inactivity and dire unemployment (ἀργία καὶ ἀπραξία) will render his life unworthy of the name and what could be more monstrous than this? I shrink from saying, for the very thought is a blasphemy, that quiescence will entail as a consequence the death of God." The same argument was employed by the Epicureans. "Moreover I would put to both of you the question," says Velleius the Epicurean, "why did these deities suddenly awake into activity as world-builders after count-less ages of slumber? For though the world did not exist, it does not follow that ages *(saecla)* did not exist; ... but from the infinite past there has existed an eternity not measured by limited divisions of time, but of a nature intel-ligible in terms of extension, since it is inconceivable that there was ever a time when time did not exist. Well then, Balbus, what I ask is, why did your Providence remain idle all through that extent of time of which you speak?" (Cicero *ND* 1.9.21–22). Cf. Diels, *Dox. Graec.*, pp. 209–301; Lucr. 5.168. A simi-lar argument had already been employed by Parmenides, DK B.8, 9–10: "What need would have made it grow, beginning from non-Being, later or sooner?"

41. Cf. Spinoza, *Eth.* 1.33, sch. 2: "But since in eternity there is no when nor before nor after, it follows from the perfection of God alone that He nei-ther can decree nor could ever have decreed anything else than that which He has decreed, that is to say, God has not existed before His decrees and can never exist without them."

42. See *Det.* 160, and Selections from Philo, n. 205.

43. See n. 22 above.

44. Of Plato's Receptacle, J. B. Skemp writes that "it is more real than the 'images' of the Forms which appear in it" ("*Hyle* and *Hypodoche*," in *Ar-istotle and Plato in the Mid-Fourth Century*, ed. I. Düring and G. E. L. Owen [Göteborg, 1960], p. 207).

45. See Winston (cited in n. 9).

46. See A. N. M. Rich, "The Platonic Ideas as the Thought of God," *Mnemosyne*, ser. 4, v. 7, fasc. 1 (1964): 123–33; W. Theiler, *Die Vorbereitung des Neuplatonismus* (Berlin/Zürich, 1964), pp. 1–60; C. J. de Vogel, *Philosophia* I (Assen, 1969): 372–77; J. H. Loenen, "Albinus' Metaphysics. An Attempt at Rehabilitation," *Mnemosyne*, ser. 4, 10 (1950): 44–45; Dillon, pp. 29, 95.

47. Bousset, p. 144, n. 1 suggests that Philo may be referring to Jewish opponents who understood the Aristotelian doctrine of the eternity of the world as teaching its eternal creation through God.

48. See Winston (cited n. 15), p. 170, n. 1.

49. See *Op.* 16, 19 and passim; *Mut.* 27; *LA* 2.1.2.

50. "The religion of the Cosmic God, or of the Cosmos as a god, or even of the stars, was the current form of personal religion among the majority of educated pagans, from Cleanthes in the third century B.C.E. to Simplicius

NOTES

in the fifth century C.E." (A. J. Festugière, *Personal Religion among the Greeks* [Berkeley and Los Angeles, 1954]: 51). See also Festugière 2, *passim*.

51. It should also be noted that according to Philo's own analysis of time (*Op.* 26; *Aet.* 53), it would be absurd to say "there was a time when the world was not," since time and world are for him correlative (cf. Aristotle *Phys.* 8.125b11ff.; Philoponus *Aet. M.*, pp. 145–47, Rabe). As to Philo's characterization of God's creative act as one of βούλησις (*Op.* 16), Wolfson comments: "Following Scripture and Plato, Philo conceives the act of creation as an act of will and design (i.e., not a necessary result of God's nature)" (1.315). This statement is as incorrect for Plato as it is for Philo, for the Demiurge of the *Timaeus* acts in accordance with his unchangeable nature, which is good (or more precisely the source of the good), and Philo is here faithfully following his master. Cf. J. Rist, *Eros and Psyche* (Toronto, 1964), p. 76: "for although the *Demiourgos* may be said to will creation, he does not choose it as one of two alternatives. He simply wills it because it is good; being good means doing good, and the *Demiourgos* is thus 'beyond' choice."

52. Wolfson 1.358.

53. *Ebr.* 166–205; *Jos.* 125–43. See Selections from Philo, n. 257.

54. See the excellent discussion in Bréhier, pp. 182–83. Cf. *Mos.* 1.165, where the miracle is called "a mighty work of nature" (μεγαλούργημα τῆς φύσεως). See D. G. Delling, "Wunder, Allegorie, Mythus bei Philo von Alexandreia," *Wissensch. Zeitschr. d. M. Luther Univ. Halle-Wittenberg*, 6:5 (1957): 713–40. For the Skeptics' use of εὔλογος and πιθανός, see V. Brochard, *Les Sceptiques grecs* (rep. Paris, 1969), pp. 110, 135.

55. For the Stoic theory of *pneuma*, see S. Sambursky, *Physics of the Stoa* (London, 1959), pp. 1–48; Hahm, pp. 153–74; and for their own use of it in explaining the miracles of divination, see Cicero *ND* 3.39.32. (On the complete flexibility of matter, cf. Diels, *Dox. Graec.*, p. 307, line 22. For its use by Wisd. in order to explain the miracle of the Red Sea, see Winston, p. 331; cf. Selections from Philo, n. 384.

56. It may well be that Cicero is utilizing the exaggerated version of an overzealous defender of the Stoic theory of divination. The Stoic theory was severely attacked by philosophers like Carneades and Diogenianos. Among the Stoics themselves, however, only Panaetius seems to have dissented (Cic. *Divinat.* 1.6).

57. For other examples see Wolfson 1.350–04. It may be noted that Philo tells the story of Balaam in *Mos.* 1.269–74 without mentioning the incident of his speaking ass, and in *Cher.* 32–35 he completely allegorizes the story. See Delling (cited in n. 54), p. 717.

58. *Deus* 32. For Philo's concept of time, see Selections from Philo, n. 119. The tendency to incorporate the biblical miracles into the original order of nature is also found in rabbinic literature (*M. Abot* 5.6; *BR* 5.3. See Wolfson, 1:351, n. 24; Urbach, p. 95. Cf. Augustine's doctrine of the *semina*, which,

implanted into the cosmos at the time of its creation, produce the miracles (*De Trin.* 3.8; *De Gen. ad Litt.* 6.14; 9.16–18. See Grant (cited n. 25), pp. 218ff. Philo, like the rabbis, emphasized the miraculous and truly marvelous character of the natural order itself, in contrast to the unfamiliar events that amaze us with their strange novelty (*Mos.* 1.212–13. See Selections from Philo, n. 382). The obverse of the tendency to incorporate the miraculous into the order of nature was the attempt of the Occasionalists to incorporate the order of nature into the category of the miraculous. A Jewish version of this notion was Nahmanides's doctrine of "hidden miracles" (in his commentary to Exod. 6:3), and the astrological version of Abraham b. Ezra. A midway position was the doctrine of Bahya b. Pakuda and Judah Halevi (*Kuzari* 109), which blends a hidden natural order within that which is manifest in order to regulate all cosmic events in accordance with the biblical doctrine of divine retribution. Even Maimonides, in his *Treatise on Resurrection*, adopts this doctrine. See G. Scholem, *Ursprung und Anfänge der Kabbala* (Berlin, 1962), pp. 400–401.

59. Cf. *Deus* 53ff.; *Somn.*1.237; *Fragments of Philo Judaeus*, ed. J. R. Harris (Cambridge, 1886), p. 8; *QG* 2.54. Johann Mosheim, in his long note on Philo in his Latin translation of R. Cudworth's *True Intellectual System of the Universe* (1773), had already suggested that there were two systems in Philo, the popular religion on the one hand and the more sublime and recondite on the other. See T. H. Billings, *The Platonism of Philo Judaeus* (Chicago, 1919), pp. 6–7. For Philo's very frequent resort to mystery terminology in order to represent the secret level in his theological doctrines, see Lilla, pp. 148–49; Nikiprowetzky, pp. 17–28.

60. This section is a condensed version of D. Winston, "Was Philo a Mystic," a chapter in a book on Jewish Mysticism, edited by J. Dan, to be published by The Association for Jewish Studies.

61. See N. Smart, "Mysticism, History of," in the *Encyclopedia of Philosophy*, ed. P. Edwards.

62. See P. Merlan, *Monopsychism, Mysticism Metaconsciousness* (The Hague, 1963), pp. 14ff.

63. See Plotinus 5.3.17; 6.9.11. Cf. J. Rist, *Plotinus, The Road to Reality* (Cambridge, 1967), pp. 213–30.

64. See P. Merlan, *From Platonism to Neoplatonism* (The Hague, 1960), pp. 97, 105; H. Krämer, *Der Ursprung der Geistmetaphysik* (Amsterdam, 1967), pp. 207–18, 351–58; H. Happ, *Hyle* (Berlin, 1971), pp. 208–41; J. Dillon, "The Transcendence of God in Philo," *Colloquy 16*, Center for Hermeneutical Studies (Berkeley, 1975); Festugière 4.1–140.

65. It is possible that Eudorus was influenced by the first Hypothesis of Plato's *Parmenides*. See Dodds, *Class Quart* (1928), pp. 135ff. Moreover, Philo himself may be referring to the aforementioned philosophers in *Somn.* 1.184: "Others maintain that the Uncreated resembles nothing among created

things, but so completely transcends them that even the swiftest understanding falls far short of apprehending Him."

66. Although Philo generally affirms that God is ἀσώματος and ἄποιος, at *LA* 3.206 he asserts that we cannot even make negative statements of God. Cf. Albinus *Did.* 10.4, Louis; Proclus *In Parm.* 7.68–76; *Platonic Theology* 2.109. See Selections from Philo, n. 233.

67. See Drummond 2.17–34; Wolfson 2.94–164.

68. *Phileb.* 27 BC: "The first then I call the Unlimited, the second the Limit, and the third the being that has come to be by mixture of these two." A similar triadic configuration reappears in the mysticism of the *Zohar.* The sefirot of Wisdom and Intelligence represent the Logos, while those of Love and Stern Judgment are its dynamic polar principles, the Unlimited and Limit, which in this case are balanced and anchored in the *sefirah* of Compassion.

69. Wolfson has correctly pointed out that "though Philo used many negative descriptions of God, he does not say outright that, as a result of the unknowability and ineffability of God, He is to be described by negations. Nor does he apply the principle of negation as an interpretation of those predicates in Scripture which are couched in positive form" (*Studies in the History of Philosophy and Religion* [Cambridge 1973], p. 117). Philo also hints at another way of predicating of God, i.e., the process of κατ' ἀφαίρεσιν, which consists of depriving the object of knowledge of any sensible attribute (*Deus* 55–56; cf. Albinus, *Did.* 165.14). See also J. Whittaker, "Neopythagoreanism and Negative Theology," *Symbolae Osloenses* 44 (1969): 109–25; Lilla, p. 221. Although Philo's *via eminentiae* put God beyond the good, the beautiful, the One, the *archē*, knowledge, blessedness, and happiness, we are nowhere told that He is beyond being (like Plato's Good, which is ἐπέκεινα τῆς οὐσίας: *Rep.* 6.509B). It may be inferred, however, from the fact that God alone is ὄντως ὄν that his being is of an altogether different order than that of all else. This is made explicit by Philo at *Det.* 160. See Selections from Philo, n. 205.

70. Seneca writes: "One thing is practically settled, that there is some difference between philosophy and wisdom. Nor indeed is it possible that that which is sought and that which seeks are identical." Other Stoics, he continues, "have maintained the two cannot be sundered." Cf. Cicero *Leg.* 1.22: "And what is more godlike . . . than reason, which, once it is full grown and brought to perfection, is rightly called wisdom?"

71. Cf. Seneca *Ep.* 89.4; Cicero *Off.* 2.25; *Tusc.* 4.25.57; *SVF* 2.36; Diels, *Dox. Graec.* 273a13; IV Macc. 1:16.

72. See *Mos.* 2.48, 181; *Abr.* 16, 60; *Op.* 143; *Spec.* 1.31, 155; 2.13; 3.46–47, 112, 137; 4.204; *Decal.* 132; *Mig.* 128; *Virt.* 132, 18; *Plant.* 49; *Ebr.* 142 (cf. *SVF* 3.613); *Prob.* 160; *Det.* 52; *Agr.* 66; *QG* 4.90; *PT Kil'ayim* 1.7; *BT Kiddushin* 39a.

NOTES

Cf. I. Heinemann, "Die Lehre vom ungeschriebenen Gesetz im jüdischen Schrifttum," *HUCA* 4 (1927): 149–71.

73. See Heinemann, pp. 475–78. Cf. *Her.* 213 (where Moses is designated "the interpreter of Nature's facts"), 182, 179; *Op.* 53–4, 77; *Post.* 102.

74. For πίστις in Greek philosophy, see Lilla, chap. 4; Rist (cited n. 63), pp. 231–46; Billings, pp. 72–75. Cf. especially the *pistis* characterizing the Stoic wise man (*SVF* 3.548). The opposite of πίστις is called by Philo οἴησις, τῦφος, κενὴ δόξα, ἀφροσύνη, φιλαυτία (*Mut.* 176; *Spec.* 1.10; *Somn.* 248–66, 162, 192; *Her.* 106). It consists in giving to the senses or to the thought based on them that trust which should be bestowed on God alone. Cf. Plato's denunciations of φιλαυτία in *Laws* 731D–732.

75. Cf. Epictetus fr.1 (Stobaeus *Eclog.* 2.1.31).

76. I. Heinemann, "Philo als Vater der mittelalterlichen Philosophie?" *Theolog. Zeits.* 6 (1950): 99–116.

77. See *QE* 2.124; *Conf.* 41; *Mig.* 103; *Conf.* 63, 146; *Deus* 31; *Her.* 205; *Fug.* 112; *Mos.* 2.134; Eusebius *PE.* 7.13.1; *LA* 3.96.

78. See Plato, *Laws* 886A; *Phileb.* 28E; Aristotle fr.12a; Ross; Cicero *ND.* 2.31–39; 15–19; Epictetus 1.6; Ps. Aristotle *De Mundo* 6; Xenophon *Mem.* 1.412–19; Albinus *Did.* chap. 10; Wisd. 13:1–9; Rom. 2:20.

79. For Philo's employment of the cosmological proof, see *Post.* 167; *Fug.* 12; *Mut.* 54; *Post.* 28.

80. Cf. Plato, *Symp.* 211C: ὥσπερ ἐπαναβαθμοῖς χρώμενα. For the history of this image in medieval Arabic and Jewish philosophy, see A. Altmann, *Studies in Religious Philosophy and Mysticism* (London, 1969), pp. 41–72; also B. Zak, "R. Solomon Alkabetz' Attitude towards Philosophic Studies," *Eshel Beer-Sheva* (Beer-Sheva, 1976), pp. 288–306 (Heb).

81. Chroust interprets Philo's direct way of knowing God in the light of Sextus Empiricus's statement (*Adv. Phys.* 1.20–22) that Aristotle used to say (*On Philosophy*, fr.12a, Ross) that men's thoughts of the gods originated from two sources: the personal experience of the soul and the phenomena of the heavens. "It arose from events which concern the soul because of the inspired states of the soul which occur in sleep and because of prophecies." As we have already indicated, however, Philo says nothing of prophetic inspiration when he discusses the direct approach to God. See A. H. Chroust, " 'Mystical Revelation' and 'Rational Theology' in Aristotle's 'On Philosophy,' " *Tijdschrift voor Filosofie* 34 (1972): 500–12; idem, *Aristotle* (London, 1973), 2.159–74. Cf. E. Vanderlinden, "Les divers modes de connaissance de Dieu selon Philon d'Alexandrie," *Mélanges de Sciences Religieuse* 4 (1947): 285–304; H. Jonas, "The Problem of the Knowledge of God in the teaching of Philo of Alexandria," in *Commentationes Judaico-Hellenisticae in Memoriam Johannes Lewy* (Jerusalem, 1949), pp. 75–84 (Heb); idem, *Gnosis und spätantiker Geist* (Göttingen, 1954), 2:1.70–121. According to Bréhier (pp. 197ff.) and Vanderlinden, Philo is re-

ferring to a direct mystical contact with the Deity, resulting from a deep longing for Him.

82. See R. Robinson, *Plato's Earlier Dialectic* (Oxford, 1953), pp. 156–79.

82a After my manuscript had already been sent to the publisher, I received a copy of M. Dragon-Monachou's *The Stoic Arguments for the Existence of God* (Athens, 1976) and note that he too sees in some of the Stoic arguments anticipations of the ontological argument. He also correctly refers to Diogenes of Babylon's restatement of Zeno's first argument for the existence of God (Sextus *Math.* 9.133) as an anticipation of the ontological formula which describes God as a being whose essence involves existence (pp. 41–50; 92–96).

83. See *Op.* 8, 144; *LA* 3.2, 81, 203; *Cher.* 44, 46, 86; *Sacr.* 101; *Det.* 54–56; *Post.* 4, 28; *Deus* 7, 22, 52, 56; *Plant.* 35.

84. There were four generic kinds of *pathē*: fear *(phobos)*, lust *(epithymia)*, mental pain *(lypē)*, mental pleasure *(hēdonē)*. The three *eupatheiai* (Lat. *constantiae*) were: wish or well-reasoned appetite *(boulēsis)*, caution or well-reasoned avoidance *(eulabeia)*, joy or well-reasoned elation *(chara)*. (Cf. Cicero *Tusc.* 4.14; D.L. 7.116; Virgil *Aen.* 6.733.) See especially F. H. Sandbach's excellent analysis in his *The Stoics* (London, 1975), pp. 24–27; A. Bonhöffer, *Epictet und die Stoa* (Stuttgart, 1890), pp. 284ff.

85. *Abr.* 201–204; *Fug.* 166–67; *Somn.* 1.160; *Sobr.* 8; *Congr.* 36; *Det.* 46; *Mut.* 1. For Moses, see *LA* 3.128–34, 140–47; *QG* 4.177; *QE* 1.15; *Mig.* 67.

86. For the Stoic debate on whether the wise man will get drunk, see J. Rist, *Stoic Philosophy* (Cambridge, 1969): 18–19. In *Cont.* 73 and *QG* 2.67, however, Philo suggests that the use of wine is superfluous, and in *Agr.* 35, *Mos.* 2.211, and *Legat.* 42 he warns against effeminate music and the frantic excitement brought on by dancers and the scandalous scenes of mimes.

87. Cf. Aristotle *EN.* 1147b31–33; D.L. 7.94, 86; Arius Didymus, ap. Stobaeus 2.53.18; Albinus *Did.* 32.7, Louis; Plato *Phileb.* 53C.

88. See Sandbach (cited n. 84), p. 62: "If the pleasantness of experience of touch, sight, taste, smell and hearing was thought to be good and important, a pleasure arose that was passionate and to be censured (Cicero *Tusc.* 4.20), but the agreeable feelings themselves were not condemned by any Stoic, although there was no agreement on their exact status. Cleanthes denied that they were 'in accord with nature' or had any value in life, Archedemus thought that they were natural but without value, like the hairs in the armpit, while Panaetius believed some to be natural and others not." Cf. Zeller, *Stoics, Epicureans and Sceptics* (rep. New York, 1962), pp. 237–38.

89. Cf. *LA* 3.107, where ἡδονή is considered the passion par excellence.

90. Cf. Plato, *Phaed.* 67E, 64A; *Her.* 292; *Cont.* 34; *Conf.* 106; *Mig.* 9, 16, 204; *Deus* 2; *Her.* 239–40; *Fug.* 91; *LA* 1.103.

91. For the contemplative mode of prayer in Hasidism, see R. Shatz-Uffenheimer, *Quietistic Elements in Hasidic Thought* (Jerusalem, 1968), pp. 22–31, 95–110 (Heb).

92. Cf. Dodds, pp. 74–79.

93. See H. Lewy, *Sobria Ebrietas* (Giessen, 1929). Cf. the expressions *al-sahw al-thani*, "the second sobriety," and *sahwu'l-jam'*, "sobriety of union," of the Sufi mystic Ibn 'al-Farid of Cairo (1182–1235). See R. A. Nicholson, *The Idea of Personality in Islam* (Cambridge, 1923), p. 19.

94. In *QG* 3.3, Philo writes that "the heavenly singing does not extend or reach as far as the Creator's earth, as do the rays of the sun, because of his providential care for the human race. For it rouses to madness those who hear it, and produces in the soul an indescribable and unrestrained pleasure. It causes them to despise food and drink and to die an untimely death through hunger in their desire for the song. For did not the singing of the Sirens, as Homer says (*Od.* 12.39–45), so violently summon listeners that they forgot their country, their home, their friends and necessary foods?" (Cf. Plato, *Phaedr.* 259BC; *Cont.* 35; *Prob.* 8; Hesiod, *Shield* 395; Plutarch *Quaest. Conviv.* 9.14.6).

With this we may compare the statement of R. Isaac Napha that the angel of the Lord opened the ears of Sennacharib's troops who were besieging Jerusalem (II Kings 19:35) and they heard the song of the *Ḥayyoth*, or Heavenly Living Creatures, and died (*BT Sanhedrin* 95b). See G. Scholem, *Jewish Gnosticism* (New York, 1965), p. 27. Nicholson, *Mystics of Islam* (1914), pp. 63–64, writes: "Hujwiri gives anecdotes of persons who were thrown into ecstasy on hearing a verse of the Koran or a heavenly voice or poetry or music. Many are said to have died from the emotion thus aroused.... Pythagoras and Plato are responsible for another theory, to which the Sufi poets frequently allude, that music awakens in the soul a memory of celestial harmonies heard in states of preexistence."

95. Cf. R. T. Wallis, "Nous as Experience," in *The Significance of Neoplatonism*, ed. R. B. Harris (Norfolk, Va., 1976), pp. 133ff.

96. See H. Chadwick, "Philo," in *The Cambridge History of Later Greek and Early Medieval Philosophy*, ed. A. H. Armstrong (Cambridge, 1967), pp. 150–54.

97. See Dodds, p. 70 ("Persons who are of the opinion that [mystical] union is possible I shall call 'mystical theorists'; persons who believe that they have themselves experienced it I shall call 'practising mystics': the first class of persons of course includes the second, but not vice versa"). Cf. Festugière 2.554, n.1 for the term "intellectual mysticism" applied by J. M. Murry to himself.

98. The view that the Therapeutae were not Jews, but Christians, was predominant during the whole of the Middle Ages. After Protestant criticism had overthrown this view, opinions on the Therapeutae became divided. Some considered them as representatives of a philosophical tendency within Alexandrian Judaism; others identified them with a branch of Essenism, and yet others denied them all historic reality, regarding *On the Contemplative Life*

NOTES

as a romance. In the nineteenth century Graetz revived the opinion of the Church fathers, declaring the Therapeutae to be Christian ascetics of the second and third century C.E., and the *De Vita Contemplativa* the work of a Christian belonging to the Gnostic or Montanistic circle, who wishes to idealize the ascetic mode of life. Graetz's view was defended with great ingenuity by P. E. Lucius (*Die Therapeuten und ihre Stellung in der Gesichichte der Askese* [Strasburg, 1879]), and his position received the assent of scholars such as Zeller, Schürer, and Harnack. L. Massebieau, however, decisively refuted Lucius's thesis, demonstrating that the style of the treatise is so completely Philonic that in the whole book there is scarcely a sentence that could not be supported by parallels from the other writings of Philo. See L. Cohn, "The Latest Researches on Philo of Alexandria," *JQR* 5 (1893): 38–42.

99. Although Philo's conversion is assumed by Eusebius, he does not attribute it to Peter's preaching. There is, however, an account of Philo's baptism in the *Acta Joannis* of Pseudo-Prochorus (fifth century) (ed. T. Zahn [Erlangen, 1880], pp. 110–12). J. Bruns concludes: "That there was a Philo legend in written form anterior to Eusebius can scarcely be doubted. Insofar as it can be reconstructed from the works of Eusebius, Jerome, Photius, and, with due reserve, Pseudo-Prochorus, it told of Philo's baptism (by John, with no locale given), his second visit to Rome, his friendship with Peter, and his authorship of the Book of Wisdom." Bruns conjectures that the written account used by Eusebius came from Hegesippus ("Philo Christianus, The Debris of a Legend," *HTR* 66 [1973]: 141–45). See also Billings, chap. 1. It is Jerome who quotes a proverb "current among the Greeks", ἢ Φίλων πλατωνίζει ἢ Πλάτων φιλωνίζει, either Philo platonizes, or Plato philonizes (*Vir. Illust.* 11).

100. See S. A. Poznanski, "Philon dans l'ancienne littérature judéoarabe," *REJ* 50 (1905): 10–31.

101. *Me'or 'Enayim: Imre Binah*, chap. 4.

102. My view is thus in sharp contrast to that of Harry Wolfson, who sees in Philo and Spinoza two antipodal philosophical poles. What Philo built up, says Wolfson, Spinoza remorselessly tore down (Wolfson, 2.458–60). As I have pointed out above, however, Philo was not an original philosopher, and the similarities of his thought with that of Spinoza are inherent in the Middle Platonic and Neopythagorean character of his philosophy, which was already well on its way in his age toward becoming the full-blown monistic world view soon to be exemplified by Plotinus.

103. It may also be noted that just as Philo described the intelligible world, which was an immediate creation of God and created by him from eternity, as the elder son of God, whereas the sensible world is called his younger son, and time, which is not an immediate creation of God but the offspring of the sensible world, is described as a grandson of God (*Deus* 31), so does Spinoza characterize the immediacy of the two infinite modes of ex-

tension and thought by saying of motion that it is "a Son, Product, or Effect created immediately by God," and of understanding that it too is "a Son, Product, or Effect created immediately by God." (*Short Treatise* 1.9. This terminology does not occur, however, in the *Ethics*.) The same designations reappear in Plotinus 5.8.12–13; 5.5.3. Cf. Numenius, Fr. 21, Des Places.

104. It should also be noted that the rabbis were not unmindful of the dangers inherent in a philosophical exegesis of Scripture such as Philo's, which readily lent itself to distortion by sectarians with dualistic tendencies. See A. F. Segal, *Two Powers in Heaven* (Leiden, 1977), pp. 159–81. Nor could they ignore the threat to the performance of the *miṣwôt* latent in the Philonic allegory.

THE CONTEMPLATIVE LIFE

1. The subtitle is "The Fourth Part Concerning the *Aretai*," which is given in all the manuscripts. Colson has pointed out that "the title of Περὶ ἀρετῶν [*On the Wonderful Works of God*] is given by Eusebius (*HE* 2.18) to the treatise of which the *Embassy to Gaius* as we have it is a part, and he says (ibid., 2.5) that this had five books and speaks of the sufferings of the Jews in Alexandria as being described in the second book. The subtitle therefore affirms that *De Vita Contemplativa* was the fourth book of this treatise" (LCL 9.518).

2. For Philo's accounts of the Essenes, see *Prob.* 75–91 (pp. 249–52 of the present volume) and *Hypoth.* 11.1–11.18, extracted by Eusebius from what he designates as Philo's *Apologia pro Iudaeis*. According to Daumas, Lyon 29.11–12, the reference here is undoubtedly to the latter. For an extensive bibliography on the Therapeutae and the Essenes, see E. Schürer, *The History of the Jewish People in the Age of Jesus Christ*, rev. and ed. G. Vermes, F. Millar, M. Black (Edinburgh, 1979) 2.555–97. For a detailed comparison of Philo's description of the Therapeutae with his delineation of the career of Abraham, see S. Sandmel, *Philo's Place in Judaism* (Cincinnati, 1956), pp. 194–96.

3. Cf. *Spec.* 1.191; *Sacr.* 121; *Mig.* 124 (see p. 244 below); Josephus *JW* 2.136. Soul therapy begins, according to Philo, with the aid of philosophy's healing art during the third stage of life, the age of maturity, and those who succeed in this attain, in the fourth and final stage, complete spiritual health and strength (*Her.* 299). See G. Vermes, *Post-Biblical Jewish Studies* (Leiden, 1975), pp. 30–36; "Essenes, Therapeutae, Qumran," *Durham University Journal* 52 (1960): 97–115.

4. Similarly Cornutus (*Theologia*, chap. 19, Lang) says of Hephaestus ἐκ τοῦ ἧφθαι ὠνομασμένος, and like Philo in *Decal.* 54, identifies ῞Ηρα with ἀήρ (cf. Plato *Cratylus* 404C; D.L. 7.147; Diod. 1.12). For Poseidon, cf. Cornutus, chap. 4. On these etymologies, see P. Decharme, *La critique des tra-*

ditions religieuses chez les Grecs (Paris, 1904), pp. 291–303; F. Buffière, *Les mythes d'Homère et la pensée grecque* (Paris, 1956), pp. 60–65, 104–105, 168; W. Burkert, "La Genèse des choses et des mots: Le papyrus de Derveni entre Anaxagore et Cratyle," *Les Études Philosophiques* (1970), pp. 443–55.

5. Cf. Ps. 134:17. Criticism of images as lifeless is already implied in the famous utterance of Heraclitus, DK B.5: "Moreover, they talk to these statues as if one were to hold conversation with houses, in his ignorance of the nature of both gods and heroes." Timaeus of Tauromenium used the adjective ἄψυχος as a term of reproach for statues of the gods (*FGH* 566, F32). Cf. Philo *Decal.* 76: "Let no one, then, who has a soul worship a soulless thing"; Plato *Laws* 931A; Epictetus 2.8.20; Philo *LA* 1.6; Wisd. 13:17. For Philo's attacks on idolatry, see *Decal.* 52ff.; *Spec.* 1.13ff.; *Congr.* 133. Cf. Wisd. 13–15, and my detailed commentary to these chapters in the *Anchor Bible* (New York, 1979).

6. Thersites is an ugly foul-tongued fellow, who rails at Agamemnon (Iliad 2.211ff.), until beaten into silence by Odysseus. Cf. Plutarch *Moral.* 18A.

7. Cf. *Agr.* 54; *Abr.* 25; *Sobr.* 40; *Somn.* 1.248; *Jos.* 258; *Mos.* 1.153; *Spec.* 2.23; *Virt.* 5; *Praem.* 54; Plato *Laws* 631C (though with Plato, the "seeing wealth" is wealth in the literal sense used wisely; with Philo, wisdom or virtue itself); Aristophanes *Plutus* 90.

8. Cf. *Prov.* 2.12–13. This story about Anaxagoras and Democritus was a common theme in Greco-Roman literature. See Plutarch *Pericles* 16; Plato *Hipp. Mai.* 283A; D.L. 2.6; Cicero *Tusc.* 5.114–115; *Fin.* 5.87; Horace *Ep.* 1.12.12–13; Seneca *Prov.* 6.2; Philostratus *VA* 1.13; *VS* 517.

9. Hippocrates, *Aphorisms* 1.1 reads as follows: "Life is short, the Art [of medicine] long, opportunity fleeting, experiment treacherous, judgment difficult" (cited again at *Somn.* 1.10). Cf. the somewhat similar statement of R. Tarfon: "The day is short and the task is great, and the laborers are sluggish, and the recompense is ample, and the Master of the house is urgent" (*M. Aboth* 2.15).

10. Ἀβίων in Iliad 13.6 is understood by some scholars as a proper name, by others as "having no fixed subsistence," i.e., nomads. Philo evidently takes it in the latter sense.

11. κενὴ δόξα or κενοδοξία, empty imagining, is an Epicurean term that appears with very great frequency in Philo as one of his favorite "theme" words. We read in Epicurus's *K.D.* 30: "Such pleasures are due to idle imagination (κενὴν δόξαν) and it is not owing to their own nature that they fail to be dispelled, but owing to the empty imaginings (κενοδοξίαν) of the man" (i.e., a mental picture of some object, which does not really contribute to pleasure, causes us to desire it). Cf. *K.D.* 15 and 29; Usener, p. 456; Ps-Aristeas 8; IV Macc. 2:15, 8:19; Wisd. 14:14; Philo *Mut.* 94–96; *Mig.* 19, 21; *Jos.* 36; *Legat.* 114; *Praem.* 100; *Virt.* 7; *QG* 3.47; *Somn.* 1.255; 2.47–62 (where the expression κενὴ δόξα is repeated eight times).

12. Cf. *Praem.* 17–18; *Virt.* 214; *LA* 2.85; Mark 10:29; D.L. 7.17–18 (ἀπο-δημοῦντα ἐπὶ τοῖς ὅροις ἀνεπιστρεπτεῖν: a precept of Pythagoras). See I. Lévy, *La légende de Pythagore de Grèce en Palestine* (Paris, 1927), pp. 231–34.

13. We read in Plutarch *Moral.* 166D: "There is a law even for slaves who have given up all hope of freedom, that they may demand a sale, and thus exchange their present master for one more mild." See G. Glotz, *La cité grecque* (Paris, 1928), p. 305. Cf. Justinian *Inst.* 1.8.

14. A temperate climate is one of the characteristic traits of Greek utopian communities; cf. Diod. 5.19.5; 2.47.1. See D. Winston, "Iambulus' Islands of the Sun and Hellenistic Literary Utopias," *Science-Fiction Studies* (Nov. 1976), 10,3,3: 223. For the influence of climate on intelligence, cf. Philo *Prov.* 2.109; Cicero *ND* 2.17, 42.

15. For μοναστήριον LSJ give the meaning "hermit's cell." The word is first found here, and reappears only in Patristic literature.

16. Cf. Iamblichus *VP* 107.

17. Chaeremon (ap. Porphyry *De Abstin.* 4.6) tells us that the Egyptian priests "always kept their hands within their garments."

18. For the place of women in the synagogue, see E. L. Sukenik, *Ancient Synagogues in Palestine and Greece* (London, 1934), pp. 47–48; C. H. Kraeling, *The Synagogue* (rep. New York, 1979), pp. 23b–24a. "In Galilee," writes Kraeling, "the women probably occupied a gallery above the main floor of the synagogue, to which access was provided by a staircase on the outside of the building. At Dura the women shared equally with the men in the use of the House of Assembly, though they entered by a special door-way and sat on benches reserved especially for them. . . . Whether in admitting the women to the same room as the men the elders provided some means of physical separation beyond that of the assignment of special benches is not evident. What we learn about the means for the separation of sexes in Babylonia, presumably at weddings and when there was occasion to hear sermonic discourse, suggests that any such means were portable and makeshift. (In *BT Kiddushin* 81a, it is said that Abaye made a partition of jugs and Raba one of canes when men and women were gathered together, to avoid contact between them.) Cf. also *PT Sukkah* 5.1, 55b, where we read that after killing the men (in the Alexandrian Diplostoon), Trajan offers mercy to the women at the price of their honor, but they reply, 'Do to those above (ᶜîlayya') as you have done to those below ('arᶜayya')." "Right or wrong," notes Sukenik, "the Palestinian narrator cannot conceive of the Community Center in Alexandria otherwise than with a gallery, and that reserved for the women" (p. 48, n. 1). S. Safrai, however, has challenged the accepted view that the synagogue contained a women's gallery. In his view there is no allusion in the literature to the existence of such a gallery, and the women's court in the Temple is irrelevant because it was not for the exclusive use of women. Only once a year, during the Festival of Water Drawing, when all-night dancing took place in the Temple

court, was separation insisted on. The raised galleries in the synagogues, he believes, served various purposes but not that of a women's gallery ("Was There a Women's Gallery in the Synagogue of Antiquity?" *Tarbiz* 32 [1963]: 329–38 [Heb.]. See also *Ancient Synagogue Excavations at Khirbet Shema^c, Upper Galilee, Israel 1970–1972*, Myers, Kraabel, and Strange, The Annual of the American Scholars of Oriental Research, vol. 42, ed. D. N. Freedman [Durham, N.C., 1976]: 58, 90).

19. Cf. Josephus's description of the Essenes: "[They avoid going to stool on the Sabbath] On other days they dig a trench a foot deep with a mattock ... and wrapping their mantle about them, that they may not offend the rays of the deity [i.e. the sun], sit above it" (*JW* 2.147–48). Schürer contrasts *Test. Benjamin* 8:3, where it is said that the sun is not defiled by shining on dung and mire. (So, too, *Teachings of Silvanus* 101, 32, Robinson, p. 354.) Cf. also III Baruch 8:4–5, where it is said that the sun's beams are defiled on earth by human vice; and *Test. Levi* 3:1, where we are told that the lowest heaven is gloomy because it beholds all the unrighteous deeds of men. We may also recall the interesting exchange between one of the Magi and Amemar: "A Magus once said to Amemar: From the middle of thy [body] upwards thou belongest to Ormuzd; from the middle downwards, to Ahriman. The latter asked: Why then does Ahriman permit Ormuzd to send water through his territory?" (*BT Sanhedrin* 39a).

20. Cf. *Prob.* 8, and see Plato *Phaedrus* 259BC: "The Story goes that these locusts were once men, before the birth of the Muses, and when the Muses were born and song appeared, some of the men were so overcome with delight that they sang and sang, forgetting food and drink, until at last unconsciously they died. From them the locust tribe afterwards arose, and they have this gift from the Muses, that from the time of their birth they need no sustenance, but sing continually, without food or drink, until they die, when they go to the Muses and report who honors each of them on earth." Cf. Aristophanes *Clouds* 1360. The idea that the grasshopper needs no food except air or, more frequently, dew, goes back to Hesiod, *Shield* 395.

21. Colson translates "and on it after providing for the soul refresh the body also," and notes that "neither anointing in the literal sense nor rest from labor for the Therapeutae themselves suits the context, which is concerned with the general abstemiousness in food and mild relaxation on the Sabbath. The sense I have given to λιπαίνω is much the same as in *Spec.* 4.74 where it is applied to relieving the hard condition of the needy by charity.... It is worth noting that according to Josephus, *JW* 2.123, the Essenes abstained altogether from the use of oil. Though it is not a decisive point it is a little surprising to find the Therapeutae making a sabbatical luxury of the indulgence which the less ascetic Essenes refuse" (LCL 9.134, 520–21). On the other hand, Daumas, Lyon 29.104, n. 2 points out that in Jewish practice it was forbidden to anoint the body with oil during periods of mourning and fasting

NOTES

(II Sam. 14:2; Dan. 10:3; *M. Ta^canit* 1.6; *Yoma* 8.1), and it is to this that our text alludes. Unlike the Essenes who rejected all anointing of the body with oil, the Therapeutae allowed it on the Sabbath. It should also be noted that although the Essene avoidance of oil was usually attributed to their general asceticism, J. Baumgarten (*Studies in Qumran Law* [Leiden, 1977], pp. 88–97) has demonstrated that it is to be understood rather as resulting from their scruples concerning levitical purity.

22. Chaeremon (ap. Porphyry *De Abstin.* 4.6) tells us that the Egyptian priests "at those times in which they were not employed in purifying themselves, were accustomed to eat bread with hyssop, cut into small pieces. For it is said that hyssop very much purifies the power of bread."

23. Cf. Seneca *Ep.* 8.5: "Hold fast, then, to this sound and wholesome rule of life; that you indulge the body only so far as is needful for good health.... Eat merely to relieve your hunger; drink merely to quench your thirst"; *Ep.* 18.9: "[Epicurus] boasts that he himself lived on less than a penny, but that Metrodorus, whose progress was not yet so great, needed a whole penny."

24. Conybeare's reading ἀντὶ λασίου δορᾶς, which has the better manuscript authority, is based on the belief that "no excrementitious matter is pure and clean, and it is from forms of surplus that wool, fur, hair, and nails originate and grow" (Plutarch *Moral.* 352D). The Therapeutae therefore scrupled to wear fur or skin, as being a dead and unclean refuse of animals, and wore linen only. Colson objects, however, that χλαῖνα would have to be understood as a "linen garment," whereas it was frequently, if not usually, made of wool. Daumas, on the other hand, dismisses Colson's objection and accepts Conybeare's reading.

25. Cf. *Plant.* 160.

26. See Odyssey 9.373: "And from his gullet came forth wine and bits of human flesh (ψωμοί τ' ἀνδρόμεοι), and he vomited in his drunken sleep."

27. Cf. *Spec.* 3.96: ἐν σπονδαῖς ἄσπονδα ἔπαθεν; *Gig.* 51; *Conf.* 46. The theme of war-in-peace was common in the Cynic-Stoic diatribe literature of the first century C.E. Cf. Ps-Heraclitus *Ep.* 7; Ps-Diogenes *Ep.* 28.

28. ἀντὶ ἀθλητῶν ἄθλιοι—A common pun in antiquity. Cf. Galen *Protrep.* 31.

29. H. A. Harris writes: "This is the only piece of evidence we have to show that a Greek umpire, like a modern boxing referee, sometimes separated contestants by stepping between them" (*Greek Athletics and the Jews* [Cardiff, 1976], p. 90).

30. Cf. *Ebr.* 221; Ps-Aristotle *Probl.* 871a 8–9.

31. Reading γόνου with Cohn. Colson believes γόνου a misprint for γόνυ. Bormann adopts the reading of F: ὑπὸ τῶν γονάτων, "beneath the groin."

32. Literally, "with twisted (or braided) double folds of cord."

NOTES

33. Colson notes: "αἴθυια ("sea-gull"?) is taken as a type of voracity with the same verb ἐμφορεῖσθαι in *LA* 3.155 and *Det.* 101. Philo is the only author quoted for this usage, as the other passage cited by Stephanus, Athenaeus 7.283C, is not to the point. LSJ do not notice it at all."

34. Colson, with some hesitation, and Bormann adopt Cohen's transposition of sections 53–55 with his insertion of some ten omitted words. Conybeare and Daumas, however, translate the manuscript version. My translation follows Cohen's reading.

35. See Xenophon, *Symp.* 2.1ff.; Plato, *Symp.* 173A. Philo's polemical description of these banquets is clearly grossly unfair.

36. Cf. *Spec.* 3.34; Plato *Laws* 838E.

37. See Plato *Symp.* 189Dff. It may be noted that the rabbis echo the myth of the androgyne creature. See *BR* 8.1.

38. Conybeare, Smirnov, and Colson take δι' ἑπτὰ ἑβδομάδων to mean "after seven sets of seven days" or "after an interval of seven weeks," whereas Schürer, Massebieau, Heinemann, Lévy, Geoltrain, Bormann, Daumas/Miguel, and Elizarova take it to mean "every seven weeks." See the recent discussion of V. Nikiprowetzky, "Le *De Vita Contemplativa* Revisité," *Sagesse et Religion, Colloque de Strasbourg* (1976), pp. 105–125. Nikiprowetzky's objection to the rendering "every seven weeks" on the basis of *Cont.* 89, which he takes to imply that the fiftieth day was not a holiday but a profane day, seems to me indecisive. The text may simply indicate that the chief celebration in common of these special holidays took place in the evening and through the night. The plying of their usual "philosophical trade" beginning with the next morning naturally involved the Therapeutae in no profanation of the holiday. For the Qumran evidence that throws light on these seven celebrations, see J. M. Baumgarten, *Studies in Qumran Law* (Leiden, 1977), pp. 131–142. The evidence from the newly discovered *Temple Scroll* makes it possible, in Baumgarten's words, "to view the pentecontad feasts of the Therapeutae as a reflex of the [3] first fruit festivals at Qumran. The former, no longer directly related to the agricultural seasons, could readily be extended beyond the season of the harvests. An excellent example of such a development is available from the liturgical calendar of the Nestorian Christians."

39. That is, 3, 4, 5, are sides of the primal right-angled triangle and $3^2 + 4^2 + 5^2 = 50$. Cf. *Spec.* 2.176; *Mos.* 2.80; Plutarch *Moral.* 373 EF.

40. I follow Cohen in bracketing these words (so too Bormann), although Conybeare and Colson try to defend them.

41. Cf. *Congr.* 5; *QG* 3.29; Wisd. 4:1; 8:2–3.

42. Cf. Epictetus 3.3.5: "That is why the good is preferred above every form of kinship. My father is nothing to me, but only the good"; Mark 3:35.

43. A common rhetorical device. Cf. *QG* 4.168; *Jos.* 125.

44. Cf. *Spec.* 1.148; 1.94; The image derives from Plato, *Tim.* 70E: "There they tethered it [the appetitive part of the soul] like a wild beast."

NOTES

45. Cf. Iamblichus *VP* 99.

46. The notion of the Law as a living being derives from Plato, *Phaedrus* 264C, where Socrates says that "every discourse must be organized, like a living being, with a body of its own, as it were, so as not to be headless or footless, but to have a middle and members, composed in fitting relation to each other and to the whole." Cf. *QG* 3.3; M. Aurelius 4.40; 5.8.

47. Cf. II Cor. 3:6: "For the written code kills, but the Spirit gives life."

48. For the cultic aspect of the meal, cf. *Cont.* 74. See P. Geoltrain, "Le Traité de la Vie Contemplative de Philon d'Alexandrie," *Semitica* 10 (1960): 20; B. Bokser, "Philo's Description of Jewish Practices," *Colloquy 30 of the Center for Hermeneutical Studies* (Berkeley, 1977), and literature there cited.

49. The LXX reading prescribes salt with the showbread, though the Hebrew does not.

50. There is evidence that a variety of modes were in use by Alexandrian Jews in their chanting of the Psalm, and Clement of Alexandria, who praised the majestic psalmody of the Alexandrian Jews, singled out one of these modes as the *Tropos Spondeiakos,* apparently a modification of the Dorian mode (*Paedagogus* 2.4). See E. Werner, "The Attitude of the Church Fathers to Hebrew Psalmody," *RR* 7 (1943): 349–53. "The Qumran *Hodayoth,* which are chiefly individual prayers, some of them expressing the concerns of a leader, would find a satisfactory *Sitz im Leben* in the context of a ceremony parallel to that of the Therapeutae during which the president and each member recited a hymn in succession" (Schürer, 2.595. For the vigil, cf. 1 *QS* 6.7–8: "And the Congregation shall watch in community for a third of every night of the year, to read the Book and to study Law and to pray together."

51. Cf. Sir. 39:5; *BT Berakot* 9b: "The *watikin* [i.e., those 'strong' in their piety] used to finish it [the recital of the *Shema*] with sunrise"; Josephus *JW* 2.128: "Before the sun is up they [the Essenes] utter no word on mundane affairs, but offer to him certain prayers which have been handed down from their forefathers, as though entreating him to rise"; Iamblichus *VP* 256. M. Smith quotes Lieberman as saying that Josephus's account misinterprets the use of Isa. 60:1, known from Genizah fragments to have been recited in morning prayers ("Essenes in Josephus and the Philosophumena," *HUCA* 29 (1958): 288, n. 55). For further examples, see A. J. Festugière, 4.245, n. 3.

52. The notion of friendship with God is an ancient and widespread motif. Cf. Isa. 41:8; II Chron. 20:7; 22:7, Vulgate; Exod. 32:11, LXX; Jub. 30:20–21; *Apoc. of Abr.* 9 and 10; *Test. Abraham* A 15,16; James 2:23; *Sib Or* 2:245; Philo, *Sobr.* 56; *Mos.* 1.156; *Her.* 21; *Prob.* 44; *Abr.* 129; *LA* 3.204. For further references see my Anchor commentary on *Wisdom of Solomon,* pp. 188–89; and E. Peterson, "Der Gottesfreund," *ZKG* n.f. 5, 42 (1923): 161–202.

NOTES

THE GIANTS

1. In Philo's great scheme, the pair of commentaries *De Gigantibus—Quod Deus Sit Immutabilis* resumes the exegesis of Genesis after a brief gap, occasioned by the rather intractable material, genealogical in nature, that comprises Genesis, chap. 5. The previous treatise, *On the Posterity and Exile of Cain*, took us to the end of chap. 4, the birth of Seth.

2. Philo's exegesis of Gen. 6:1 is at first sight surprising. Why should the growth of population and the birth of daughters in itself be a bad thing? This can partly be explained, perhaps, by the nature of the preceding chapter, "The Book of the Generations of Adam," where each of the patriarchs is described as producing both sons and daughters, culminating with Noah (v. 32), who engenders only sons (cf. *BR* 26.4, Th-Alb:246); and partly also because the concepts of multiplicity and the female had definite negative connotations in contemporary Platonism (particularly in the Pythagorean wing of it) to which Philo was fully alive. The juxtaposition of the fewness and maleness of Noah's progeny, with the pullulating anonymous femininity of what follows him, was something too striking for Philo to miss.

3. Doctrine of symmetrical contrast: "good/bad," "few/many." For the rarity of the good, cf. *LA* 1.102; *Ebr.* 26; *Mig.* 59, 51, 63, 123; *Mut.* 34–56, 213; *Virt.* 10; *Abr.* 19; *Prob.* 63, 72; *Agr.* 180; Plato *Phaedo* 90A.

4. The principle that opposites are most easily recognized by opposites is perhaps a development of the principle that "knowledge of the contraries is the same" (Aristotle, *Top.* 105b 25). Cf. Plato, *Ep.* 7.344 AB (virtue and vice must be learned together just as the truth and error about any part of being must be learned together); Chrysippus ap. Gellius *NA* 7.1 (*SVF* 2.1169): opposites can only be known through opposites. This principle seems also to be operative at *Deus* 122, where the point is that only at the appearance of a sense of good (or of conscience) does evil become recognizable. Cf. *LA* 1.46; 3.73; *Ebr.* 186; *Her.* 213: "For the two opposites together form a single whole, by the division of which the opposites are known." (Philo attributes this principle to Heraclitus, but insists that Moses had already discovered it; cf. *QG* 3.5.)

5. The Equation of the female with the lower parts of our nature, the passions of the irrational soul, is a basic Philonic image (e.g., *Sacr.* 103). See Baer.

6. For the principle that opposites arise from opposites, see Aristotle *Phys.* 188b21ff.; *De Caelo* 310a 23ff.; *Gen. Corr.* 331a14. See G. E. R. Lloyd, *Polarity and Analogy* (Cambridge, 1966), pp. 15–171.

7. The present section shows both that the Middle Platonic theory of daemons was well developed by Philo's time and that he was well acquainted with it. The analysis of the true relation between the terms "daemon," "an-

gel" and "soul" is for Philo a matter of some importance. Plato, in an influential passage of the *Timaeus* (90 A), had identified the rational part of the soul as the daemon of each man, and later Platonism made no very clear distinction between daemons and angels. What Greek philosophers call daemons, says Philo, Moses is accustomed to call "angels." Angels and daemons are, for Philo, merely terms for souls performing certain roles. Evil angels, so-called, are simply souls that have descended into corporeality, and have been fascinated by the pleasures associated with it. As to the reading οἱ ἄγγελοι τοῦ θεοῦ in Gen. 6:2 in place of οἱ υἱοὶ τοῦ θεοῦ, this must have been the tradition available to him, and is one of Philo's more interesting departures from the LXX text as we have it (apart from a corrector of the Codex Alexandrinus). It seems as if someone in the Alexandrian tradition was offended, as well he might be, by the idea of God's having sons, and glossed "sons" by the less offensive term ἄγγελοι (cf. P. Katz, *Philo's Bible* [Cambridge, 1950], pp. 20–21).

8. The other passage in which Philo sets out his daemonology (or angelology) is *Somn.* 1.135–143, in connection with the exegesis of Jacob's ladder (Gen. 28:12). The ladder symbolizes the element of Air, which is the abode of souls. *BR* 26.5, Th-Alb: 247 reflects a similar motivation to deny that the biblical passage is literally referring to fallen angels. R. Simeon b. Yoḥai says the reference is to the sons of judges, and curses those who insist that it refers to the sons of God. For a discussion of Philo's various explanations for the incarnation of souls, see Winston, pp. 26–28.

9. A parallel argument to this is given by Apuleius, *De Deo Socratis,* chap. 8, showing it to be part of the Platonic tradition. Apuleius's source may well be Varro (ap. Augustine *CD* 7.6), whose source in turn might be Posidonius, though possibly also Antiochus of Ascalon. Cf. Plato *Epinomis* 984BC; Arist. *Gen. Anim.* 3.762a18ff.; Cicero *ND* 2.42; Sextus *Math.* 9.86; D.L. 8.32. See also Plato, *Tim.* 40A and 41BC, where it is laid down that all varieties of living things must exist, in order that the cosmos may be complete (cf. Philo *Prov.* 2.110).

10. Philo is the first attested user of the word πυρίγονα (cf. *Aet.* 45), but the "fire-born creatures" are introduced first by Aristotle (*HA* 5.19, 552b). The connection with Macedonia, which Philo makes again at *Plant.* 12, is not derivable from Aristotle's account, which describes the creatures as appearing in copper-smelting furnaces in Cyprus, and is of mysterious provenance (cf. Cicero *ND* 1.103).

11. The doctrine of stars and planets as pure souls takes its origin from Plato's *Tim.* 40A–D. Cf. *Op.* 27, 73; 144; *LA* 2.10; *Cher.* 23; *Deus* 46; *Somn.* 1.135; *Spec.* 1.19; *QG* 4.157; *Plant.* 12. In *Op.* 144 Philo speaks of the stars as "spiritual and divine natures" that are "not without bodies." Wolfson (1.364) believes that this represents Philo's own view, whereas the doctrine of the stars as pure souls represents the views of others.

NOTES

12. Cf. *Prov.* 2.24; 1.18; 2–67, 102; *Prob.* 76; *Aet.* 126. On the origins of the physical theory envisaged here, cf. *Legat.* 125–26, and Smallwood's commentary ad loc.

13. Image borrowed from Plato *Tim.* 43A.

14. The conjunction of soul with body, says Aristotle (*Protrep.* B107, Düring), is reminiscent of the Etruscan custom of torturing captives "by chaining dead bodies face to face with the living." The body is for Philo, at best, a necessary evil (*LA* 3.72–73; cf. *Her.* 272), for it is a corpse, a shell-like growth, the dwelling place of endless calamities, wicked by nature and a plotter against the soul (*LA* 3.69; *Conf.* 177; *Agr.* 25; *Mig.* 21; *Somn.* 2.237; *Flac.* 159).

15. This notion derives from Plato *Symp.* 202E (cf. *Epinomis* 985B), where the function of the δαίμων is "interpreting and transporting human things to the gods and divine things to men; entreaties and sacrifices from below, and ordinances and requitals from above.... Through it are conveyed all divination and priestcraft concerning sacrifice and ritual and incantations, and all soothsaying and sorcery." Cf. *Somn.* 1.141; *Plant.* 14; *Abr.* 115.

16. The contrast between immortal/mortal and γνήσιος/νόθος (genuine/spurious) is frequent in Philo, and thoroughly Platonic. Cf. *Deus* 151–52; Plato *Laws* 631BC; *Rep.* 469A, 535C–536A, 587B.

17. Every being possessed of a human soul has some ἔννοια of the good at some time. This can be seen as an application of the Stoic concept of κοιναὶ ἔννοιαι (literally, common notions) which are imprinted on human reason. In the writings of Epictetus we find the Natural Law grounded in the προλήψεις or preconceptions, which the Stoics believed were common to all men (1.22.1; 2.11; 4.1.41; cf. Cicero *Fin.* 5.4.3; *Tusc.* 3.2 (*semina innata virtutum*); Seneca *Benefic.* 4.17.4: "Of all the benefits that we have from nature, this is the greatest, the fact that Virtue causes her light to penetrate into the minds of all; even those who do not follow her, see her." *Ep.* 108.8; Musonius 2.14, Lutz. Cf. *LA* 1.34–35, 38; *Det.* 86.

18. Cf. Ps-Aristotle *De Mundo* 394b8; *QG* 1.90; *Det.* 83; Empedocles DK B.100; Plato, *Cratylus* 410B; *SVF* 2.471. See O. Gilbert, *Die meteorologischen theorien des griechischen Altertums* (Leipzig, 1907), pp. 512ff.; A. Leisegang, *Der Heilige Geist* (Leipzig-Berlin, 1919), pp. 15–75.

19. Cf. *Det.* 83–90; *Congr.* 25; *Mut.* 219; *Jos.* 146; *Virt.* 55; Plato *Phaedrus* 247D: ἐπιστήμῃ ἀκηράτῳ τρεφομένη (θεοῦ διανοία); *Laws* 735C.

20. This is the Platonic doctrine of the imparting of spiritual qualities without loss to the source. Cf. *Det.* 90; *Spec.* 1.47; *Wisd.* 7:27. For the concept see Ennius, quoted by Cicero *Off.* 1.51; Ps-Aristotle *De Mundo* 398b 10ff.; Seneca, *Ep.* 41; M. Aurel. 8.57, 7.59; Numenius, Fr. 14, Des Places (a torch lighting another does not lose anything of its own light, nor is the teacher's learning diminished when he imparts it to his pupil [cf. Plot. 6.5.8; 4.9.5]. There is an analogy in the Zoroastrian tradition, Ormuzd's creation of the

NOTES

Bounteous Immortals being compared to the lighting of a torch (*Ayadgar I Jamaspiq*, ed. G. Messina [Rome, 1939], 3.3–7. See also *Shir Hashirim R.* on Cant. 3:10; *BT Sanhedrin* 39a; *BR* 68.9; *Tanḥ* Buber, *Beha'alotka* 22; Plot. 1.7.1; 5.3.12; 5.4.2; 3.8.10; Justin, *Dial.* 128 ad fin; Tertullian *Apol.* 21.10–13; Lactantius *Div. Inst.* 4.29. 4–5; Augustine *Conf.* 9.5.1.

21. Cf. *Post.* 112; *Jos.* 130; *Prov.* 2.21. The same image and phraseology is found in Plutarch *Moral.* 804E.

22. βαρυνόμεναι καὶ πιεζόμεναι is a frequent collocution in Philo. See *Deus* 14; *Det.* 16; *Ebr.* 104, 214; cf. *LA* 3.152; *Spec.* 4.114. A reminiscence of Plato *Phaedo* 81C: "And such a soul is weighed down (βαρύνεται) by this and is dragged back into the sensible world." A fragment of the Pythagorean Onatas states that "the earthly mixture of the body defiles the purity of the soul" (Thesleff: 140, 9) and Ecphantus taught that on earth man "is weighed down by a large portion of earth" (Thesleff: 79, 3). See also Wisd. 9:15; Jos. *JW* 7.346; Plutarch *Moral.* 353A; Epictetus 1.1.15; *CH Asclepius* 1.9; Seneca *Ep.* 65, 16; Plotinus 6.9.8.16.

23. Cf. *Plant.* 16–27; *Det.* 85; *QG* 4.46; Xenophon *Mem.* 1.4.11; Plato *Tim.* 90A–D; Cicero *ND* 2.140. See A. Wlosok, *Laktanz und die philosophische Gnosis* (Heidelberg, 1960), pp. 8–69.

24. The theme of the "real man" is very common in Philo and in Greek literature. See *Her.* 231; *Fug.* 71; *Somn.* 1.215, 124–25; 2.167; *Det.* 23; *Fug.* 131; *Jos.* 71; *Spec.* 1.303; *Congr.* 97; *Plant.* 42; *Prob.* 111; Plato *Rep.* 589B; *Alcibiades I* 130C; *Phaedo* 111C; *Laws* 919B; Aristotle *EN* 1166a; Cicero *Somn. Scip.* [*Rep.* 6]26; *Tusc.* 1.52. For a detailed discussion see J. Pépin, *Idées grecques sur l'Homme et sur Dieu* (Paris, 1971), pp. 71–86.

25. Note Philo's indifference to the Hebraism here, as so often. Rabbinic exegesis, attuned to the slightest superfluity of expression in Scripture, derives an additional legal ruling (i.e., that Gentiles are included in the prohibition) from the ἐπαναδίπλωσις or doubling of the word 'îš (*Sifra, Aharê* 9–13; *BT Sanhedrin* 57b). Here the doubling simply indicates for Philo "the real Man."

26. For the famous story concerning Diogenes the Cynic, see D.L. 6.41.

27. For the nature of Philo's asceticism, see Introduction, pp. 30–32.

28. Although the Epicurean distinction between necessary and unnecessary desires had been already anticipated by Plato (*Rep.* 558Dff.; cf. *Tim.* 70E), Philo's contrast of the gifts of nature with those of κενὴ δόξα or empty opinion (*Praem.* 100; *Virt.* 7; *QG* 3.47; *Somn.* 1.255) in addition to his contrast between necessary and unnecessary desires points to his dependence on an Epicurean source. (See Usener, *Epicurea* 456; Cicero *Tusc.* 5.93; D.L. 10.149; *K.D.* 30.) For other possible Epicurean echoes in Philo, see Bréhier, pp. 263–64.

29. The comparison of the passions with wild beasts is very frequent

325

NOTES

in Philo: *LA* 1.69; 2.9–11, 92; 3.156; *Sacr.* 62; *Plant.* 43; *Conf.* 24, 110; *Mig.* 219; *Abr.* 32; *Spec.* 2.9; *Praem.* 59, 88. The image is Platonic (*Tim.* 70E; *Rep.* 588C). Cf. n. 41 on *Cont.* 74.

30. Philo is fond of the image of rabid dogs whose bite is irremediable. See *Prob.* 90; *Cont.* 40. "During the early stages of the disease a rabid animal is most dangerous because it appears to be healthy and may seem friendly but will bite at the slightest provocation" (*Ency. Brit.* s.v. Rabies [1963], 18.863a).

31. For ὀλιγοδεία, see *Virt.* 6–9; *Praem.* 99–100; *Somn.* 1.9, 97, 124–25, 173–74; 2.159–60, 195; *Prob.* 77, 84; *Op.* 164; *Ebr.* 58, 214–15; *Mos.* 2.185; *QG* 23.48; *LA* 2.17; 3.140–143, 147, 154, 236; *Sacr.* 59; *Mut.* 103; *Det.* 101. Cf. Xenophon *Mem.* 1.6.10; 1.3.5–6; Musonius (in Stobaeus 751, 526.16, 173). Wendland has pointed out the parallels between numerous passages in Philo and Musonius, and argued that they must have a common origin in Cynic-Stoic diatribe. See P. Wendland, *Philo und die Kynisch-Stoische Diatribe*, Beiträge zur Gesch. d. griechischen Philosophie (Berlin, 1895); and D. R. Dudley, *A History of Cynicism* (London, 1937), pp. 186, 32, 69, 189–201.

32. Rejection here of the Peripatetic view. Happiness is independent of any external goods. Cf. *LA* 2.16–18. See Dillon, pp. 147–48.

33. Cf. *Mos.* 2.212; *Cher.* 123; Plato *Prot.* 313CD (Sophists as crooked market traders); *Soph.* 231D; Lucian, *Bion Prasis* (cut-rate sale of philosophies).

34. Cf. *Ebr.* 43. Some corruption seems to have crept in here. Wendland conjectured ἡ ἀσυγκρίτων σύγκρισις. Colson suggests the following reconstruction: οὔκουν <εἰ> τὸ μὲν σαρκός ἐστιν ἄλογος ἡδονή, τὸ δὲ ψυχῆς καὶ τοῦ παντὸς ὁ νοῦς τῶν ὅλων, ὁ θεός ἐφάμιλλος [τε] ἢ [ἀ] συγκρίτων ἡ σύγκρισις, εἰ μὴ . . ., i.e., "Then if the first is . . ., and the second is . . ., the comparison is not an evenly balanced one or between two really comparables, unless we are prepared to admit . . ." etc. Wendland's emendation may perhaps make good sense, if we assume Philo to be speaking ironically, but the reading of H, which omits μή after εἰ, seems to me to give a rather easier sense, and it is this reading I have followed in my translation.

35. Cf. Plato *Apol.* 28E–29A; *Deus* 34; *Ebr.* 145; *Cher.* 32; *Det.* 142; *Aet.* 65; *Cont.* 11; *Decal.* 104, 178; also Epictetus 1.16–21; 1.9.16; IV Macc. 9:23.

36. The rabbis interpreted Lev. 18:6 in a similar manner. *Sifra, Aḥarê* 9.1: "I am the Lord" (Lev. 18:6). I am the judge to punish, and faithful to reward. Cf. *Wayyikra R.* 23.9.

37. Cf. *LA* 3.4; *Sacr.* 67; *Det.* 153; *Post.* 14, 30; *Deus* 57; *Conf.* 136; *Somn.* 1.62; 2.221; Seneca *Ep.* 41.1–2; 83.2; Epictetus 1.14; 2.8.9–14: "You are bearing God about with you, you poor wretch, and know it not. . . . But when God himself is present within you, seeing and hearing everything. . . ."

38. Philo explains God's designation as κύριος as a reference to his ἐξουσία or sovereignty, and his designation θεός as a reference to his ἀγαθότης or goodness. To the former he applies the adjectives βασιλική, ἀρχική, νομοθετική and κολαστήριος, whereas for the latter he employs

326

the adjectives ποιητική, εὐεργετική, χαριστική, δωρητική, ἵλεως. For Philo's doctrine of the Powers, see Introduction, pp. 23–24.

39. Σοφία is here identified with the *pneuma* or Logos of God pervading the universe, as a force both cosmological and ethical. For the relationship of σοφία to Logos, see U. Früchtel, *Die kosmologischen Vorstellungen bei Philo von Alexandrien* (Leiden, 1968), pp. 172–83. Cf. especially *Fug.* 97 and 109.

40. According to the Stoics, whom Philo is following, the Wise Man is no longer separated from virtue, whereas those making progress (προκόπτουτες) are still liable to reverse course and slip back into their former habits. Cf. *LA* 1.89.

41. For βεβαιότης cf. *SVF* 3.510: ὅταν αἱ μέσαι πράξεις αὗται προσλάβωσι τὸ βέβαιον καὶ ἐκτικόν καὶ ἰδίαν πῆξιν τινὰ λάβωσι. For πῆξιν cf. *Agr.* 160; *LA* 2.55.

42. The ideal of εὐστάθεια or inner calm and stability is a central theme running through Philo's writings. Cf. *Post.* 23, 27–29; *Cher.* 19; *Somn.* 1.158; 2.219; *Virt.* 32; *Legat.* 113; *Conf.* 130–132; *Fug.* 174; *Abr.* 27; *Ebr.* 76, 100; *Sacr.* 8; *Flac.* 135. For the earliest application of the term εὐσταθής to the human soul see Democritus, DK B.191. Cf. also Epicurus, Fr. 11, Bailey; Epictetus 1.29; *SVF* 3.280; Musonius Rufus, Fr.38 Lutz; Ps-Aristeas 261; Aristobulus, *FPG*:224; Wisd. 8:16; *CH* 13:20; *Gospel of Philip* 119.13–15; Plotinus 6.9.11; 4.8.1; Plato *Rep.* 532E. See H. Gomoll, *Der stoische Philosoph Hekaton* (Bonn, 1933), pp. 21ff.; Y. Amir, "A Religious Interpretation of a Philosophical Concept in Philo," (Heb.), Memorial Volume for Prof. BenZion Katz (Tel Aviv, 1970), pp. 112–17; P. Vielhauer, *Aufsätze zum Neuen Testament* (München, 1965), pp. 215–34; O. Hofius, *Katapausis* (Tübingen, 1970), pp. 75–90.

43. Cf. *Deus* 23; *Conf.* 30, 32; *Mut.* 87, 183; *Somn.* 2.220, 227; *Abr.* 170; *Prob.* 29, κατὰ τὰ αὐτὰ καὶ ὡσαύτως ἔχουσαν is a basic Platonic phrase, e.g., *Phaedo* 78D.

44. The equation of the High Priest with the Logos is a common one in Philo (cf. *Fug.* 108ff.; *Mig.* 102; *Somn.* 1.215), but here it must plainly refer simply to human reason.

45. Cf. *Mig.* 71–81; *Mos.* 2.129–130. The Stoic distinction between λόγος ἐνδιάθετος and λόγος προφορικός goes back to Plato (*Theaet.* 190A, 206D; *Soph.* 263E) and Aristotle (*Anal. Post.* 1.10.76b24), though without the cosmic dimensions Philo here presupposes. See M. Pohlenz, *Die Stoa* (Göttingen, 1959) 1.39; K. Otte, *Das Sprachverhältniss bei Philo von Alexandrien* (Tübingen, 1968), pp. 131–42.

46. Cf. *LA* 2.59–60; *Cher.* 31; *Sacr.* 84; *Ebr.* 34; *Mig.* 90, 192; *Mut.* 199; *Somn.* 1.43; *Abr.* 236; *Spec.* 1.63; 4.71; *Prob.* 43. The image of stripping goes back to some extent to the myth of the *Gorgias* 523Aff. It is also common in Gnostic texts. See H. Jonas, *The Gnostic Religion* (2nd ed., Boston, 1963), p. 166; W. Bousset, *Die Himmelsreise der Seele* (rep. Darmstadt, 1960); J. Rist, *Plotinus* (Cambridge, 1967), pp. 188–91; Dodds, pp. 94–95.

47. Cf. *Post.* 14; *Mut.* 7; *Mos.* 1.158; for the use of this image in Gregory of Nyssa, see J. Daniélou, "Mystique de la Ténèbre chez Grégoire de Nysse," *Dict. de la Spiritualité*, ed. M. Viller (Paris, 1932ff.), pp. 1872–85.

48. This corresponds to nothing in Philo's existing Life of Moses. A detailed arithmological discussion of 120 is given in *QG* 1.91.

49. Moses, like Plato, is a stern censor of the arts. Philo is thinking of the Second Commandment (Exod. 20:3). Cf. *Ebr.* 109; *Decal.* 66, 156; *Spec.* 1.28–29; *Her.* 169; Wisd. 14:18–21; Cicero *ND* 1.42, 77; Seneca *Ep.* 88.18; Clement of Alexandria 4. See J. Gutmann, "The Second Commandment and the Image in Judaism," *No Graven Images* (New York, 1971), pp. 12–14.

50. There is a close parallel to Philo's triadic distinction of Men of Earth, Men of Heaven, and Men of God in Plato's three classes of men: the philosopher or lover of wisdom, the lover of victory and the lover of gain (*Rep.* 581C; cf. *Phaedo* 68BC); and in Aristotle's distinction of three types of life, the Life of Enjoyment, the Life of Action, and the Life of Contemplation (*EN* 1095b 17ff). This doctrine of the three lives goes back to Pythagoras, who compared human life to a festival celebrated with magnificent games: "for at this festival some men whose bodies had been trained sought to win the glorious distinction of a crown, others were attracted by the prospect of making gain by buying or selling, whilst there was on the other hand a certain class, and that quite the best, of free-born men, who looked neither for applause nor gain, but came for the sake of the spectacle and closely watched what was done. So also we, as though we had come from some city to a kind of crowded festival, leaving in like fashion another life and nature of being, entered upon this life, and some were slaves of ambition, some of money; there were a special few who, counting all else as nothing, closely scanned the nature of things; these men gave themselves the name of lovers of wisdom (for that is the meaning of the word philosopher)." (Cicero *Tusc.* 5.3.8; cf. Iamblichus *VP* 58). For a similar Stoic distinction, see D.L. 7.130; Plutarch *Moral.* 8A.

51. For παραθήγων καὶ ἀκονῶν cf. *Fug.* 125; *Congr.* 25; *Ebr.* 159. For the image, cf. Isocrates *Antid.* 261ff.

52. There is a conscious reminiscence here of the *Phaedrus* myth (especially 249C: ἀνακύψασα εἰς τὸ ὂν ὄντως).

53. For Philo, Abraham is a paradigm of conversion—specifically from the state of an οὐράνιος, as cosmos-bound intellectual, who (coming as he does from Chaldaea) is one of those who worships the heavenly bodies rather than their Creator. There is a reference here to the Stoics, and in particular the heliolatrous tendencies developed a generation or so before Philo by Posidonius (F 17, 20, Kidd); cf. Wisd. 13:1–9 (cf. F. H. Sandbach, *The Stoics* [London, 1975], pp. 72–75). For Abraham's practice of astrology, see G. Vermes, *Scripture and Tradition in Judaism* (Leiden, 1973), pp. 76–83.

54. According to A. Hanson, this derivation is apparently from the three Hebrew words: *'ab, bōr,* and *hôm* or *hamô.* In the LXX *bōr* and *bārôr* are

occasionally rendered by ἐκλεκτός and ἠχεῖν is a frequent translation of *hôm* and *hāmô* (*JTS* n.s. 11 [1967]: 128–39). Another possibility is that it derives from *'ab* and *ra'am*.

55. The allegorization of the Royal Road of Num. 20:17–20 is a favorite of Philo's; cf. *Deus* 140–166.

56. The image of adulterating the coinage is common in Philo: *Post.* 89, 98; *Congr.* 159; etc. Its remote origin presumably lies in the story told of himself by Diogenes the Cynic, as to why he was expelled from his native city (D.L. 6.20).

57. The rabbis deduced from Gen. 10:9 that Nimrod knew his Master and intentionally rebelled *(marad)* against him (*Sifra, Beḥuqqotay* 2.2). Cf. *BT Pesaḥim* 94b; Ps-Jonathan ad loc.

SELECTIONS FROM PHILO'S OTHER WORKS

1. For ἰλυσπώμενος, cf. Plato *Tim.* 92A: "And inasmuch as there was no longer any need of feet for the most foolish of these same creatures, which stretched with their whole body along the earth, the gods generated these footless and wriggling (ἰλυσπώμενα) upon the earth." Cf. also *Her.* 238.

2. Cf. *Spec.* 1.37; *Op.* 70; Plato *Phaedr.* 246ff.

3. For the image of the lookout, cf. *Spec.* 3.48; Plato *Rep.* 445C; *Polit.* 272E; Numenius, Frs. 2 and 12, Des Places.

4. The reference may be to the troubles of 38–41 C.E. described in the *In Flaccum* and *Legatio ad Gaium* (although Heinemann cavalierly dismissed this).

5. Cf. *Praem.* 37.

6. Cf. Plato *Phaedo* 109E; *Phaedr.* 246Dff., 249C, 251BC, 256B. Philo's dreamworld, as that of most Middle Platonists, is dominated by what Bachelard has aptly called an "Icarus complex" (quoted by Mosès, ad loc.); cf. *Her.* 126–28, 234; *Op.* 70–71; *LA* 3.71, 84; *Det.* 27, 86–90; *Plant.* 24–25; *Somn.* 1.139; *Spec.* 1.37, 207; 2.45, 230; *Mut.* 66–67, 179–80; *Mig.* 184; *Praem.* 121–22. The verbs employed in these passages are usually: αἰθεροβατεῖν, μετεωροπολεῖν, μετεωρίζεσθαι. See M. Harl, Lyon 15.119, n. 2; R. M. Jones, "Posidonius and the Flight of the Mind in the Universe," *Classical Philology* 21 (1926): 97–113; Dodds, pp. 7ff.; cf. n. 602 below.

7. Cf. *QG* 4.234: "But let all thanks be given to a gracious and beneficent one who does not permit the mind to be emptied and bereft of an excellent and most divine form when it descends into an earthly body and is burned by the necessities and flames of desire, for these are a true Tartarus, but he permits it to spread its wings sometimes and to behold heaven above and to taste of that sight."

NOTES

8. "If it is asked," writes Colson, "why this eloquent outcry is introduced at this point, I think it is enough to say that it is a natural literary device marking that he is just halfway through his great subject. Such prologues at pauses in a long disquisition are not, I think, uncommon. They appear, for instance in Quintilian" (LCL 7.631).

9. For impregnation by God, cf. *Cher.* 44–45; *Cont.* 68; *Congr.* 7; *Her.* 118–19; *Deus* 5.

10. For the suddenness of the revelation; cf. *Sacr.* 78–79; *Somn.* 1.71; Plato *Symp.* 210E; *Ep.* 7.341CD.

11. Cf. *Cher.* 27; *LA* 2.32, 85; *Somn.* 2.252.

12. For the sexual imagery, cf. Prov. 7:4; Sir. 15:2; Wisd. 8:2–16; *Kobel. R.* 9.9; *Mid. Mishle* 5.18. The Dead Sea Psalms scroll has provided us with a portion of the original poem at the end of Ben Sira (51:13ff.) in which form it constitutes a series of artful double entendres each of which possesses an erotic as well as a moralistic sense:

> I was a young man before I had erred
>> when I looked for her.
> *She came to me in her beauty*
>> when finally I sought her out.
> . . .
> And she became for me a *nurse;*
>> to *my teacher* I give my *ardor.*
> I purposed *to make sport:*
>> I was zealous for pleasure,
>> without *pause.*
> I *kindled* my desire for her
>> *without distraction*
> I bestirred my desire for her,
>> *and on her heights I do not waver.*
> I spread my hand(s) . . .
>> and perceive her *unseen parts.*

(Translation, verbatim, by J. A. Sanders, *The Dead Sea Psalms Scroll* [Ithaca, 1967], p. 115.)

13. For the same succession of technical terms, see *Somn.* 1.205; *Agr.* 137; *Post.* 104; cf. *LA* 3.121; *Somn.* 1.28.

14. Cf. Plato *Euthyd.* 271C: "These two men are absolutely omniscient (πάσσοφοι): I never knew before what 'all-round sportsmen' (παγκρατια-σταί) were."

15. πνεῦμα is used here in the Stoic sense of ἕξις, the pneumatic current that bonds all things. Cf. *Aet.* 86; *Deus* 35; *Her.* 242; *Op.* 131; *Praem.* 48.

16. Cf. Seneca *De Constantia Sapientis* 9.5: "Just so in the sacred games

330

many have won the victory by wearing out the hands of their assailants through stubborn endurance. Do you, then, reckon the wise man in this class of men—the men who by long and faithful training have attained the strength to endure and tire out any assault of the enemy"; *De Ira* 2.14.2: "Nor is it difficult to subdue the spirit, since even athletes, concerned as they are with man's basest part, nevertheless endure blows and pain in order that they may drain the strength of their assailant and strike, not when anger, but when advantage, prompts."

17. Euripides, *TrGF* Fr.275.

18. ἤδη γοῦν is frequently the formula through which Philo introduces a reference to a personal experience. Cf. *Ebr.* 177; *Prob.* 26.

19. According to legend, pigeons tended and fed the infant Semiramis, who had been exposed by her mother, the goddess Derceto (the Phoenician Artagatis, represented at Ascalon as half woman, half fish). Since that time the pigeon has been honored as a goddess by the inhabitants of Syria (Diodorus 2.4.2–6).

20. Cf. *LA* 2.32.

21. Cf. *Post.* 7; *Abr.* 68, 99, 119; *Mut.* 60; *Prob.* 82; *Cont.* 28–29, 78; *Somn.* 1.73, 102, 164; 2.8; *Her.* 221; *Decal.* 1; *Spec.* 1.327; *Jos.* 28.

22. Cf. *Abr.* 236, 147, 200; *Sacr.* 131; *Plant.* 36; *Spec.* 2.147; 3.178.

23. τροπικὰς ἀποδόσεις.

24. A reminiscence of the Platonic myth of the Cave (*Rep.* 7.514ff.).

25. Cf. *Conf.* 14; *Somn.* 1.92–102; *Sobr.* 33; *Abr.* 217; *QG* 4.168.

26. For Philo's use of the collocution σώματα καὶ πράγματα, see Colson, LCL 4.573. In a number of cases πράγματα signifies things belonging to the mental world, ideas in fact. This curious usage may derive from the Stoic use of *pragma* to mean *lekton* as attested in *SVF* 2.173, and especially D.L. 7.57. Cf. also the use of *pragma* in Plato *Protag.* 330BD.

27. Cf. Heraclitus, DK B.123: φύσις δὲ καθ' Ἡράκλειτον κρύπτεσθαι φιλεῖ (Nature likes to hide). Cf. *Fug.* 179.

28. Reading with Colson < οὐκ > ἀκριβοῦς ἐρεύνης φαυλίσαντες. Arnaldez retains the manuscript reading.

29. For Wendland's expunging of στοιχείῳ περιττεύει see Colson, LCL 5.588.

30. For a discussion of Wendland's reading of the Greek text, see Colson, LCL 5.588.

31. Cf. *QG* 1.53; 3.43, 53; *Conf.* 2–13; *Agr.* 157; *Abr.* 178.

32. Cf. *LA* 1.43; 2.19; *Deus* 59; *Op.* 154, 157.

33. According to Epicurus, the Gods are anthropomorphic, for they appear to us only in human shape (Cicero *ND* 1.46). This is also likely on a priori grounds, for the human figure is the most beautiful figure we know, and it is therefore likely that the figure of the gods is similar. Moreover, since the gods, like men, possess the power of reason, they must also have human

form (*ND* 1.48). "Yet their form is not corporeal, but only resembles bodily substance; it does not contain blood, but the semblance of blood" (*ND* 1.49). The gods are merely patterns of fine atoms lacking the density to constitute a solid body. They are "images" (εἴδωλα), because their nature is continuously reconstituted by a moving stream of "images," discrete arrangements of fine atoms that possess similar form (Usener 355). See J. M. Rist, *Epicurus* (Cambridge, 1972), pp. 140–146; A. A. Long, *Hellenistic Philosophy* (London, 1974), pp. 46–49. Arnaldez (ad loc.) believes that it is more likely the Epicurean relegation of the gods into deep space (the *intermundia*, spaces between the individual cosmic systems: Lucretius 5.146ff.), and the gods' utter lack of concern with human affairs that is at the heart of Philo's attack here (cf. *Somn.* 1.184 for the *intermundia*).

34. That is, their worship of animals; cf. *Mos.* 2.193; *Legat.* 163; *Cont.* 8.

35. Cf. *Somn.* 2.246; *LA* 3.4; *Det.* 13–15, 95, 155, 167; *Congr.* 44; *Plant.* 32, 113; *Post.* 51; *Deus* 21–22, 133; *QE* 2.34.

36. Cf. *Aet.* 56; *Cont.* 63; *Op.* 2; *Spec.* 1.28, 79; *Mig.* 76; *Sacr.* 13, 76; *Post.* 165; *Decal.* 66, 156; *Ebr.* 109; *Her.* 169; *Gig.* 58.

37. Cf. *Cher.* 48–49; *Sacr.* 60; *Post.* 173; *Gig.* 54; *Plant.* 26; *Fug.* 85; *Abr.* 122; *Mos.* 2.71; *Decal.* 41; *Virt.* 178; *QG* 4.8; *Praem.* 121; *Prov.* 2.40; Philo's use of mystery terminology was based on an accepted usage among Greek philosophers. Cf. Plato *Symp.* 210A; *Phaedr.* 250B, E; *Gorg.* 497C; *Meno* 76E; Gellius *NA* 20.5; Themistius *Orationes* 26.319D, Dindorf; Plutarch, *Moral.* 382D, 383A, 718CD, 422E; *SVF* 2.42, 1008; Epiphanius *Adv. Haer.* 3.2.9; Albinus *Did.* 179.33–34; 182.8, Hermann; Josephus *Ag. Ap.* 2.188. See A. D. Nock, *Essays on Religon and the Ancient World* (Oxford, 1972), pp. 459–68; Wolfson 1.24–25, 43–55; Nikiprowetzky, pp. 14–28; Lilla, pp. 144–58.

38. Philo's authority in Deuteronomy for this section is 23:17–18, where the LXX contains the following addition to the Masoretic text: "there shall be no τελεσφόρος ('sorceress') among the daughters, nor τελισκόμενος ('initiate') among the sons." Whatever the LXX means, Philo clearly understood both words as referring to initiation into the mysteries. We similarly find mystery terminology in the LXX translation of Num. 25:3: καὶ ἐτελέσθη Ἰσραὴλ τῷ βεελφεγώρ, i.e., they were consecrated or initiated into the mysteries of Baal Peor. Cf. Amos 7:9, LXX. See Y. Gutman, *The Beginnings of Jewish-Hellenistic Literature* (Jerusalem, 1958–1963) 1.144–45.

39. A Platonic theme; see *Phaedr.* 247A; *Symp.* 210A; cf. *Prob.* 13; *Spec.* 2.249; *Her.* 213; *Somn.* 2.282; Wisd. 7:13; Sir. 20:30–31; Ps-Aristotle *De Mundo* 391a17: πᾶσιν ἀφθόνως μεταδοῦναι βουληθεῖσα (the divine soul wished to impart to all unstintingly). There is a stele from about 200 B.C.E. recording the decree conferring citizenship of Samia on an otherwise unknown philosopher, Epicrates of Heraclea, because he "communicated without stint" (μεταδιδοὺς ἀφθόνως). See M. N. Tod, "Sidelights on Greek Philosophers," *JHS* 77 (1957): 135.

NOTES

40. Reading with Colson: δι' ἀνέμων τε καὶ αὐρῶν. Cf. *Spec.* 2.172; *Virt.* 93.

41. This principle reached its apogee in the hermeneutics of R. Akiba, which employed the rules of *ribbûy* and *mi^cut*. According to this method (which Akiba inherited from his teacher Nahum of Gimzo), the particles *'ap, gam, et,* indicate an inclusion or amplification; the particles *'ak, raq, min,* point to a limitation, exclusion or diminution (*Tosef. Shevuot* 1.7; *BT Shevuot* 26a; *Ḥagigah* 12a. Akiba was opposed by R. Ishmael, whose thirteen hermeneutical principles did not include this farfetched methodology.

42. Cf. *LA* 3.147.

43. Philo's preoccupation with arithmology (a term introduced by A. Delatte, *Études sur la littérature pythagoricienne* [Paris, 1915], p. 139, and referring to the study of the mathematical relationships between numbers and their cosmic significance) is clearly indicated by the fact that of the 172 sections of *Opificio Mundi,* 40 or about 23 percent are devoted to the number seven. Arithmology, as H. Moehring has correctly noted, allowed Philo to stress the universal character of the Jewish tradition, which is therefore the most "natural" of religions. See his article "Arithmology as an Exegetical Tool in the Writings of Philo of Alexandria," *SBL Seminar Papers* (1978) 1.191–227. One of Philo's sources concerning the number seven is the treatise Περὶ Ἑβδομάδων, completely extant only in two early medieval Latin translations. The Greek text has been lost except for a number of fragments. A Parisian manuscript goes as far as the middle of chapter five, and the remainder of the Greek text of this chapter has been preserved in Philo *Op.* 105 and other arithmological writings. J. Mansfeld assigns a first century B.C.E. date to the first part of the treatise *On the Sevens* (*The Pseudo-Hippocratic Tract* ΠΕΡΙ ἙΒΔΟΜΑΔΩΝ 1–11 *and Greek Philosophy* [Assen, 1971], p. 229, and 156–204).

44. John Lydus (*De Mensibus,* p. 33, 14–15) attributes this idea to Philolaus, a Pythagorean contemporary with Socrates. Cf. *LA* 1.15; *Mos.* 2.210; *QG* 2.12; 3.49; *QE* 2.46; *Spec.* 2.56; *Her.* 170, 216; *Cont.* 65; *Decal.* 102. The Pythagoreans had assimilated the number seven to Athena. See Lydus, p. 48, 2–5; Stobaeus *Ecl.* 1.1.10; Aristotle *On the Pythagoreans* Fr. 13, Ross: "Since the number seven neither generates nor is generated by any of the numbers in the decad, they identified it with Athena. For the number 2 generates 4, 3 generates 9 and 6, 4 generates 8, and 5 generates 10, and 4, 6, 8, 9, and 10 are also themselves generated, but 7 neither generates any number nor is generated from any; and so too Athena was motherless and ever-virgin."

45. For the identification of Athena and Nike, cf. Sophocles *Philoct.* 134; Euripides *Ion* 454ff.; 1528ff.

46. Cf. *Congr.* 89–94; *Decal.* 20–31; *Spec.* 4.105–106. For other arithmological passages, see *Op.* 47–52; *Plant.* 117–125; *Spec.* 2.176–78; *QG* 1.91; 2.5; 3.3, 38, 49. Further discussion on the decad may be found in M. Alexandre, Lyon 16.242–44.

NOTES

47. Sheshai would normally be associated with the Hebrew word *šēš*, six, and *šiší*, sixth. In his *Onomasticum Sacrum* (Tübingen, 1706), Hiller explains the name of this giant as meaning "6 cubits long." Philo must have consulted an ancient onomasticon written in Greek and read ἐκτός, outside, instead of ἕκτος, sixth (the breathings were no longer distinguished in his period, and accents were often omitted). The clear implication, as E. Stein long ago pointed out, is that Philo knew little Hebrew and having recourse only to the LXX probably did not recognize in Σεσείν the Hebrew word *šiší*, (*Die allegorische Exegese des Philo aus Alexandreia* [Giesen, 1929], p. 21).

There is now papyrological evidence that makes it evident that Philo did indeed make use of Greek onomastica. In three passages (*Gig.* 50; *Mut.* 103; *Agr.* 43) he explains the name Jethro, 'Ιοθόρ in Greek, by περισσός. "Amir pointed out," writes Rokeah, "that in all other cases Philo uses the Attic form περιττός. Moreover in the same sentences, after using the form περισσός he reverts to the Attic style and uses περιττός in his own syntactical construction. He does this also when he gives the meaning of the Hebrew without stating that it is a translation (*Sacr.* 50). Amir argued that this interchange of dialects in a writer who took pains to write in a pure style can only be explained on the assumption that there was in front of Philo, in writing, the form περισσός as a translation of 'Ιοθόρ, and that, as Philo wrote, he did not think himself privileged to change it. Amir added that he did not dare say whether this was a bare list of biblical names and their Greek equivalents, or a literary essay which contained etymological explanations. In any case, it is difficult to suppose that this document contained only the explanation of the name Jethro. Therefore, said Amir, whoever wishes to attribute to Philo a knowledge of the original language of the Bible will no longer be able to make use of Philo's explanations of Hebrew names as evidence. . . . Now three cases of περισσός as over against about seventy cases of περιττός is very telling, even if there were no strict distinction between the Attic and the *Koinē* as argued by H. D. Mantel. Indeed, I cannot see any other satisfactory explanation of this phenomenon than the above suggested. In fact we have at our disposal part of this compilation in the Greek onomastica, the Oxyrhyncus Papyrus, and Hieronymus' *Onomasticon.* (Ax. AB15 reads Ιεθερ περισσος.) With their help we can solve almost all the problems that the Philonian etymologies pose" (D. Rokeah, "A New Onomasticon Fragment from Oxyrhynchus and Philo's Etymologies," *JTS* N.S. 19 [1968]: 76–77; Y. Amir, "Explanation of Hebrew names in Philo," *Tarbiz* 31 [1962–1963]: 98–99 [Heb.]; Y. Kohen-Yashar, "Did Philo of Alexandria Know Hebrew?" *Tarbiz* 34 [1964–1965]: 337–45 [Heb.]).

48. The three terms Philo uses here as possible descriptions of the universal term "mankind" refer respectively to the views of Aristotle, Plato, and the Stoics with regard to universals. See Wolfson 1.412.

49. Cf. *Mut.* 80, 122, 146; *Cher.* 51; *QG* 4.155.

NOTES

50. This corresponds to most of the manuscript readings of Exod. 33:18; LXX: δεῖξόν μοι τὴν σεαυτοῦ δόξαν. Vat. B. reads: ἐμφάνισον μοι σαυτόν. Cf. *QE* 2.45.

51. Here and in 330 below, Philo explicitly identifies the δυνάμεις with the Platonic Forms, while *Cher.* 51 may imply it. For the relationship between the Forms or "ideas" and the powers, see Introduction, pp. 23–24.

52. There seems to be an allusion here to Aristotle's criticism of the Platonic Forms. At *Met.* 991a21, Aristotle asserts that "to say that the Forms are patterns, and that other things participate in them, is to use vacuous phrases (κενολογεῖν) and poetical metaphors." Cf. *Ethica Eudemia* 1.8.1217b22: "That if we are to speak about it concisely, we say that in the first place to assert the existence of a Form not only of good but of anything else is to speak abstractly and vacuously (λέγεται λογικῶς καὶ κενῶς)." Cf. Plato's own remark in *Tim.* 51C: "And it is merely an idle assertion of ours that there always exists an intelligible Form of every object, whereas it is really nothing more than a verbal phrase (πλὴν λόγος)." Aristotle simply added the adjective κενός. For the Epicurean caution against the use of κενοὶ φθόγγοι or words devoid of meaning, see *Epistula ad Herodotum* 1.38; *K.D.* 37; and for the Stoic rejection of the Platonic Forms, see *SVF* 1.65.

53. See Deut. 23:1, LXX: "He that is crushed (θλαδίας) or mutilated in his private parts shall not enter into the assembly of the Lord."

54. For the mind as hot and fiery, see *Fug.* 133; *Mut.* 180; cf. *Mig.* 165; *Her.* 309; *SVF* 3.305; 2.446; Diels, *Dox. Graec.* 303, 11.

55. Cf. *Fug.* 100; *Spec.* 1.307; *Sacr.* 59–60; *QG* 1.57; *Op.* 21; *Plant.* 50; *Mos.* 2.99. For a discussion of Philo's theory of Powers, see Introduction.

56. Cf. *QG* 2.16, 51, 75; 3.39; 4.2, 8, 30; *QE* 2.62, 68; *Conf.* 171–73; *Abr.* 121–130; *Legat.* 6; *Fug.* 94–105. See Dahl and Segal, "Philo and the Rabbis on the Names of God," *JSJ* 9:1 (1978): 1–28.

57. A Stoic conception. See D.L. 7.138–39; "Reason (νοῦς) pervades every part of the cosmos just as does the soul in us. Only there is a difference in degree; in some parts there is more of it, in others less."

58. There is a lacuna here. For the idea, cf. Plato *Tim.* 41A.

59. Another lacuna, which Wendland restores as follows: οὐκ ἐπινοεῖται περὶ τόπον, οὐ κατα < λαμβανόμενον, εἰ μὴ κατὰ > τὸ ε ἶναι μόνον. Colson suggests as an alternative: ἐπινοεῖται πέρα τοῦ εἶναι κατὰ τὸ εἶναι μόνον ("is conceived of as transcending the idea of being in any particular place and in terms of existence only"), for which he compares Aristotle *Phys.* 4.1.208b29.

60. Cf. *Conf.* 166; *Mos.* 2.132.

61. Scholars have found it difficult to fit in the two powers of this passage with Philo's theory of the Creative and Regent Powers (see E. Goodenough, *By Light Light* [rep. Amsterdam, 1969], p. 205, n. 44). I should like to suggest the following explanation. From the perspective of the Divine cre-

ativity, the Unlimited or Indefinite Dyad represents God's goodness or love, his infinite overflow or productivity, which the Logos equilibrates by means of Limit, which regulates the rampaging overflow through its precise delimitations (cf. *Plant.* 10). From the human perspective, however, the Unlimited represents the destructive ravages of uncontrolled desire (cf. Plato *Phileb.* 31A), which man's reason maintains in some measure of equilibrium by means of Limit, which reins in desire's insatiable riot with its saving, punishing sovereignty. Since the world is generated when beneficent Limit "brings the Unlimited to completion," the cosmos and the human race are a mixture of these two powers (cf. *Phileb.* 27BC: "The first then I call the Unlimited, the second the Limit, and the third the being that has come to be by the mixture of these two"). Sometimes, says Philo, the evil becomes greater in this mixture, and all creatures live in torment (cf. Proclus *Elements*, prop. 159: "But at some points Limit is dominant in the mixture, at others the Unlimited"). This mixture is also both in the wicked and in the wise, though not in the same degree of predominance. In the souls of the foolish, the Unlimited predominates, whereas in the souls of the noble it is beneficient Limit that is predominant. Cf. J. Daniélou, *Philon D'Alexandrie* (Paris, 1958), pp. 53–57, who concludes that this singular Philonic passage is under the influence of two different sources, an Essene exposition of the doctrine of the two spirits and an exposition of dualist philosophy bringing into relief Egyptian philosophical schools (Plutarch *Is. et Os.* 369Bff.).

62. The reverse appears to be the view of R. Schneur Zalman of Liadi, founder of Ḥabad Hasidism. The vitality of all the worlds, the supernal and the lower, and the transformation of the "nothing" into something, says Zalman, is constituted by the primordial thought of the divine will "I wish to be king," and there is no king without a people. See Y. Jacobson, "The Doctrine of Creation in Schneur Zalman," *Eshel Beer Sheva* (Jerusalem, 1976), pp. 340–41 (Heb.).

63. Cf. *QE* 2.66.

64. Cf. *Somn.* 2.254; *Conf.* 146. πολυώνυμος is also employed by the Stoic Cleanthes for Logos-Zeus in the opening line of his famous hymn (*SVF* 1.537). Cf. also Ps-Aristotle *De Mundo* 401a12: "Though he [Zeus] is one, he has many names (πολυώνυμος), according to the many effects he himself produces"; D.L. 7.135, 147; *CH* 5.10; Irenaeus *Adv. Haer.* 1.2.31; *Acta Petri et Pauli* 35. In the highly syncretistic Isis cult, we find this goddess bearing so many cult names that she is often called μυριώνυμος (Plutarch *Moral.* 372E). An Oxyrhynchus papyrus (no. 1380: early second century C.E.) gives us a long invocation of her. (See A. D. Nock, *Conversion* [Oxford, 1933], pp. 150–51; Apuleius *Metamorphoses* 11.5.) Comparable is the epithet πολυώνυμος used of Isis in the post-Augustan Anubis-hymn from Cius in Bithynia and *P. Oxy.* 11.1380, 97 and 101. This epithet is used also of Demeter, with whom Isis was

identified as early as the fifth century B.C.E. (Herodotus 2.59), and of Hades (*Homerici Hymni* 2.18). See J. W. Griffiths, *Plutarch De Iside et Osiride* (Cardiff, 1970), pp. 502–503; and Winston, pp. 179–80.

65. See Prov. 8:22, LXX, cited by Philo *Ebr.* 31.

66. Cf. *Conf.* 146; *Ebr.* 92; *Mut.* 125; *Somn.* 254; *QG* 1.4,57; 3.40; 4.23.

67. Cf. *LA* 3.175; *Det.* 115–18, 160; *Her.* 191; *Fug.* 138.

68. Cf. *LA* 1.45.

69. See note 26 above.

70. Cf. *Her.* 127, 130; *Abr.* 22–23, 87.

71. Reading with Colson μουσικῆς, as in a quotation of the passage by Eusebius, where the μούσης of the manuscripts is so reproduced.

72. Cf. *Apocalypse of Abraham* 10, where the angel Jaoel declares that he is the one who, according to God's commandment, restrains the threatening attack of the living creatures of the Cherubim (i.e., the "holy Ḥayyoth" of Ezekiel 1) against one another; and *Tanḥ. Bereshit*, Buber, commenting on Job 25:2, and indicating that God keeps peace among the angels; *Shir Hashirim R.* 8.11; *Pesikta Rabbati* 97b, Friedmann; *PRK* 5; *BT Sanhedrin* 99b; *Somn.* 2.114.

73. Reading with Wendland: πειθοῖ συναγωγῷ.

74. Cf. *LA* 1.37; *Her.* 188; *Det.* 90; *Gig.* 27 *QE* 2.68, 118.

75. Cf. *Somn.* 2.188.

76. Within the framework of the intercourse of God with the soul, God or Sophia or *aretē* takes the dominant, active, male role, sowing the seed and impregnating the soul. The double gender of Sophia finds a close analogy in the *Zohar*, where we read: "This king [the third *Sefirah*, Intelligence], although he is a supreme king, is female in relation to the supreme point [the second *Sefirah*, Wisdom], which is completely hidden. But though female, he is male in relation to the lower king [the sixth *Sefirah*, Beauty or Compassion] (2.3a). Cf. Plutarch *Moral.* 368C, where Selene is both male and female.

77. Cf. *Abr.* 101–102.

78. The words ἐκ προσώπου are equivalent to the Aramaic *min qodām*, used to avoid anthropomorphism. Cf., for example, *Targum Onkelos*, Gen. 20:3.

79. Cf. *Mut.* 259–260; *Congr.* 170–74; *Her.* 191; *Det.* 118; *LA* 2.86; 3.162–64, 169–76; *Somn.* 2.242–47. Cf. also Prov. 9:5. See P. Borgen, *Bread From Heaven* (Leiden, 1965), pp. 111–114. The identification of manna with wisdom is suggested in a late midrash (*ShR* 25.7, where Exod. 16:4 about the manna is combined with Prov. 9:5 about wisdom. See Borgen, p. 156).

80. Cf. *Ebr.* 152; *Somn.* 2.183; *Deus* 155–58.

81. Cf. *Prov.* 1.6; *Aet.* 83.

82. A Stoic formulation. See *SVF* 2.300, 312; cf. Aristotle *Phys.* 8.4.255a, 12–15; 254b. 27–33; *Gen. Corr.* 2.9.335b, 29–31. Cf. *Prov.* 1.22.

83. Plato *Tim.* 29E.

NOTES

84. οὐσία is here a Stoic term. Cf. *SVF* 1.85: τὸ μεὶν οὖν πάσχον εἶναι τὴν ἄποιον οὐσίαν τὴν ὕλην; 2.311: ἀκίνητος οὐσία ἐξ αὐτῆς καὶ ἀσχημάτιστος.

85. Cf. *Op.* 171; *LA* 3.78; *Cher.* 127; *Post.* 143–45; *Deus* 108; *Plant.* 2–7; *Her.* 160; *Somn.* 2.45; *Mos.* 2.266–67; *Spec.* 4.187; *QG* 1.55, 64; 4.160; *Abr.* 203.

86. The rabbis entertain a similar notion. See *BR* 10.10, Th-Alb: 85. Cf. *Her.* 156.

87. God does not praise the ὕλη or primordial matter but only the works of his own art, i.e., ὕλη itself is not a work of God's art. For a discussion of Philo's theory of creation, see Introduction.

88. This seems to be in direct contradiction to what Philo says in *Prov.* 1.6–9 (p. 109 of this book). For an attempt to resolve the contradiction see Introduction, p. 17.

89. Cf. *Somn.* 2.19; *Op.* 171; *Plant.* 6–7.

90. Cf. *BR* 1.1, where R. Hoshaya of Caesarea, a Palestinian Amora of the third century, states that the Torah served as God's paradigm in his creation of the world. It was long ago suggested by J. Freundenthal (*Hellenistische Studien* [Breslau, 1875] 1.73) that Philo was very likely the rabbi's source for this Platonic concept. (In 1881 Grätz [MGWJ] had suggested that Origen, who had settled in Caesarea in 231, may have been R. Hoshaya's intermediate source. See also Bacher, *JQR* 3 (1891): 357–60). Urbach, however, has correctly noted that Philo's emphasis on the location of the Intelligible World in the mind of God is missing in the midrash (pp. 175–76). Cf. also *M. Abot* 3.23: "R. Akiba said, Beloved are Israel to whom was given a precious instrument wherewith the world was created"; *Sifre Deut.* 48; *BT Nedarim* 62a.

91. Cf. *LA* 1.1, 21–24; *QG* 1.2, 19.

92. Cf. *BT Berakot* 55a: "At the time when the Holy One, blessed be He, said to Moses; Go and tell Bezalel to make me a tabernacle, an ark and vessels, Moses went and reversed the order, saying, Make an ark and vessels and a tabernacle. Bezalel said to him: Moses, our Teacher, as a rule a man first builds a house and then brings vessels into it; but you say, Make me an ark and vessels and a tabernacle. Where shall I put the vessels that I am to make? . . . Moses replied: Perhaps you were in the shadow of God *(beṣēl ēl)* and knew!"

93. Cf. *Mig.* 5–6.

94. Cf. Wisd. 8:3: "She [Wisdom] magnifies her noble birth by enjoying intimacy (συμβίωσιν) with God, and the Master of All loved her"; Plato *Rep.* 490B, where the lover of knowledge is said to have intercourse with reality, to bring forth intelligence and truth, and to find release from "travail"; *Symp.* 212A.

95. Cf. Plutarch *Moral.* 1001A: "Also in the case of a maker, such as a builder is or a weaver or one who produces a lyre or a statue, his work when done is separated from him, whereas the principle of force emanating from

the parent is blended in the progeny and cohibits its nature, which is a fragment or part of the procreator. Since, then, the universe is not like products that have been molded or fitted together but has in it a large portion of vitality and divinity, which God sowed from himself in the matter and mixed with it, it is reasonable that, since the universe has come into being a living thing, God be named at the same time father of it and maker."

96. The other son is the νοητὸς κόσμος or Intelligible World.

97. Cf. *Op.* 77, 84; *Spec.* 3.83; 4.14.

98. Cf. Plato *Tim.* 91E: "And the wild species of animal that goes on foot is derived from those men who have paid no attention at all to philosophy nor studied at all the nature of the heavens, because they ceased to make use of the revolutions within the head and followed the lead of those parts of the soul which are in the breast. Owing to these practices they have dragged their front limbs and their head down to the earth, and there planted them, because of their kinship therewith; and they have acquired elongated heads of every shape, according as their several revolutions have been distorted by disuse. On this account also their race was made four-footed and many-footed, so that they might be dragged down still more to the earth."; Xenophon *Mem.* 1.4.11.

99. Cf. Plato *Tim.* 90D: "The motions akin to the divine part in us are the thoughts and revolutions of the universe."

100. Our text of the LXX lacks the word λαβών. For the variant readings of the biblical text in Philo, see P. Katz, *Philo's Bible* (Cambridge, 1950); and the remarks of D. Gooding and V. Nikiprowetzky in the Introduction to *Philo's De Gigantibus and Quod Deus*, ed. with introduction and commentary by D. Winston, J. Dillon, and V. Nikiprowetzky (forthcoming).

101. For the heavenly and earthly man in Philo, see Baer (cited in *The Giants*, n. 5), pp. 21–35.

102. Cf. *LA* 1.32–42, 88–90; 92–95; 2.4; *QG* 1.8; 2.56.

103. Two opposed attitudes on the development of man range through Greek literature almost from the very beginning. One sees early man living in innocent bliss and carefree abundance, a state that is forfeited in the course of time. This view is sometimes designated as chronological primitivism. The antipodal view holds that man once lived like a wild beast, and only by a gradual ascent with the aid of the arts achieved a more humane and abundant life. For a collection of all the relevant texts, see A. O. Lovejoy and G. Boas, *Primitivism and Related Ideas in Antiquity* (Baltimore, 1935). See also Waldemar Graf Uxkull-Gyllenband, *Griechische Kultur Entstehungslehren* (Berlin, 1924); and T. Cole, *Democritus and the Sources of Greek Anthropology* (Ann Arbor, 1967). Adhering to the biblical text, Philo here follows the former view. The notion of gradual deterioration is also prominent in Jewish apocalyptic. Cf., for example, IV Ezra 14:16: "For the weaker the world grows through age, so much the more shall evils increase upon the dwellers on earth." Plato's po-

sition seems to be on the side of the anti-primitivists. He relegates the Golden Age to another cosmic era (in the myth of the *Politicus*); such a mode of life, he implies, might have been true in topsy-turvydom, where ἄμαξα τὸν βοῦν ἕλκει, or where you "meet a bark and it dogs at you" (see R. J. E. Tiddy, *The Mummers' Play* [Oxford, 1923], pp. 171–72). In *Laws* 678–80, Plato envisages the remnants of the cyclic floods as living in an ethical Golden Age. The simplicity of their economy in which there was neither poverty nor wealth, and their dull, unclever minds (what Preuss termed their *Urdummheit* or primal stupidity) eliminated injustice or war. This middle position is echoed in Seneca's *Ep.* 90.44: "But no matter how excellent and guileless was the life of the men of that age, they were not wise men. . . . Still, I would not deny that they were men of lofty spirit and—if I may use the phrase—fresh from the gods. For there is no doubt that the world produced a better progeny before it was yet worn out. . . . It was by reason of their ignorance of things that the men of those days were innocent; and it makes a great deal of difference whether one wills not to sin or has not the knowledge to sin." Cf. Sextus *Math.* 9.28: "And some of the later Stoics declare that the first men, the sons of Earth, greatly surpassed the men of today in intelligence (as one may learn from a comparison of ourselves with the men of the past), and that those ancient heroes possessed, as it were, in the keenness of their intellect, an extra organ of sense and apprehended the divine nature and discerned certain powers of the Gods"; Juvenal *Sat.* 15.69. Cf. also Lucretius 2.1144–74, although Philo would not accept the premise of the Epicurean argument concerning the growth and decay of worlds.

104. Cf. *Op.* 154; *Virt.* 203–205; *Plant.* 44–45; *Somn.* 2.70.

105. Cf. Plato *Tim.* 32C–33.

106. Untranslatable word-play, borrowed from Plato *Tim.* 55CD. ἄπειρος means both "infinite" and "inexperienced," "unskilled."

107. Cf. *Op.* 9–11.

108. Cf. Plato *Rep.* 546B; Augustine *CD* 11.30.

109. Cf. *Op.* 67; *LA* 1.3–4.

110. The Stoic definition (*SVF* 2.509ff.). Cf. *Aet.* 4.

111. This is Plato's teaching in the *Tim.* 38B.

112. This phrase is another example of Philo's profound assimilation to Greek philosophical modes.

113. Cf. *LA* 1.2, 19–20; *QG* 1.1, Gr. Fr.

114. Cf. Epictetus 2.8.20; "And the Athena of Pheidias, when once it had stretched out its hand and received the Nike upon it, stands in this attitude for all time to come, but the works of God are capable of movement, have the breath of life, can make use of external impressions and pass judgment upon them."

115. Euripides, *TrGF*, Fr. 839.

NOTES

116. Cf. *LA* 1.18; *Cher.* 87; *Gig.* 42.

117. Cf. *Mos.* 1.283; *Somn.* 1.182; *Decal.* 47.

118. For the cosmos as God's son, cf. *Ebr.* 30; *Mos.* 2.134; *Spec.* 1.96; Plutarch *Moral.* 1001B and 373A. The contrast between the elder son who stays at home with his father and the younger son who wanders abroad finds an interesting parallel in Plotinus 5.8.12–13 and 5.5.3 (originally parts of a single work). For Plotinus the sensible world is God's youngest son Zeus, who alone appears "without," whereas his elder brothers remain with their Father (Nous-Kronos), who "abides bound in identity," and gives the sense-world to his son (now apparently regarded as the World-Soul) to rule. Note also in 5.8.13 and 5.5.3 the genealogical language used of the three Plotinian hypostases, of which the highest (the One) is the grandfather of the World-Soul.

119. For Philo's concept of time, cf. *Fug.* 57; *Jos.* 146; *LA* 3.25; *Mut.* 11, 267; *Her.* 165; *Sacr.* 76; *Mig.* 139; *Ebr.* 48. See J. Whittaker, *God Time Being* (Oslo, 1971); S. Lauer, "Philo's Concept of Time," *JJS* 9 (1958): 39–46.

120. For the Stoic σπερματικοὶ λόγοι or seminal principles, see *SVF* 1.102, 98; 2.580, 1074, 1027, 780; 3.141. The seminal principles in the cosmos or any other living thing are the principles contained in the seed of any thing that determines what it shall be and how it shall behave during its life. See Hahm, pp. 75–76.

121. Aristotle (*Gen. Anim.* 741b 21) compares Nature to a runner covering a double course (διαυλοδρομούσης) and retracing her steps toward the starting point whence she set out. Cf. *Deus* 36; *Mut.* 117; *Spec.* 1.338; 2.246; *Plant.* 9, 76, 125; *Aet.* 58. Cf. Harris (cited in *The Contemplative Life*, n. 29), pp. 58ff.

122. Cf. Epictetus 1.12–16; Seneca *NQ* 7.27.4. Philo's cosmic principle of love is reminiscent of Eryximachus's conception of love in Plato's *Symposium* 186A, which is itself a reflection of Empedocles's cosmology. It may also be seen in Aristotle's famous line that describes the Unmoved Mover causing motion "as being an object of love" (κινεῖ δὲ ὡς ἐρώμενον: *Met.* 12.1072b 4). Jaeger has suggested that Aristotle's notion is identical with the third of Plato's hypotheses explaining heavenly motions (*Laws* 898E: "or the soul has no body at all, but guides the motion of the star by some extraordinary and wonderful power") (*Aristotle* [Oxford, 1948], p. 142. Cf., however, G.E.R. Lloyd *JHS* (1968): 165). In medieval Jewish thought, the idea of cosmic love as the origin and goal of the universe and the power permeating all things found exuberant expression in Judah Abravanels's famous *Dialoghi D'Amore*, first published in Rome in 1575, and one of the most influential philosophical works of the sixteenth century.

123. In order to explain man's exalted and unique position among earth creatures, Philo provides a detailed account of the scale of being, beginning with ἕξις or cohesion, which holds the cosmos together and prevents its dis-

integration into the void (*SVF* 2.540, 552–53). In describing the next level, that of φύσις (growth or nature), exemplified by the plant world, Philo characteristically employs a vivid imagery. He then continues with the level of ψυχή (life), which is characterized by sensation, impression (φαντασία), and impulse. Finally he turns to a description of man's unique superiority over the animals, and ends with a eulogistic account of the human intellect, which emphasizes its indestructibility and its freedom.

124. The cosmic pneuma, according to the Stoics, has a fourfold function. In the form of ἕξις it provides unity and quality; in the form of φύσις, nutrition and growth, in the form of ψυχή, sensation and movement; and in the form of νοῦς or λόγος, it provides rationality. Inanimate objects possess only ἕξις; plants possess in addition φύσις; irrational animals possess ψυχή; and man and the cosmos possess also ψυχὴ λογική or reason (*SVF* 2.473, 460, 634, 714–16, 804, 1013). See Hahm, pp. 136–74.

125. Pneumatic motion has two phases, a movement into itself and a movement out of itself, or movements back and forth, either from the center of the cosmos to its extreme boundaries or from the center of any given entity to its surface (*SVF* 2.442, 471, 551). S. Sambursky, *Physics of the Stoics* (London, 1959), pp. 21–48.

126. Philo is fond of this image. Cf. *Mut.* 117; *Spec.* 1.338, 2.246; *Plant.* 76, 125; *Aet.* 58; *Op.* 44, 47. See also n. 121 above. The main point of the comparison is simply to emphasize that the motion is one that returns on itself and need not indicate that it is necessarily sequential. As Sandbach puts it, Philo "must intend a continuous stream of which at any moment part is moving outward, part turning, part coming back" (*The Stoics* [London, 1975], pp. 77–78).

127. αἴσθησις/εἴσθεσις is apparently an attempt to understand Plato's etymologizing at *Tim.* 43A 5–6.

128. Cf. *SVF* 2.56; *LA* 3.36; *Post.* 57; Plato *Phaedr.* 276D.

129. Cf. *LA* 2.22–23; *Her.* 137; *Somn.* 1.136; *Aet.* 75.

130. According to Plutarch *Sollert. Anim.* 974A (= DK B.154), "Democritus declares that we have been their [the animals'] pupils in matters of fundamental importance: of the spider in weaving and mending, of the swallow in homebuilding, of the sweet-voiced swan and nightingale in our imitation of their song."

131. Cf. Philo's spirited descriptions of the vine in *Deus* 38 and *Mut.* 162. He undoubtedly had personal acquaintance with them. One of the earliest steps taken by the Ptolemies to satisfy the ever-growing demand of the Greek inhabitants of Egypt for wine was an extensive planting of vines of various kinds. See M. Rostovtzeff, *Social and Economic History of the Hellenistic World* (Oxford, 1941), 1.353–54.

132. Cf. *Anim.* 40: "It is said that Aristogiton, one of those valiantly in-

volved in making Athens a prominent city, had a stubborn horse which, upon appearance in the hippodrome, pretended to be lame. But it gave up cheating when it was eventually detected by the breeders."

133. Cf. *Anim.* 45: "A hound was after a beast. When it came to a deep shaft which had two trails beside it—one to the right and the other to the left, and having but a short distance yet to go, it deliberated which way would be worth taking. Going to the right and finding no trace, it returned and took the other. Since there was no clearly perceptible mark there either, with no further scenting it jumped into the shaft to track down hastily. . . . The logicians call this thoughtful reckoning 'the fifth complex indemonstrable syllogism': for the beast might have escaped either to the right or to the left or else may have leaped." The same example is found in Plutarch *Sollert. Anim.* 969 B.

134. The Stoics, Epicureans, and Peripatetics held that animals lacked reason. (They had ψυχή, φαντασία, and ὄρεξις, but not λόγος, ἐπιθυμία, or θυμός.) Nor do they have affections, since the latter are defined as contrary to reason, though Seneca grants that they have what may be called quasi-emotions. Animal art is born, not taught (*nascitur . . . non discitur: Ep.* 121.23). Pythagoras (D.L. 8.30), on the other hand, was apparently the first to have asserted that animals have νοῦς and θυμός, and Empedocles endowed both animals and plants with reason (Sextus *Math.* 8.286; DK B.110; cf. Sextus *Math.* 9.127). The Skeptic Carneades led the attack against the Stoic view, and Alexander's disquisition in the first half of Philo's *De Animalibus* undoubtedly follows the line of his argumentation. (For the Skeptic Arguments, see Sextus *Hypotyp.* 1.62–77; Porphyry *De Abstin.* 3; Plutarch *Sollert. Anim.*). Philo's refutation of Alexander probably depends on some Stoic treatise. See G. Tappe, *De Philonis libro qui inscribitur* Ἀλέξανδρος ἢ περὶ τοῦ λόγου ἔχειν τὰ ἄλογα ζῶα (Göttingen, 1912).

135. Cf. *Mut.* 184.

136. Cf. *LA* 1.91. The description of God as the soul of the universe is Stoic (*SVF* 1.532). Cf. also Deut. 4:19; Wisd. 13:1–9; *Decal.* 52–53; *Cont.* 3; *Conf.* 173; Plato *Cratylus* 397D.

137. The Stoics divided entities into discrete (διεστῶτα), contiguous (συναπτόμενα), and unified (ἡνωμένα). See *SVF* 2.366 ("some bodies are composed of separate elements, such as a fleet or an army, others of elements joined together, as a house or a ship, and still others form together an intimate union, as in the case with every living creature"); 367–68 ("unified bodies are those ruled by one ἕξις, as a stone or a log, ἕξις being the binding *pneuma* of a body"). In unified structures each of the elements subsists only in coexistence with the rest, and is not able to exist if the organization as a whole disintegrates. The Stoic term for this form of coexistence was "sympathy" (συμπάθεια), and analogies from the living organism were given to

exemplify this condition: when a finger is cut, the whole body shares in its condition (Sextus *Math.* 9.80). "Philo takes ἕν in the full sense of the Stoic ἡνωμένον and argues that if the world is ἡνωμένον it must be composed of the same elements throughout and this will effect συμπάθεια. Sextus (*Math.* 9.78) puts the Stoic argument in much the same way but in reverse order. Only ἡνωμένα exhibit συμπάθεια and since there is συμπάθεια between the parts of the Cosmos, the Cosmos must be an ἡνωμένον σῶμα" (Colson, LCL 4.565).

138. A reminiscence of Plato *Tim.* 41A: "For though all that is bound may be dissolved, yet to will to dissolve that which is fairly joined together (καλῶς ἁρμοσθέν) and in good case were the deed of a wicked one."

139. Cf. *Her.* 97–99; *Abr.* 70; *Somn.* 1.161.

140. Cf. Plato *Tim.* 32C: "For these reasons and out of these materials, such in kind and four in number, the body of the Cosmos was harmonized by proportion (δι᾽ ἀναλογίας) and brought into existence."

141. Cf. Plato *Phaedo* 86b.

142. Cf. *Post.* 58; *Plant.* 28; *Mig.* 220; *Mos.* 2.135; *Prov.* 140; D.L. 142–43; Plato *Tim.* 30B–31B; *QG* 4.188; *Op.* 82; *Spec.* 1.210.

143. This title assimilates the nature of Moses to that of a philosopher. Cf. *Her.* 30; *Ebr.* 98; *Op.* 8; *Her.* 279 (where Israel is similarly so assimilated); *Mos.* 2.216.

144. Cf. *QG* 3.5.

145. See Exod. 34:28; Deut. 9:9; cf. *QG* 3.3.

146. Cf. *Plant.* 122; *Her.* 163; *Legat.* 85; *QE* 1.6. The inquirers into natural philosophy are undoubtedly the Pythagoreans (cf. *Her.* 152).

147. Cf. *QG* 2.14: "Now the square numbers are splendor and light, consisting of an equality of sides. But the oblong numbers have night and darkness because of their inequality, for that which is excessive casts a shadow on that which falls under the excess."

148. For the etymology of ἐνιαυτός, cf. Plato *Cratylus* 410D.

149. ἐπέχρησεν, literally "lent itself," "put itself at the service of" (Colson, LCL 8.153, note b).

150. Democracy is equated here with ἰσότης. What Philo thought of what would be vulgarly termed "democracy" he makes plain in *Agr.* 45–46, where he terms it ὀχλοκρατία or mob rule, "the very worst of bad constitutions, the counterfeit of democracy, which is the best of them." He contrasts democracy and ochlochracy again at *Conf.* 108, where he identifies the distinctive mark of democracy as being that it honors ἰσότης, which must be taken as denoting "geometrical equality," giving to each his due. At *Deus* 176, we are told that the world is a democracy because the Logos apportions to each race and nation its due. Cf. Aelius Aristides, *To Rome* 60: "But a common democracy of the earth has been set up under one man, the best, as ruler and orderer; and all come together as in a common marketplace, each to re-

ceive what is worthy of him." C. G. Starr points out that hints of the concept that the Roman Empire is the perfect democracy may be found in the first century in such phrases as Philo's remark that Augustus was "the distributor to every man of what was suited to him" (*Legat.* 147), and its roots may well go back into the Hellenistic period, even though we cannot detect them. ("The Perfect Democracy of the Roman Empire," *American Historical Review* 58:1 [1952]: 1–16. See also E. Langstadt, "Zu Philos Begriff der Demokratie," *Gaster Anniversary Volume* [London, 1936], pp. 349–64; Colson, LCL 8.437–39). Cf. also *Abr.* 242; *Virt.* 180.

151. "The portrayal of the universe as divided into three parts can be taken as Pythagorean in general inspiration, but also as deriving, perhaps, ultimately from Xenocrates (Fr. 5 Heinze). It is he who is responsible for the triadic scheme appearing, later, in the myth of Plutarch's essay *On the Face in the Moon.* . . . Philo's assigning of the two chief powers each to a division of the cosmos is a remarkable development, and this passage stands alone in Philo's work. There are, certainly, suggestions elsewhere that the Regal Power is somewhat lower on the scale of perfection than the Creative Power (*Fug.* 97ff.). What we have here, however, is the projection of this hierarchy onto the cosmic plane, with the Regal Power presiding over the lowest level, the sublunary realm." (Cf. Plutarch *Moral.* 393A ff.). (Dillon, pp. 168–70).

152. The Presocratics had already taught the mutual interchange of the elements. Pythagoras, for example, taught that "the elements interchange and turn into one another completely" (D.L. 8.25). The principle behind this doctrine was clearly stated by Diogenes of Apollonia (DK B.2., cf. Plato *Tim.* 49 BC; *Phaedo* 72B; Arist. *Gen Corr.* 337, 1–7). By the Hellenistic age it was a commonplace of Greek philosophy that the stuff out of which the world is made is ἄποιος ὕλη, and that therefore the elements were mutually interchangeable (Sextus *Phys.* 2.312; D.L. 7.150, 8:25; Epictetus 3.24; *SVF* 2.405–11).

153. Contrast *Her.* 228, where Philo denies the existence of a cosmic void, "the existence of which is implied in the marvelmongers' fable of the general conflagration." The connection of the Stoic theory of the general conflagration with that of the void is explained in *Aet.* 102.

154. The Stoics repeated the Platonic eulogy of the sphere (D.L. 7.140).

155. For βαρυδαιμονίας, cf. Plato *Phaedr.* 248C: καί τινι συντυχίᾳ χρησαμένη λήθης τε καὶ κακίας πλησθεῖσα βαρυνθῇ.

156. For a discussion of Philo's doctrine of incarnation, see Winston pp. 27–28.

157. Cf. *Gig.* 6–18 (pp. 62–64 in this volume); *Plant.* 14; *Conf.* 77–78, 174, 176–77; *Somn.* 1. 135–43; *Spec.* 1.66; *QG* 1.42, 4.157; *QE* 2.13.

158. Cf. *Cher.* 120–21.

159. This classification is Stoic. It is more usually stated in the form that the soul has eight parts, the ἡγεμονικόν being reckoned as one. See *SVF* 2.827ff.

NOTES

160. See Plato *Tim.* 69E, 90 A.

161. A frequent comparison in Philo; cf. *Spec.* 4.123, 3.111; *Conf.* 17–21; *Somn.* 1.32; Cicero *Leg.* 1.26.

162. Reading with Colson: μετὰ ἀσωμάτων ἀσύγκριτοι ἄποιοι, *QE* 2.46.

163. Philo adapts from the Attic orators the technical language used of a wife who formally claimed divorce from her husband. If the husband did not agree, an ἀπολείψεως δίκη had to be brought before the Archon. Cf. *Det.* 143.

164. For the notion of the illusory self, cf. Plato *Symp.* 207 DE: "It is only for a while that each live thing can be described as alive and the same, as a man is said to be the same person from childhood until he is advanced in years: yet though he is called the same he does not at any time possess the same properties; he is continually becoming a new person"; *Theaet.* 154A, 166B.

165. According to Sextus Empiricus (*Math.* 7.234), some Stoics distinguished two usages of the term ψυχή: they applied it quite generally to "that which holds together the whole compound," and specifically they used it to refer to the ἡγεμονικόν or ruling part. Cf. *Mig.* 5; *Det.* 9; *Op.* 66 (the "soul as soul" or "the soul's soul" refers to the ἡγεμονικόν). Cf. also Plato *Tim.* 30B; Lucr. 3.275 (*anima animae*).

166. Cf. *Det.* 92; *Spec.* 4.123; *QG* 2.59.

167. Cf. Plato *Phaedo* 64C.

168. Cf. *Det.* 48.

169. Cf. Plato *Gorg.* 493A; *Cratylus* 400 B.

170. In fashioning the mortal parts of man, the young gods, according to Plato, "imitating their own Maker, borrowed (δανειζόμενοι) from the Cosmos portions of fire and earth and water and air, as if meaning to pay them back" (*Tim.* 42E). Cf. Ps-Plato *Axiochus* 367b2: "Nature is like a small money-lender; if we do not repay the debt of life promptly, she comes down on us and takes sight or hearing, or often both, as pledges for a settlement." For further references, see Winston, pp. 286–87.

171. Cf. Aristotle *De Caelo* 1.2–3, where it is said that while the four elements have a rectilinear, the ether or fifth element has a circular movement. Cf. also *Somn.* 1.21; *QE* 2.14.

172. Cf. *Somn.* 2.133; *Cher.* 2.

173. For the teleological argument, see Diogenes of Apollonia, DK B.3; Plato *Laws* 886A; *Phileb.* 28E; Aristotle Fr. 12a, Ross; Cicero *ND* 2.37–39, 15–19; Epictetus 1.6; Ps-Aristotle *De Mundo* 399b–400a; Xenophon *Mem.* 1.4.2–19; Seneca *Benefic.* 4.6; Albinus *Did.* chap. 10; Apuleius *De Mundo* 22, 24, 35; *SVF* 2.1009; Galen *De Usu Partium* 17.1, 1.8; *CH* 5.5–8, 11.6–14; Sextus *Math.* 9.22–27; Wisd. 13:3–5. See A. S. Pease, "Caeli Enarrant," *HTR* 34:3 (1941): 163–200.

NOTES

Jubilees 12:17 implies that Abraham arrived at the knowledge of the existence of God through celestial observations (cf. Josephus *Ant.* 1.7.1).

174. Cf. *Somn.* 1.203–204; *Spec.* 1.32–35, 3.187–89; *QG* 2.34.

175. Philo often refers to Deut. 32 as "the greater Song" in distinction from that in Exod. 15; cf. *LA* 3.105.

176. For ἐκ προσώπου τοῦ θεοῦ, see note 78.

177. The context, in my opinion, makes it virtually certain that we ought to read not ἐναργεία but ἐνεργεία. Philo is arguing that knowledge of the true Creator of the universe, unlike that of the false idols, does not depend on hearsay evidence, since his existence is clearly revealed by his dynamic cosmic activity, which may be observed with the eye. We have here, then, the cosmological argument, not the incipient or proto-ontological argument, which depends on ἐνάργεια, or the self-evidence, of certain propositions implied by our definitions and constituting analytical truths. ἀπόδειξις should therefore be taken here not in its technical meaning of "demonstration," but in the general sense of "exposition." See Introduction, pp. 26–30.

178. Cf. *Post.* 19, 28; *Conf.* 98; *Fug.* 12; *Mut.* 54.

179. Cf. *Somn.* 1.53; Anaximenes DK B.2; Xenophon *Mem.* 1.1.11; Plato *Phaedr.* 229E.

180. Cf. *Her.* 301; *QG* 3.3, 4.51.

181. Cf. *Abr.* 74; *Fug.* 213; *Somn.* 1.53–58; *Spec.* 1.18.

182. Cf. Plato *Tim.* 92C, where the Cosmos is called "a perceptible God made in the image of the Intelligible" (εἰκὼν τοῦ νοητοῦ θεὸς αἰσθητός). Philo adds the qualification "seeming."

183. Cf. *QG* 4.110.

184. See Note 37.

185. Cf. *Plant.* 27; *Somn.* 1.206.

186. Cf. *Det.* 86–87; *Abr.* 79–80.

187. The meaning is that sensible reality has only a semblance of form, since in its essence it is indeterminate. In Platonism and Neopythagoreanism, the dyad, or principle of matter, is designated ἀόριστος, undefined, indeterminate. See note 189 below.

188. Cf. *Spec.* 3.187.

189. Cf. *Somn.* 2.70. There appears to be a reference here to the Pythagorean doctrine. See D.L. 8.25: "The principle of all things is the monad or unit; arising from this monad the undefined dyad or two serves as material substratum to the monad, which is cause." Cf. *LA* 1.3 (two is an image of matter).

190. For Philo's notion of the direct apprehension of God, see Introduction, pp. 26–30.

191. See *The Giants* 20, note 17.

191a. Cf. Xenophon *Mem.* 1.4.9; Cicero *Tusc.* 1.50–51.

192. The implication is that this is not an accurate expression. Cf. *Mig.* 179 and 181 where the possible danger of this expression, as tending to suggest that God is contained in the universe, is pointed out. The expression is Stoic. (*SVF* 2.774; 1.532).

193. Cf. *Post.* 15, 20; *Mut.* 10; *Op.* 69.

194. A similar notion is found in Greek religious thought. The statue of the Delian Apollo held the graces in his right hand and bow and arrow in his left. This gave rise to an allegorical interpretation, namely, that the god holds the bow in his left hand "because he is slower to chastise if man repents" (Callimachus Fr. 114.8–11, Pfeiffer; cf. Apollodorus's *Peri Theōn, FHG* 244 F15; Philo *Legat.* 95). See R. Pfeiffer, *Ausgewählte Schriften* (München, 1960), pp. 55ff.

195. Although the image is biblical, there may also be a reminiscence of Iliad 24.527: "For two urns are set upon the floor of Zeus of gifts that he giveth, the one of ills, the other of blessings."

196. Cf. Wisd. 12:10; *Spec.* 1.58.

197. Cf. Wisd. 13:3; Plotinus 1.6.9.42; 5.1.4.1ff.

198. Cf. *Spec.* 2.53, 55; *Abr.* 202; *QG* 4.188. For a good discussion, see P. Boyancé, *Le Culte des Muses chez les Philosophes grecs* (Paris, 1937), pp. 219–27.

199. Cf. Aristobulus, *FPG*:224, 24: "The clear statement in our Law that God rested on it [the Sabbath], was not set down as meaning, as some assume, that God is no longer active, but in the sense that their order (i.e. of heaven and earth) reached its completion thus to be arranged for all time."

200. Cf. Ps-Aristotle *De Mundo* 398b 23: "God does not take upon himself the toil of a creature that works and labors for itself, but uses an indefatigable power, by means of which he controls even things that seem a great way off"; 398b 14: "The most divine thing of all is to produce all kinds of result easily by means of a single motion."

201. Cf. the similar rabbinic interpretation in *Mek.* to Exod. 17:6, Lauterbach 2.133: "I will be standing there before you, etc. God said to him: Wherever you find the mark of man's feet, there I am before thee." The Hebrew *lepānêkā* is local in meaning, but the LXX takes it temporally, as does the *Mekilta.*

202. For tensional motion, see Selections from Philo, note 125.

203. Cf. *Mut.* 15; *Abr.* 119–122.

204. As Colson points out, "in *Timaeus* 69D ἀναγκαίως is used of the way in which the inferior agents in the Creation performed their somewhat baffling tasks. It has been rendered there 'as best they might' (LSJ). Moses is faced with a task more baffling even than theirs. It is to express in human speech the Name of God. He does it 'as best he may.' " (LCL 2.497).

205. We find precisely the same notion in the anonymous commentator (Porphyry?) on Plato's *Parmenides,* Fr. 2 (fol. 4, lines 19–28): "For it is not He

NOTES

who is non-existent and incomprehensible for those wishing to know Him, but it is we and all existing things who are nothing in relation to Him. And this is the reason it has been impossible to know Him, because all other things are nothing in relationship to Him, whereas acts of knowing perceive the similar through the similar. It is therefore we who are the nothing in relationship to Him, whereas He alone is the only true Existent (if you understand it in the sense indicated) in relationship to all things that are posterior to Him (τὰ μετ' αὐτοῦ)." See P. Hadot, *Porphyre et Victorinus* (Paris, 1968), 1.119; 2.76.

206. See *The Giants,* note 42.

207. Cf. *Somn.* 2.219, 237.

208. Cf. *Op.* 23; *Abr.* 203.

209. Cf. Plato *Phaedo* 83A.

210. Cf. Plato *Tim.* 71B, where the liver acts as a mirror.

211. For the use and meaning of the appellation *makôm* in rabbinic literature, see Urbach, pp. 58–63. According to Urbach, the term *makôm* represents an indigenous Jewish development and was used metonymously for the God who reveals himself in the place he has chosen. It is thus an appellation indicating the closeness of God.

212. The very similar statement of R. Jose b. Ḥalafta (second century) is probably derived from the Philonic formulation: "R. Jose b. Ḥalafta said: "We should not know if God were an appendage to the world, or if the world were his appendage, had not he himself said, 'Behold, there is a place by me' (Exod. 33:21). He is the place of the world; the world is not his place. So the world is an appendage to him; he is not an appendage to the world" (*Mid. Teh.* on Ps. 90:1, 195b, Buber). Cf. Sallustius 2; Porphyry *Lettera ad Anebo,* ed. Sodano, p. 4, 3–8; Origen *C. Cels.* 6.71. For Gnostic and Patristic parallels to the Philonic formula "containing, not contained," see W. R. Schoedel, "Topological Theology and Some Monistic Tendencies in Gnosticism," *Essays on the Nag Hammadi Texts in Honour of Alexander Böhlig,* ed. M. Krause (Leiden, 1972), pp. 88–108. Cf., for example, *The Teaching of Silvanus,* pp. 100–101: "Consider these things about God: he is in every place; on the other hand, he is in no place. With respect to power, to be sure, he is in every place, but in the exaltation of his divinity nothing contains him. Everything is in God, but God is not in anything" (Robinson, pp. 353–54); Hermas *Man.* 1.1; Clem. Alex. *Strom.* 6.39; Justin *Dial.* 127.2; Theophilus *Ad. Aut.* 2.3; Irenaeus *Haer.* 1.15.5. *C.H.* 5.10; 12.23; 2.12–17 Hippolytus *Haer.* 6.32; Eudemus, ap. Damascius *De Principiis* 125 bis. See also Wolfson 1.247–51, 317–22; Festugière 2.545–47.

213. *LA* 1.44, 3.6–7, 51; *Post.* 7; *Sobr.* 63; *Conf.* 136; *Mig.* 182–83, 192; *Fug.* 75; *Somn.* 1.185.

214. Cf. *Decal.* 178; *Conf.* 98.

215. ἴσως ἄν τις ἐπιζητήσειε, διὰ τί. . . . Didymus the grammarian

NOTES

(second half of the first century B.C.E. and beginning of the first century C.E.) likes to introduce his disquisitions with ζητεῖται, διὰ τί, etc., and the ζητή-ματα constituted a notable part of the philologic, the philosophic, and the juridic literature. The Hebrew *lidrôš* in Ezra 7:10 is correctly translated by LXX: ζητῆσαι to inquire (see S. Lieberman, *Hellenism in Jewish Palestine* (New York, 1950, pp. 47–48). Cf. Demetrius (earliest known Greco-Jewish writer; lived during the reign of Ptolemy IV: 221–204 B.C.E.): ἐπιζητεῖν δέ τινα πῶς οἱ Ἰσραηλῖται ὅπλα ἔσχον ἄνοπλοι ἐξελθόντες (*FPG*: 179). R. Pfeiffer writes: "Aristotle had apparently drawn up a list of 'difficulties' of interpretation in Homer with their respective 'solutions'; this custom of ζητήματα προβάλλειν may have prospered at the symposia of intellectual circles. . . . Although certain circles of the Alexandrian Museum seem to have adopted this 'method' of ζητήματα, which amused Ptolemaic kings and Roman emperors, as it had amused Athenian symposiasts, the great and serious grammarians disliked it as a more or less frivolous game. It was mainly continued by the philosophic schools, Peripatetics, Stoics, Neoplatonists, and by amateurs, until Porphyry arranged his final collection of Ὁμηρικὰ ζητή-ματα in the grand style, in which he very probably still used Aristotle's original work" (*History of Classical Scholarship* [Oxford, 1968], pp. 69–70, 263). (Cf. also *Deus* 86: οἱ ζητητικοὶ τῶν κυρίων ὀνομάτων; *Det.* 76; *Conf.* 5).

216. Philo raises exactly the same question as the author of the *Wisdom of Solomon* (11:17–23) and his first answer is similar to that given in Wisd. 11:23. Cf. also *Koheleth R.* 5.8.4, where God is said to have punished Titus with the most insignificant creature, the mosquito.

217. παῖς, as if from παίζων, playing.

218. "The essence of will," writes H. H. Brinton, "is purposeful activity yet such activity is generated by want. How then can we have activity as a final goal? Boehme answers by calling the perfect state 'play.' In 'play' life expresses itself in its fullness; therefore play as an end means that life itself has intrinsic value. . . . When Boehme is speaking of God's life as it is in itself he refers to it as 'play' " (*The Mystic Will* [New York, 1930], pp. 217–18; cited by N. O. Brown, *Life against Death* [Middletown, 1959], p. 33). Cf. *BT A.Z.* 3b, where it is said by R. Judah in the name of Rav that God spends the last quarter of every day playing with Leviathan.

219. Cf. *Cher.* 85–86; *Spec.* 2.53, 55; *Abr.* 202; *Plant.* 167–70.

220. The expression νοῦς ἡγεμών, popularized by the Stoa, is already found in Plato *Laws* 963A.

221. Cf. *Congr.* 115; *Post.* 1.4.

222. Cf. *Conf.* 98; *Plant.* 35.

223. Criticism of literal interpreters. Cf. *Deus* 21; *Somn.* 1.102; *Conf.* 14; *Mig.* 45. See M. J. Shroyer, "Alexandrian Jewish Literalists," *JBL* 55 (1936): 261–84.

NOTES

224. For the rabbinic attitude to anthropomorphism, see Wolfson, 1.135ff; M. Kadushin, *The Rabbinic Mind* (New York, 1965), pp. 273–87; A. Marmorstein, *The Old Rabbinic Doctrine of God* II. *Essays in Anthropomorphism* (New York, 1937) (rep. 1968 Ktav).

225. Cf. Aristotle *Phys.* 2.3, 194b 32.

226. Elsewhere we are told that God gives the principal boons in his own person, whereas the secondary ones, i.e., those involving riddance from ills, are bestowed by his Angels and λόγοι (*LA* 3.177–78; *Fug.* 67; *Conf.* 181). For the Logos as God's ὄργανον in creating the world, cf. *LA* 3.96; *Mig.* 6.

227. No doubt, as Colson suggests, partly aimed at the Stoics, who held the cosmos and/or the heavens to be the οὐσία θεοῦ (*SVF* 1.164; Colson, LCL 3.485).

228. Perhaps a reference to the Stoic concept of διαστροφή or κατ-ήχησις, wrong instruction acquired in childhood that stands in the way of the attainment of wisdom (*SVF* 3.228–236; cf. Plato *Tim.* 87B).

229. Cf. *Cher.* 15. The same notion is expressed by Plato in *Rep.* 389B. Cf. *SVF* 3.554–55, 2.132.

230. Cf. *Mos.* 1.42; *Decal.* 12; *LA* 3.129–31.

231. Note the use of the masculine here (τὸν ὄντα), as opposed to neuter elsewhere in the passage.

232. Cf. *Deus* 72; *Conf.* 134; *Congr.* 115; *Somn.* 1.234–37.

233. Heinemann correctly points out that Philo is here echoing the Skeptical school rather than expressing his usual views. Elsewhere he passionately affirms that God is ἀσώματος and ἄποιος. On the *via negativa* and *via eminentiae*, see Introduction, pp. 22–24.

234. Cf. *LA* 1.36, 51; *Somn.* 1.66–67.

235. Cf. *Ebr.* 198; *Her.* 248.

236. Hyperbaton is defined as an "arrangement of words or thoughts changed from the consecutive order."

237. "Wendland suspected ἐπιστάτῃ and proposed παλαιστῇ, but Philo conceives of the angel rather as a master of the contest (ἀγωνοθέτης) training his pupil by wrestling with him" (Colson, LCL 5.151).

238. Cf. *Abr.* 51.

239. Χαλδαϊστί. Philo frequently uses "Chaldean" in the sense of Hebrew, especially with reference to language: *Abr.* 8, 12, 99, 201; *Mos.* 1.5; 2.224; *Praem.* 14, 31, 44.

240. This title has its biblical origin in Gen. 32:31, where Jacob after wrestling with the angel and receiving the name Israel, exclaims "I have seen God." The phrase "a man seeing God" as the interpretation of Israel occurs twenty-three times in Philo, who seems to be drawing on an earlier tradition. It is found in the lost Jewish apocryphon *The Prayer of Joseph* (Origen *In Joh.* 2.25 = *PG* 14.168–69); in Christian sources presumably dependent on Philo

351

(Clem. Alex. *Paed.* 1.9; [*PG* 8.341]; Origen *Princ.* 4.3; (*PG* 11.395); *PE* 11.6; Jerome *Lib. de Nomin. Hebr.*, Exod. (*PL* 23.1039); Hippolytus *Contra Noetum* 5 (*PG* 10.809); in two Jewish (?) prayers: *Constitutiones Apostolorum* 7.36.2, 8.15.7; and in *Seder Eliyyahu Rabbah* 27. Cf. also the Coptic Gnostic treatise *On the Origin of the World* (2.5) 105 (Robinson, p. 166), where, amidst Cherubim and Seraphim, there stands near to Sabaoth "a first-born called Israel," i.e., "the man who sees God." The etymology may derive either from reading Yisrael as a contraction of 'iš rāāh 'ēl, "a man who saw God," or the equivalent of yašur 'ēl, "he sees God." See E. Stein, *Die allegorische Exegese des Philo aus Alexandria* (Giessen, 1929), pp. 20ff.; E. Sachsse, "Die Etymologie und älteste Aussprache des Names Israel," *ZAW* 32 (1914): 3 (derives Israel from šur); P. Borgen (cited n. 79), pp. 115–18, 175–79; J. Z. Smith, "The Prayer of Joseph," *Religions in Antiquity,* ed. J. Neusner (Leiden, 1968), pp. 253–94.

241. Philo defines God in Platonic terms. Cf. *Gig.* 45; *Decal.* 81; *Spec.* 1.277, 2.53.

242. Inferring the existence of God from his created works is inferior to the higher intuition of the Israel-soul, which conceives it as an analytical truth. See Introduction, pp. 26–30.

243. δορυφόρος is a favorite word of Philo to describe the relationship of God to his powers, viewed as the bodyguard of an oriental king. Cf. *Deus* 109; *Sac.* 59; *Abr.* 122; *Spec.* 1.45; *QE* 2.67.

244. Cf. *Praem.* 40; *Her.* 187; *Abr.* 123; *Cont.* 2; *QG* 2.54, 4.140; *QE* 2.68; *Mig.* 40–41.

245. Cf. *LA* 3.161; *Det.* 90; *Plant.* 18; *Somn.* 1.34; *Mut.* 223: "Reasoning is a short word, but a most perfect and most divine activity, a fragment of the soul of the universe, or, a more devout way of putting it for those following the philosophy of Moses, a close imprint of the divine image." For the Greek sources, see n. 537 below.

246. Cf. *Det.* 161–62.

247. ὑπὸ θεοῦ γίνεται καὶ δι' αὐτοῦ.

248. For the notion of a spiritual libation, cf. *LA* 2.56; *Ebr.* 152.

249. The image of mixing-bowls is Platonic (*Tim.* 41 DE).

250. Cf. *LA* 2.51; *Agr.* 80.

251. Philo is here following Stoic doctrine. The seven parts of the soul growing out of the *hegemonikon* and extending through the body are compared to the tentacles of an octopus (*SVF* 2.836). Chrysippus uses another analogy: "In the same way as a spider in the center of the web holds in its feet all the beginnings of the threads, in order to feel by close contact if an insect strikes the web, and where, so does the ruling part of the soul, situated in the middle of the heart, check on the beginnings of the senses, in order to perceive their messages from close proximity" (*SVF* 2.879). (This analogy probably goes back to Heraclitus: DK B.67a.) Cf. *LA* 3.57; *Fug.* 182 (where the

hegemonikon's power is described as pneumatic, and as extending to the eyes a visual pneuma [ὁρατικὸν πνεῦμα τείνοντος], an accoustical one to the ears, a smelling one to the nostrils, etc.).

252. φαντασία δέ ἐστι τύπωσις ἐν ψυχῇ. Cf. *LA* 1.30. Philo is influenced by Plato's *Theaetetus*, as were later Platonists in general (Arius Didymus, ap. Eusebius *PE* 11.23.3–6; Plutarch *Moral.* 373B), but also by Stoic doctrine (*SVF* 2.55–56).

253. Cf. *SVF* 1.484.

254. This description of the process by which the mind acquires concepts is peculiar, in that it seems to revert to the more primitive doctrine of the Old Stoa (Zeno, Cleanthes), disregarding the more sophisticated model proposed by Chrysippus, according to which each new image introduces a "modification" (ἑτεροίωσις) into the *hegemonikon* (*SVF* 2.56) rather than impressing anything upon it. Philo is perhaps influenced here by what he (or some intermediate source) takes to be the doctrine adumbrated in the *Theaetetus* 191C. Cf. *Op.* 166 and *Her.* 181, where he accepts the same doctrine.

255. A reference to the Stoic doctrine of ὁρμή (resulting in οἰκείωσις), and ἀφορμή (resulting in ἀλλοτρίωσις), arising from the reaction of the soul to the impressions it receives (*SVF* 3.169–77).

256. Cf. Plato *Laws* 863C, 732A; *Phileb.* 48E.

257. There follows Philo's version of the tropes of Aenesidemus, omitting two of the ten as they are stated by Sextus Empiricus (*Hyp.* 1.36ff.) and Diogenes Laertius 9.79–88. (Aristocles in Eusebius *PE* 14.18, 760b, speaks of only nine tropes.) The τρόποι or "modes" are critical arguments designed to bring about suspense of judgment (ἐποχή). See H. von Arnim, *Quellenstudien zu Philo von Alexandria*, Philologische Untersuchungen (Berlin, 1888), pp. 53–100; V. Brochard, *Les Sceptiques Grecs* (rep. Paris, 1969), pp. 253ff.; C. L. Stough, *Greek Scepticism* (Berkeley and Los Angeles, 1969), pp. 67–105. Cf. *Conf.* 125–26.

258. Cf. *Sobr.* 24; Ps-Longinus *De Sublimitate* 44.3.4.

259. Cf. Plato *Gorg.* 485D; Demosthenes 3.32.

260. Cf. *Mut.* 10. Contrast the true philosophers in *Congr.* 142.

261. Cf. *Her.* 243.

262. For the different opinions mentioned in this section, see Colson, LCL 4.574. Cf. *Agr.* 143–44; *Ebr.* 199–202; *Congr.* 67.

263. See note 240.

264. Cf. *Conf.* 140; *Abr.* 57, 60, 164; *QG* 3.32; Plato *Theaet.* 201 B.

265. Cf. *Cont.* 16, n. 8.

266. Cf. *SVF* 1.399.

267. For the various philosophers exemplifying these different views, see P. Wendland, "Eine doxographische Quelle Philons," *Sitzungsberichte der Berliner Akademie* 23 (1897): 1074ff.; and Colson, LCL 5.594–95.

NOTES

268. Colson writes: "αὐτῷ is difficult. To refer it to σῶμα understood from σώμασι as in the translation is possible, but strange. Mangey αὐτός. Perhaps αὐτῶν as in MS., partitive genitive after ποῦ. Or it may be an insertion from αὐτῷ below" (LCL 5.310, n. 5).

269. Cf. *LA* 1.91–92; *Mig.* 137.

270. Reading with Whitaker: <ὅν> οἶκον ὠνόμασε.

271. Wendland excludes the whole of the last sentence as a Christian interpolation describing the celestial city. For the textual difficulties in this passage, see Colson, LCL 5.602–603. Both Colson and Savinel suppose the last sentence to be genuine.

272. For Philo's conception of πίστις, see Introduction, pp. 24–26.

273. Reading with Mangey and Heinemann ὄντως instead of οὕτως.

274. Cf. *Sacr.* 12–14; *Op.* 45–46; *Conf.* 30–31; *Abr.* 268.

275. Cf. *Her.* 98; *Mut.* 181.

276. Philo is not condemning medicine, but only those who believe that it constitutes a self-sufficient agent and do not realize that it is merely an instrument of God (*LA* 3.178).

277. Cf. *Spec.* 1.252.

278. Cf. *Somn.* 1.119.

279. Cf. *LA* 1.16–18; *Mig.* 190–191; *Somn.* 1.72, 81–84, 118–19; *Mos.* 1.274, 283, 2.6; *Spec.* 1.65, 4.49, 192; *QG* 3.9; 4.196; *QE* 2.49.

280. Wendland (note on *Somn.* 1.1) has called attention to the resemblance between Philo's classification of prophetic dreams and that of Posidonius in Cicero *Divinat.* 1.64. According to Posidonius there are three ways in which men dream as a result of divine impulse: (1) The soul is clairvoyant of itself because of its kinship with the gods. (2) The air is full of immortal souls, already clearly stamped with marks of truth. (3) The gods in person converse with men when they are asleep. See Bréhier, p. 186; Colson, LCL 5.593; Wolfson 2.55–59.

281. Cf. *Somn.* 1.1–2; *Mig.* 190–91.

282. This passage is inspired by Plato *Tim.* 71–72.

283. What Philo seems to be saying is that they are too grand and complex to be dealt with as an aside to an encomium of Moses and must be analyzed in a separate treatise dedicated solely to that topic.

284. For Philo's theory of prophecy, see my study in the forthcoming volume on Hellenistic Judaism of the McMaster University project, *Judaism and Christianity in the Graeco-Roman Period: The Process of Achieving Normative Self-Definition.*

285. Cf. *Spec.* 2.189.

286. Cf. *LA* 1.36.

287. Philo begins by describing what is clearly a corporeal phenomenon (air shaped into a flaming fire, sounding forth an articulate voice), but then abruptly allegorizes it into an incorporeal one (the hearing that takes place

is that of the mind, not a sense-organ). Cf. Plutarch *Moral.* 588D–589E, where the *daimonian* of Socrates is explained in a somewhat similar manner.

288. Cf. *Spec.* 2.189, 3.7; *Praem.* 2.

289. Cf. *Cher.* 123; *Spec.* 2.244. For Philo's doctrine of worship, see J. Laporte, *La Doctrine Eucharistique chez Philon D'Alexandrie* (Paris, 1972). For Philo's spiritualization of the sacrificial cult, see N. Nikiprowetzky, "La spiritualisation des sacrifices et le cult sacrificiel au Temple de Jérusalem chez Philon d'Alexandrie, *Semitica* 17 (1967): 97–116; L. W. Thompson, "Hebrews 9 and Hellenistic Concepts of Sacrifice," *JBL* 98:4 (1979): 567–78.

290. A Stoic definition (Sextus *Math.* 9.123).

291. Cf. *Sobr.* 58; *Spec.* 2.35.

292. Cf. *Her.* 112–13; *Cher.* 94–97; *Fug.* 41; *Mut.* 49, 124; Plato *Laws* 716E.

293. Cf. *Agr.* 130; *Plant.* 164; *Her.* 123; *Spec.* 1.191, 203, 275, 283–84, 2.35.

294. Cf. *Her.* 82.

295. Cf. *Ebr.* 94.

296. Following with Colson and Heinemann's punctuation, who puts the full stop after ἄβατον, rather than Cohen, who puts it after θυσίαις.

297. Cf. Seneca *Benefic.* 1.6.3: "The honor that is paid to the gods lies, not in the victims for sacrifice, though they be fat and glitter with gold, but in the upright and holy desire of the worshipers. Good men, therefore, are pleasing to the gods with an offering of meal and gruel; the bad, on the other hand, do not escape impiety although they dye the altars with streams of blood."

298. Cf. Ps-Aristeas 170; *BT Menahot* 104b: "R. Isaac said, Why is the meal-offering distinguished in that the expression 'soul' is used therewith (Lev 2:1)? Because the Holy One, blessed be He, said, 'Who is it that usually brings a meal-offering? It is the poor man. I account it as though he had offered his own soul to Me." Cf. also *M. Menahot* 13.11.

299. Cf. *Spec.* 1.201, 277; *Plant.* 107–108.

300. See Exod. 20:25: "But if you make me an altar of stones, do not build it of hewn stones." Cf. Josephus *Ag. Ap.* 1.198.

301. Philo gives an allegorized form of the legend in Hesiod *Theog.* 50ff., where Zeus lay for nine nights with Mnemosyne, who after a year bore the Nine Muses at a birth. Mnemosyne was known as the mother of the Muses to Alcman (8.9), Eunelus (16), Solon (1.1), *Hymn to Hermes* (429), etc.

302. Philo is following the LXX (ἀνοίξω), which differs from the Hebrew.

303. Cf. the saying of the Persian Sufi Abu 'l-Hasan Khurqāmī (died 1033 C.E.): "When thou givest to God thy nothingness, He gives to thee His All" (R. A. Nicholson, *The Mystics of Islam* [London, 1963], p. 138).

304. Cf. *Her.* 226.

305. Cf. *Mut.* 12.

306. Cf. *Mig.* 122.

NOTES

307. LXX reads μείζων ἡ αἰτία μου τοῦ ἀφεθῆναί με. Cf. QG 1.73 where Philo takes this to mean that Cain is punished by being abandoned by God, not that his guilt is too great to be overlooked (Marcus).

308. Probably, as Aucher suggests, a reference to Exod. 19:22, where LXX reads μήποτε ἀπαλλάξη ἀπ' αὐτῶν κύριος (Marcus).

309. Cf. *Decal.* 81; *Det.* 86; *Abr.* 58; *Praem.* 14; *Somn.* 1.38.

310. Cf. *Somn.* 1.149, 2.251; *Virt.* 188; *Fug.* 117; *Praem.* 123. We have here a favorite conception of the Late Stoa, which was frequently used by Philo. Cf. Plato *Tim.* 90C; Epictetus 2.8.14: "It is within yourself that you bear Him, and do not perceive that you are defiling Him with impure thoughts and filthy actions. Yet in the presence of even an image of God you would not dare do anything of the things you are now doing. But when God Himself is present within you, seeing and hearing everything, are you not ashamed to be thinking and doing such things as these, O insensible of your own nature, and object of God's wrath!"; Seneca *Ep.* 83: "Nothing is shut off from the sight of God. He is witness of our souls, and he comes into the very midst of our thought—comes into them, I say, as one who may at any time depart"; Wisd. 1:4; I Cor. 3:16.

311. Cf. Theophilus *Ad Autol.* 1.2: "As a burnished mirror, so ought man to have his soul pure. When there is rust on the mirror, it is not possible that a man's face be seen in the mirror, so also when there is sin in a man, such a man cannot behold God."

312. Cf. *Mig.* 31; *Post.* 32; *QE* 2.61; *Mos.* 217; *Abr.* 54. The Stoic mythographer Cornutus (mainly following Chrysippus), in his *Summary of the Traditions concerning Greek Mythology* (chap. 9), allegorized Justice (Δίκη) and the Graces (Χάριτες), explaining that the Graces are God's sources of grace and beneficence to men. Cf. Seneca *Benefic.* 1.3.2ff. See Bréhier, pp. 147–48.

313. Cf. *Post.* 21; *LA* 3.47.

314. Cf. Plotinus 6.9.11.18.

315. Cf. *Abr.* 170; *Op.* 71; *Somn.* 1.71, 165; *LA* 3.84; *Deus* 138; *Her.* 68; *Post.* 92; *Plant.* 22–25.

316. Cf. *LA* 3.253; *QG* 1.51.

317. The inadequacy of language for the expression of truth receives great emphasis in the Platonic *Seventh Letter*. At 341C it is denied that the science of ultimate truth is expressible in words like other sciences. The reason is the inadequacy of the "the four," names (ὀνόματα), definitions (λόγοι), sensible images (εἴδωλα) and human knowledge based on these, to express the nature of "the Fifth," i.e., the Pure Form (342 Aff.). (Although the terms εἶδος and ἰδέα are not used in the *Letter*, it is clear that this is what is meant by such phrases as ὅ δὴ γνωστόν τε καὶ ἀληθῶς ἐστιν ὄν: 342B.) The Letter describes two ways of knowing the Forms, an imperfect way based on words and on the Forms' sensible images, and one that transcends these. Similarly, one of the ways in which νόησις in the *Republic* was claimed to

356

be superior to διάνοια was in dealing with the Forms themselves and making no use of their sensible images (εἰκόνες) (510B, 511Aff.). The *Cratylus* too refers to the need for a faculty that will grasp Realities by themselves (αὐτὰ δι' αὐτῶν) and independently of names (ἄνευ ὀνομάτων), since only so can we be sure that our application of names is correct (438 DE). (Cf. Plutarch *Moral.* 589C (thoughts of daemons have no need of verbs or nouns); Plotinus 4.3.30.5ff.; 5.5.1.38–39.) For an excellent discussion, see R. T. Wallis, "Nous as Experience," *The Significance of Neoplatonism*, ed. R. B. Harris (Norfolk, Va., 1976), pp. 121–53.

318. Cf. *Her.* 71–72; *Det.* 158–59; *LA* 3.83; *Abr.* 60ff.

319. The word play ἔγνω/ἀπέγνω is lost in the English. For the notion of self-despair see also *Mig.* 134: "The final aim of knowledge is to hold that we know nothing." Cf. R. Nahman of Bratzlav's frequent statement: "The end of knowledge is [the realization] that we do not know." (*Hayyey Moharan* II [Shivḥey Moharan] 2.42, p. 20). See A. Green, *Tormented Master* (Alabama, 1979), p. 294. Cf. also Nicholas of Cusa's well-known phrase *Docta Ignorantia.*'

320. Cf. *Somn.* 1.212; *Sacr.* 55; *Mig.* 134.

321. A passage in diatribe style, frequent in Philo's writings. See H. Thyen, *Der Stil der jüdisch-hellenistischen Homilie* (Göttingen, 1955).

322. Cf. *LA* 1.82; 3.41–42, 47; *Somn.* 2.232.

323. Cf. *LA* 2.51, 3.126; *Post.* 12; *Somn.* 1.243, 252; *Gig.* 44; *QG* 4.20.

324. *LA* 1.82; *Her.* 7.4.

325. Cf. *Op.* 100; *Post.* 64; *Decal.* 102; *Spec.* 2.59; *LA* 1.15–18. The identification of seven with both light and Logos was already made by Aristobulus (*FPG:* 224); cf. Philolaus DK A.12.

326. For the rest of the soul in God, cf. *Post.* 28; *Somn.* 2.228; *Fug.* 174; *LA* 1.6.

327. For a Pythagorean exposition of the hexad, cf. Anatolius, ap. *Theol. Ar.* p. 42, 19, De Falco; Theo of Smyrna, p. 102, 4ff., Hiller. Cf. *Op.* 13; *LA* 1.4, 16; *Post.* 64; *Spec.* 2.58–59, 64. Hannah has transcended the βίος πρακτικός, symbolized by the hexad, to attain to the βίος θεωρητικός, symbolized by the hebdomad, the number proper to the Logos and to God himself. For the notion of moving up the scale of being described in terms of numbers, cf. *Congr.* 103–105; *The Discourse on the Eighth and Ninth* (CG 6.6, Robinson, p. 294): "Lord, grant us a wisdom from thy power that reaches us, so that we may describe to ourselves the vision of the eighth and the ninth. We have already advanced to the seventh, since we are pious and walk in thy law."

328. See note 317 above. Cf. *Gig.* 52; *Plant.* 126: *Ebr.* 69, 94; *Mig.* 12; *Her.* 71–72; *Spec.* 1.272.

329. That is, representative of the genus beloved of God.

330. LXX: εἶδον τὸν τόπον οὗ εἱστήκει ὁ θεὸς τοῦ Ἰσραήλ.

331. The LXX read *lebēnat* rather than *libnat*.

NOTES

332. Cf. *Mos.* 1.158; *Post.* 14, 69.

333. For a discussion of the extrovertive and introvertive types of mystical experience, see Dodds, pp. 79–84.

334. Cf. *Det.* 89; *Congr.* 133–34; *Spec.* 1.207.

335. Cf. Xenophon *Mem.* 1.4.17; *CH* 11.19–20.

336. Cf. Aristotle *EN* 10.7.8, 1178a: "For little though it [the intellect] be in bulk, in power and in worth it is far above all the rest."

337. Cf. *CH* 12.1; Plotinus 5.2; Manilius *Astronomica* 2.115–29, 4.923–35.

338. Cf. *Fug.* 169.

339. Cf. *Sacr.* 78–79; *Mig.* 35.

340. Reminiscent of Plato *Phaedr.* 249C: "And this is a recollection of those things which our soul once beheld, when it journeyed with God and, lifting its vision above the things which we now say exist, rose up into real being (ἀνακύψασα εἰς τὸ ὄν ὄντως). And therefore it is just that the mind of the philosopher only has wings."

341. Cf. *A.P.* 9.406: "Alas for those who drink water: they are mad but with a temperate madness (μανίην σώφρονα μαινόμενοι)." The reference is apparently to a group of less inspired poets who are mockingly said to be mad with a temperate madness. Cf. also Plutarch *Moral.* 156D: κρατῆρα νηφάλιον, a nonintoxicating bowl. For a detailed study of the expression μέθη νηφάλιος, see H. Lewy, *Sobria Ebrietas* (Giessen, 1929). Lewy believes that Philo originated the expression himself, but this seems to me very unlikely. In any case, he has failed to note the closest parallel, *A.P.* 9.752, which explains the contradiction in Cleopatra's ring which bore a figure of the goddess Drunkenness (Μέθη) engraved on an amethyst, the stone of sobriety. The epigram reads as follows: "I am Drunkenness, the work of a skilled hand, but I am carved on the sober stone amethyst. The stone is foreign to the work. But I am the sacred possession of Cleopatra: on the queen's hand even the drunken goddess should be sober (νήφειν καὶ μεθύουσαν ἐδει)." According to Tarn, "this gives the meaning of the figure; it was that Sober Drunkenness (μέθη νηφάλιος) 'mother of virtue,' which was to play such a part in Philo of Alexandria, and for long afterwards, as the expression of the Mystic Wisdom or divine Joy of Life. In origin it was connected, on the Greek side, with the 'drunkenness without wine' (ἄοινον μέθην) of the Bacchic women (Plutarch *Moral.* 291A); and what the ring, which is called a 'sacred possession,' presumably did signify was that Cleopatra, like Arsinoe II,was an initiate of Dionysus." (*Cambridge Ancient History* 10.38–39)

342. Cf. Plato *Soph.* 254A: "Whereas the Philosopher, whose thoughts constantly dwell upon the nature of reality, is difficult to see because his region is so bright; for the eye of the vulgar soul cannot endure to keep its gaze fixed on the divine"; *Rep.* 515C (διὰ τὰς μαρμαρυγὰς ἀδυνατοῖ καθορᾶν).

343. Cf. *Ebr.* 145; *Fug.* 32, 166; *LA* 1.84; 3.82; *Prob.* 13; *Mos.* 1.187; *Cont* .12, 89.

NOTES

344. Following the reading of the Greek fragment: προσκολληθῶσι θεῷ.

345. ἐν αὐγῇ καθαρᾷ is a Platonic echo, *Phaedr.* 250C4.

346. Cf. *LA* 3.88: ὁ γὰρ ζωοπλάστης θεὸς ἐπίσταται τὰ ἑαυτοῦ καλῶς δημιουργήματα.

347. Cf. *Mig.* 186; *Spec.* 3.189.

348. For the theory of the succession of Empires, see J. W. Swain, "The Theory of the Four Monarchies, Opposition History under the Roman Empire," *Classical Philology* 35 (1940): 1–21; D. Flusser, "The Four Empires in the Fourth Sibyl and in the Book of Daniel," *Israel Oriental Studies* 2 (1972): 148–75.

349. It is noticeable that Philo studiously avoids mentioning Rome, though the whole tendency of the passage suggests that Rome too will have her day of reckoning. (Cf. *Praem.* 169, where again the Romans, depicted as pawns in God's larger historical plan, are not mentioned by name.) For Philo's political polemic "in code" or "by innuendo" see the somewhat imaginative portrayal of E. Goodenough, *The Politics of Philo Judaeus* (New Haven, 1938), pp. 21–63.

350. Cf. Aristotle *Phys.* 4.14, 223b25ff.: "For we say that human affairs and those of all other things that have natural movement and become and perish seem to be in a way circular, because all these things come to pass in time and have their beginning and end as it were 'periodically'; for time itself is conceived as 'coming round' "; Polybius 38.22.2; 29.21.3–6. *A.P.* 9.74. Festugière (2.523–26) suggests that Philo's source may have been Demetrius of Phalerum's Περὶ τύχης (Fr. 39, Jacoby = Pol.29.21; Diod. 31.10). Cf. E. Bayer, *Demetrius Phalereus der Athener* (Tübinger Beiträge 36. Stuttgart-Berlin, 1942), pp. 164ff.

351. On Philo's concept of democracy, see n. 150.

352. Cf. *Jos.* 131–41; *QG* 4.43; *Mos.* 1.31.

353. Cf. *SbR* 12.5. A fourfold classification of the ten plagues found in *Shibbole ha-Leket* (ed. Buber, p. 194) by Zedekiah b. Abraham Anaw (flourished at Rome in 13th cent.) corresponds exactly to their fourfold classification by Philo.

354. That God is altogether good and cannot be the direct cause of evil was a fundamental doctrine of Plato (*Tim.* 42D, *Rep.* 379B) and the Stoics (*SVF* 2.1168–1186). *Tim.* 41–42, where the Demiurge deputizes "younger Gods" to create the mortal kinds and especially the mortal parts of the human soul "to the end that He might be blameless in respect of its future wickedness" (42D), is closely parallel to Philo's interpretation here. The rabbis held a similar view. Cf. *Sifra Beḥukkōtay* 4; *Lament. R.* on 3.38; *BR* 3.5, *Th-Alb:*23.

355. Cf. *Conf.* 168–82; *Fug.* 68–72; *Mut.* 30–32.

356. Cf. *Conf.* 180–82.

357. Cf. *Fug.* 67; *Deus* 57.

NOTES

358. Cf. Prov. 19:3; Sir. 15:11: "Say not: 'From God is my transgression,' for that which He hateth made He not." We find virtually the same words in an ancient Egyptian text: "Beware lest thou say: Every man is according to his own character; ignorant and learned are all alike; Fate and upbringing are graven on the character in the writing of God himself" (A. Gardiner, *Hieratic Papyri in the British Museum*, 3d ser. [London, 1935], p. 43). Similarly, we read in the *Egyptian Coffin Texts:* "I did not command [men] that they do evil, (but) it was their hearts which violated what I have said" (*ANET*: 8); I Enoch 98:4: "Sin has not been sent upon the earth, but man of himself has created it"; Ps. Sol. 3:5: "The righteous stumbleth and holdeth the Lord righteous."

359. Cf. *Sacr.* 106; *Det.* 122; *Agr.* 128–29; *Op.* 149; *Plant.* 53; *Cont.* 178; *QG* 1.68, 1.89.

360. Cf. *Deus* 19; *Somn.* 2.116; *Prov.* 2.84. See n. 526.

361. Philo's view is identical with that of the Stoics. See Plutarch *Moral.* 1065B, where Chrysippus is quoted as saying: "The evil which occurs in terrible disasters has a rationale *(logos)* peculiar to itself; for in a sense it too occurs in accordance with universal reason, and so to speak is not without usefulness in relation to the whole. For without it there could be no good."

362. The meaning of the text (ἢ οὐκ ἀποδέον) is unclear. As for God's use of tyrants, cf. Plutarch *Moral.* 552F: "Indeed the Deity has actually made use of some of the wicked as chastisers of others—public executioners, one might say—and then blasted them; this is true, I believe, of most tyrants."

363. Similar descriptions of fire in *Congr.* 55; *Spec.* 4.26. For the idea, cf. *Decal.* 136.

364. Same comparison between law and providence in Ps-Aristotle *De Mundo* 400b15.

365. This distinction between the primary works (προηγούμενα ἔργα) and secondary effects (ἑπόμενα καὶ ἐπακολουθοῦντα) of nature is Stoic. See Gellius *NA* 7.1.8: "[Chrysippus], however, does not think that it was nature's original intention to make men subject to disease; for that would never have been consistent with nature as the source and mother of all things good. 'But,' said he, 'when she was creating and bringing forth many great things which were highly suitable and useful, there were also produced at the same time troubles closely connected with those good things that she was creating'; and he declared that these were not due to nature, but to certain inevitable consequences, a process that he himself calls κατὰ παρακολούθησιν. 'Exactly as,' he says, 'when nature fashioned men's bodies, a higher reason and the actual usefulness of what she was creating demanded that the head be made of very delicate and small bones. But this greater usefulness of one part was attended with an external disadvantage; namely, that the head was but slightly protected and could be damaged by slight blows and shocks.' " This example of the head derives from Plato's *Tim.* 74E–75C.

360

NOTES

366. Cf. Cicero *ND* 3.86–90.

367. Cf. Origen *Commentary on Genesis* 1.28, *PG* 12–26; Nemesius 62, 14. The Stoics found a use even for wild animals, bugs, and mice. See *SVF* 2.1173, 1152 (The gods made horses "in order that they might assist us in battle, dogs, that they might hunt with us, and leopards, bears, and lions, for the sake of exercising our fortitude"), 1163 ("Well in the fifth book concerning Nature after having said that bugs are useful in waking us up and mice in making us attentive about putting things away carefully"). For similar rabbinic apologetics, see *BR* 10.7, Th-Alb:79: "Our rabbis said: Even those things which you may regard as completely superfluous to the creation of the world, such as fleas, gnats, and flies, even they are included in the creation of the world, and the Holy One, blessed be He, carries out his purpose through everything, even through a snake, a scorpion, a gnat, or a frog . . ."; *Kohelet R.* 5.8; *BT Shabbat* 77b: "R. Judah said in Rab's name: Of all that the Holy One, blessed be He, created in his world, He did not create a single thing without purpose. [Thus] He created the snail as a remedy for a scab; the fly as an antidote to the hornet ['s sting]; the mosquito [crushed] for a serpent['s bite]; a serpent as a remedy for an eruption."

368. Cf. *Praem.* 149; *QG* 1.74; *Kohelet R.* 5.8.5: "R. Tanḥuma and R. Menaḥma related the following incidents. A man was once standing by the river and he saw a frog carrying a scorpion and conveying it across the river. He exclaimed, 'Surely it is engaged on performing its mission.' The frog conveyed the scorpion across; the latter performed its mission and was carried back to its place. Then a sound of wailing was heard in the city, 'A scorpion has stung so-and-so and he has died.' "

369. See *Prov.* 2.95–96.

370. φυτὸν οὐράνιον, heavenly plant, is a *vox Platonica* (*Tim.* 90A). Cf. *Det.* 85; *Plant.* 17.

371. This encomium of Greece was a common theme (τόπος), undoubtedly borrowed from Plato (*Tim.* 24C). Cf. Cicero *De Fato* 4.7: "Athens has a rarified climate, which is thought also to cause sharpness of wit above the average in the population"; *Vita Pythag.* (ap. Photius, *Biblioth.* 249) (attributed by W. Theiler to Eudorus of Alexandria, who has left his mark on Philo) contains the same statement. Cf. *Prob.* 140. For the influence of the air, see *The Contemplative Life*, n. 14.

372. See DK B.118. See Colson, LCL 9.546–47.

373. Reading ψυχωθῆναι, as suggested by Colson, instead of ὑψωθῆναι of the manuscripts.

374. It is interesting to find Philo here defending the Greek mythmakers and insisting that their writings must be allegorized. Indeed, not content with the Stoic exegesis of Homer and Hesiod, Philo even provides new allegorizations of his own. Cf. *Conf.* 170; *QG* 1.92; 4.8; *QE* 2.102; *Plant.* 129. See J. Pépin, *Mythe et Allégorie* (Paris, 1976), pp. 234–38. For a good summary of

those passages in which Philo attacks pagan mythology, see Wolfson 1.32–36. (Cf. *Op.* 1, 157; *Det.* 125; *Gig.* 58).

375. Contrast Philo's attitude at *Decal.* 54. Cf. *SVF* 2.1066–1067, 1075; D.L. 7.147.

376. Cf. *Legat.* 99.

377. Cf. D.L. 3.5.

378. This formula is frequently repeated by Philo. Cf. *Mos.* 1.94; *Abr.* 175; *Jos.* 244; *Spec.* 4.127; *Virt.* 26; *QG* 1.32, 2.47, 4.17.

379. Reading with Wendland τέως instead of τάχα of manuscripts.

380. Cf. *Mos.* 1.211, 2.154.

381. Cf. *Mos.* 1.174 cited above, and 2.261. For detailed discussion, see Introduction.

382. The rabbis similarly emphasized the miraculous and truly marvelous character of the natural order itself, in contrast to the unfamiliar events that amaze us with their strange novelty. Cf. *Sifra, Shemini* 5.53b, p. 218, Finkelstein: "When R. Akiba read this verse [the verses in Lev. 11 enumerating the various birds and reptiles] he used to say 'How manifold are thy works, O Lord!' (Ps. 104:24) Thou hast creatures that live in the sea and creatures that live upon the dry land; if those of the sea were to come upon the dry land they would die, and if the land creatures go into the sea they would die. Thou hast creatures that live in fire and creatures that live in air, if those of the fire were to come into the air they would die, and if those of the air would go into the fire they would die. The one's source of vitality is death for the other and the one's sphere of existence spells death for the other. 'How manifold are thy works, O Lord!' " Cf. *BR* 20.9, Th-Alb:192–193: "R. Eleazar said: Redemption is likened to the earning of a livelihood, and the reverse: just as redemption requires the working of wonders, so does the earning of a livelihood require the same ... R. Joshua b. Levi said: Sustenance requires more effort than the dividing of the Reed Sea, for it is written, 'who split apart the Sea of Reeds' (Ps. 136:13), and 'Who gives food to all flesh' (Ps. 136:25)." See Urbach, pp. 92–93.

383. For ὑπηρετήσοντα, to minister, cf. Wisd. 19:6 (ὑπηρετοῦσα ταῖς σαῖς ἐπιταγαῖς).

384. Cf. *Mos.* 2.267: "For, as God called up His most perfect work, the world, out of non-being into being, so He called up plenty in the desert, altering the elements to meet the pressing need of the occasion, so that instead of the earth the air bore food for their nourishment." By employing the formula μεταβαλὼν τὰ στοιχεῖα, Philo is undoubtedly referring to the Greek philosophical theory of the interchange of the elements (cf. D.L. 8.25; Sextus *Math.* 10.312; *SVF* 405–07, 409–10, 413 and n. 152 above). For the use of this theory in even more explicit terms by the author of *The Wisdom of Solomon*, see my Anchor Bible commentary on that book, pp. 330–32.

385. Cf. *Mos.* 1.117: "At the same time she [Nature] rejoices to employ

her science in works of manifold variety, and thus out of contrarieties form the harmony of the universe. And therefore she supplies the benefit of water to some from heaven above, to others from the springs and rivers below"; *Fug.* 180: "For what the sky is in winter to other countries, this the Nile is to Egypt in the height of summer: The one sends the rain from above upon the earth, the other, strange to say, rains up from below and waters the fields." Philo is here employing the typically Egyptian view of rain for his own purposes. Addressing the god, the Egyptian worshiper acknowledged his goodness to Egypt: "Thou makest the Nile in the lower world and bringest it whither thou wilt, in order to sustain mankind, even as thou hast made them. Thou makest that whereon all distant countries live. Thou has put (another) Nile in the sky, so that it may come down for them ... in order to moisten their fields in their townships ... The Nile in the sky, thou appointest it for the foreign peoples and for all the beasts of the highland which walk upon feet, whereas the (real) Nile, it comes from the lower world for (the people of) Egypt" (*Aton Hymn* 9–10; cited by J. A. Wilson, *Before Philosophy* [Baltimore, 1949] p. 46). The Palestinian version of the manna miracle naturally sees the matter in simpler terms: "R. Simeon b. Gamaliel says: Come and see how much beloved the Israelites are by Him by whose word the world came into being. Because they are so much beloved by Him, He made the upper region like the lower and the lower like the upper. In the past the bread came up from the earth and the dew would come down from heaven, as it is said: 'The earth yielding corn and wine; yea, His heavens drop down dew' (Deut. 33:28). But now things have changed. Bread began to come down from heaven and the dew came up from the earth, as it is said: 'Behold, I will cause to rain bread from heaven' and it says: 'And the layer of dew came up.' " (v. 14) (*Mek.* on Exod. 16:4, Lauterbach 2.102. Cf. *ShR* 25.2 and 6).

Borgen's attempt (pp. 7–13, cited n. 79 above) to deduce from Philo's version that it must be an awkward reworking of a Palestinian tradition seems to me at best indecisive. It is just as likely that Philo, who as a non-Egyptian writing in the Roman period would not have ordinarily described the phenomenon of rain as the early Egyptians did (note his words at *Fug.* 180: "strange to say, rains up from below"), thought he could diminish the strangeness of the miracle of the manna raining down from heaven by using Egypt as an illustration of a country where the unusual reversal of raining up from below is the normal routine of nature. If he were simply recording a Palestinian tradition, the chances are he would have left it unaltered.

386. For Wisdom dwelling in a cloud, cf. Sir. 24:4; I Baruch 3:29; *On the Origin of the World*, CG 2.5, 106.5–6 (Robinson, p. 166). From the parallel passage in *Her.* 203–205 it is clear that Philo is referring here to the Logos, which, while in itself invisible, is depicted nevertheless as flashing forth a continuously bright light. Cf. Ezekiel the Tragedian, *Exagoge* 94–99 (*FPG*: 210, 33–211, 4): "What then? I will go forward and behold / this wondrous sign

(τεράστιον μέγιστον), that passes man's belief. (Then God speaks to him:) ... The place thou standest on is holy ground; / And from this bush God's word (or Logos?) shines forth to thee (θεῖος ἐκλάμπει λόγος) ... Of mortal birth, thou canst not see my face; / Yet mayest thou hear the words I came to speak." Although Philo seems nowhere else to speak of the Logos as "shining forth" (ἐκλάμπειν), he does describe it at *Cher.* 30 as "hot and fiery" (ἔνθερμον καὶ πυρῶδη) (and at *Fug.* 134 he speaks of νοῦς as an ἔνθερμον καὶ πεπυρωμένον πνεῦμα). The fact is that Philo is capable of using various kinds of metaphorical expression concerning the Logos, which are not meant to be taken literally.

387. Cf. *LA* 2.46, 69, 93; 3.33, 136–37; *Cher.* 57, 66, 71.

388. Philo is adapting Plato *Phaedr.* 243D: ποτίμῳ λόγῳ οἷον ἁλμυρὰν ἀκοὴν ἀποκλύσασθαι.

389. Philo here utilizes a piece of Stoic grammar. According to the Stoic philosopher Apollodorus of Athens (fl. c. 140 B.C.E., a pupil of Panaetius): "Reflexive predicates (ἀντιπεπονθότα) are those among the passive, which although in form passive, are yet active operations, as 'he gets his hair cut' (κείρεται): for here the agent includes himself in the sphere of his action" (D.L. 7.64; *SVF* 2.183). The application of the term ἀντιπεπονθότα in Philo suggests that its grammatical meaning was not so much that of the ordinary middle (I shave myself) as that of the causative middle ("I get myself shaved"). Cf. *LA* 3.201; *Decal.* 31. Philo uses the distinction between the passive and middle or reflexive use of κείρω to illustrate what should be one's attitude to adversity. One may submit to it willingly, like a man going to have his hair cut, or unwillingly, like a sheep going to the shearing. This is only an alternative image to that employed by Chrysippus and Zeno: "Just as a dog tied to a cart follows while being pulled, if it is willing to follow, making its own self-determination comply with necessity; yet it will be in all respects subject to compulsion if it is unwilling to follow. So it is too with men" (*SVF* 2.975; cf. Seneca *Ep.* 107.11: *volentem ducunt fata, nolentem trahunt*). For further illustrations from Stoic writings, see D. Winston, "Freedom and Determinism in Philo of Alexandria," *SP* 3 (1974–1975): 67, n. 29. On Apollodorus, see Colson, LCL 2.484; Dillon, p. 179.

390. Cf. Seneca *De Consolatione ad Polybium* 10.4.5: "If anyone should be angry that he has had to pay back borrowed money—especially that of which he had the use without paying interest—would he not be considered an unfair man? Nature gave your brother his life. . . . If she has required from him from whom she wanted it an earlier payment of her loan, she has but used her own right." See n. 170.

391. Cf. *Post.* 42.

392. Cf. *Conf.* 127; *Fug.* 134; *Mut.* 141; *Sacr.* 2–3, 97–98; *QG* 3.3.

393. Cf. *Post.* 35; *Fug.* 172.

394. The emphatic pronoun οὗτος is used for mind four times in succes-

sion. Similar repetition of the personal pronoun is a feature of Hellenistic aretalogies or hymns of praise discovered in Egypt. See A. J. Festugière, "Le Style de la 'Kore Kosmou,'" *Vivre et Penser* 2 (1942): 50–53; CH 23 [*Kore Kosmou*] 65–68, eleven οὗτοι follow each other. See also Y. Grandgean, *Une nouvelle Arétalogie d'Isis à Maronée* (Leiden, 1975), pp. 17–18, where we find αὕτη three times in succession, after which the invocations continue in the second person. Cf. Wisd. 10:1–15, where αὕτη recurs six times in reference to Wisdom; Acts 7:35–38; Aristides *Encomium on Zeus* 43.29ff.; Philo *Legat.* 144ff.; *Praem.* 11 (where ἐλπίδι recurs three times, followed by δι' ἐλπίδα); Heb. 11, where we have a long succession of the dative of πίστις (a similar usage is already found in *CD* 2:17–3:12, where we find the repeated use of the Hebrew pronominal suffix *b*. For the encomium on mind, cf. Sophocles *Antigone* 331ff.

395. Reading χερσαῖον with Heinemann. Cf. *Spec.* 4.155: "That the creature whose element is land can float his way through the element of water" (literally, "the land-nature is able to pass through navigable nature"); *Op.* 147; Wisd. 19:19: "For land animals became aquatic, and things that swim migrated to shore."

396. Cf. Euripides *The Suppliant Women* 209: "And commerce over sea, that by exchange a country may obtain the goods it lacks"; Wisd. 14:5.

397. Cf. *Ebr.* 107: "For you have been made instruments (ὄργανα) to minister to His undying acts of grace." The Stoics similarly say: "The movements of our minds are nothing more than instruments for carrying out determined decisions since it is necessary that they be performed through us by the agence of Fate" (*SVF* 2.943).

398. The term ἄφετος is a good clue to Philo's conception of the mind's conditional freedom. This word is properly used of animals allowed to roam free (often in sacred enclosures, and sometimes preparatory to being sacrificed), instead of being bound in stalls and employed for specific tasks.

399. Philo is clearly emphasizing the limited character of the freedom bestowed by God on man. Cf. Plato *Tim.* 38B: Time was made after the pattern of the Eternal Nature, to the end that it might be as like thereto as possible (κατὰ δύναμιν); *Theaet.* 176B: "And to escape is to become like God, so far as this is possible (κατὰ τὸ δυνατόν); Philo *Abr.* 203, where God bestows χαρά on Isaac only "in so far as the recipients's capacity allows"; *Op.* 23, where God confers benefits "in proportion to the capacities of the recipients." Cf. *Tanh.* Buber, Debarim 1.

400. Philo seems deliberately to be avoiding Stoic terminology here, since neither ἐθελουργός nor αὐτοκέλευστος appears to have been used by the latter. It may well be that in those passages where he is anxious to emphasize man's freedom, relative though it be, he prefers to dissociate himself from the Stoic formulae, which were under heavy attack by those who accused the Stoics of trying to camouflage their deterministic position by coat-

ing it with innocuous but meaningless phrases that suggested some sort of human freedom. (The Cynic Oenomaus called the lot accorded to man by Chrysippus "semi-slavery." Eusebius *PE* 6.7.2 and 14; cf. Nemesius *De Nat. Hom.* 35.) On the other hand, when writing for the "initiated" and wishing to indicate the very limited nature of human freedom, he does employ the Aristotelian/Stoic formula ἐφ᾽ ἡμῖν (fragment from lost fourth book of *LA*. See Harris *Fragments*, p. 8). It is also interesting to note when ἐθελουργός and αὐτοκέλευστος are first used. In both cases, by Xenophon (*Eq.* 10.17; and *Anab.* 3.4.5): in the former case in the context of "animals" (horses) doing things willingly and spontaneously; in the latter of soldiers doing something without command from above. We may be relatively free, but we are still chattels of God. Moreover, ἐθελουργὸς καὶ αὐτοκέλευστος is a frequent collocation in Philo, and it is illuminating to examine the various contexts in which this phrase occurs. They all refer to that kind of human action which is spontaneous and not the result of external compulsion, i.e., precisely what is ordinarily meant in Greek philosophy by the term ἑκούσιον. At *Conf.* 59, for example, it refers to the Israelites' readiness to perform God's will even before learning and understanding its nature, whereas at *Mut.* 270, it refers to the relative independence of the pupil in the absence of his teacher's presence. Cf. *Det.* 11; *Mos.* 1.63; *Spec.* 1.57; 2.146, 3.127; *Prob.* 22.

401. The prime motivation of Philo in this passage, to show that man is responsible for all his actions, is very similar to that of Plato in *Tim.* 42D and *Rep.* 10.614ff. (*Rep.* 617E: αἰτία ἑλομένου, θεὸς ἀναίτιος.) For a detailed analysis of Philo's concept of freedom, see D. Winston (cited n. 389 above).

402. The Roman law on the subject of the respect due by freedmen to their masters is better reported than the Greek. Ulpian, in *Digest* 47.10.7.2, advises judges not to admit actions for insult and the like from freedmen against their former masters.

403. Cf. *Her.* 186, 272–73.

404. Cf. *Op.* 117; *Abr.* 73; Plato *Laws* 644D.

405. Cf. *QG* 4.220.

406. Philo seems deliberately to avoid the Platonic notion that the soul may become diseased through the body (cf. *Spec.* 3.10–11). He thus apparently held that a healthy soul can essentially overcome the diseased conditions of the body and that even when sick (i.e., when the εὐκρασία of its three faculties is defective), it still functions autonomously since its sickness is in no way caused by anything external (i.e., Philo seems to have believed that it was defective when it entered the body).

407. The Platonic division of the soul into λόγος, θυμός, and ἐπιθυμία, and their location respectively in the head, chest, and around the diaphragm (*Tim.* 69Eff), is frequently mentioned by Philo (e.g., *LA* 1.70–73. 3.115). In the restive horses there is an allusion to the myth in Plato *Phaedr.* 253D, where

the charioteer is to be interpreted as reason, and the two horses as spirited-ness and desire.

408. Cf. Plato *Craty.* 411E: σωφροσύνη δὲ σωτηρια . . . φρονήσεως.

409. Paradoxically it is his own free will that permits him to deny his freedom. Cf. M. Aurelius 11.20.

410. Cf. *Mig.* 194; *Abr.* 69. A large proportion of the demons in the *Testament of Solomon* have some definite astrological relationship, and mortals seem to be particularly liable to injury from demons who are συναστροί with them, i.e., belong to the same star (4.6). Chapter 18 of that work "gives a list of the 36 decans, and constitutes a piece of astrological material taken over bodily. Each decan is thought of as a demon causing certain diseases, and the means for counteracting them are detailed. Here the astrological entity does not *belong* to the demon, or the demon to it, but *is* the demon. In other words, the astral deities of paganism have become demons" (C. C. McCown, *The Testament of Solomon* [Leipzig, 1922], p. 46).

411. A school argument; cf. Cicero *Divinat.* 2.97; Sextus *Math.* 5.92: Favorinus, ap. Gellius *NA* 14.1.27.

412. Cf. Sextus *Math.* 5.55ff.

413. For a discussion of Philo's refutation of astral fatalism, see D. Amand, *Fatalisme et liberté dans l'antiquité grecque* (Louvain, 1945). Amand (pp. 84–85) attributes Philo's refutation to the scholastic tradition of the New Academy, but it is not impossible that he may owe some of his arguments to the master of Middle Stoicism, Panaetius, who had certainly rejected the school's doctrine in this matter (Cicero *Divinat.* 2.88); (D.L. 8.149). See M. Hadas-Lebel, Lyon 35.89.

414. Cf. *Her.* 300–301; *QG* 3.13.

415. Cf. Plato *Laws* 720; Cicero *Leg.* 2.14: "But I think that I should follow the same course as Plato, who was at the same time a very learned man and the greatest of all philosophers, and who wrote a book about the Republic first, and then in a separate treatise described its Laws. Therefore, before I recite the law itself, I will speak in praise of that law"; Josephus *Ant.* 1.21–24.

416. Cf. Cicero *Leg.* 1.61.

417. Cf. *Op.* 143; *Ebr.* 142; *Somn.* 2.174; *Mos.* 2.47–52, 211; *Spec.* 2.13, 3.32, 4.203–206, 212; *Prob.* 37, 62; *QG* 1.27, 4.90, 184; *QE* 2.1.

418. LXX, however, reads: ἐφύλαξε, not ἐποίησε.

419. Cf. Aristotle *Topica* 140a6, where the following is given as an example of a bad definition: "Law is a measure or image (εἰκών) of the naturally just"; Plato *Polit.* 297C: "But our one right form of government must be sought in some small number or one person, and all other forms are merely, as we said before, more or less successful imitations (μιμήματα) of that."

420. Cf. *Abr.* 275–76.

NOTES

421. Cf. *SVF* 1.262: "Moreover, the much-admired Republic of Zeno, the founder of the Stoic sect, may be summed up in this one main principle: That all the inhabitants of this world of ours should not live differentiated by their respective rules of justice into separate cities and communities, but that we should consider all men to be of one community and one polity, and that we should have a common life and order common to us all . . ."; 3.322, where Chrysippus exposes the ridiculous varieties in laws and customs.

422. "This term for the Stoic ideal of the world conceived of as a state and expressed in the word κοσμοπολίτης, occurs also in *Op.* 19 and *Mos.* 2.51. It is not quoted from any other writer than Philo in this sense" (Colson, LCL 6.156, n. a).

423. Cf. *Sacr.* 111. Philo's interpretation is based on Num. 28:2, where bemôᶜ adô is rendered by the LXX as ἐν ἑορταῖς μου, and the series of sacrificial laws for the holidays opens with the daily offering. "It is no doubt a consideration with him that the inclusion serves to make the perfect number 10, but he could have obtained this otherwise by including the 'Basket'" (*Spec.* 2.215). (Colson, LCL 7.335, n. a).

424. Retaining with S. Daniel the reading of the manuscripts, ὡς τῶν, as (being that of) men who . . .

425. Philo shares the exceptional view of the Stoic philosopher Musonius Rufus (c. 30–101 C.E.) that only intramarital coition for the sake of procreation constitutes lawful intercourse. Cf. Musonius, Fr. 12, Lutz, p. 87. (μόνα μὲν ἀφροδίσια νομίζειν δίκαια τὰ ἐν γάμῳ καὶ ἐπὶ γενέσει παίδων συντελούμενα . . . τὰ δέ γε ἡδονὴν θηρώμενα ψιλὴν ἄδικα καὶ παράνομα, κἂν ἐν γάμῳ ᾖ). Philo's language is similar: θήρα γὰρ αὐτὸ μόνον ἡδονῆς ἀκράτορος . . .); cf. *Spec.* 3.113. As A. C. van Geytenbeek has pointed out, Plato (*Laws* 835 Dff.) speaks about a law that would regulate all sexual problems in an ideal manner and would contain a measure forbidding all intercourse that does not intend παιδοποιία. Later however it appears that he merely forbids extramarital intercourse (841 DE). Ps-Ocellus (*De Univ. Nat.* 4) contrasts pleasure as an aim with procreation, but when he goes on to say that the children of those who have had intercourse for the sake not of procreation but of pleasure are despised by gods and men, it appears that he, too, thinks of extramarital intercourse only. Philo and Clement, concludes Geytenbeek, are the only moralists who share Musonius's opinion. (For Clement, see *Strom.* 3.7.58, 11, 71–72; *Paed.* 2.10 90–102.) (*Musonius Rufus and Greek Diatribe* [Assen, 1962], pp. 71–73. The rabbinic view was not quite as harsh as that of Philo. A priest, even though he has had a wife and children, shall not marry a woman incapable of procreation, since such is included in the term of harlot mentioned in the Torah. Since Israelites were not commanded concerning the harlot, they are not included under this prohibition under the circumstances mentioned (*BT Yebamot* 61a–62b;) cf. *Tosef. Yeb.* 8.4. On the oth-

er hand, "If a man married a woman and remained with her for ten years and she has not yet given birth, he is not allowed to neglect further the duty of procreation" (*BT Yebamot* 64a; cf. Plato *Laws* 784B). The later attitude to this problem is epitomized by R. Jacob Tannenbaum of Hungary in a Responsum dated 1893: "The Sages of previous generations have dealt at length with the matter and, it seems, could not find it in their hearts to permit in actual practice divorce against her will or the taking of a second wife because of childlessness" (*Responsa Naharei Afars'mon, E.H.*, no. 18). The rabbinic attitude toward sexual pleasure is well summarized in the following statement of Maimonides: "But a man's own wife is permitted to him and, with her, he is allowed to do as he pleases. He may cohabit with her whenever he pleases, kiss her wherever he pleases, and cohabit naturally or unnaturally. . . . Still, the way of piety is not to be frivolous about this but to approach it with holiness, and not deviate from the natural (M.T. Issurei Biah 21.9)." See D. M. Feldman, *Birth Control in Jewish Law* (New York, 1968), pp. 36–41, 88–89.

426. Philo's attitude here is similar to that relayed in two midrashic sources—from the days when plural marriage was permitted even in practice. "It happened once that a woman in Sidon had lived ten years with her husband without bearing him a child. They came to R. Simeon b. Yohai and requested to be parted from one another. He said to them: I adjure you, just as you have always shared a festive board together, so do not part save with festivity." During the feast the husband asked his wife to choose any article she wanted and take it with her to her father's house as a token of his love. When he awoke from his inebriated state, he found himself in her father's house. There was nothing in the world, she insisted, that she cared for more than he. They returned to the rabbi, who prayed for them and they became fertile (*Shir Hashirim R.* 1.4.2; *PRK* 22, Mandelbaum: 327).

427. Cf. *Spec.* 3.46, 112, 176; *Prob.* 79, 160; *Cont.* 70.

428. At *Spec.* 3.110, Philo derives the prohibition against exposure of infants from Exod. 21:22 *a minori ad maius*. Both Plato and Aristotle object to bringing up all children on social grounds, and have no moral objections against abortion (ἄμβλωσις) and exposure (ἔκθεσις) (Plato *Rep.* 372C, 459–461C; *Laws* 740 Bff.; Aristotle *Polit.* 1265ab, 1326ab). Polybius (36.17.5ff.) complains of ἀπαιδία and ὀλιγανθρωπία in Greece and attributes this to people's carelessness and avarice: They bring up one or two children only, in order to be able to provide them with luxury. Condemnation of exposure came mostly from the Stoics. Epictetus (1.23.7–10) rejects Epicurus's advice not to bring up children as unnatural: "But a sheep does not abandon its own offspring, nor a wolf; and yet does a man abandon his?" Musonius Rufus argued for the raising of all children as something expedient and profitable (Fr. 15, Lutz; cf. Hierocles, von Arnim, p. 55; Themistius *Or.* 26, 235a). Philo's protest against the cruelty of exposure is largely missing in the writings of

the Greek moralists. See van Geytenbeek (cited n. 425), pp. 78–88. For the Jewish opposition to exposure, cf. Hecataeus of Abdera, ap. Diodorus 40.3.8 (M. Stern, *Greek and Latin Authors on Judaism* [Jerusalem, 1976], p. 29); Josephus *Ag. Ap.* 2.202; *Sib Or* 3.765; Ps-Phocylides 184–85. See Stern, p. 33; Heinemann, pp. 392ff.; P. van der Horst, *The Sentences of Pseudo-Phocylides* (Leiden, 1978), pp. 232–34.

429. Cf. *Spec.* 4.149; Ps-Aristotle *De Mundo* 400b30: "God is a law to us, impartial and admitting no correction or change; he is surely a stronger and more stable law than those inscribed on tablets."

430. Cf. Cicero *Rep.* 3.33. For a discussion of the origin and development of natural law theory in Greek thought, see D. Winston, "Philo's Ethical Theory," *ANRW* (forthcoming).

431. Cf. *Det.* 146; *Her.* 7; *Jos.* 48, 68, 215, 262; *Spec.* 1.203, 235, 3.54; *Virt.* 206; *Praem.* 84, 163; *Prob.* 99, 124; *Flac.* 7; *Legat.* 165. For Philo's theory of conscience, see D. Winston (cited n. 430).

432. Cf. *LA* 1.46.

433. Cf. *Deus* 126, 128, 182; *Op.* 128; *Fug.* 117–18, 203, 207; *Somn.* 1.91; *Decal.* 87.

434. Cf. *Somn.* 1.149, 2.37, 251; *Sob.* 62; *Fug.* 117; *Virt.* 188; *Praem.* 123; *QE* 2.51.

435. Cf. note 317.

436. Literally "old of old."

437. Philo, through his usual mode of "creative" etymology, derives ὄνος from πόνος and πρόβατον (probably correctly) from προβαίνω. Cf. *Somn.* 1.198.

438. Cf. *Deus* 92–93.

439. Cf. *Mig.* 170–71.

440. Cf. *LA* 3.173–77; *Mig.* 80–81.

441. Cf. *Gig.* 64; *Deus* 143, 162–63; *Mig.* 146; *Spec.* 4.168.

442. For this division of Stoic doctrine, see D.L. 7.40.

443. Cf. *LA* 1.57; *Mut.* 74–75.

444. According to the Stoics the wise man will not be aware of the moment of his transition to wisdom (*SVF* 3.539–42). Philo here employs the distinctive Stoic terminology attached to the various stages: διαληλυθότες σοφοί and πῆξις (cf. *LA* 2.55). Chrysippus, who speaks only of two stages (as Epictetus 4.2, but unlike Seneca *Ep.* 75.9, who reports a threefold classification of certain philosophers), says of the man who has advanced to the point where he only just falls short of wisdom or perfection: "He fulfills all appropriate actions in all respects and omits none; but his life is not yet in a state of well-being. This supervenes when these intermediate actions acquire the additional property of firmness (τὸ βέβαιον), habituation (ἑκτικόν) (i.e., consistency), and their own proper fixity (ἰδίαν πῆξιν)" (*SVF* 3.510).

445. Cf. *Fug.* 202, 213; *Somn.* 2.270.

446. The vow of the Nazarite is called (as in *LA* 1.17) "the great vow" from Num. 6:2 (ὃς ἂν μεγάλως εὔξηται εὐχήν).

447. Reading ἑκουσίων of the manuscripts. "Wendland wrote ἀκουσίων, i.e., the ideal course is to avoid both kinds of offense, the next best to avoid the voluntary and to minimize the involuntary" (Colson *LCL* 3.200, n.l).

448. Cf. Wisd. 1:16: "But godless men have summoned Death through word and deed; thinking him a friend they pined for him, and made a pact with him, for they are worthy to be members of his party."

449. Cf. *Somn.* 1.115, 151; *Gig.* 60–64.

450. Sarah symbolizes for Philo generic virtue: *LA* 2.82; 3.218, 244; *Cher.* 3ff., 41; *Det.* 59; *Post.* 130; *Her.* 62, 258; *Fug.* 128; *Mut.* 61, 77, 255; *Abr.* 206; *QG* 4.122. Philo attributes this symbolism to φυσικοὶ ἄνδρες, natural philosophers or students of the (higher) truths of Nature (*Abr.* 99). On the sovereignty of virtue, cf. *LA* 1.65; *Mut.* 80; *Virt.* 188; *Prob.* 154.

451. Cf. *Mig.* 126; *Mut.* 267; *QG* 3.60.

452. For this tripartition of the virtuous life, cf. *Post.* 85ff. (where it is derived from Deut. 30:14); *Mut.* 236–37; *Mos.* 2.212; *Virt.* 183–84; *Prob.* 68; *QG* 7.11.

453. Virtue arrives late in the life of man. Cf. *Sacr.* 15–16: "when the age of maturity brings the great change and quenches the fiery furnace of the passions"; *Sobr.* 26: "the desire for moral excellence is a later birth"; *Her.* 294–96; *QG* 4.157. Describing Plato's theory of education, H. I. Marrou sums up: "Only at the age of fifty would those who have survived and surmounted all these trials finally arrive at their goal: the contemplation of pure Goodness. As Malraux says in *La Condition Humaine,* 'It takes fifty years to make a man . . .' " (*A History of Education in Antiquity* [London, 1956], p. 77).

454. Cf. Albinus *Did.* 28.4, Louis; Crantor, ap. Stobaeus 2.206.26; "Crantor said that one could not be initiated into the great mysteries before being initiated into the lesser, nor arrive at philosophy before being exercised in the encyclical studies"; Synesius of Cyrene *Dion* 5.3.

455. Cf. *Deus* 4; *Congr.* 89, 95–96, 98, 101; *Sacr.* 72ff.; *Her.* 113–25.

456. M. Alexandre retains the manuscript reading τὸ ἕν, arguing that Philo sometimes uses this mathematical expression for God (*Agr.* 54; *Deus* 11; *LA* 2.2). The hebdomad must be turned toward the One, because seven is related to one, being engendered by it (*LA* 1.15; *Post.* 64ff.; *Deus* 11–13; *Decal.* 102; *Her.* 216; cf. *Theol. Arith.* 8.54, p. 72, de Falco 7–9).

457. Plato is fond of this image: cf. *Rep.* 531D, 532D; *Laws* 722DE, 723AB, etc.; Albinus *Did.* 7.4, Louis; Synesius *Dion* 4.4.

458. Cf. *LA* 1.57: "For some of the arts and sciences are theoretical indeed but not practical, such as geometry and astronomy, and some are practical, but not theoretical . . . but virtue is both theoretical and practical; for clearly it involves theory, since philosophy, the road that leads to it, involves it through its three parts, logic, ethics, physics; and it involves conduct, for

virtue is the art of the whole of life, and life includes all kinds of conduct."
That virtue is the art of the whole of life is an echo of a Stoic formulation
(*SVF* 3.560; Seneca *Ep.* 95.7–8, 55–57).

459. "Astronomy of an elementary kind was regularly included among
the Encyclia, but is not named by Philo in his other lists of the subjects,
doubtless because, as often in other writers, it is regarded as a branch of geometry. Cf. Quintilian 1.10.46" (Colson, LCL 4.577). See also M. Alexandre,
Lyon 16.38, who points out that astronomy occupied both a privileged position in Philo's scheme, inasmuch as the contemplation of the world leads to
its Creator, as well as a perilous one, since it could lead to the deification of
the universe.

460. Cf. *LA* 3.244; *QG* 3.19.

461. Cf. *Somn.* 1.205; *QG* 3.19, 20, 25, 27, 32, 33.

462. Cf. *Sacr.* 78ff.; *Abr.* 23; Epictetus 1.2.25–26; Ps-Plutarch *Moral.* 12c.

463. Cf. *Agr.* 137. For the power of music to charm the soul, see P.
Boyancé, *Le Culte des Muses chez les philophes grecs* (Paris, 1937), pp. 101ff.; M.
Détienne, *Homère, Hésiode et Pythagore* (Brussels, 1962), pp. 28–29. Cf. Plato
Tim. 47 DE.

464. Cf. Plato *Gorg.* 508A: "You have failed to observe the great power
of geometrical equality amongst both gods and men: you hold that self-advan-
tage is what one ought to practice, because you neglect geometry."

465. See *The Giants* n. 51.

466. Cf. Aristotle *Rhet.* 1.1.1; 1.1.7; *SVF* 2.48, 94; 1.75. Aristotle speaks of
rhetoric as being ἀντίστροφον (counterpart), παραφυές (offshoot), μόριον
(part), and ὁμοίωμα (copy) of dialectic.

467. Cf. note 381 above.

468. Cf. *Somn.* 2.10; *Agr.* 9; *Prob.* 160; Arcesilaus (ap. Stobaeus 2.31.28):
"One may not give children immediately after their birth the fruits of Demeter, that are so lovely and nourishing, but only the nurses' milk"; I Cor.
3:1–3; Heb. 5:12.

469. Cf. *Cher.* 105; *Mut.* 228–29; *Agr.* 9; *Mig.* 29; *Spec.* 1.343; *Prob.* 160.

470. Cf. *Det.* 43.

471. Cf. *The Giants*, n. 33.

472. Cf. *SVF* 1.203: "The followers of Zeno say figuratively: character is
the fountainhead of life, from which particular actions flow."

473. Cf. *Somn.* 1.107–108.

474. Cf. *QG* 2.49; Plato *Laws* 729C.

475. Cf. Isocrates *Antid.* 267: "I would, therefore, advise young men to
spend some time on these disciplines, but not to allow their minds to be os-
sified (κατασκελετευθεῖσαν) by these barren subtleties ..."; Ps-Plutarch
Moral. 70: "And it was a clever saying of Bion, the philosopher, that, just as
the suitors, not being able to approach Penelope, consorted with her maid-
servants, so also do those who are not able to attain to philosophy wear them-

372

selves to a shadow (κατασκελετεύουσι) over the other kinds of education which have no value"; Epictetus 2.23.41: "Some persons are captivated by all these things and stay where they are; one is captivated by style, another by syllogisms, another by some other 'inn' of that sort, and staying there they molder away (κατασήπονται) as though they were among the Sirens"; Seneca *Epistles* 88 and 89.

476. Cf. *Somn.* 1.28; M. Alexandre translates "nuances."

477. Cf. *QG* 3.23; *Ebr.* 51.

478. Cf. *QG* 1.6, 3.43. This definition of philosophy is Stoic (*SVF* 2.35, 36; Cicero *Offic.* 2.5; *Tusc.* 4.26.57, 5.3.7; Seneca *Ep.* 31.7; 89.4; IV Macc. 1:16–17).

479. Cf. Aristotle *Met.* 996b11: "Inasmuch as Wisdom is the most sovereign and authoritative kind of knowledge, which the other sciences, like slaves, may not contradict." For a discussion of this formula in Philo, see Introduction, pp. 24–25.

480. The lacuna is filled by Wendland as follows: νομοθετική, δι᾽ ἧς προστάττει ἃ δεῖ, πέμπτη δ᾽ ἡ.

481. For a resolution of the apparent contradictions in Philo's descriptions of Logos and Sophia (contrast *Fug.* 97 with *Fug.* 109), see Drummond 2.207–211; Wolfson 1.258–61; Früchtel (cited in *The Giants* n.39), pp. 177–78. In *LA* 1.63, Philo explicitly identifies Sophia with Logos. Cf. Wisd. 9:1–2.

482. The derivation of θεός from τίθημι is frequent in Philo (cf. *Abr.* 121; *Conf.* 127; *Mut.* 29; *Mos.* 2.99; *QE* 2.62, 68). It was also traditional with the Greeks (Herodotus 2.52).

483. In Philo's grading of the human capacities to know God, that which is based on love is higher than that based on fear. Cf. *BT Sotah* 31a: "R. Simeon b. Eleazar says: Greater is he who acts from love than he who acts from fear, because with the latter [the merit] remains effective for a thousand generations but with the former it remains effective for two thousand generations"; *ARN* B. 10, p. 26, Schechter. Maimonides *M. T. Teshuvah* 10.6: "One cannot love God except through the knowledge with which one knows Him and the love is in proportion with the knowledge"; Aquinas *Summa Theologica*, Prima Secundae, Quaest. 27, Art. 2. Similarly, according to Spinoza, man loves God "solely because he has a knowledge of God" (*TTP* 4), but it is the third kind of knowledge, the intuitive and immediate kind of knowledge that is the source of this love, though the second kind of knowledge may lead to the third kind (*Ethics* 5.27–33). For ἀνάγκη σωφρονιζούσῃ νουθετεῖται, cf. *Legat.* 7: ἡ κόλασις νουθετεῖ καὶ σωφρονίζει.

484. A Stoic formulation (*SVF* 3.314; Cicero *Leg.* 1.6.18). Cf. *LA* 1.94; *Deus* 53; *Mig.* 130; *Jos.* 29; *Mos.* 2.4; *Praem.* 55.

485. Naḥmanides (to Exod. 20:8) connects the positive commandments with the love of God, and the negative with the fear of God, and asserts that the former are therefore superior to the latter. Philo's scheme is somewhat different, since he makes the νομοθετική, or Legislative Power, spring from

the Regent Power, which is connected with the fear of God, but, like Nahmanides, he rates the positive commandments above the negative.

486. There is a verbal connection between ἵλεως and ἱλαστήριον as
there appears to be between the Hebrew *kapparah* and *kapporet*, although the
etymology of the technical term *kapporet*, ark-cover, remains uncertain.

487. Reading with the manuscripts ἀφιδρυμένος. Wendland's modification ἐφιδρυμένος is unnecessary. ἀφιδρυμένος contains the notion of ἀφ-
ίδρυμα, image, and thus carries on the thought of εἰκών. (See Colson, LCL
5.584).

488. Cf. *Deus* 116; *Spec.* 1.300; *QE* 2.68.

489. Cf. *Mut.* 225; *Deus* 75.

490. Cf. *Sacr.* 6–7; *Mig.* 29.

491. Cf. *Mut.* 39, where the wise men are described as inspired by an
ἔνθεον μανίαν, a God-inspired frenzy.

492. Cicero complains that "far too much attention is devoted by the
Stoics, principally by Chrysippus, in drawing an analogy between diseases of
the soul and diseases of the body" (*Tusc.* 4.23). Avoiding their exaggerations,
he notes how efficacious is the medicine applied by philosophy to the diseases
of the soul (4.58), and insists that human nature has in itself all means of calm-
ing the soul (4.62). In a paean to philosophy, he exclaims: "O philosophy,
thou guide of life, o thou explorer of virtue and expeller of vice! Without thee
what could have become not only of me but of the life of man altogether?"
(5.5). Similarly, in giving a few practical hints as to how a man can prevent
himself from becoming a victim of his passions, Spinoza refers to them as
"remedies against the emotions (*Ethics* 5. Praef., end), and the irrational emotions themselves are described by him as a sickness of the mind." (*Eth.* 5.
Prop. 10, Schol.).

493. Cf. *Conf.* 146; *Mig.* 174; *Somn.* 1.66, 117, 148, 238–41; *QG* 3.34.

494. A common division in Greek educational theory. Cf. Plato *Meno* 70
A; Protagoras DK. B.3; *Dissoi Logoi* 6 DK 2.414; Isocrates *Antid.* 186–88; Aristotle *Polit.* 1332a38; *EN* 1103a14; 1170a 11–12; D.L. 5.18; *SVF* 3.214; Antiochus of Ascalon (Cicero *Acad. Post.* 1.20, 38); Arius Didymus (Stobaeus 2.38.3,
2.51.5); Ps-Plutarch *Moral.* 2AB, 3A; Plutarch *Moral.* 443C; Albinus *Did.*
182.3–5; Apuleius *De Plat.* 2.222–23; Maximus of Tyre *Or.* 1.5d; Clement
Strom. 1.31.5, 1.34.1.

495. Cf. *Somn.* 1.167–69.

496. Cf. *BR* 44.12, Th–Alb:433: "God said to Abraham: You are a prophet, not an astrologer"; *BT Nedarim* 31a: "God said to Abraham: Go forth from
your astrological speculations, Israel is not subject to planetary influences";
Jubilees 12:17. For the view that the Chaldean doctrine here criticized is to be
traced to Aristotle's early work *De Philosophia*, see J. Pépin, *Théologie cosmique
et Théologie chrétienne* (Paris, 1964), pp. 286–91.

497. Cf. *Virt.* 212–19.

498. See Selections from Philo, n. 454.

499. A proverbial expression, used by Philo also at *Somn.* 1.44; *Decal.* 84. Cf. Plato *Phaedo* 99D.

500. Cf. *Gig.* 47–60; Wisd. 13:6. We may recall the beautiful verses of the Jewish philosopher and poet Ibn Gabirol (eleventh century) in his famous poem *The Royal Crown:* "Thou art God, and all creatures are thy servants and worshipers; and thy glory is undiminished in spite of those who worship aught save thee—for the aim of all is to reach unto thee. But they are as blind ones, their faces are set eagerly on the King's Highway, but they have lost their way" (stanza 8). In Islam, the Ikhwan As-Safā (tenth century) held that there was an element of truth in every religion, and therefore believed that everyone should be left free to embrace the religion he chooses (*Rasā'il* 3.86–90; 4.54–65). This trend of thought had already been a distinctive characteristic of the *Bhagavad Gita* (between fifth and second centuries BCE). The Supreme Being, according to the Hindu view, permits and takes benign delight in all the different illusions that beset the beclouded mind of man: "Whatever form [whatever God], a devotee with faith desires to honor, that very faith do I confirm in him [making it] unswerving and secure. Firm-established in that faith he seeks to reverence that [God] and thence he gains his desires, though it is I who am the true dispenser" (7.21–22, trans. Zaehner [Oxford 1969]). Cf. the remark of Maximus of Tyre (second century CE): "If a Greek is stirred to the remembrance of God by the art of Pheidias, an Egyptian by paying worship to animals, another man by a river, another by fire—I have no anger for their divergences; only let them know, let them love, let them remember" (2.10; p. 29.9 Hobein).

501. Cf. *Post.* 88; *Virt.* 184; *Praem.* 81; *Prob.* 96; *QG* 4.110.

502. Cf. *Spec.* 2.62.

503. Cf. *QG* 1.49. For a full discussion of this theme in Philo, see Baer.

504. The division of virtue into four classes goes back to Plato (*Phaedo* 69C; *Rep.* 427Eff.; *Laws* 631C; cf. Aeschylus *Seven against Thebes* 610; Xenophon *Mem.* 3.9.1–5, 4.6.1–12; Isocrates *De Pace* 63; Demosthenes 18.215). Two of the cardinal virtues are dealt with by Aristotle in *EN* 3, and the other two in *EN* 5 and 6, but he has no fourfold scheme as such. The Epicureans similarly rejected the cardinal division, though they were at pains to show how all four virtues minister to pleasure (Cicero *Fin.* 1.42–54). The Stoics, however, accepted it together with the Platonic notion that they implied one another ($\dot{\alpha}\nu\tau\alpha\kappa o\lambda o\nu\theta\dot{\iota}\alpha$) and Zeno expressed three of the cardinal virtues in terms of the fourth, wisdom (*SVF* 3.255, 256–61). Philo repeats the fourfold division, though he sometimes substitutes $\epsilon\dot{\nu}\sigma\dot{\epsilon}\beta\epsilon\iota\alpha$ for $\varphi\rho\dot{o}\nu\eta\sigma\iota\varsigma$ (*Spec.* 4.147; *Decal.* 119). Like Wisd. 8:7, he derives them from the Wisdom or Logos of God. (The actual phrase "the cardinal virtues" seems to derive from St. Ambrose *In Lucam* 5. Cf. also IV Macc. 1:18, 5:23.

505. A reminiscence of Prov. 8:30.

NOTES

506. Cf. *LA* 1.66–69, 72; *Post.* 128; *Sacr.* 84; *Deus* 95.

507. The words "on your breast" are not in the Hebrew.

508. Pleasure as an irrational emotion ($\pi\acute{\alpha}\theta$ος) must be distinguished from its innocent sense of "agreeable physical feelings." See Introduction, p. 31.

509. Cf. Aristotle *EN* 2.1105a 9–11.

510. Cf. *LA* 3.246.

511. Cf. Plato *Rep.* 612B; Aristotle *EN* 10.6.1176b, 8–9; D.L. 1.89, 127; *M. Abot* 1.3; *Sifre Deut.* 306; *BT Ta*ᶜ*anit* 7a.

512. Cf. *Sobr.* 15.

513. Cf. *Deus* 150; *Ebr.* 200–202. On the question of external goods, see my "Philo's Ethical Theory," *ANRW* (forthcoming) and Dillon, pp. 146–48.

514. Cf. *Conf.* 18ff.; *Ebr.* 201.

515. Cf. *Mig.* 86–88.

516. Homer Od. 14.258.

517. Proper motivation for a right action was especially emphasized by the Stoics (*SVF* 3.516–17; Cicero *Fin.* 3.59. Cf. *LA* 1.99, 3.210; *Cher.* 14; *Decal* 177).

518. A variation of the example given by Plato *Rep.* 331C–332B, and Aristotle *EN* 5.8.1135b3ff. Philo gives the same example again at *Plant.* 103; *Cher.* 14; *Spec.* 4.67. Cf. *Decal.* 172 ("using honesty as a screen for dishonesty").

519. Nietzsche emphasized the same point. "Nietzsche found it ridiculous to consider a Cesare Borgia unhealthy in contrast to an emasculated man who is alleged to be healthy (J 197). When Nietzsche was criticized on that account, he clarified his point in another book, three years later (G IX 37). He now explained that he did not favor 'the abolition of all decent feelings' but that he was not sure 'whether we have really become more moral.' Perhaps we have just become emasculated, and our failure to do evil is to be ascribed merely to our inability to do evil" (W. Kaufmann, *Nietzsche* [New York, 1968], p. 224). Cf. Clement of Alexandria *Strom.* 4.36.2.

520. "The use in boxing of the *caestus* or leathern thong loaded with lead or iron is best known from the description in Virgil's *Aen.* 5.405ff. Mr. Whitaker's ingenious suggestion of $\sigma\iota\delta\eta\rho o\tilde{\upsilon}\nu$ $\tau\rho o\pi\acute{o}\nu$ for $\sigma\iota\delta\acute{\eta}\rho o\upsilon$ $\tau\rho\acute{o}\pi o\nu$ ('like iron') may perhaps be questioned on the ground that $\tau\rho o\pi\acute{o}\varsigma$ is the thong used for fastening the oar to the thole. But it may have been used more generally, and if so gives an excellent sense. The construction of the ordinary reading is not quite clear" (Colson, LCL 3.491).

521. The works of Philo teem with the terminology of the games and with the picture of the *Agon* of virtue. For the *Agon* of virtue as holy, cf. *Mig.* 200; *Mut.* 81; *Praem.* 4, 52; *Abr.* 48; IV Macc. 17:11–16; *Wisd.* 4:2. See V. C. Pfitzner, *Paul and the Agon Motif* (Leiden, 1967), pp. 38–48.

522. Cf. *Deus* 120; *Plant.* 168; *Her.* 49, 290; *Fug.* 146; *Abr.* 270–71; *Praem.* 112; *Legat.* 142; *QE* 2.20. We have here a very widespread literary theme. Cf.

376

Menander Fr. 553, Körte: "Not from white heads has wisdom always sprung; Nature gives it to some men while they're young" (J. M. Edmonds, *The Fragments of Attic Comedy* [Leiden, 1957], 3. B810); Cicero *Tusc.* 5.5, 1.45; Seneca *Ep.* 78.28 (Quoting Posidonius): "A single day among the learned lasts longer than the longest life of the ignorant"; 93.2; Plutarch *Moral.* 111D; Virgil Aen. 9.311; Wisd. 4:8; *BT Kiddushin* 32b. See E. R. Curtius, *European Literature and the Latin Middle Ages* (New York, 1953), pp. 98–101.

523. Cf. *LA* 2.59; *QG* 4.201.

524. Cf. *Plant.* 44–45; *Congr.* 36; *QG* 4.165. For the theme of ἁπλότης in Philo and elsewhere, see J. Amstutz, ΑΠΛΟΤΗΣ (Bonn, 1968).

525. An allusion to the unquoted part of the text: "And they shall enslave them, and afflict them, and humble them four hundred years."

526. For the Stoic doctrine of the four passions, see *SVF* 1.211; 3.386ff.

527. For συστέλλεται, cf. *SVF* 3.391: λύπη μὲν οὖν ἐστιν ἄλογος συστολή.

528. Cf. Democritus DK B.62: "Virtue consists, not in avoiding wrongdoing, but in having no wish thereto"; *BT Yoma* 29a: "Lustful thoughts are even worse than lustful deeds"; *Shabbat* 64a: "Though we escaped from sin, yet we did not escape from meditating upon sin."

529. Reading with Colson γέρα ὄντα instead of γέμοντα of the manuscripts.

530. Cf. *Deus* 19; *Prov.* 2.84. The same sentiment is clearly expressed by Plato *Laws* 903 BD: "Let us persuade the young man by arguments that all things have been arranged by the overseer of the universe for the security and excellence of the whole. . . . Each of these parts down to the smallest feature of its condition or activity is under the direction of ruling powers, which have perfected every minutest detail. And you, you stubborn man, are one of these parts, minute though you are, which always contributes to the good of the whole. . . . creation occurs not for your sake but you occur for the sake of the universe. . . . You are peeved because you fail to realize how what is best for you is best for the universe as well as yourself." Cf. M. Aurelius 9.39: "Either there is one intelligent source, from which as in one body all after things proceed—and the part ought not to grumble at what is done in the interests of the whole or there are atoms, and nothing but a medley and a dispersion"; Plotinus 2.9.9.75.

531. Cf. *Jos.* 26. Plutarch (*Moral.* 102D) advocates μετριοπάθεια in bereavements in similar terms and proceeds to quote Crantor the Academician's Περὶ πένθους to the same effect. The same passage from Crantor is quoted by Cicero *Tusc.* 3.12. (Cf. Plato Rep. 603E) Since Philo's highest ethical ideal is ἀπάθεια we should have expected him to have described Abraham's grief and tears at his wife's death as constituting nothing more than "a sting and minor soul contractions" (*morsus* [δηγμός] *et contractionculae* [συστολαί] *quaedam animi:* Cicero *Tusc.* 3.82), in accordance with Stoic teaching, but he

may have felt such technical language to be out of place here. Although the Stoics did not consider δηγμός (compunction) to be a *pathos*, neither did they consider it a *eupatheia*, but placed it in the category of an automatic bodily reaction such as pallor, shuddering, or contraction of the brow (Epictetus, Fr. 9 (180); Seneca *De Ira* 2.3; *De Consol. ad Polyb.* 17.2; 18.5–6; Ep. 57.3; 71.29. 99.15). (Although Epictetus ordinarily speaks of δηγμός as a *pathos*, he does, on one occasion, describe it as an automatic bodily reaction [3.24.108].) The Stoics were frequently attacked on this account for fudging and resorting to linguistic quibbles in order to escape from reality (Plutarch *Moral.* 449a). Philo, on the other hand, classified it as a *eupatheia* (*QG* 2.57). He was either following some minor Stoic disciple who, sensitive to the criticisms hurled at the Stoics, had elevated δηγμός into a *eupatheia*, or else he simply did it on his own. He could therefore have described Abraham's behavior in this case as another example of his *apatheia/eupatheia*, but the technicalities involved in such an explanation probably deterred him, and he preferred to invoke the Peripatetic ideal of *metriopatheia* instead. For the Stoic theory of *apatheia/eupatheia*, see Introduction, p. 30. See also Bréhier, p. 254, n. 7; A. Bonhöffer, *Epictet und die Stoa* (Stuttgart, 1890), pp. 307–11; J. Dillon and A. Terian, "Philo and the Stoic Doctrine of Εὐπάθειαι," *SP* (1976–1977): 17–24.

532. Cf. *Op.* 83; *QG* 2.27.

533. Cf. *Virt.* 13.

534. Cf. *Shir HaShirim R* 1.2.2: "Let Him kiss me with the kisses of His mouth." R. Yohanan said: "An angel carried the utterances [at Mount Sinai] from before the Holy One, blessed be He, each one in turn, and brought it to each one of the Israelites and said to him, 'Do you take upon yourself this commandment?' ... The Rabbis, however, say: The commandment itself went in turn to each of the Israelites and said to him, 'Do you undertake to keep me?' ... He would reply, 'Yes, yes,' and straightway the commandment kissed him on the mouth and taught him Torah"; *PRK* Piska 12, Braude-Kapstein, p. 249: "R. Levi said: The Holy One appeared to them as though He were a statue with faces on every side [a *Janus Quadrifons*], so that though a thousand men might be looking at the statue, they would be led to believe that it was looking at each one of them. So, too, when the Holy One spoke, each and every person in Israel could say, 'The Divine Word is addressing me.' Note that Scripture does not say, 'I am the Lord your God,' but 'I am the Lord Thy God, [thy very own God].' "

535. Cf. *QG* 2.60; *Det.* 164; *Spec.* 4.414.

536. Cf. *Spec.* 3.83; Plato *Laws* 869B: "For outrage he will be liable to most heavy penalties, and likewise for impiety and sacrilege (ἱεροσυλίας), since he has robbed his parent of life (ψυχὴν συλήσας); 931E: "For the shrine which is an ancestor is marvellous in our eyes, far beyond that which is a lifeless thing."

537. The theme of man's kinship (συγγένεια) with God occurs in Plato

and is a characteristic teaching of the Stoa. Plato writes in *Tim.* 90A: "We declare that God has given to each of us, as his daemon, that kind of soul which is housed in the top of our body and which raises us—seeing that we are not an earthly but a heavenly plant—up from earth toward our kindred (ξυγγένειαν) in the heaven." Cf. I *Alcib.* 133BC; *Protag.* 322A; *Tim.* 41D, 90C; *Laws* 726A; Posidonius F 187, 6, Kidd: "[The cause of the *pathē* is] not following the daemon within us which is akin and of like nature with the one that orders the whole universe." Epictetus 1.9; 2.8.11 ("You are a fragment [ἀπόσπασμα] of God ... why then are you ignorant of your own kinship?"); 3.13.14; Sext. *Math.* 7.93; Plotinus 6.9.8.29; Wisd. 8:17, 2:23. Diogenes of Apollonia had already taught that "the air within us has perception because it is a small part (μόριον) of the God" (DK A.19). See E. des Places, *Syngeneia* (Paris, 1964).

538. Cf. *Praem.* 92; *Spec.* 1.317; *Mos.* 1.314.

539. A reminiscence of Job 1:21.

540. The sectarian law of *CD* (11.12: "No one shall urge on his servant, his maidservant, or his hireling on the Sabbath") agrees with Philo's proscription of a slave's doing any work at all for the master, even if it did not violate the Sabbath, a view entirely unknown to Tannaitic Halakah. See S. Belkin, *Philo and the Oral Law* (Cambridge, Mass., 1940), p. 203; L. H. Schiffman, *The Halakah at Qumran* (Leiden, 1975), pp. 120–21.

541. For a discussion of Philo's views on slavery, see my "Philo's Ethical Theory," *ANRW* (forthcoming).

542. This was the Stoic view (Cicero *Fin.* 3.67; D.L. 7.129), but is in agreement with biblical teaching (Gen. 1:26).

543. Cf. *Spec.* 2.79–85, 89–90, 123; 3.137; *Cont.* 70.

544. See Exod. 23:11; Lev. 25:6.

545. Cf. *Spec.* 2.138, 141; 4.97, 219–25; *Mos.* 1.249; *Virt.* 28, 51.

546. On the question of the *telos,* or purpose of life, Philo follows Eudorus's adoption of "likeness to God" (ὁμοίωσις θεῷ). Cf. Aelian *VH* 12.59; Longinus 1.2; Strabo 10.3.9. (Since Philo's discourse on Nature often passes over imperceptibly into speaking about God, he could hold on equally well to the Stoic *telos* formula of consonance with Nature.) Theiler traces this to an anonymous *Life of Pythagoras* (ap. Photius 249) dependent on Eudorus. Cf. *Fug.* 63, where he quotes Plato *Theaet.* 176 AB; *Laws* 716CD; *Op.* 144; *Virt.* 8, 168, 204–205; *Spec.* 4.188; *Decal.* 73; *LA* 2.4; *QG* 4.188. The idea of *imitatio Dei* was also distinctively Jewish. See *Mek. Shirta* 3, Lauterbach 2.25; *BT Shabbat* 113b; *Sotah* 14a; A. Marmorstein, *Studies in Jewish Theology*, ed. J. Rabbinowitz and M. Loew (London, 1950), pp. 106–21; S. Schechter, *Some Aspects of Rabbinic Theology* (New York, 1936), pp. 199ff. See W. Theiler, *Untersuchungen zur antiken Literatur* (Berlin, 1970), pp. 494–98; Dillon, pp. 145–46.

547. Cf. *Post.* 140, 150–51; *Prob.* 13.

548. Play of words in Greek, βραχίων, shoulder, and βραχύς, petty.

NOTES

549. Cf. Plato *Rep.* 411B: ἕως ἂν ἐκτήξῃ τὸν θυμὸν καὶ ἐκτέμῃ ὥσπερ νεῦρα ἐκ τῆς ψυχῆς.

550. Cf. *LA* 3.147.

551. ἐπεντρώσεις, delicacies, is an Epicurean term (Fr. 22, Arrighetti [413, Usener]).

552. Cf. *BT Ḥagigah* 12b: "Zebul is that [firmament] in which [the heavenly] Jerusalem and the Temple and the Altar are built, and Michael, the great Prince, stands and offers up thereon an offering daily. What does he offer? . . . the souls of righteous men" (following the reading given by the BaḤ, [acronym for R. Joel Sirkes]).

553. On Philo's conception of Moses, see W. A. Meeks, *The Prophet-King* (Leiden, 1967), pp. 100–31; C. R. Holladay, *Theios Aner in Hellenistic Judaism* (Missoula, 1977), pp. 103–98.

554. The LXX reads "my servant" (τοῦ παιδός μου), which Philo uses in *LA* 3.27. The notion of friendship with God is an ancient and widespread motif. Cf. Isa. 41:8; II Chron. 20:7, 22:7, Vulgate; Exod. 32:11, LXX; Jubilees 30:20–21; *Apoc. Abraham* 9 and 10; *Test. Abraham* A 15.16; Wisd. 7:27; James 2:23; *Sib Or* 2.245; Qur'an 4:124; Philo *Mos.* 1.156; *Her.* 21; *Prob.* 44; *Abr.* 129; *LA* 3.204; *Cont.* 90; *BT Menaḥot* 53b; *Tosef. Berakot* 7.13; *Sifre Num.* 115 and *Sifre Deut.* 352, Finkelstein, p. 409; *Mek.* on Exod. 12:11 and 15:17. In Greek literature, cf. Plato *Laws* 716 CD; *Tim.* 53D; *Symp.* 193B; *Rep.* 621C; Epictetus 2.17.29, 4.3.9; D.L. 6.37, 72; etc. For further references, see Winston, pp. 188–89.

555. For the paradoxical nature of the wise man, see *SVF* 3.589ff. Cf. *Post.* 138; *Agr.* 41; *Plant.* 67–68; *Somn.* 21243–44; *Prob.* 19–22.

556. Cf. *Somn.* 1.177.

557. Cf. *BT Berakot* 28b. For the many rabbinic parallels to the great impact the righteous have on their environment, see R. Mach, *Der Zaddik in Talmud und Midrasch* (Leiden, 1957), pp. 117–24.

558. Cf. *Sacr.* 1.21., 124–25; *QG* 2.11, 3.44; *QE* 1.21.

559. Cf. *Op.* 82; Plato *Tim.* 47BE.

560. Cf. note 205 above.

561. Cf. *Gig.* 48; *Abr.* 27; *Post.* 24; *Somn.* 1.174; *QG* 3.39.

562. See *The Giants*, n. 3. Cf. Seneca *Ep.* 42.1 (The wise man, like the Phoenix, appears only once in five hundred years); *Tranq. An.* 7.4; *SVF* 3.545: "Wherefore an account of their extreme magnitude and beauty we seem to be stating things which are like fictions and not in accordance with man or human nature."

563. For Jewish and Muslim legends of hidden righteous ones, see G. Scholem, *Judaica* (Frankfurt am Main, 1963), pp. 216–25; Cf. R. A. Nicholson, *The Mystics of Islam* (London, 1914), pp. 123ff. Cf. *Abr.* 22–24; *Prob.* 63–64, 72.

564. Gen. 6:9, cf. *Deus* 117.

565. For a discussion of *eupatheia*, see Introduction, p. 30.

NOTES

566. Cf. *LA* 3.86; *Spec.* 2.55, 185.

567. Cf. *Her.* 253; *Det.* 122.

568. "On the value of πρόληψις *(praemeditatio)* as alleviating λύπη *(aegritudo)*, see the discussion in Cicero *Tusc.* 3.24–34 and 52ff., where the opinion is represented as Cyrenaic in opposition to the Epicurean that it was futile to dwell on evils beforehand. But it was also to some extent a Stoic view *(SVF* 3.482)" (Colson, LCL 7.624). Seneca expresses it well: "The wise man comes to everything with the proviso 'if nothing happens to prevent it'; therefore we say that he succeeds in everything and nothing happens contrary to his expectation, because he presupposes that something can intervene to prevent his design" *(Benefic.* 4.34; cf. *Tranq. An.* 13.2–3; *Ad Marc.* 9–11; *Ad Polyb.* 11, 1; *Ep.* 63, 15, 99.32, 107.3–4. See C. G. Grollios, *Seneca's Ad Marciam, Tradition and Originality* (Athens, 1956), pp. 44ff.; C. E. Manning, "Seneca's 98th Letter and the *Praemeditatio Futuri Mali,*" *Mnemosyne* 29, fasc. 3:301–04.

569. Cf. *Mut.* 237ff.

570. Following Colson: "The phrase as it stands is an obscure, though perhaps not impossible, way of expressing what I have translated it by, but the change of καθάπερ into καθ' ὅπερ would make it feasible" (LCL 8.276–77, n. 3).

571. The Sorites was "a set of statements which proceed, step by step, through the force of logic or reliance upon a succession of indisputable facts, to a climactic conclusion, each statement picking up the last key word (or key phrase) of the preceding one" (H. A. Fischel, "The Use of Sorites in the Tannaitic Period," *HUCA* 44 [1973]: 119–51). For detailed illustration, see Winston, pp. 154–55. (Cf. Cicero *Leg.* 1.7.23; *Fin* 4.50; M. Aurelius 12.30; Epictetus 1.14.10.)

572. Colson translates: "known also by the appropriate name of the Seven" (" 'appropriate,' because ἑπτά is supposed to be derived from σεμνός and σεβασμός; cf. *Op.* 127") (See his detailed discussion, LCL 9.512–13.)

573. Following Colson's suggested reading: ἐν ᾗ πρεσβεύεται λόγων ἔργα.

574. Cf. *Spec.* 3.100. See Colson's extended discussion LCL 7.635–36.

575. On Philo's understanding of the term "Gymnosophists," see LCL 9.513–14.

576. For the relation of this description of the Essenes to those in the *Hypothetica* (11.148), see Colson's extended note, LCL 9. 514–16.

577. See *The Giants*, n. 12.

578. Cf. *Plant.* 158; *Mig.* 201.

579. γνήσιος is here used of children, not as usual in antithesis to νόθος, but in the literal as opposed to the figurative sense. Cf. *Legat.* 62, 71; *Spec.* 4.184 (Colson, LCL 9.60, n. a).

580. Cf. *QG* 4.206. Philo is here reflecting Stoic doctrine. See Sextus *Math.* 7.38 (= *SVF* 2.132): "Hence, too, its [truth's] possessor is a Sage (for he

possesses knowledge of things true), and he never speaks falsely, even if he says what is false, because he does not utter it from an evil but from a cultivated disposition. For just as the doctor who says something false respecting the cure of his patient . . . is not lying though he says something false (for in saying it he has regard to the cure of the person in his charge)—and just as the best commanders, when, as often, they concoct messages from allied States for the encouragement of the soldiers under their command, say what is false yet are not liars because they do not do this with a bad intention—and just as the grammarian, although when giving an example of a solecism he utters a solecism, is not guilty of bad grammar . . . so also the Sage . . . will at times say something false but will never lie because his mental disposition is not assenting to what is false." Cf. *SVF* 3.554, 177. See also A. A. Long, "Language and Thought in Stoicism," *Problems in Stoicism*, ed. A. A. Long (London, 1971), pp. 98ff.; S. Lieberman, *Greek in Jewish Palestine*, (New York, 1942) pp. 142–43.

581. Cf. Plato *Gorg.* 493A; *Cratyl.* 400B. There is a veiled reference here to that unpleasant story about the Etruscans that they tied live men to corpses as a punishment (Aristotle *Protrep.* fr. 10b, Ross). (Noted by Leisegang in his note to *Gig.* 15; cf. Dillon, p. 149). Cf. *Deus* 2; *Conf.* 106; *Mig.* 16; *Fug.* 54–55; *Jos.* 71; *QG* 4.152.

582. Cf. *LA* 2.8, 71; *Gig.* 38, 43.

583. Cf. *Ebr.* 69–71; *Deus* 2; *Her.* 64–66.

584. Cf. M. Aurelius 4.41: "Thou art a little soul bearing up a corpse, as Epictetus said" (not found in the latter's extant works).

585. Cf. *Agr.* 25.

586. Cf. *Gig.* 29–31, 34–35, 38, 43; *Cher.* 40–41.

587. Omitting τῶν after τινὰ with HL (Colson, LCL 2.214, n. a).

588. Cf. Plato *Symp.* 205E: "For men are prepared to have their own feet and hands cut off if they feel these belongings to be harmful"; Matt 5:29.

589. Cf. Plutarch *Moral.* 505D: "Zeno the philosopher [of Elea] . . . bit his tongue through and spat it out at the despot."

590. Cf. *Praem.* 31–32; *Somn.* 2.164–65; *QG* 2.68, 4.188.

591. Cf. Plato *Soph.* 264A: "Thought is conversation of the soul with itself"; *Theaet.* 189E.

592. That is, Plato. The allusion is to the *Timaeus*, where ὕλη is described as "Mother and Receptacle of this generated world" (51A), and as "nurse of all becoming" (49A). As Heinemann has correctly noted, however, Philo's description does not reproduce the Platonic view accurately, since Plato had applied the terms "mother" and "nurse" only to the Receptacle and not to sensible matter.

593. Cf. *Fug.* 14.

594. See note 468 above.

595. The section that follows is in the style of the diatribe, the popular

NOTES

moral invective so characteristic of the Hellenistic period. See T. G. Burgess, "Epideictic Literature," *Studies in Classical Philology* 3 (1902): 89–261; P. Wendland, *Die hellenistisch-römische Kultur in ihren Beziehungen zu Judentum und Christentum* (Tübingen, 1912), pp. 39–50; *Philo und die kynisch-stoische Diatribe* (Berlin, 1895); R. Bultmann, *Der Stil der paulinischen Predigt und die kynisch-stoische Diatribe* (Göttingen, 1910); H. Thyen (cited in n. 321), pp. 9, 63.

596. Homer, Odyssey 21.294.

597. Cf. Dio Chrysostom 20, where we are told that it is illegitimate to flee the opportunity to serve one's country and one's friends: "The mind should accustom itself to do and think what is essential to it everywhere, even in a perfect din as well as in perfect quiet. Otherwise seclusion and quiet offer no advantage and no greater safeguard, for men who are fools, to keep them from conceiving and committing many strange and wicked deeds" (20.26); Seneca *Ep.* 56. See Bréhier, p. 268.

598. Cf. *Mig.* 208–209; *Mut.* 39ff.

599. An allusion to Plato *Phaedr.* 247A. Cf. *Spec.* 2.249; *Prob.* 13.

600. See *Theaetetus* 176AB.

601. Cf. *Abr.* 87.

602. "In the recurrent *topos* of the flight of the soul through the universe . . . we can trace a growing contempt for all that may be done and suffered beneath the moon" (Dodds, pp. 7ff.). Cf. Cicero *Somn. Scip.* 3.16; Seneca *NQ* 1, praef. 8; Ps-Aristotle *De Mundo* 1, 391a 18ff. To Gregory of Nyssa, human affairs are but the play of children building sand castles which are promptly washed away. See Dodds, p. 10; Festugière, 2.449ff.

603. Cf. *Mut.* 45; *Ebr.* 80–87; *QG* 3.42.

604. Cf. *Spec.* 4.168; *Deus* 144ff.; *Post.* 101; *Gig.* 64; *Mig.* 146–47.

605. Philo frequently emphasizes the ideal of ὀλιγοδεία, frugal contentment, for the less one needs the closer one is to God. Cf. Xenophon *Mem.* 1.6.10, 1.3.6; Musonius Rufus, Fr. 18a, Lutz; *Somn.* 1.97, 120–126, 2.47–64; *Praem.* 99–100; *QG* 2.67; *Ebr.* 214–15; *Cont.* 37–39. For a detailed analysis of this theme and the parallel Cynic and Stoic sources, see Wendland (cited in n. 595).

606. Cf. *Cont.* 18.

607. Contrast *Plant.* 166, where it is said that the wise man will indulge in heavy drinking, though in the more moderate manner of the ancients. Cf. *Legat.* 82; *QG* 2.68.

608. Cf. *Her.* 45–46.

609. Cf. Josephus *Ag. Ap.* 1.213.

610. Cf. Plato *Theaet.* 183D; Lucian *Piscator* 9.

611. Cf. Plato *Laws* 656D, 799A, 819A.

612. These words are reminiscent of what was said of Pythagoras: "Aristotle relates in his work on the Pythagorean philosophy that the following division was preserved by the Pythagoreans as one of their greatest secrets—

that there are three kinds of rational living creatures—gods, men, and beings like Pythagoras" (Aristotle, *On the Pythagoreans*, Fr. 2, Ross). Cf. Plato *Soph.* 216C: "And though I do not think he is a god at all, I certainly do think he is divine, for I give that epithet to all philosophers"; Philo *Virt.* 177. See the literature cited in n. 553.

613. Cf. *Prob.* 96; Iamblichus *VP* 176.

614. Cf. *Abr.* 235.

615. Exod. 33:11.

616. Exod. 20:21. Cf. *Mut.* 7; *Post.* 14; *Gig.* 54. Cf. *The Giants*, n. 47.

617. A saying of Menander, Fr. 724, Kock; cited by Philo at *Abr.* 134.

618. Cf. Josephus *Ag. Ap.* 2.277–79; Luke 16:17; Matt. 5:18.

619. Cf. Josephus *Ag. Ap.* 279–85.

620. For the meaning of ἐνηχεῖν, see Colson, LCL 5.588.

621. Reminiscent of *CH* 13 (Asclepius).

622. Cf. *Spec.* 1.66–97; Josephus *Ant.* 3.179–87; Wisd. 18:24. Plutarch 382C; Heraclitus Rhetor *Quaest. Hom.* 43. For a comparison between Philo's and Josephus's accounts, see Früchtel (cited in *The Giants*, n. 39), pp. 98–100; J. Daniélou, "Le symbolique cosmique au Temple de Jérusalem chez Philo et Josèphe," *Symbolisme cosmique des monuments religieux* (Paris, 1953), pp. 1–65.

623. Retaining the μιμημάτων of the manuscripts with Colson.

624. The Son here is the World. Cf. *Spec.* 1.96; *Deus* 31.

625. "The Prophets look back to the past, the time of Israel's youth in the desert, when she was betrothed to Yahweh (Jer. 2:2; Hos. 13:5; Amos 2:10). They condemn the comfort and luxury of urban life in their own day (Amos 3:15; 6:8), and see salvation in a return at some future date, to the life of the desert, envisaged as a golden age (Hos. 2:16–17; 12:10). . . . But nomadism itself is not the ideal; rather it is that purity of religious life and that faithfulness to the Covenant, which was associated in Israel's mind with its former life in the desert. . . . We shall encounter this mystique of the desert again in the last days of Judaism, among the sectaries of Qumran." (R. de Vaux, *Ancient Israel* [New York, Toronto, London, 1961], p. 14). See also the critical discussion by S. Talmon, "The 'Desert Motif' in the Bible and in Qumran Literature," *Biblical Motifs* (Cambridge, 1966), pp. 31–63.

626. For τῦφος, vanity, cf. Sextus *Math.* 8.5 (Monimus the Cynic said "that 'All things are vanity' (τῦφον), that is to say, a vain fancy (οἴησις) that non-existents are existent"). Cf. Kohelet 1:2.

627. See *The Giants*, n. 49.

628. The rabbis similarly derived many teachings from one verse: "In R. Ishmael's School it was taught: 'And like a hammer that breaketh the rock in pieces' (Jer. 23:29), i.e., just as [the rock] is split into many splinters, so also may one Biblical verse convey many teachings" (*BT Sanhedrin* 34a).

629. See n. 534.

630. Cf. *Sobr.* 54; *QG* 2.75, 3.39.

NOTES

631. A Platonic phrase (*Tim.* 69D).

632. Although in reality only an aspect of the Logos (the κολαστικὴ or βασιλικὴ δύναμις), there are passages in Philo, an author who loves to multiply images, where Justice as assessor (πάρεδρος), surveyor, and ruler of all things, seems, as here, to acquire an independent existence (*Mut.* 194; *Jos.* 48; *Mos.* 2153; *Spec.* 4.201). Cf. Wisd. 9:4, 11.20; Hesiod *Op.* 259; Pindar *Olympia* 8.22 (where Themis is designated as the *paredros* of Zeus; Euripides *Medea* 843; Sophocles *Oedipus Coloneus* 1382; Aelius Aristides *Orationes* 2; *Orphic Hymns* 62; Plato *Laws* 715E, 872E; *Epinomis* 988E; Ps-Demosthenes (= *Orphicorum Fragmenta* 23, Kern) 25.11. See R. Hirzel, *Themis, Dike und Verwandtes* (Leipzig, 1907), pp. 138ff., 412ff.; Bréhier, pp. 149ff.

633. πρύτανις is often applied to the gods. Cf. *Somn.* 1.142 (τὸν παμπρύτανιν); Pindar *Pythia* 6.24; Aeschylus *Prom.* 170. Wisd. 13:2 applies it to the sun and moon (cf. Plutarch *Moral.* 601A).

634. Circumcision was frequently the target of pagan ridicule. Josephus tells us that Apion derided the practice of circumcision, which was rather stupid of him, since the Egyptian priests themselves practiced it. "I cannot, therefore, but regard the penalty which Apion paid for maligning his country's laws as just and appropriate. An ulcer on his person rendered circumcision essential; the operation brought no relief, gangrene set in, and he died in terrible tortures" (*Ag. Ap.* 2.137–43). Martial addresses a Jewish rival four times as "circumcised poet" *(verpus poeta)* (11.94; cf. 7.30). Namatianus believed that circumcision was at the root of all the folly of the Jews (*De Reditu Suo* 1.389). Juvenal thinks that a Roman has reached his lowest point when, after adopting diverse Jewish customs he has himself circumcised (14.99). Strabo looked on circumcision as one of the fruits of the superstition into which the Jewish religion had degenerated (16.2.37). See J. N. Sevenster, *The Roots of Pagan Anti-Semitism in the Ancient World* (Leiden, 1975), pp. 132–35.

635. Tacitus nevertheless remarks that the Jews adopted circumcision to distinguish themselves from other peoples by this difference (*Hist.* 5.5). Josephus quotes the passage in which Herodotus discusses the origins of circumcision: "The Colchians, the Egyptians and the Ethiopians are the only nations with whom the practice of circumcision is primitive. The Phoenicians and the Syrians of Palestine admit that they learnt it from the Egyptians" (*Ag. Ap.* 1.169; Herodotus 2.104). Diodorus says that the Colchians and the Jews are descended from the Egyptians and from them learnt circumcision (1.28.3; 1.55.5). Celsus argues that the Jews must not fancy that they are holier than other people because they are circumcised, for the Egyptians and Colchians did this before they did (Origen *Cont. Cels.* 1.22; 5.41). See Sevenster (cited n. 634), p. 134. "There is indisputable evidence that circumcision was practised in Egypt, but it is insufficient to determine how widespread the practice was. The evidence of Egyptian texts and reliefs is collected by Jonckheere, 'La circoncision des anciens égyptiens,' *Centaurus* I.3 (1951): 212–34.

NOTES

There are only seven passages in the whole of Egyptian literature relating to circumcision, but representations of the god Min and the drawing of the hieroglyph of the male organ suggest that it was common" (A. Burton, *Diodorus Siculus, Book I, A Commentary* [Leiden, 1972], p. 121).

636. Retaining with S. Daniel the reading of the best manuscripts λογιζομένους ὡς οὐκ εἰκός. Cohn and Colson: λογιζομένους, ὡς εἰκός.

637. Cf. *Spec.* 21.163.

638. Cf. Maimonides *Guide* 3.49: "Similarly with regard to circumcision, one of the reasons for it is, in my opinion, the wish to bring about a decrease in sexual intercourse and a weakening of the organ in question, so that this activity be diminished and the organ be in as quiet a state as possible."

639. Cf. *QG* 3.47, 48.

640. The earliest instance in Greek literature of the notion of the cosmos as a temple is in Ps-Plato *Epinomis* 983E–984B. Cf. Chrysippus ap. Cicero *ND* 3.26; *Rep. (Somn. Scip.)* 6.15; Plutarch *Moral.* 477C; Ps-Heraclitus *Ep.* 4 (H. W. Attridge, *First-Century Cynicism in the Epistles of Heraclitus* [Missoula, 1976], p. 59); Euripides Fr. 968; Seneca *Ep.* 90.28; *Benefic.* 8.7.3; Heb. 8:2, 9:11.

641. The same justification is found in Josephus *Ag. Ap.* 2.193; cf. *Ant.* 4.201.

642. Cf. *Flac.* 89, and Box's note ad loc.; II Macc. 3:19; Menander, Fr. 546, Edmonds: "You leave the zone, dear, proper to a wife, / The yard; the front-door bounds a lady's life; / To pursue into the street snapping and snarling / Like this, is what a dog does, Rhodé darling." "Philo's discussion of the sphere and ideal conduct of women is to be compared with a similar discussion by the Pythagorean female philosopher Phintys. In praising the chief virtue of women as *sōphrosynē* she points out that loyalty to her husband is the chief duty of a woman.... While there is much virtue that should be shared alike by both sexes, man's peculiar virtue is to be brave in war and to carry on public affairs, woman's is to remain within doors and to await and cherish her husband.... She may attend the public sacrifices to the patron god of the city ... but she is to leave the house, not after dark or in the evening, but only when the market place is full and she is attended by one or, better, two companions holding her hand. Such excursions are also allowed for the sake of paying a call, or for the household shopping" (E. R. Goodenough, *The Jurisprudence of the Jewish Courts in Egypt* (rep. Amsterdam, 1968), pp. 130–31. For the Greek text, see Thesleff, pp. 151ff. Cf. Plato *Meno* 71E. See also Heinemann, pp. 231–49; W. A. Meeks, "The Image of the Androgyne," *HR* 13:3 (1974): 165–208, esp. 176–77. For other Philonic passages referring to women, see *Ebr.* 55, 60; *Legat.* 319; *Op.* 151, 103; *QG* 1.25, 27, 33, 37, 4.15; *Fug.* 128; *Agr.* 73; *Hypoth.* 7.3 (cf. Josephus *Ag. Ap.* 2.201), 11.14.

643. Cf. *QG* 4.165; *Jos.* 38.

644. Cf. *Virt.* 19; *QG* 1.26.

645. "Possibly τὸ ἱερόν may have become in the diaspora a conventional

name for the synagogue as the best possible substitute for the temple, particularly in Alexandria where the synagogue was said to have been especially magnificent and famous; and so too with the common collocation εὐχὰς καὶ θυσίας for the due performance of all religious rites possible" (Colson, LCL 7.640). Reform and today also many Conservative synagogues are designated as Temples.

646. Cf. *Virt.* 21: "With the further object of guarding against the manish-woman as much as the womanish-man."

647. γυναῖκες need not be bracketed, as by Cohen.

648. Philo here accepts a punishment that he severely criticizes in *Spec.* 2.244–248. At 178, however, Philo says of the literal explanation only that it is the one commonly and widely stated, and clearly prefers the allegorical. Cf. Goodenough, *Jurisprudence* (cited n. 642), pp. 132–33.

649. Cf. Aelian *VH* 10.1; Pausanias 5.6.7.

650. The same allegorical interpretation is given in *Somn.* 2.69.

651. Literally, the "twin" [glands]. δίδυμοι is the term used in LXX.

652. According to Philo, this was precisely Adam's sin (*Somn.* 2.70). Jewish mystics offered a similar interpretation of Adam's sin.

653. Philo is probably thinking of Heraclitus DK B.101 (cf. Herodotus 1.8). It is a favorite notion of Philo's: cf. *Ebr.* 82; *Sacr.* 34; *Mos.* 1.274; *Spec.* 4.137; *Conf.* 140–41.

654. Cf. *QE* 2.9; *Conf.* 141; Ps-Demosthenes, *Against Stephanus* 2.6–7; *Against Eubulides* 4; *Against Leochares* 55.

655. On μακρόθεν see Colson, LCL 8.432; A. Mosès, Lyon 25.351–52.

656. See Deut. 14:4–5; cf. *QE* 2.101. On the identification of the animals, see A. Mosès, Lyon 25.357–58.

657. See Lev. 11:3ff.; Deut. 14:6ff. For the allegorical interpretation of the parted hoof and the chewing of the cud, cf. *Agr.* 131–145; Ps-Aristeas 150ff.

658. Philo is following the LXX, in which both Lev. 11:3 and Deut. 14:6 include the word "two"; διχηλοῦν ὁπλὴν καὶ ὀνυχιστῆρας ὀνυχίζον δύο χηλῶν, parting the hoof and making divisions of two claws. The Masoretic text does not include the word "two" in Lev. 11:3.

659. Cf. Hesiod *Op.* 287–92.

660. See Lev. 11:42. Cf. *LA* 3.139.

661. Reading with Heinemann καὶ συρμῷ instead of ἢ συρμῷ.

662. The "snake-fighter" is the LXX translation of the Hebrew *ḥāgāv* (Lev. 11:22) (New JPS version renders it "grasshopper"). Cf. *Op.* 163.

663. See *The Giants*, n. 22.

664. Cf. *Prov.* 2.91, 103 [56]; *Jos.* 3; *Mos.* 1.60. This justification is of Stoic origin: Cicero *ND* 2.161; *SVF* 2.1173. A more severe attitude toward hunting may be found in *QG* 2.82: "Hunting is as far removed as possible from the rational nature." For the disapproving rabbinic attitude toward hunting, see

the responsum of R. Ezekiel Landau (1713–1793), in S. B. Freehof, *A Treasury of Responsa* (Philadelphia, 1963), pp. 216–19.

665. Cf. *Mig.* 90: "And to let go nothing that is part of the customs fixed by divinely empowered men greater than those of our time"; Zaleucus (lawgiver of Italian Locri) ap. Stobaeus 4:126, 1.1, Wachsmuth-Hense: πάτρια τὰ κάλλιστα.

666. As the enacted laws of the Torah are nothing but "memorials of the life of the ancients" (*Abr.* 5), who were themselves "living laws" (νόμοι ἔμψυχοι), so too are the orally inherited customs of these patriarchs. Cf. *Virt.* 194: "And the lives of those who have earnestly followed virtue may be called unwritten laws." The unwritten laws, like those that are written, are thus also identical with the laws of nature. (See Mosès, Lyon 25.360–61). Cf. also *Legat.* 115.

667. Cf. Responsa of R. Sherira Gaon: " 'set up by previous generations' (Deut. 19:14), from this we deduce that custom is a matter of consequence" (cited by B. Epstein, *Torah Temimah*, ad loc.). As A. Mosès has pointed out, Prov. 22:28 would have been more apt, but Philo undoubtedly preferred to cite the Pentateuch.

668. Cf. Aristotle *Rhetoric* 1375a15: "So too, again [wrong acts are greater], when a man offends against the unwritten laws of right, for there is greater merit in doing right without being compelled [and therefore the violation of them is more discreditable]; now the written laws involve compulsion, the unwritten do not." Cf. *PT Sanhedrin* 11.4: " 'And your mouth like choicest wine' (Cant. 7:10). R. Simeon b. Ba, Said in the name of R. Yohanan: the oral law *(dibrê sôferîm)* is closely akin [*dôdim*] to Scriptural law *(dibrê Torah)* and is more beloved than Scriptural law, 'for your love is more delightful than wine.' (Cant. 1:2)." Wolfson maintains that, although Philo often uses "unwritten law" in the Greek sense, in some places in his works, as here, there are references to the Jewish oral law (1.188–94).

669. Retaining the reading of the manuscripts: τὰ μὲν γενόμενα ἡγεμονικά, τὰ δ' ὡς ὑπήκοα καὶ γενησόμενα. Cohn prints: τὰ μὲν [γενόμενα] < ὡς > ἡγεμονικά, τὰ δ' ὡς ὑπήκοα, and translates: "destined the former to be subjects, the latter to be rulers."

670. Cf. *Mos.* 2.46ff.

671. See Gen. 27:40: "You shall serve your brother." Cf. *Congr.* 176; *Virt.* 208–09; *LA* 3.88–89, 193.

672. Cf. *LA* 1.108; *Her.* 214; *Spec.* 4.61; *QG* 3.5, 4.152, 167.

673. Cf. II Macc. 6:12; Wisd. 3:5; 12:22; *Assumption of Moses* 12:11–12; Josephus *Ant.* 4.6.6, 3.15.1; *Psalms of Solomon* 13:4–10.

674. The use of the word προτέλεια derives from the mystery imagery. Cf. Albinus *Did.* 28.4. See n. 454 above. Cf. *Congr.* 5; *Abr.* 89.

675. Typical diatribe-style exclamation.

676. Triadic asyndeton, proper to passages of heightened emotion.

NOTES

677. A reference to the Orphic tag σῶμα — σῆμα. Cf. *Somn.* 1.139.

678. See n. 240 above.

679. The Israelite borrowing of gold and silver vessels from the Egyptians had been a special target of the anti-Semitic literature of the Greco-Roman age, and Jewish writers found it necessary to provide some sort of apologetic defense. Cf. Wisd. 10:17; *Jubilees* 48:18; Ezekiel *Exagogē (FPG:* 213, line 5ff.); Artapanos *(FPG:* 195, line 4); Pompeius Trogus (ap. Justinus's Latin epitome of his *Historiae Philippicae* 36.2.13); *BT Sanhedrin* 91a. Among Marcion's many calumnies against the Demiurge was the charge that he induced his people to spoil the Egyptians (A. von Harnack *Marcion* [rep. Darmstadt 1960], p. 280).

680. "The manuscripts vary here considerably and the construction in the text as printed is difficult. A simple emendation would be λαμβάνοντες παρ᾽ ἀκόντων ὃν and so, except that ἅ appears instead of ὃν, it is in the paraphrase of Procopius quoted in Cohn, p. 153" (Colson, LCL 6.348, n. 1).

681. Cf. Wisd. 19:14: "Others refused to welcome strangers who visited them, but these enslaved guests and benefactors."

682. Cf. *Op.* 3; *Mig.* 59; *Somn.* 1.243; *Mos.* 1.157; *Conf.* 106.

683. Cf. *Abr.* 98; *QE* 1.10.

684. The selection of Israel is here interpreted as the selection of the worthiest. Philo is very sensitive with regard to the doctrine of Israel's election and covenant. Indeed, he understands the διαθήκη of the LXX either as "testament" or else allegorizes it to mean "grace" or "Logos." See A. Jaubert, *La Notion d'Alliance dans le Judaisme* (Paris, 1963), pp. 375–442. Cf. *Spec.* 4.182.

685. Retaining with Daniel the reading of the manuscripts, προνοίας, in preference to the correction of Mangey, προνομίας, adopted by Cohn and Colson.

686. Cf. *Spec.* 2.163.

687. Philo may be echoing the Stoic idea that all people possess a κοινὴ ἔννοια, common notion, of the existence of God, whom they worship in one form or another. See Cicero *ND* 2.12 where it is said that God's existence is imprinted in every man. Cf. Sextus *Math.* 9.123–25. Epicurus held a similar view (Cicero *ND* 1.43).

688. For M. Mendelssohn's similar notion , see his *Jerusalem*, ed. A. Jospe (New York, 1969), p. 89.

689. Cf. *Praem.* 166; *Legat.* 3.

690. *Proskynesis* was performed before the Assyrian kings, in whose documents there are references to vassals prostrating themselves and kissing the king's feet (*ANET:* 275ff.). The practice was followed in the Persian court, but did not imply worship. To the Greeks, however, it was primarily an act of worship offered to a god. When Alexander attempted to introduce this custom at Bactra in 327, Greek and Macedonian opposition forced him to abandon the project. The introduction of *proskynesis* into Rome is attributed to L.

NOTES

Vitellius on his return from his province of Syria in 39 C.E. (Suetonius *Vitellius* 2.5). In admitting *proskynesis* Gaius probably intended it to connote worship (Smallwood).

691. See, for example, Hecataeus of Abdera: "In another passage Hecataeus mentions our regard for our laws, and how we deliberately choose, and hold it a point of honor to endure anything rather than transgress them" (Josephus *Ag. Ap.* 1.190–93). Cf. I Macc. 1:60–63, 2:29–38; II Macc. 6–7; IV Macc.

692. Cf. Hos. 14:6; *IV* Ezra 5:24; *Shir Hashirim R.* 6.6; *Wayyikra R.* 23.

693. Cf. *Virt.* 102–03; 178–79; Plato *Laws* 729E. On Jewish proselytism, see B. J. Bamberger, *Proselytism in the Talmudic Period* (Cincinnati, 1939).

694. Cf. Isa. 11:6–9. "Philo never mentions Isaiah by name, but quotes from him four times (*Somn.* 2.172; *Mut.* 169; *Praem.* 158; *LA* 2.69) as one of the prophets and once (*Her.* 25) without any indication that it is a quotation" (Colson, LCL 8.456).

695. Reading ὅμορα of the manuscripts, instead of Cohn's ὅμοῖα supposing that καὶ βλαβερὰ has fallen out, or ὁμοίως βλαβερὰ should be substituted (Colson, LCL 8.366, n. 2).

696. So Num. 24:7, LXX: "There shall come forth a man from his seed and he shall rule over many nations." The Hebrew is completely different. Cf. *Targum Onkelos* ad loc.: "The king anointed from his sons shall increase, and have dominion over many nations."

697. See Exod. 23:28; Deut. 7:20.

698. Lev. 26:3–4; Deut. 11:13–14.

699. Adopting Colson's suggestion ἀσκηθεῖσι (agreeing with οἷς).

700. Cf. Wisd. 7:7ff and my commentary ad loc.

701. See Lev. 26:40ff., LXX; Deut. 30:1ff.

702. See Lev. 26:42. Colson notes that the idea of the departed saints acting as intercessors, a genuinely Jewish idea, is unique in Philo.

SELECTED BIBLIOGRAPHY

The literature on Philo is vast, but there are excellent bibliographies available to guide the reader. The older literature is fully detailed by Goodenough and Goodhart in E. R. Goodenough, *The Politics of Philo Judaeus* (New Haven, 1938; rep. Hildesheim, 1967). An excellent annotated bibliography for the years 1937–1962 is provided by L. Feldman, *Studies in Judaica: Scholarship on Philo and Josephus* (1937–1962) (New York, n.d.). For the years 1924–1934, there is R. Marcus, "Recent Literature on Philo," *Jewish Studies in Memory of George A. Kohut* (New York, 1935), pp. 463–91. Feldman's bibliography is updated by Antonio V. Nazzaro, *Recenti Studi filoniani* (1963–1970) (Naples, 1973). Further bibliographies are provided in every issue of *Studia Philonica*, published by The Philo Institute, beginning in 1972. Earle Hilgert's *Bibliographia Philoniana*, 1935–1975, will appear soon in *ANRW*, in a volume that will also include P. Borgen's "Philo of Alexandria: A Critical and Synthetical Survey of Research Since World War II." A useful survey of earlier Philonic research may be found in Thyen, "Die Probleme der neueren Philoforschung," *Theologische Rundschau* 23 (1955–1956): 230–46.

Günther Mayer's *Index Philoneus* (Berlin, New York, 1974) now supplements H. Leisegang's index (volume 7 of the *Editio maior* of Philo, ed. L. Cohn and P. Wendland, 7 vols. in 8 books [Berlin, 1896–1930]), and a computerized concordance to Philo by P. Borgen of the University of Trondheim in Norway is nearing completion.

There are German, French, and English translations of Philo with very useful notes: *Die Werke Philos von Alexandria in deutscher Übersetzung*, Band I–VII, hsgeg. von L. Cohn, fortgeführt von I. Heinemann, M. Adler, H. Lewy, J. Cohn, W. Theiler (Breslau 1909–1964); *Les Oeuvres de Philon d'Alexandrie publiées sous le patronage de l'Université de Lyon*, par R. Arnaldez, J. Pouilloux, C. Mondésert (Paris, 1961ff.), vols. 1–34ᴬ, and 35 (cited in this book as Lyon, followed by the volume number); *Philo with an English translation*, by F. H. Colson (and G. H. Whitaker for vols. 1–4), Loeb Classical Library (Cambridge, Mass., London) vols. 1–10, plus two supplementary volumes containing the *Questions and Answers on Genesis and Exodus* (1953), translated from the Armenian by R. Marcus. There are fully annotated editions of Philo's *In Flaccum* and *Legatio ad Gaium* by H. Box (London, 1939), and E. M. Smallwood (Leiden, 1961) respectively.

In spite of the plethora of books on Philo, there is still no fully satisfactory study of his work. The best available is E. Bréhier, *Les idées philosophiques et religieuses de Philon d'Alexandrie*[3] (Paris, 1950). An older but very useful briefer account is T. H. Billings, *The Platonism of Philo Judaeus* (Chicago, 1919). Although J. Drummond's *Philo Judaeus* (London, 1888; rep. Amsterdam, 1969) is now antiquated, its philosophical analysis still has important insights to offer. The large monographs by W. Völker, *Fortschritt und Vollendung bei Philo von Alexandrien* (Leipzig, 1938), and H. A. Wolfson, *Philo: Foundations of Religious Philosophy in Judaism, Christianity and Islam* 2 vols. (Cambridge, Mass., 1947), are indispensable for their very rich presentations of data, but are perversely one-sided in their interpretations. E. R. Goodenough's many studies on Philo, including his *An Introduction to Philo Judaeus*[2] (Oxford, 1962) are very stimulating, but highly idiosyncratic. A very useful introduction for the beginner is S. Sandmel's *Philo of Alexandria: An Introduction* (New York, Oxford, 1979), but it is weak on philosophical issues. (See also his earlier study *Philo's Place in Judaism* [Cincinnati, 1956; rep. New York, 1971].) J. Daniélou's *Philon d'Alexandrie* (Paris, 1958) is a very readable brief introduction, and *Philon d'Alexandrie*, Lyon 1966: Colloque. Centre national de la recherche scientifique (Paris, 1967) offers a splendid series of articles dealing with various facets of Philo's work. The best brief chapters on Philo are that of H. Chadwick, in *The Cambridge History of Later Greek and Early Medieval Philosophy*, ed. A. H. Armstrong (Cambridge, 1967), pp. 135–57; and J. Dillon, in *The Middle Platonists* (London, 1977), pp. 139–83, which is especially important for Philo's philosophical sources.

A fundamental study on Philo's relationship to Palestinian Judaism and Greek culture is I. Heinemann, *Philons griechische und jüdische Bildung* (Breslau, 1932; rep. Hildesheim, 1962). V. Nikiprowetzky, *Le commentaire de l'écriture chez Philon d'Alexandrie* (Leiden, 1977) is a very rich study of Philo's exegetical approach. U. Früchtel, *Die kosmologischen Vorstellungen bei Philo von Alexandrien* (Leiden, 1968), is an excellent study of the cosmological motifs in Philo's writings, and R. C. Baer, *Philo's Use of the Categories Male and Female* (Leiden, 1970) is an interesting account of this aspect of Philo's imagery. For Philo's philosophical sources, one may consult M. Pohlenz, "Philo von Alexandria," *Nachrichten von der Gesellschaft der Wissenschaften in Göttingen*, Philologisch—historische Klasse (1942), pp. 409–87; H. J. Krämer, *Der Ursprung der Geistmetaphysik* (Amsterdam, 1967), pp. 264–92; and W. Theiler, "Philo von Alexandria und der Beginn des kaiserzeitlichen Platonismus," *Parusia, Festschrift für J. Hirschberger* (Frankfurt, 1965; rep. in *Untersuchungen zur antiken Literatur* [Berlin, 1970], pp. 484–

BIBLIOGRAPHY

501); "Philo von Alexandria und der hellenisierte Timaeus," in *Philomathes: Studies . . . Philip Merlan,* ed. R. B. Palmer, R. Hamerton-Kelly (The Hague, 1971), pp. 21–35.

Philo's love of sport and his detailed knowledge of it is well documented in H. A. Harris, *Greek Athletics and the Jews,* ed. I. M. Barton, A. J. Brothers (Cardiff, 1976), pp. 51–95. For the relationship between Wisdom of Solomon and Philo, see D. Winston, *The Wisdom of Solomon* (New York, 1979), pp. 59–63; for Philo and Hebrews, see R. Williamson, *Philo and the Epistle to the Hebrews* (Leiden, 1970); and L. K. K. Dey, *The Intermediary World and Patterns of Perfection in Philo and Hebrews* (Missoula, 1975); and for Philo and Patristic literature, see P. Heinisch, *Der Einfluss Philos auf die älteste christliche Exegese* (Münster 1908); S. R. C. Lilla, *Clement of Alexandria* (Oxford, 1971); and E. Lucchesi, *L'Usage de Philons dans l'oeuvre exégétique de Saint Ambroise* (Leiden 1977).

INDEX TO PREFACE,
FOREWORD, INTRODUCTION AND NOTES

INDEX

Chroust, A.H., 311, n. 81.
Chrysippus, 5, 13, 322, n. 4; 352, n. 251; 353, n. 254; 356, n. 312; 360, n. 361, n. 365; 364, n. 389; 366, n. 400; 368, n. 421; 370, n. 444; 374, n. 492; 386, n. 640.
Cicero, 5, 20, 29, 307, n. 40; 308, n. 55, n. 56; 310, n. 70, n. 71; 311, n. 78; 312, n. 84, n. 88; 316, n. 8; 317, n. 14; 323, n. 9, n. 10; 324, n. 17, n. 20; 325, n. 23, n. 24, n. 28; 328, n. 49, n. 50; 331, n. 33; 346, n. 173; 348, n. 191a; 354, n. 280; 361, n. 366, n. 371; 367, n. 411, n. 413, n. 415, n. 416; 370, n. 430; 373, n. 478, n. 484; 374, n. 492, n. 494; 375, n. 504; 376, n. 517; 377, n. 522, n. 531; 379, n. 542; 381, n. 568; 383, n. 602; 386, n. 640; 387, n. 664; 389, n. 687.
Circe, 5.
Claghorn, G.S., 305, n. 35.
Claudius, 35.
Cleanthes, 5, 29, 307, n. 50; 312, n. 88; 336, n. 64; 353, n. 254.
Clement of Alexandria, xii, 321, n. 50; 328, n. 49; 349, n. 212; 352, n. 240; 368, n. 425; 374, n. 494; 376, n. 519.
Cleopatra, 358, n. 341.
Cohen, 320, n. 34, n. 40; 387, n. 647.
Cohen-Yashar, 303, n. 19; 334, n. 47.
Cohn, L., 302, n. 14; 314, n. 98; 319, n. 31; 355, n. 296; 386, n. 636; 388, n. 669; 389, n. 680, n. 685; 390, n. 695.
Cole, T., 339, n. 103.
Colson, F.H., xv, 315, n. 1; 318, n. 21; 319, n. 24, n. 31; 320, n. 33, n. 34, n. 38, n. 40; 330, n. 8; 331, n. 26, n. 28, n. 29, n. 30; 333, n. 40; 335, n. 59; 337, n. 71; 344, n. 137, n. 149; 345, n. 150; 346, n. 162; 348, n. 204; 351, n. 227, n. 237; 353, n. 262, n. 267; 354, n. 268, n. 271, n. 280; 355, n. 296; 361, n. 372, n. 373; 364, n. 389; 368, n. 422, n. 423; 371, n. 447; 372, n.

459; 374, n. 487; 376, n. 520; 377, n. 529; 381, n. 568, n. 570, n. 572, n. 573, n. 574, n. 576, n. 579; 382, n. 587; 384, n. 620, n. 622; 386, n. 636; 387, n. 645, n. 655; 389, n. 680, n. 685; 390, n. 694, n. 695, n. 699, n. 702.
Contemplation, 21, 35, 41, 312, n. 91.
Conybeare, 319, n. 24; 320, n. 34, n. 38, n. 40.
I Corinthians, 3:1–3, 372, n. 468; 3:16, 356, n. 310.
Conford, F.M., 304, n. 23, n. 24.
Cornutus, 315, n. 4; 356, n. 312.
Crantor, 14, 305, n. 35; 306, n. 37; 371, n. 454; 377, n. 531.
Creation, eternal, 7, 9, 13, 14, 15, 16, 17, 27, 307, n. 47; *ex nihilo*, 7, 8, 11, 12; and God, 7, 8, 9, 10, 11, 12, 13, 14, 15, 16, 18, 27, 303, n. 19; 305, n. 29; 314, n. 103; 347, n. 177; 349, n. 212; 362, n. 382, n. 384; and primordial matter, 7, 8, 9; temporal, 7, 13, 14, 15, 16, 17, 305, n. 35; 308, n. 51.
Cudworth, R., 309, n. 59.
Culpepper, R.A., 302, n. 12.
Curtius, E.R., 377, n. 522.
Cynics, 5, 319, n. 27; 383, n. 605.

Daemons, 322, n. 7; 323, n. 8; 324, n. 15; 379, n. 537.
Dahl, 335, n. 56.
Damascius, 349, n. 212.
Dan, J., 309, n. 60.
Daniel, 10:3, 319, n. 21.
Daniel, S., 368, n. 424; 386, n. 636; 389, n. 685.
Daniélou, J., 328, n. 47; 336, n. 61; 384, n. 622.
Daumas, 315, n. 2; 318, n. 21; 319, n. 24; 320, n. 34, n. 38.
Debarim, I., 365, n. 399.
Decharme, P., 315, n. 4.
De Falco, 357, n. 327.
Delatte, A., 333, n. 43.
Delling, D.G., 308, n. 54, n. 57.

INDEX

INDEX

INDEX

Jaeger, 341, n. 122.
James, 2:23, 321, n. 52; 380, n. 554.
Jaoel, 337, n. 72.
Jaubert, A., 389, n. 684.
Jeremiah, 2:2, 384, n. 625; 23:29, 384, n. 628.
Jerome, 36, 314, n. 99; 352, n. 240.
Job, 1:21, 379, n. 539; 25:2, 337, n. 72.
John, 314, n. 99.
Jonathan, Pseudo-, 329, n. 57.
Jonas, H., 311, n. 81; 327, n. 46.
Jonckheere, 385, n. 635.
Jones, R.M., 329, n. 6.
Jose b. Halafta, R., 349, n. 212.
Josephus, 2, 315, n. 3; 318, n. 19, n. 21; 321, n. 51; 325, n. 22; 332, n. 37; 347, n. 173; 355, n. 300; 367, n. 415; 370, n. 428; 383, n. 609; 384, n. 618, n. 619, n. 622; 385, n. 634, n. 635; 386, n. 641, n. 642; 388, n. 673; 690, n. 691.
Joshua b. Levi, R., 362, n. 382.
Jospe, A., 389, n. 688.
Jove, 5.
Judah, R., 350, n. 218; 361, n. 367.
Judah Abravanel, 341, n. 122.
Judah Halevi, 309, n. 58.
Judaism, cf. also Philo; Alexandrian, 1, 4, 37, 313, n. 98; 315, n. 1; 321, n. 50; 387, n. 645; customs of, 385, n. 634; Hellenistic, 354, n. 284; and Theraputae, 313, n. 98.
Justin, 7, 325, n. 20; 349, n. 212.
Justinian, 317, n. 13.
Justinus, 389, n. 679.
Juvenal, 340, n. 103; 385, n. 634.

Kadushin, M., 351, n. 224.
Katz, P., 323, n. 7; 339, n. 100.
Kaufmann, W., 376, n. 519.
Khurqāmī, Abu 'l-Hasan, 355, n. 303.
II Kings, 19:35, 313, n. 94.
Kraabel, 318, n. 18.
Kraeling, C.H., 317, n. 18.
Krämer, H.J., 306, n. 36; 309, n. 64.
Krause, M., 349, n. 212.
Kustas, G.L., 304, n. 22.

Lactantius, 325, n. 20.
Landau, R. Ezekiel, 388, n. 664.
Langstadt, E., 345, n. 150.
Laporte, J., 355, n. 289.
Lauer, S., 341, n. 119.
Lauterbach, 363, n. 385; 379, n. 546.
Law, Mosaic, 25, 302, n. 14; and philosophy, 24; and Sabbath, 348, n. 199.
Leisegang, A., 324, n. 18.
Leisegang, H., 305, n. 32; 306, n. 38.
Levi, R., 378, n. 534.
Leviticus, 2:1, 355, n. 298; 11, 362, n. 382; 11:3ff, 387, n. 657, n. 658; 11:22, 387, n. 662; 11:42, 387, n. 660; 18:6, xii, 326, n. 36; 25:6, 379, n. 544; 26:3-4, 390, n. 698; 26:40ff, 390, n. 701; 26:42, 390, n. 702.
Lévy, 320, n. 38.
Lewy, Hans, xv, 313, n. 93; 358, n. 341.
Lieberman, S., 301, n. 1; 321, n. 51; 350, n. 215; 382, n. 580.
Lilla, 303, n. 18; 305, n. 34; 306, n. 38; 309, n. 59; 310, n. 69; 311, n. 74; 332, n. 37.
Lindeskog, G., 304, n. 25.
Lloyd, G.E.R., 322, n. 6; 341, n. 122.
Loenen, J.H., 307, n. 46.
Loew, M., 379, n. 546.
Logos, 385, n. 632; and creation, 9, 16, 23, 26, 303, n. 16; 336, n. 61; 344, n. 150; 351, n. 226; and light, 363, n. 386; as manifestation of God, 21, 23, 26, 364, n. 386; and miracles, 21; and *nous*, xii; and number, 357, n. 327; powers of, 24; as Sophia, 327, n. 39; 373, n. 481; 375, n. 504; union with, 36; vision of, 34.
Long, A.A., 332, n. 33; 382, n. 580.
Longinus, 379, n. 546.
Longinus, Pseudo-, 353, n. 258.
Lovejoy, A.O., 339, n. 103.
Lucian, 326, n. 33; 383, n. 610.
Lucius, P.E., 314, n. 98.
Lucretius, 307, n. 40; 332, n. 33; 340, n. 103; 346, n. 165.

403

INDEX

INDEX

Nicholas of Cusa, 357, n. 319.
Nicholson, R.A., 313, n. 93, n. 94; 355, n. 303.
Nietzsche, 376, n. 519.
Nike, 333, n. 45; 340, n. 114.
Nikiprowetzky, Valentin, xv, 301, n. 4, n. 6, n. 7; 303, n. 20; 309, n. 59; 320, n. 38; 332, n. 37; 339, n. 100; 355, n. 289.
Nimrod, 329, n. 57.
Noah, 322, n. 2.
Nock, A.C., 332, n. 37; 336, n. 64.
Nous, xii, 23.
Number, xiii, 333, n. 43.
Numbers, 6:2, 371, n. 446; 20:17-20, 329, n. 55; 24:7, 390, n. 696; 25:3, 330, n. 38; 28:2, 368, n. 423.
Numenius, 315, n. 103; 324, n. 20; 329, n. 3.

Ocellus, Pseudo-, 368, n. 425.
Odysseus, 5, 316, n. 6.
Oenomaus, 366, n. 400.
Onatas, 325, n. 22.
Ontological Argument, 28-30, 312, n. 82a; 347, n. 177.
Origen, xii; 338, n. 90; 349, n. 212; 351, n. 240; 361, n. 367; 385, n. 635.
Ormuzd, 318, n. 19; 324, n. 20.
Orpheus, 4.
Otte, K., 327, n. 45.
Owen, G.E.L., 307, n. 44.

Panaetius, 308, n. 56; 312, n. 88; 364, n. 389; 367, n. 413.
Parmenides, 307, n. 40; 309, n. 65.
Pausanius, 387, n. 649.
Pearson, B.A., 302, n. 15.
Pease, A.S., 346, n. 173.
Penelope, 372, n. 475.
Pentateuch, xi, xii, xiv, 2; 388, n. 667.
Pépin, J., 301, n. 10; 305, n. 35; 325, n. 24; 361, n. 374; 374, n. 496.
Peter, 35, 314, n. 99.
Peterson, E., 321, n. 52.

Pfeiffer, R., 348, n. 194; 350, n. 215.
Pfitzner, V.C., 376, n. 521.
Pheidias, 340, n. 114; 375, n. 500.
Philo, cosmology of, 13; family of, 1-2; and Hellenism, xi, xii, xiii, xv, 1, 2, 3, 4, 11, 17, 24, 340, n. 112; 362, n. 384; 388, n. 668; and Judaism, xi, xii, xv, 1, 2, 3, 4, 6, 10, 11, 17, 36, 37, 333, n. 53; 339, n. 103; 351, n. 240; 388, n. 668; 389, n. 684; mysticism of, 16, 21-35, 41, 311, n. 81; 358, n. 341; and Platonism, xii, xiii, 1, 2, 3, 9, 10, 14, 16, 36, *passim* pp. 301-390; style of, xv, 1, 17; themes of, xv; translation of, xv, 36, 302, n. 14.
Philo, works of, *De Abrahamo*, 23, 24, 28, 33, 34, 302, n. 12, n. 13; 310, n. 72; 312, n. 85; 316, n. 7; 321, n. 52; 322, n. 3; 324, n. 15; 326, n. 29; 327, n. 42, n. 43, n. 46; 331, n. 21, n. 22, n. 25, n. 31; 332, n. 37; 335, n. 56; 337, n. 70, n. 77; 338, n. 85; 344, n. 139; 345, n. 150; 347, n. 181, n. 186; 348, n. 198, n. 203; 349, n. 208; 350, n. 219; 351, n. 238, n. 239; 352, n. 243, n. 244; 353, n. 264; 354, n. 274; 356, n. 309, n. 312, n. 315; 357, n. 318; 362, n. 378; 365, n. 399; 366, n. 404; 367, n. 410, n. 420; 371, n. 450; 372, n. 462; 373, n. 482; 376, n. 521, n. 522; 380, n. 554, n. 561; 380, n. 563; 383, n. 601; 384, n. 614, n. 617; 388, n. 666, n. 674; 389, n. 683; *De Aeternitate Mundi*, 12, 14, 302, n. 14; 305, n. 31; 306, n. 38, n. 39, n. 40; 308, n. 51; 323, n. 10; 324, n. 12; 326, n. 35; 330, n. 15; 332, n. 36; 337, n. 81; 340, n. 110; 341, n. 121; 342, n. 126, n. 129; 345, n. 153; *De Agricultura*, 310, n. 72; 312, n. 86; 316, n. 7; 322, n. 3; 324, n. 14; 327, n. 41; 330, n. 13; 331, n. 31; 334, n. 47; 344, n. 150; 353, n. 262; 355, n. 293; 360, n. 359; 371, n. 456; 372,

INDEX

INDEX

INDEX

INDEX

413

INDEX

n. 430, n. 431; 380, n. 554; 381, n. 571.

Wisdom, 1:4, 356, n.310; 1:14, 303, n. 19; 1:16, 371, n. 448; 2:23, 379, n. 537; 3:5, 388, n. 673; 4:1, 320, n. 41; 4:2, 376, n. 521; 4:8, 377, n. 522; 7:7, 390, n. 700; 7:13, 330, n. 39: 7:27, 324, n. 209; 380, n. 554; 8:2–3, 320, n. 41; 8:2–16, 330, n. 12; 8:3, 338, n. 94; 8:7, 375, n. 504; 8:16, 327, n. 42; 8:17, 379, n. 537; 9:1–2, 373, n. 481; 9:4, 385, n. 632; 9:15, 325, n. 22; 10:1-15, 365, n. 394; 10:17, 389, n. 679; 11:20, 385, n. 632; 11:23, 350, n. 216; 12:10, 348, n. 196; 12:22, 388, n. 673; 13:1-9, 17, 311, n. 78; 328, n. 53; 343, n. 136; 13:2, 385, n. 653; 13:3, 348, n. 197; 13:3–5, 346, n. 173; 13:6, 375, n. 500; 14:5, 365, n. 396; 14:14, 316, n. 11; 14:18–21, 328, n. 49; 16:24, 304, n. 21; 18:24, 384, n. 622; 19:6, 362, n. 383; 19:14, 389, n. 681; 19:19, 365, n. 395.

Wlosok, A., 325, n. 23.

Wolfson, H.A., xi-xiii, 3,9-12, 18, 22, 23, 24, 26, 27, 303, n. 16; 304, n. 25; 308, n. 52, n. 57, n. 58; 310, n. 67, n. 69; 314, n. 102; 323, n. 11; 332, n. 37; 334, n. 48; 349, n. 212; 351, n. 224; 354, n. 280; 362, n. 374; 373, n. 481; 388, n. 668.

World, creation of, 7-18; higher, xii; intelligible, xii, 10, 16, 61, 314, n. 103; 338, n. 90; 339, n. 96; physical, 19, 27; sensible, 9, 11, 23, 304, n. 20; 314, n. 103; 325, n. 22; 341, n. 118; uncreated, 14.

World-Soul, 341, n. 118; 352, n. 245.

Xenocrates, 6. 14, 305, n. 35; 345, n. 151.

Xenophon, 5, 311, n. 78; 320, n. 35; 325, n. 23, 326, n. 31; 339, n. 98; 346, n. 173; 347, n. 179; 348, n. 191a; 358, n. 335; 366, n. 400; 375, n. 504; 383, n. 605.

Yoḥanan, R., 378, n. 534; 388, n. 668.

Zaehner, R.C., 375, n. 500.

Zahn, T., 314, n. 99.

Zak, B., 311, n. 80.

Zaleucus, 388, n. 665.

Zalman of Liadi, R. Schneur, 336, n. 62.

Zedekiah b. Abraham Anaw, 359, n. 353.

Zeller, 312, n. 88.

Zeno, xiii, 5, 6; 312, n. 82a; 353, n. 254; 364, n. 389; 368, n. 421; 372, n. 472; 375, n. 504; 382, n. 589.

Zeus, 336, n. 64; 341, n. 118; 348, n. 195; 355, n. 301; 385, n. 632.

Zohar, 310, n. 68; 337, n. 76.

Zoroastrianism, 324, n.20.

414

INDEX TO TEXTS

415

INDEX

138, 139, 140, 141, 164, 167, 180, 192, 242, 282; God as, 181, 193, 251, 277, 278; passive, 96; universal, 139; of universe, 125, 132.

Chaldeans, 70, 113–114, 122, 125, 222, 246, 268, 271.

Cherubim, 89, 91, 217–218.

Circumcision, 81–82, 196, 277–279.

Commander, 85–86.

Commandments, the, 277, 292.

Compassion, 75, 216, 221, 290, 291.

Conscience, 202–203, 229, 297.

Contemplation, desire for, 95; of the Existent, 68, 164; and God, 78, 170, 242; of heaven, 158; of the intelligible, 134, 155, 159, 287; and Jews, 272, 292, 293; of Law, 55; life of, 41–57, 86, 259, 261; of nature, 57, 122, 146; and philosophy, 53, 75; of realities, 52; and Scripture, 79; of universe, 75, 88, 159, 193.

Corybants, 53, 173.

Cosmogony, 96–99.

Cosmological Argument, 124–125.

Cosmology, 109–118.

Creation, Cf. also Universe, World; ceaseless, 107, 109, 132; and change, 104, 105, 286; and the good, 97; and matter, 88, 96–99, 109, 144; mortal-, 142; narrative of, 104–105, 271, 286; simultaneous, 106, 107; worship of, 42, 96.

Customs, 285, 291–292.

Cyclops, 48.

Daemons, 62, 118, 123.

Decalogue, The, 156.

Demeter, 42.

Democritus, 44.

Deuteronomy, 1:43–44, 229; 5:5, 94; 5:31, 68, 133, 173, 242; 8:5, 138; 10:9, 169, 218; 16:20, 255; 16:21, 187; 19:14, 285; 19:17, 226; 26:17–18, 248; 27:9, 211; 28:14, 208; 30:12ff., 233; 32:4, 219; 32:34, 131;

32:39, 125; 33:3f., 198; 33:6, 207; 34.5, 242; 34:6, 243; 34:7, 69; 34:10, 153.

Dreams, 150, 154–155; and God, 154, 193.

Dyad, 129, 223, 282.

Ecstasy, 153, 154, 173, 220, 266.

Eden, 80, 92, 225, 226.

Edom, 208, 287.

Elements, and creation, 97, 144, 148, 176, 193, 271; fifth, 117, 148; and Forms, 88; interchange of, 117–118; and life, 62; and Moses, 269; and proportion, 114, 117; and punishment, 176; worship of, 42.

Emotions, irrational, 227; and moderation, 235; rational, 246, 248, 252; vehement-, 241.

Empedocles, 184.

Enoch, 245.

Enos, 229.

Epicureans, 81.

Er, 180, 254.

Eros, 51.

Esau, 193, 232, 252, 259.

Essence, of existents, 88, 269; of God, 88, 124–125, 141; and universe, 117.

Essenes, 41, 249–252.

Ethics, 187–253.

Etymology, 86, 90.

Eupathia, 240–253.

Euripides, 77.

Eusebius, 71.

Evil, 48, 75, 82, 119, 131, 136, 144, 152, 163, 164, 176, 177, 179, 180, 181, 218, 220, 226, 232, 236, 245, 246, 262, 274, 275, 277, 279, 286.

Exegesis, 70.

Existent, the, and allegory, 81; contemplation of, 68, 164; and emotion, 138, 141; fear of, 141; goodness of, 131, 178; ineffable, 142; and intelligibles, 217; knowledge of, 124–125, 141, 142, 168–169, 171; love for, 141, 171; migration to, 243; place of, 159;

INDEX

Infanticide, 201.

Isaac, 136, 142, 153, 178, 192, 205, 220, 221, 231, 246, 257, 258, 259.

Isaiah, 50:4, 162.

Ishmael, 231.

Israel, 122, 143, 147, 169, 214, 240–241, 272, 286–293.

Jacob, 142, 153, 178, 192, 193, 207, 215, 221, 232, 259.

Jerusalem, 78, 86.

Jethro, 68.

Jews, 196, 225, 249, 267, 270, 279, 286, 289–291, 292.

Joseph, 193, 199, 202, 255.

Joy, 57, 75, 81, 95, 136–137, 164, 166, 172, 179, 227, 243, 246, 248, 252, 257, 258, 279.

Judgment, faculties of, 146, 194, 229; of intelligibles, 152; of Moses, 185; of truth, 264.

Justice, and equality, 45, 53, 97, 116, 214, 276; and God, 97, 126, 277; and guilt, 194; and Israel, 290; lacking, 62, 195, 268; nature of, 277; perfect, 86; seeking of, 255; and wisdom, 212.

Knowledge, and creation, 101, 102; desire for, 47, 52, 65, 117, 148, 166, 186, 190, 193, 268; of God, 124–129, 130, 140, 141–143, 169, 172, 186, 217, 223, 255; God's, 98, 99, 101, 102, 128, 141, 177; is infinite, 208; and inspiration, 89; of intelligibles, 150; lacking, 145; light of, 210; limits to, 147, 148; perfect, 43, 168; pure, 64; -self, 120, 125, 130, 137, 168, 169, 194, 278; of substance, 137, 150; and teaching, 205–206; theory of, 143–150; and virtue, 227.

Laban, 259.

Law, 132; absolute, 126; copies of, 198, 282; dietary-, 282–284; and fatalism, 195, 196; and Forms, 88, 101; from God, 270, 272;

interpretation of, 55; of Israel, 288–289, 292, 293; and justice, 234; and Moses, 239, 267–286; Natural, 197–202; of necessity, 119, 135, 148; and symbol, 79, 281, 282.

Leah, 192.

Levi, 169.

Levites, 261.

Leviticus, 1:1, 127, 166; 2:14, 108; 6:20, 126; 7:34, 241; 8:2, 241; 8:21, 241; 9:14, 242; 11:21, 118; 16:1ff., 254; 16:2, 68; 16:16, 93; 16:34, 68; 17:11, 121; 18:6, 65; 19:24, 160; 25:6, 245; 26:5, 297; 26:10, 122, 206.

Life, active, 41, 259, 261, 264, 267; blessed, 44; in body, 63; contemplative, 41–57, 86, 259, 261, 267; earthly-, 108; eternal, 217; for God, 208, 212; of God, 108; good-, 227, 240, 276; holy, 46; illumination of, 83; immortal, 63; improvement of, 66, 291; -models, 215; mortal, 69, 75, 172, 262; and nature, 198, 199, 200; pure, 75, 250; of sage, 68, 69, 198; of soul, 121–122, 168; stages of, 120; ways of, 212, 267.

Light, and Existent, 213; of God, 127–129, 139, 153, 164; human, 153; intelligible, 222; and Logos, 202; of mind, 46, 154, 173; sacred, 159; sensible, 139, 154, 159, 223; and wisdom, 159.

Logos, 184; as Angel, 178; not created, 94; and creation, 97, 100, 101, 132, 139, 175–176, 193, 216, 242, 297; as Divine Mind, 87–95; as Image, 101, 126, 171, 217; and law, 198, 199; as mediator (unifier), 89, 93–94, 101, 139, 178, 193, 216, 241; name of, 143; and primal Cause, 89, 95, 117; as Sophia, 92; not uncreated, 94; vision of, 171, 172.

Lycurgus, 202.

Magi, 249.

Maleness, 225.

419

INDEX

Man, called upward, 166–167, 169; capacity of, 216–218; creation of, 100, 102–105, 126, 137, 176–177, 245, 272; degeneration of, 103–104; earthly, 103, 272; end of, 137; first-, 103–104; and Form, 87; freedom of, 53, 194, 195, 197, 239, 248; and God, 189, 190, 193, 203, 238; good-, 68, 269; heavenly, 102, 103, 272; as image, 100, 101, 103, 137, 143, 176; as microcosm, 114–115; and mortality, 121, 151, 184, 191; nature of, 65, 87, 103, 126, 146, 177, 218, 219, 237, 250, 267, 273, 292; nothingness of, 168–169; perfect, 209; -of Practice, 127, 142; true, 66, 202, 229.

Manna, 93, 186, 276.

Matter, chaotic, 89; and dyad, 282; escape from, 168; and Form, 96; lifeless, 42; pre-elemental, 88; primordial, 96–99; sensible, 258.

Mercy, 152.

Mercy-Seat, 89, 91, 217–218.

Messianic Age, 294–298.

Mind, cf. also Body; all-encompassing, 75; apprehension of, 62, 63, 88, 172; champions of, 192; Divine, 87–95, 99–100, 109, 170, 268; eyes of, 75, 88; heavenly, 70; as image, 268; and inspiration, 144, 156, 165, 169; light in, 46, 154; and Logos, 143, 165–166; in man, 93, 102, 123, 125–126, 127, 143, 170, 172, 192–194, 221, 268; nature of, 149, 159, 201, 268; passivity of, 187; perfection of, 204; powers of, 145, 172; purified, 126, 144, 157–158, 159, 164, 169, 171, 205, 297; and reason, 201, 202; rules man, 144, 145, 149, 158, 242–243; and senses, 102, 144–147, 167, 171, 194, 244; states of, 187–188; and tension, 266–267; Universal, 96, 125–126, 134, 135, 137, 170, 194; and virtue, 198, 214, 253, 254.

Miracles, 174, 185–187.

Miriam, 56.

Misanthropy, 291.

Mnemosyne, 160.

Monad, 128, 283; conformity with, 170; dyad, 129, 282; and Existent, 42; and first cause, 281–282; and God, 131; Indivisible, 68.

Moral Development, 209–210.

Moses, 52, 56, 62, 64, 65, 68, 69, 71, 76, 80, 81, 83, 84, 86, 87, 88, 89, 92,95, 96, 98, 100, 101, 104, 105, 107, 113, 114, 115, 118, 121, 123, 125, 126, 127, 131, 132, 133, 136, 137, 139, 141, 144, 151, 153, 154, 155, 160, 161, 162, 163, 164, 165, 166, 167, 168, 171, 172, 173, 176, 177, 185, 191, 192, 196, 197, 198, 199, 206, 208, 212, 213, 217, 219, 220, 221, 224, 231, 233, 238, 240, 241, 242, 244, 245, 253, 257, 264, 267–286, 287, 288, 290, 291.

Movement, and generation, 85; and God, 86, 107, 132, 133, 141, 154, 193; and Mind, 96; and soul, 145, 219; and time, 106, 108; of universe, 147, 148; of world, 106, 108.

Munificent, the, 89.

Muses, 183, 184.

Music, 76, 173, 205, 213, 214, 225, 255, 266, 268; of Spheres, 115.

Mysians, 44.

Mysteries, divine, 82; of Existent, 140, 166; and God, 164, 191, 223, 254; and initiation, 46, 69, 83, 126, 140, 184, 236; pagan, 83; and symbols, 184.

Mysticism, 164–174.

Mythology, 52; and angels, 62; and giants, 69; and God, 139, 160; and Hades, 123; and law, 197–198; and proselytes, 293; and Scripture, 79, 80, 82, 92, 105.

Naid, 80.

Nature, contemplation of, 57, 122, 146, 183, 247; created, 165, 292; of creation, 96–97; enemies of, 200–201, 206; female, 280–282; of

INDEX

421

INDEX

244, 259; *De Mutatione Nominum*, 80, 143, 208, 218, 219, 220, 234, 245, 262; *De Opificio Mundi*, 85, 86, 96, 97, 100, 101, 102, 103, 104, 105, 106, 107, 109, 137, 144, 173, 175, 177, 198; *De Plantatione*, 94, 161, 167, 169, 257; *De Posteritate Caini*, 81, 86, 125, 133, 134, 145, 151, 208; *De Praemiis et Poenis*, 129, 153, 180, 265, 286, 291, 294; *Quod omnis Probus Liber sit*, 77, 202, 249, 252, 286; *De Providentia*, 77, 78, 99, 109, 118, 181, 182, 183, 185, 197; *Quaestiones et Solutiones in Exodum*, 91, 92, 118, 165, 174, 225, 273, 293; *Quaestiones et Solutiones in Genesim*, 84, 90, 117, 119, 137, 164, 166, 203, 229, 252, 253, 266, 267; *Quis Rerum Divarum Heres sit*, 89, 93, 94, 97, 98, 115, 119, 121, 123, 147, 152, 154, 162, 163, 169, 191, 212, 228, 233, 244; *De Sacrificiis Abelis et Caini*, 108, 132, 138, 152, 206, 207, 243; *De Sobrietate*, 165, 231, 243; *De Somniis*, 79, 84, 86, 95, 115, 135, 148, 149, 150, 155, 166, 169, 172, 173, 209, 221, 234, 235; *De Specialibus Legibus*, 76, 79, 83, 88, 89, 117, 155, 159, 192, 200, 201, 225, 236, 238, 239, 240, 248, 264, 279, 282, 285, 289, 290, 291, 293, 294; *De Virtutibus*, 163, 195, 201, 248, 264, 291, 294, 295, 296, 297, 298; *De Vita Mosis*, 136, 156, 163, 176, 185, 186, 187, 224, 225, 263, 267, 268, 269, 270, 271, 272, 274, 288, 289.

Philo, Works of, *The Contemplative Life*, 41–57; *The Giants*, 61–71.

Philolaos, 85.

Philosophy, 115, 131, 147; contemplative, 53; desire for, 44, 46, 47, 57, 76, 245; divisions of, 209; and Moses, 96, 98, 269; natural, 116; as royal road, 208; so-called, 146, 245; study of, 224, 249, 251, 289; and wisdom, 215–216.

Piety, 42, 46, 57, 82, 105, 128, 141, 175, 187, 196, 210, 213, 224, 225, 250, 255, 256, 263, 264, 266, 279.

Place, 135.

Plato, 51, 118, 184.

Pleasure, and body, 53, 63, 64, 66, 67, 69–70, 104, 121, 123, 168, 228, 236, 255, 259; control of, 260; and evil, 226–227; and knowledge, 255; life of, 267; love of, 227, 284; and mind, 278; and passion, 252, 265; rejection of, 242, 265, 294.

Poetry, 184–185, 205.

Polytheism, 105.

Poseidon, 42.

Powers, Creative-, 89, 90–91, 98, 117, 216, 218, 223; of Existent, 178; and Forms, 88–89; functions of, 91–92; of God, 88, 89–92, 96, 98, 108, 125, 133, 136, 143, 144, 156, 160, 165, 166, 176, 185, 205, 216, 217; of God's goodness, 89, 178, 180, 224; of God's sovereignity, 68, 89, 114, 176, 180, 224, 238; Gracious-, 216, 217, 218, 224, 244; intelligible, 88; and Logos, 100, 218; of nativity, 195–197; Punitive-, 89, 177–178; Regent-, 91–92, 177–178, 216, 217, 218, 223, 224.

Prayer, 46, 53, 57, 153, 157–158, 163, 165, 178, 199, 213, 225, 274, 289, 290, 295, 297.

Predestination, 196.

Priest, High, 273–274, 289.

Prophecy, 143, 153–156, 186.

Prophets, 46, 64, 68, 69, 70, 142, 153, 169, 266, 269, 272, 294.

Proselytes, 293–294.

Proverbs, 8:22, 102.

Providence, 98, 174–176, 195, 197, 267, 297.

Psalms, 23:1, 158; 77:49, 63; 78:49 (A.V.), 63.

Punishment, 135–136, 164, 176, 178, 179, 180, 181, 182, 195, 224, 236, 256, 277, 285, 297.

Purification, of mind, 126, 144, 157–158, 159, 164, 169, 171, 205,